IMPLEMENTING TRAUMA

A Handbook

Edited by C. Nadine Wathen and Colleen Varcoe

The need for health and social services to be trauma- and violence-informed has never been so pressing. In the wake of COVID-19, racial violence intensified and violence against women spiked globally. Mental health for many is worsening, while the ongoing toxic drug overdose crisis provides horrendous evidence of the impact of trauma, violence, stigma, and social inequities. Service providers across sectors are increasingly impacted by these dynamics and, without supportive environments, are burning out.

Implementing Trauma- and Violence-Informed Care aims to support health and social service organizations and providers to create environments, policies, and practices to mitigate the harms of structural and interpersonal violence and the trauma that ensues. The book is organized around case examples of trauma- and violence-informed care (TVIC) implementation and impact in diverse settings, providing how-to guidance for getting started, sustaining momentum, and assessing outcomes. The book describes the importance of TVIC at multiple levels, from individual practices to organizational protocols and system-level policies, emphasizing TVIC's alignment with system transformation goals. In doing so, the book presents TVIC as a call to action to improve service user experiences and outcomes, efficient and effective use of resources, and the health and well-being of staff, while addressing and reducing health and social inequities.

C. NADINE WATHEN is a professor and Canada Research Chair in Mobilizing Knowledge on Gender-Based Violence in the Arthur Labatt Family School of Nursing at Western University.

COLLEEN VARCOE is a professor emeritus in the School of Nursing at the University of British Columbia.

Implementing Trauma- and Violence-Informed Care

A Handbook

EDITED BY
C. NADINE WATHEN AND COLLEEN VARCOE

UNIVERSITY OF TORONTO PRESS
Toronto Buffalo London

© University of Toronto Press 2023
Toronto Buffalo London
utorontopress.com
Printed in the USA

ISBN 978-1-4875-2925-3 (cloth)   ISBN 978-1-4875-2928-4 (EPUB)
ISBN 978-1-4875-2926-0 (paper)   ISBN 978-1-4875-2927-7 (PDF)

Library and Archives Canada Cataloguing in Publication

Title: Implementing trauma- and violence-informed care: a handbook /
  edited by C. Nadine Wathen and Colleen Varcoe.
Names: Wathen, C. Nadine, 1968– editor. | Varcoe, Colleen, 1952– editor.
Description: Includes bibliographical references.
Identifiers: Canadiana (print) 20230200311 | Canadiana (ebook) 2023020032X |
  ISBN 9781487529253 (cloth) | ISBN 9781487529260 (paper) |
  ISBN 9781487529284 (EPUB) | ISBN 9781487529277 (PDF)
Subjects: LCSH: Psychic trauma – Patients – Care – Case studies. |
  LCSH: Victims of violent crimes – Care – Case studies. |
  LCSH: Psychic trauma – Case studies. | LCSH: Violence – Case studies. |
  LCSH: Public health – Case studies. | LCSH: Social service – Case studies. |
  LCGFT: Case studies.
Classification: LCC RC552.T7 I47 2023 | DDC 616.85/21–dc23

Cover design: BW&A Books/Chris Crochetiere
Cover image: Annie Spratt/Unsplash

We wish to acknowledge the land on which the University of Toronto Press operates. This land is the traditional territory of the Wendat, the Anishnaabeg, the Haudenosaunee, the Métis, and the Mississaugas of the Credit First Nation.

University of Toronto Press acknowledges the financial support of the Government of Canada, the Canada Council for the Arts, and the Ontario Arts Council, an agency of the Government of Ontario, for its publishing activities.

 Canada Council   Conseil des Arts
for the Arts   du Canada

 ONTARIO ARTS COUNCIL
CONSEIL DES ARTS DE L'ONTARIO
an Ontario government agency
un organisme du gouvernement de l'Ontario

Funded by the   Financé par le
Government   gouvernement
of Canada   du Canada

This volume is dedicated to the innovators and champions who found, and sometimes created, opportunities to bring a trauma- and violence-informed, equity-promoting, social justice lens to their own thinking and practice, and to their organizations and broader communities. This collection is a testament to their vision, perseverance, and commitment to sharing knowledge to support better care for all, especially those who need it most.

We also dedicate this work to Dr Eugenia Canas, who lived brilliantly, but not nearly long enough.

Trauma- and violence-informed care is essentially about reconnecting with our humanity and to the values that underpin why we went into a service profession in the first place. It means treating yourself, and those with whom you interact, with respect, kindness, and compassion, or, put another way, "Don't be an a**hole."

Contents

Illustrations xi
Tables xiii
Foreword by Josée G. Lavoie xv
Preface and Acknowledgments xix
Abbreviations xxi

Introduction 3
COLLEEN VARCOE AND NADINE WATHEN

Section One: The Case for Trauma- and Violence-Informed Care 9

1.1 Trauma, Violence, Health, and Well-Being 11
MARILYN FORD-GILBOE, KAREN CAMPBELL, AND LISA HESLOP

1.2 Integrating Understanding of Structural and Systemic Violence into Trauma- and Violence-Informed Care 25
COLLEEN VARCOE AND ANNETTE J. BROWNE

1.3 Leveraging Implicit Bias Recognition and Management Curricula to Advance Trauma- and Violence-Informed Care 39
JAVEED SUKHERA

1.4 Vicarious Trauma, Moral Distress, and Compassion Fatigue/Burnout through a Structural Lens 58
COLLEEN VARCOE

1.5 The Principles of Trauma- and Violence-Informed Care   72
NADINE WATHEN AND COLLEEN VARCOE

Section Two: TVIC Implementation Case Studies   83

2.1 Taking Organizational-Level Action: Creating a Context for Implementing TVIC in Health Care Settings   85
ANNETTE J. BROWNE AND COLLEEN VARCOE

2.2 Trauma- and Violence-Informed Mental Health Interventions: Our Work with Indigenous Men   99
VICTORIA SMYE, VIVIANE JOSEWSKI, PAUL GROSS, ILORADANON EFIMOFF, LYANA PATRICK, AND SANDY LAMBERT

2.3 Population Health and Trauma- and Violence-Informed Approaches: A Leadership Role for Public Health   115
SUSAN M. JACK, HEATHER LOKKO, AND NADINE WATHEN

2.4 The Trauma- and Violence-Informed Classroom, K–12   138
SUSAN RODGER, KATHY HIBBERT, MATTHEW SEREDA, AND JACQUELINE SPECHT

2.5 Developing and Implementing Trauma- and Violence-Informed Physical Activity Programing   152
FRANCINE DARROCH, GABRIELA GONZALEZ MONTANER, JESSICA WEBB, MICHELLE PAQUETTE, AND COLLEEN VARCOE

2.6 Becoming Trauma- and Violence-Informed in Policing   166
MARGARET MACPHERSON, SUSAN MACPHAIL, AND TANAZ JAVAN

Section Three: Cutting across Contexts   179

3.1 Cultural Safety and Trauma- and Violence-Informed Care: Integrated Services for Indigenous Peoples   181
VICTORIA SMYE, BILL HILL, COLLEEN VARCOE, ANNETTE J. BROWNE, CHANTEL ANTONE, LISA JACKSON, AND LLOY WYLIE

3.2 The Nexus of Trauma, Violence, Chronic Pain, Substance Use, and Stigma   201
COLLEEN VARCOE

3.3 Enhancing Public Understanding: Shifting Narratives on Trauma, Violence, and Mental Health 214
NADINE WATHEN AND JESSICA CARSWELL

3.4 Emerging Considerations for Trauma- and Violence-Informed Care: Lessons from Post-Genocide Rwanda 227
AIMÉE JOSÉPHINE UTUZA, VINCENT SEZIBERA, AND HELENE BERMAN

3.5 Thinking through Gaps and Support Needs: What Newcomer and Migrant Worker Interventions Teach Us about Trauma- and Violence-Informed Care 243
SUSANA CAXAJ, JENNIFER SANDU, AND TANAZ JAVAN

Section Four: Bringing It All Together 259

4.1 How Organizations Take Up Trauma- and Violence-Informed Care 261
TANAZ JAVAN, JENNIFER SANDU, AND NADINE WATHEN

4.2 Strategies, Tools, and Resources for Integrating Trauma- and Violence-Informed Care across Settings 279
COLLEEN VARCOE, NADINE WATHEN, ANNE-MARIE SANCHEZ, AND SCOTT COURTICE

4.3 Development of a Core Trauma- and Violence-Informed Care e-Learning Curriculum 295
EUGENIA CANAS, SAMRIDHI PRADHAN, AND NADINE WATHEN

4.4 Thinking Structurally: Using Trauma- and Violence-Informed Care to Reimagine Service Systems 310
MARGARET MACPHERSON AND NADINE WATHEN

4.5 But Does It Work? Evaluating T(V)IC Initiatives 334
NADINE WATHEN, JENNIFER MACGREGOR, AND BRENNA SCHMITT

Conclusion 349
NADINE WATHEN

Contributors 355

Illustrations

1.1.1 Common features of post-traumatic stress 13
1.3.1 A visual depiction of how the elements of transformative learning theory align with those of implicit bias recognition and management curricula 44
1.4.1 Interrelated concepts of vicarious trauma, compassion fatigue/burnout, and moral distress 63
1.5.1 Principles of trauma- and violence-informed care 75
2.1.1 Key dimensions and strategies for equity-oriented health care 87
2.2.1 Housing conditions – single room occupancy 108
2.2.2 Housing conditions – second-level housing 109
2.4.1 Example of a trauma- and violence-informed care heuristic 147
2.5.1 CBPR-specific process 155
3.1.1 Okwari: Kowa space, Parkwood, London, Ontario 186
3.2.1 Chronic pain and differential experiences of harm and stigma 202
4.2.1 TVIC action kit – phases and steps 282
4.3.1 Sample case illustration 307
4.4.1 Ecological model on DV/IPV and EA 312
4.4.2 The ecological framework – a solutions focus 326

Tables

1.1.1 How you read the clues matters: Bad behaviour or trauma? 15
1.3.1 Comparing features of TVIC and IBRM 51
2.1.1 Examples of TVIC-specific actions in EQUIP implementations 95
2.3.1 Steps to guide development and implementation of population health approaches for the primary prevention of trauma and violence 119
2.3.2 Trauma-informed review: Areas of assessment 121
2.3.3 Process for becoming a trauma- and violence-informed organization 126
2.3.4 Lessons learned from COVID-19: Public health leadership to orient services and systems to TVIC 130
2.4.1 TVIC principles applied to Case 1: Global read aloud 145
2.4.2 TVIC principles applied to Case 2: Maya's journey through the system 146
2.5.1 Principles of TVIPA as co-defined by the community 157
4.3.1 Transformative learning phases 303
4.5.1 Trauma- (and violence-) informed measures 337

Foreword

I have been working with Indigenous communities and organizations for more than thirty years, first as a service provider (nutrition, health promotion) and more recently as a researcher. Working in the 1990s in Inuit communities in the Kivalliq region (then part of the Northwest Territories, now part of Nunavut), and later in Saskatchewan First Nations health organizations (affiliated with the Peter Ballantyne Cree Nation and the Prince Albert Grand Council) gave me a unique opportunity to witness the impact of colonialism on Indigenous people's everyday lives. And I was often left to reflect on how little progress had been made at extending the benefits of Canadian society (especially timely access to health care) to rural and remote environments. I recalled similar conversations with my father in the communities in which I grew up (remote mining towns). Although my ancestry is different (French from Quebec), the organizational challenges I witnessed in Indigenous communities seemed familiar, though compounded by social exclusion, marginalization, endless jurisdictional bickering, and racism. I was often left to wonder why it was acceptable for rural, remote, and Indigenous communities to constantly struggle for access to timely care.

Predictably, my research has focused on improving access to responsive and respectful primary health care across Canada, Australia, and New Zealand and, more recently, in circumpolar countries. I was initially interested in the mechanisms Canada was putting in place to support Indigenous self-determination, especially in the area of health care. My PhD research compared the policy discourses in Canada, Australia, and New Zealand and contrasted these with the funding pathways in place to support Indigenous-controlled health organizations. An analysis of funding contracts showed how contractual mechanisms implemented in the name of accountability have created environments in which funding has remained siloed and allocated based on distant perceptions of local needs, thus undermining opportunities for local innovation and better care. My work highlighted how a transfer of responsibility without associated resources and space to innovate can serve rhetorical arguments while perpetuating inequities. I have since been working with Indigenous communities to help document systemic barriers to equity and identify policy remedies. Working closely with Indigenous political organizations has ensured that the results of our work are presented at policy tables to which researchers are rarely invited. Although this is changing, governmental inertia remains an obstacle to improvements.

I first met Colleen Varcoe in 2006, when I was applying for funding for a study to be led by Dr Annette Browne. Over the course of that study I led an analysis of the funding and policy contexts in which two marginalized Indigenous health organizations operated, and demonstrated how the funding pathways created by federal and provincial governments to fund these organizations undermined their ability to recruit and retain qualified staff and made it harder for them to set up innovative programing to better serve their populations. Colleen is a leader in implementation research in the areas of harm reduction, trauma- and violence-informed techniques, and cultural safety in equity-promoting health care. Her research focuses on equity-promoting interventions for emergency departments as well as on interventions to help women who have suffered partner violence reduce the health repercussions of that violence. Working with Colleen on that initial study allowed me to connect my system-based and structurally focused work to patient's experiences.

Through Colleen and Annette, I met Nadine Wathen, who studies measures to lessen health inequities, the science of knowledge mobilization, and how the health and social service sectors respond to gender-based violence. She places a special emphasis on creating person-centred interventions that improve health equity and assist, in a trauma- and violence-informed way, individuals who are marginalized and/or facing gender-based violence. She is steadfastly devoted to a partnership approach to research and information-sharing and has headed several federally supported research efforts as well as global research and knowledge mobilization networks.

After Colleen and Nadine asked me to provide a foreword, I started to read this handbook and could not put it down. Its objective is to expand trauma- and violence-informed care, taking into consideration historical, colonial, systemic, and individual trauma. Importantly, it highlights the structural and systemic issues that perpetuate trauma and calls for actions at individual, systemic, and structural levels. In section 1, it discusses relevant frameworks: cultural safety, harm reduction, trauma-informed care, and trauma- and violence-informed care. The book as a whole centres the principle of culture as treatment (chapter 3.1), which hinges on grounding all programs and interventions in the languages, cultural knowledges, and ways of knowing and doing of the people these programs are aiming to support. These frameworks emerged from various discussions and traditions, and the consolidation of this work greatly increases this book's usefulness.

This handbook offers tangible strategies for implementation, distilled into actionable principles. For example, at the end of chapter 3.2, providers are called upon to assume that people living with chronic pain have faced disbelief, dismissal, and discrimination; to assume that people who are labelled as substance-using will have experienced stigma and discrimination, especially if they face poverty, housing instability, racism, and other forms of structural violence; to inquire about and acknowledge people's experiences of stigma; to recognize chronic pain; and to support people's own analyses of their experiences with trauma and violence, the pain they feel, and the challenges they may be experiencing related to substances.

This handbook resonates with my current focus. I have had the privilege of working with a group of Inuit Elders and the Manitoba Inuit Association for more than seven years, focusing on the development of Inuit-centred services that will better meet the needs of Inuit living in Manitoba and of Inuit who travel from Nunavut to access services in Manitoba. Recently, we were asked to develop trauma-informed Inuit-centred programing as a means to address colonial trauma. We have been working with the Arviat Nunavut–based Aqqiumavvik Society to learn more about Inuit values and the processes they use to restore balance after conflict or trauma. Inuit distinguish between trauma with which they have always been familiar (hunger, accidental death, conflict) and colonial trauma. Inuit had a system to address the former. Colonial trauma has impacted Indigenous communities across Canada and beyond. As we heard from Elder Joe Karetak from Arviat, "it is not the past, it is continuous and relentless." The systematic undermining of community and family structures and processes that had once served to support individuals and families through their experiences of trauma only exacerbated the situation. Many families have been living in a stigmatizing cycle of trauma, passed down from one generation to the next. Tools and mechanisms had once existed to support individuals' and families' efforts to recover after trauma; these tools had been taken away and new forms of trauma had been added to the mix. Elders from the Aqqiumavvik Society taught us that all work with Inuit should be based on three fundamental values: humility, respect, and love. This principle, a cornerstone of the concept of cultural safety, extends beyond the often tokenistic and superficial adaptation of Western value-informed programs.

The case studies of successful programs presented in section 2 offer tangible evidence of this handbook's applicability to real-life situations; the examples of applications in other contexts (section 3) speak to its generalizability. In section 4, providers and system leaders review organizational practices and language and confront the structural and systemic issues undermining the health of their client populations. I found the framework provided in chapter 4.4 especially eloquent, for it visualizes opportunities for system-level actions instead of restricting itself to individual-focused ones. The authors of this chapter explain that society is a system of networks and relationships. Everyone belongs to it and contributes to it, knowingly or not. The authors emphasize the need for action at multiple levels and by multiple actors: providers, community groups, political actors, systems-level decision-makers.

I really appreciated the consolidation work undertaken in this handbook: I found the approach compelling and, given my current work, very timely. My review copy is now littered with Post-it notes and comments, making it somewhat unusable for other members of our team. While we wait for this handbook to be published, I will go back to my review copy and extract key lessons to guide our team on the development of an Inuit-centred framework that integrates TVIC to inform the development of programs at the Manitoba Inuit Association and hopefully beyond.

Josée G. Lavoie
Professor, Department of Community Health Sciences
Director, Ongomiizwin Research
University of Manitoba

Preface and Acknowledgments

Trauma- and violence-informed care (TVIC) aims to create safety for people using services by understanding the effects of trauma and its close links to health and behaviour, while also highlighting the intersecting impacts of systemic and interpersonal violence and structural inequities on people's lives. TVIC emphasizes historical *and* ongoing violence as well as the traumatic impacts of both, drawing attention to a person's experiences of past and current violence, stigma, and discrimination so that their effects are seen as residing in the individual's psychological state *and* social circumstances, and as permeating culture and society. In this edited collection, we position TVIC as a core component of equity-oriented care in health and social services. We provide case studies in diverse settings as well as "how-to" guidance for implementing TVIC in different contexts from health care to policing to education, in lower resource contexts, and when serving newcomers. We emphasize the importance of TVIC both in individual interactions and in practices and policies at the organizational, system, and societal levels. TVIC has the potential to improve experiences and outcomes for those seeking and providing care, for organizations, and for entire systems.

The past two decades have seen increased attention to the issue of "trauma-informed" approaches, but these are generally focused on the individual level – that is, on assessing "what's wrong" with people due to their personal trauma experiences and endeavouring to minimize further harm during care interactions. Relatively little attention has been paid to a "trauma- and *violence*-informed" approach, which explicitly brings in structural and systemic factors that impact people's health and well-being and that are themselves traumatizing. These factors include structural poverty, racism, sexism, and other forms of discrimination and stigma. TVIC also emphasizes organizational-level strategies to make care spaces safe for everyone – that is, those receiving and giving care and services.

The chapter authors have been drawn from the Gender, Trauma & Violence Knowledge Incubator @ Western University (GTV Incubator; https://gtvincubator.uwo.ca), a collective of researchers, community service leaders, educators, and trainees committed to research, policy, and practice. Together, they develop and evaluate TVIC education materials adaptable to a variety of contexts and tailorable to different types of learners; establish a core group of experts to deliver the training; expand and innovate TVIC and assess its impact through research, program evaluation, policy development, and advocacy; and share and mobilize new knowledge using tailored, innovative strategies. GTV Incubator projects underpin many of the chapters; thus, there is a common approach to TVIC conceptually, with deep attention to assessing contexts, adapting strategies, and evaluating impacts. We brought this collection together during the intense initial year or so of the COVID-19 pandemic. In part, it was a way to for us keep our GTV Incubator community vibrant and moving forward at a time when in-person meetings were impossible. Many of the chapters therefore reflect on the pandemic's impact on our health and social circumstances, offering arguments and strategies for why TVIC, as we emerge from this collective trauma, is more important now than it has ever been.

We take a "handbook" approach that focuses on providing guidance for practitioners and organizational and system leaders to implement TVIC. Thus, the primary audience is professionals in practice, administrators, and system leaders. However, this book will also be useful for pre-service and continuing education across a range of health and social service disciplines. It can therefore also be positioned as a classroom and/or continuing professional education resource and will be of interest to researchers and evaluators (which describes many of the chapter authors, providing ways to think about assessment and impact, locally and beyond.

We thank the chapter authors, our friends and colleagues, for their perseverance in the face of the COVID-19 pandemic, especially those who were trying to run organizations, deliver services, teach online for the first time, homeschool small children, or all of the above, while writing their chapters. Their commitment to disrupting the status quo is evident throughout.

We also thank those who have partnered in the research that underpins many of the chapters. Diverse people have shared their experiences of trauma and violence, and of services related to it – beneficial or not – through surveys, interviews, and conversations. Much of this sharing has been done in the hope that doing so will "make a difference," and we honour that hope with this book.

Jen MacGregor ensured consistency and clarity in our illustrations, created alternative text for screen readers, and brought her eagle eye to pre-production proofing efforts.

Finally, we thank Isobel McLean and Brenna Schmitt, young scholars who supported manuscript preparation, formatting, and author-nudging while completing their undergraduate degrees, almost exclusively online, during the pandemic. Their assistance has been invaluable, and their energy and passion for social justice a reason for hope.

Colleen Varcoe and Nadine Wathen

Abbreviations

ACE	adverse childhood experience
ADM	assistant deputy minister
AIFs	Active Implementation Frameworks
APA	American Psychological Association
BC	British Columbia (Canada)
CBPR	community-based participatory research
CCLC	Cross Cultural Learner Centre (London, Ontario)
CEDA	Convention on the Elimination of all Forms of Discrimination against Women
CHC	community health centre
CIHR	Canadian Institutes of Health Research
COVID-19	Coronavirus (SARS-CoV2)
CPHA	Canadian Public Health Association
CREVAWC	Centre for Research and Education on Violence Against Women and Children
CRHESI	Centre for Research on Health Equity and Social Inclusion
CWF	Canadian Women's Foundation
DTES	Downtown Eastside (of Vancouver, BC)
DUDES Club	Dudes United Defending Equality and Solidarity Club
DV	domestic violence
DVDRC	Domestic Violence Death Review Committee
EA	elder abuse
ED	emergency department
EHoCS	Equity-Oriented Health Care Scale
EMDR	eye movement desensitization and reprocessing
EOHC	equity-oriented health care
FFRP	Rwanda Women Parliamentary Forum.
GAR	government-assisted refugee
GBV	gender-based violence
GMO	Gender Monitoring Office (Rwanda)
GTV Incubator	Gender, Trauma, and Violence Knowledge Incubator @ Western University

HRV/O	honour-related violence/oppression
IBRM	implicit bias recognition and management
ICS	Indigenous cultural safety
ICTR	International Criminal Tribunal for Rwanda
IPRC	identification, placement, and review committee
IPV	intimate partner violence
ITE	initial teacher education
K–12	kindergarten to Grade 12
KL	Kilala Lelum Urban Indigenous Health and Healing Cooperative (Vancouver, BC)
LGBTQ2I+	lesbian, gay, bisexual, trans, queer/questioning, 2-sp rit, intersex, and other gender and sexual identities
LHSC	London Health Sciences Centre
LIHC	London InterCommunity Health Centre (Ontario, Canada)
LMS	learning management system
MOA	medical office assistant
MIGEPROF	Ministry of Gender and Family Promotion (Rwanda)
MLHU	Middlesex London Health Unit (Ontario, Canada)
MOH	Ministry of Health
NGM	National Gender Machinery (South Africa)
NICE	National Institute for the Care of the Elderly
NISR	National Institute of Statistics of Rwanda
NTTP	National Trauma Training Programme (Scotland)
NWC	National Women's Council (Rwanda)
OCAP	ownership, control, access, and possession
OCT	Ontario College of Teachers
PHC	primary health care
PTS/PTSD	post-traumatic stress/post-traumatic stress disorder
PHAC	Public Health Agency of Canada
RAP	Resettlement Assistance Program (Government of Canada)
RDHS	Rwanda Demographic Health Survey
ROS	Reclaiming Our Spirits
RPF	Rwandan Patriotic Front
RPN	registered practical nurse
SAWP	Seasonal Agricultural Workers Program
SJHC	St Joseph's Health Care, London
SOAR	strengths, opportunities, aspirations, and results analysis
SSPPS	Survey of Safety in Public and Private Spaces (Canada)
SRO	single-room occupancy
SWOT	strengths, weaknesses, opportunities, threats analysis
TF-CBT	trauma-focused cognitive behavioural therapy
TL	transformative learning

TVI	trauma- and violence-informed
TVIC	trauma- and violence-informed care
TVIPA	trauma- and violence-informed physical activity
UBC	University of British Columbia (Canada)
UN	United Nations
VAW[G]	violence against women [girls]
WAGE	Women and Gender Equality Canada
WHO	World Health Organization

IMPLEMENTING TRAUMA- AND VIOLENCE-INFORMED CARE

Introduction

COLLEEN VARCOE AND NADINE WATHEN

The need for health and social services to be trauma- and violence-informed has never seemed so pressing. In the wake of COVID-19, racial violence intensified and violence against women spiked globally. Mental health is worsening, with the ongoing toxic drug overdose crisis providing horrendous evidence of the impact of trauma, violence, and social inequities. Service providers across sectors are increasingly impacted by these dynamics. In the face of continually growing pressure on the health and social service sectors and the need to set priorities within finite (and likely dwindling) budgets, service providers, without guidance and supportive environments, may draw on stigmatizing social stereotypes to decide who is deserving of care. They may traumatize and retraumatize those they intend to serve. And they may themselves be harmed in the course of their efforts to provide service.

This handbook aims to help health and social service organizations, leaders, and providers create environments, policies, and practices to mitigate the harms of structural and interpersonal violence as well as the trauma that ensues. In this introductory chapter, we describe the overarching purpose of this book, discuss its importance and timeliness, describe its theoretical foundations, and give an overview of its sections.

Trauma and Violence Defined: Power Is Always at Play

This handbook is built on the premise that structural and interpersonal violence and trauma are inseparable and that violence is always an abuse of power. *Structural violence* refers to how societies are organized, or *structured*, in such a way that they do harm. For Galtung, who coined the term *structural violence*, it was interchangeable with "social injustice" (Galtung, 1969, p. 171); pointing to the element of unfairness, he asserted that such violence is present "when it is avoidable" (p. 169). Through the work of Farmer, a physician and medical anthropologist, the term has been used increasingly to understand the relationship between oppression and health. This is important because Hirschfeld argues that the limitations of structural violence as an explanatory framework for understanding health patterns have been largely ignored so that "structural violence is now used to explain all manner of health conditions and human problems that bear little connection to Galtung's or Farmer's original formulations" (Hirschfeld, 2017, p. 157). This is in part because injustice and avoidability have not been adequately scrutinized. Thus, throughout this book the term will be used to examine how things are organized in society in ways that harm people unfairly and avoidably, and we will be seeking ways to promote greater fairness and justice – a conceptualization that aligns with the definition of health inequities advanced by many as being those that "though avoidable, are not avoided and hence are unfair" (Marmot & Allen, 2014, p. S517).

Importantly, the concept of structural violence implicates us all in the task of rectifying harm. This in turn requires each of us to operate with an acute awareness of our own privilege. Farmer (2004) contends that "structural violence is violence exerted systematically – that is, indirectly – by everyone who belongs to a certain social order: hence the discomfort these ideas provoke in a moral economy still geared to pinning praise or blame on individual actors" (p. 307). Thus, throughout this book, the authors will be drawing attention not only to oppressive structures but also our roles as service providers in maintaining or disrupting those structures.

Interpersonal violence is entangled with structural violence in multiple ways. Galtung (1969) explored in depth the relationship between what he termed "personal violence," the actions of individuals, and structural violence, which is indirect and systemic. Noting that "attention has been focused more on personal than on structural violence [because] personal violence *shows*" (p. 173, italics in original), he called for attention to be paid to both, equally and symmetrically. In keeping with that summons, the chapters in this handbook keep in view the diverse links between structural and interpersonal forms of violence. It is relevant here that Galtung writes: "When one husband beats his wife there is a clear case of personal violence, but when one million husbands keep one million wives in ignorance there is structural violence. Correspondingly, in a society where life expectancy is twice as high in the upper as in the lower classes, violence is exercised even if there are no concrete actors one can point to directly attacking others, as when one person kills another" (p. 173).

To understand interpersonal violence as entwined with structural violence, we must examine patterns of abuses of power. This supports our understanding of the complexities of interpersonal violence, allowing us to discern, for example, the distinctions between understanding violence in intimate relationships as single acts and understanding it as coercive control. Thus, throughout this handbook, interpersonal forms of violence – including assault, racialized violence, sexual assault, child maltreatment, and intimate partner violence – are understood in wider contexts that encompass structural forms of violence, such as relative and absolute poverty, systemic racism, sexism/misogyny, and workplace violence. The contribution to trauma and violence of rising global inequities, ongoing armed conflict, and the patterns of displacement and migration of people will be explored, and the differential burden of trauma and violence as raced, classed, and gendered will be in constant view.

In laying the foundations for gender-sensitive, trauma-informed approaches to substance use treatment for women, Covington (2008) defined trauma as a response to overwhelmingly negative events. "Trauma is not limited to suffering violence; it includes witnessing violence as well as stigmatization because of gender, race, poverty, disability, incarceration, or sexual orientation. The terms violence, trauma, abuse, and posttraumatic stress disorder (PTSD) often are used interchangeably. One way to clarify these terms is to think of trauma as a response to violence or some other overwhelmingly negative experience (e.g., abuse)" (p. 379). In this handbook, we understand trauma in structural terms, as both individual and collective, historical and ongoing. Thus, the chapters that follow focus not only on the individual experiences of those using services, but also on entire organizations, and on service providers.

A Critical Approach to Trauma- and Violence-Informed Care: Theoretical Underpinnings

All of the authors of this handbook take a critical approach that explicitly considers power. The understanding that power is enacted in all relationships is deployed throughout to both comprehend abuses of power and the agency of all persons. An intersectional lens is deployed so as to consider multiple axes of advantage and disadvantage simultaneously. When a structural understanding is applied, intersectionality is not treated as a theory of identity (Hill Collins, 2019); rather, using Hill Collins's typology, it is used as a paradigm contributing to "shifts in thinking about how mutually constructed power relations shape social phenomena" (p. 43). Consequently, throughout this book, the core constructs of intersectionality identified by Hill Collins will be deployed: relationality, power, social inequality, social context, complexity, and social justice. Furthermore, the premises as outlined by Hill Collins underpin the chapters:

1. race, class, gender, sexuality, nationality, ethnicity, ability, age, and similar markers of power are interdependent and mutually construct one another;
2. intersecting power relations produce complex, interdependent social inequalities;

3. the social location of individuals and groups within intersecting power relations shapes their experiences within and perspectives on the social world; and
4. solving social problems within a given local, regional, national, or global context requires intersectional analyses (p. 44).

In alignment with an intersectional paradigm, a relational approach is taken in which environments and people are seen as interconnected and mutually influential. Three levels of understanding and action are considered throughout: the contextual level, the interpersonal level (among individuals), and the intrapersonal level (within individuals). The chapters that follow consider these levels as appropriate to their own focus.

Relational theory, founded on complexity theory, draws attention to how, at the contextual level, interrelated historical, physical, sociopolitical, economic, and language environments shape and are shaped by human experience (Doane & Varcoe, 2021). Thus, the historical violence experienced by specific groups, the power structures within societies and organizations, the extent to which economic systems are built on conquest and exploitation, the ways in which physical environments set the foundations for violence (think of the bars in the reception areas of health care settings), and the ways we talk about violence, trauma, and people all influence human experiences of trauma and violence. So, for example, chapter 3.4 uses the context of post-genocide Rwanda to draw attention to structural violence in ways that are useful for understanding diverse post-genocidal contexts and genocidal experiences, including in the Canadian context for those providing care to people who are newcomers to Canada, as well as those who survived or are descendants of other genocides. These ideas are then extended in chapter 3.5, in which the authors consider not only what is required when enacting trauma- and violence-informed care (TVIC) with newcomer and migrant workers and the structural influences to consider, but also what such interventions can teach us about TVIC.

At the interpersonal level, relational theory guides consideration of trauma, violence, and TVIC among individuals and, simultaneously, *in context*. That is, violence is viewed not as being comprised of isolated events between two people, but rather as patterns occurring among people arising from their given contexts. So, for example, chapter 3.1 considers violence against Indigenous people in historical and ongoing colonial contexts and as raced, classed, and gendered patterns.

At the intrapersonal level, relational theory guides attention to how biases, stereotypes, and assumptions are not merely the held beliefs of individuals; they are also manifestations of social values that maintain power and privilege. Thus, for example, chapter 1.3 approaches implicit bias from the perspective that individuals are immersed in biases in ways that require us to work to recognize and shift such thinking.

A relational approach based on complexity theory also underpins our approach to TVIC. Each principle is founded on a relational understanding of violence and trauma, as described above, and furthermore, is based on the understanding that each interaction is influential. That is, each time a provider conveys an understanding of the pervasiveness of violence and of traumatic impacts, and each time a provider seeks to create an emotionally safe environment, foster opportunities for control, and take a strength- and capacity-based approach, those actions help steer the person seeking service toward greater safety and capacity; they also contribute to a safer organizational culture and enhance the provider's practice and satisfaction. Each organization is seen as a complex adaptive system created, sustained, and influenced by both providers and recipients of service, and in turn affecting those agents.

Consequently, the contexts examined in this handbook, both in examples and in specific cases, are viewed as complex adaptive systems. Taken collectively, these diverse examples and contexts offer opportunities to consider complexity in all aspects of system assessment, design, adaptation, implementation, and evaluation. The complexity approach allows us to avoid the failures evident in many approaches to intervention development. For example, IPV interventions often fail to show positive impacts because designs are based on simplistic understandings of the problem to be solved and fail to consider the complexity of systems, organizational contexts, and people's lives (Wathen & Mantler, 2022). For decades, despite evidence of their ineffectiveness, health care responses to IPV have been narrowly focused on "screening," based on these two faulty assumptions: (a) health care providers require disclosure of a history of IPV in order to provide good care; and (b) somehow obtaining such disclosure will result in actions toward and achievement of greater safety. This overlooks the complexity of people's lives (e.g., disclosure may be fraught with danger, shame, and fear of judgment), organizations (e.g., health care providers may lack the time, knowledge, inclination, or resources to provide a supportive response beyond such disclosure), and systems (e.g., the health care system is not well designed to respond to the needs of people experiencing violence). In relation to IPV, TVIC provides a "universal" design that embraces safety for all rather than targeted planning based on disclosures that may or may not be forthcoming.

An Overview of the Handbook

This handbook has four sections. Section 1: "The Case for TVIC" provides the foundation for understanding multiple forms of violence and trauma and the relationships among them. This section draws attention to the impact of violence at the interpersonal level, to structural and systemic violence at the contextual level, and to the role of bias and stigma at the intrapersonal level.

The section concludes with an overview of the Principles of TVIC, which the remaining chapters take up. Section 2: "TVIC Implementation Case Studies" offers practical guidance and examples of taking up TVIC in diverse contexts. In section 3: "Cutting across Contexts" the authors share lessons learned in adapting, integrating, and applying TVIC principles in various contexts. This includes making explicit the link between TVIC and cultural safety by exploring TVIC's integration into services for Indigenous peoples (chapter 3.1) and in the context of the aftermath of genocide (chapter 3.4) and migration (chapter 3.5); understanding the complex interplay between trauma, violence, chronic pain, and substance use (chapter 3.2); and, at a slightly different level, taking a TVIC approach to both understanding and enhancing communication with the public, via media as well as targeted health promotion efforts (chapter 3.3). Finally, section 4: "Bringing It All Together" offers guidance to leaders, educators, practitioners, policy-makers, and evaluators, with specific attention to organizational change management, system redesign, curriculum delivery, and evaluation strategies, with practical tools for each.

REFERENCES

Covington, S.S. (2008). Women and addiction: A trauma-informed approach. *Journal of Psychoactive Drugs*, 377–85. Retrieved from https://doi.org/10.1080/02791072.2008.10400665.

Doane, G., & Varcoe, C. (2021). *How to nurse: Relational inquiry in action* (2nd ed.). Philadelphia, PA: Lippincott, Williams & Wilkins.

Farmer, P.E. (2004). An anthropology of structural violence. *Current Anthropology, 45*, 305–26. https://doi.org/10.1086/382250.

Galtung, J. (1969). Violence, peace, and peace research. *Journal of Peace Research, 6*(3), 167–91. https://doi.org/10.1177/002234336900600301.

Hill Collins, P. (2019). *Intersectionality as critical social theory*. Durham, NC: Duke University Press.

Hirschfeld, K. (2017). Rethinking "structural violence." *Society, 54*(2), 156–62. https://doi.org/10.1007/s12115-017-0116-y.

Marmot, M., & Allen, J.J. (2014). Social determinants of health equity. *American Journal of Public Health, 104*(S4), S517–S519. https://doi.org/10.2105/AJPH.2014.302200.

Wathen, C.N., & Mantler, T. (2022). Trauma- and violence-informed care: Orienting intimate partner violence interventions to equity. *Current Epidemiology Reports, 9*, 233–44. https://doi.org/10.1007/s40471-022-00307-7.

SECTION ONE

The Case for Trauma- and Violence-Informed Care

This section introduces and defines core constructs in our conceptualization of TVIC. It positions trauma and violence as both individual and social-structural phenomena that require multilevel forms of response.

SECTION ONE

The Case for Trauma- and Violence-Informed Care

1.1 Trauma, Violence, Health, and Well-Being

MARILYN FORD-GILBOE, KAREN CAMPBELL, AND LISA HESLOP

An estimated three out of four Canadian adults will experience at least one traumatic event in their lifetime (van Ameringen, Mancini, Patterson, & Boyle, 2008). However, the concept of trauma remains poorly understood. Trauma refers both to a person's exposure to an *event (or series of events)* that is/are perceived as highly threatening and uncontrollable, and to their *responses* to the event(s). Traumatic experiences or events are more than stressful; they are devastating, with the person often feeling terror, shame, helplessness, and powerlessness (Courtois, 2008). As we discuss later in this chapter, trauma overwhelms both a person's ability to cope and their biological capacity to respond to the stress associated with traumatic events (van der Kolk, 2015).

Trauma is a very common experience, but it is often hidden from view, because those who have experienced it may not talk about it openly due to stigma or pain, and also because people respond to traumatic events differently. There are, however, important clues that can alert health and human service providers to the likelihood that a person has previously experienced and/or is still experiencing trauma. Cultivating the ability to consider the nature and impact of trauma can radically change how we understand and relate to the difficulties faced by people who are accessing services or supports. This understanding positions us to think and feel differently about how services can begin to help those who have experienced trauma feel safe.

In this chapter, we highlight some key ideas about the nature and impacts of trauma in order to promote *trauma awareness* among those who design and deliver a wide range of services. Such awareness is a critical starting point for trauma- and violence-informed care (TVIC). Those who wish to read more deeply about trauma and violence are directed to the resources listed at the end of this chapter.

The Many Faces of Trauma

There is no universally accepted way of describing traumatic events, and many types of events can lead to traumatic stress. Trauma can result from exposure to a single event, such as sexual assault or the sudden death of a loved one, or through exposure to repeated or enduring events such as intimate partner violence, child abuse, or war. *Situational* traumas include the often unpredictable events that happen to individuals (such as being the victim of a crime or being in an accident), but they can also affect entire communities, such as with gang violence or natural disasters (the latter are also referred to as *collective* or *historical* traumas). The enduring harms inflicted by colonialism on Canada's Indigenous peoples are an especially poignant example of collective trauma (Monchalin, Marques, Reasons, & Arora, 2019) (see chapter 1.2).

Interpersonal trauma, the most common type of trauma globally (Benjet et al., 2016), involves violence, manipulation, or abuse at the hands of another person, often someone with whom the person has a relationship, such as a family member, friend, or a person in a position of authority (a teacher, coach, or religious leader). Interpersonal trauma involves abuse of power, violation of trust, and elements of coercive control and is often ongoing (i.e., rather than an isolated event). *Complex trauma* is often used to describe these types of events and people's responses to them because the harms are typically greater, particularly when trauma begins in childhood, and these effects can persist over a long period of time (Courtois, 2008; Herman, 1992).

Finally, given our innate capacity for empathy, it is important to note that trauma can be experienced "second-hand" (or *vicariously*) by observing or hearing about traumatic experiences that have happened to others. Trauma does not occur in a vacuum; it also takes a toll on families, workplaces, and communities. This is a critical issue for the safety and well-being of service providers and organizations alike and is a reminder that we are all vulnerable to the effects of trauma (see chapter 1.4).

Identifying Trauma "Clues"

Traumatic events are perceived as *threatening* and *uncontrollable* and can overwhelm the person's ability to manage. This *traumatic stress* can threaten a person's sense of safety and well-being. Common signs of post-traumatic stress (PTS) are shown in figure 1.1.1. These signs can be "clues" or "signals" that a person has experienced (or continues to experience) trauma. These symptoms are not a marker of personal weakness; indeed, they are an *expected* reaction to horrific and harmful experiences. Individuals can experience some or all of these symptoms at different levels of intensity and with different impacts on their lives (American Psychological Association [APA], 2013).

It can be helpful to think about PTS on a continuum. When a traumatic event is situational and time-limited (such as the death of a loved one), PTS is more likely to be *acute*, with mild to moderate impacts that usually last for

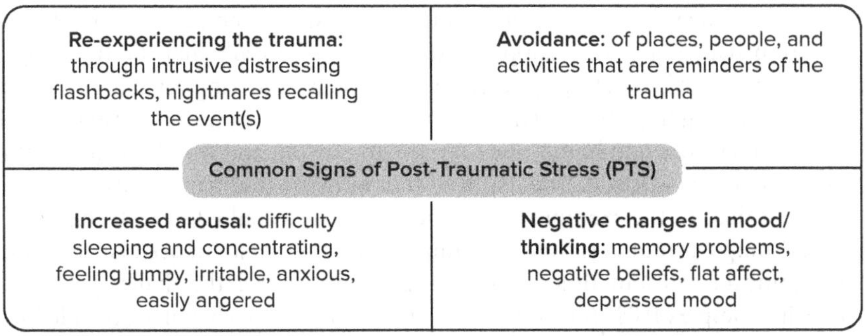

1.1 Trauma, Violence, Health, and Well-Being 13

Re-experiencing the trauma: through intrusive distressing flashbacks, nightmares recalling the event(s)	Avoidance: of places, people, and activities that are reminders of the trauma
Common Signs of Post-Traumatic Stress (PTS)	
Increased arousal: difficulty sleeping and concentrating, feeling jumpy, irritable, anxious, easily angered	Negative changes in mood/thinking: memory problems, negative beliefs, flat affect, depressed mood

Figure 1.1.1 Common features of post-traumatic stress. Copyright 2021, the authors.

short period of time. For example, a man who is assaulted during a bar fight may experience fear and anxiety from this event, along with difficulty sleeping; he may even avoid going out because of these feelings. These symptoms are likely to decrease over time as he goes about this life. In general, people are *resilient*, and acute trauma often resolves on its own with no specialized treatment (APA, 2013).

In contrast, trauma that is associated with severe, chronic traumatic experiences (e.g., sexual or physical abuse at any age, Indigenous residential schools, torture, combat) typically has more intense and enduring effects (Courtois, 2008). In this type of *complex trauma*, a person may also experience the common symptoms of PTS (such as nightmares, difficulty sleeping, or feeling depressed) more intensely along with other changes that can alter their sense of themselves, their feelings of safety, and their relationships with others (American Psychological Association [APA], 2013; Herman, 1992). Some additional indications of complex trauma include changes in:

- emotions (e.g., persistent sadness, suicidality, outbursts of anger, inability to feel joy);
- consciousness (e.g., forgetting or reliving events, feeling detached from others);
- perceptions (e.g., feeling shame, guilt, stigma, helplessness, damaged or "broken");
- relationships (e.g., mistrust of others, isolation, feeling unable to connect); and
- meaning and beliefs (e.g., hopelessness, despair, feeling without purpose).

For example, a woman with an abusive intimate partner may live in constant fear of physical, sexual, and/or psychological abuse that is both unpredictable and uncontrollable. Over time, as her partner belittles and degrades her, she may feel a growing sense of shame, entrapment, stigma, and despair that keeps her from reaching out for support. As much as she wants her life to change, she is "on watch" and sleeps poorly because she is preparing for the worst and reliving the ongoing abuse. Her energy is low, and she is on edge, irritable, and distracted at work and home. She may see no way out and wonder whether the pain of living is worth it. The depth of this woman's trauma response is much different than in the example of the man who was assaulted by a stranger in a fight. Complex trauma is especially important to understand because it results in significant and sometimes long-lasting harms. Indeed, the challenges of living with complex PTS and its associated harms are often what bring people into contact with health and human services (van der Kolk, 2015).

However, as complex trauma expert Judith Herman wrote, "all too commonly, chronically traumatized people suffer in silence; if they complain at all, their complaints are not well understood" (Herman, 1992, p. 119). The intense distress and array of symptoms reported by people who have experienced complex trauma mimic other mental health problems (van der Kolk, 2015). Without a sense of trauma awareness, care providers may not link these clues to traumatic experiences and instead misdiagnose them as mental health problems that are highly stigmatizing – most commonly borderline personality disorder, somatization disorder, or multiple personality disorder. Once labelled, the person is often blamed for their victimization (e.g., questioned why they did not leave the abusive relationship) or are accused of being manipulative, malingering, or attention-seeking (Herman, 1992). Trauma awareness helps care providers push back against the tendency to label distressing symptoms as personal deficits and, instead, contextualize, normalize, and validate these experiences as common signs of trauma.

Children can have some of the same responses to trauma as adults, such as difficulty sleeping, nightmares, depressed mood, or anxiety, but they may also have some unique responses (Bryson et al., 2017). For example, an increase in aggressive behaviour or acting out is common, and so is withdrawal from activities that were previously enjoyable. Very young children (less than six years) may be more fearful, cling to adults, or show regressive behaviour (e.g., thumb-sucking, tantrums). Older children may withdraw from their friends and lose interest in school or important rights of passage (e.g., dating). Importantly, experiences of trauma during critical periods of development and maturation can have more devastating and lifelong effects. For example, experiencing abuse by someone in a position of trust may have deep impacts on a child's self-worth, ability to trust, and sense of safety. These impacts can persist into adulthood and negatively affect their self-care, work, relationships, and many other parts of their lives (Shonkoff et al., 2012). See table 1.1.1 for examples of how to "read" trauma clues.

Table 1.1.1 How you read the clues matters: Bad behaviour or trauma?

Scenarios	A common response	A different opinion
An elderly man waits in line at a busy pharmacy for a prescription, shifting back and forth while clutching his walker. When another customer is called ahead of him, he bursts out in anger "Hey, I was here first! You people always ignore me."	The store manager tries to calm him down, but the man keeps making a scene. She notices that customers are whispering and wonders if he is high or dangerous. She asks a cashier to call the police.	The store manager tries to calm him down but gives him space. She wonders: "Is this man in pain? What is happening with him?" She offers him water and a quiet place to sit down.
A young woman with a family history of breast cancer has cancelled a mammogram appointment four times in the past year. She tells her doctor that she is "freaked out" before the procedure and that she can't sleep or function.	The doctor grows impatient with her lack of motivation and "all the drama" and reminds the woman that this is a simple test that is very easy to do.	The doctor recognizes that the woman is anxious and needs more time and support. She talks to the woman about what would help her feel more at ease.
A woman witnesses a physical assault on a neighbour during an argument with a delivery person. When a police officer arrives at her home to take her statement, she becomes flustered and gives conflicting details about what happened.	The officer taps his foot on the floor and asks her, "So, which version is the truth?" In his report, he notes that she is an unreliable witness who may be lying.	The officer calmly acknowledges that seeing an assault can be upsetting. He asks if she would like to tell what she knows after she has had a chance to become more calm.
A Grade 4 student throws a rock at another student in the school yard, injuring him. When the immediate situation is safely resolved, his teacher and principal discuss what should happen next.	His teacher tells the principal that the child acts out often, and is disruptive, "spaced out," and just not interested in school." She suggests that he be suspended for a few days and tested for ADHD.	His teacher notices that the child is tired and has been out of sorts for some time. She wonders if something is happening at home and asks the principal what can be done to support this child.

How It Works: The Embodiment of Trauma and Violence

If traumatic events cause great pain, distress, and disruption, why not put them in the past and move on? The person may *want* to move on, but these experiences continue to creep into their life because the very responses that help them survive the event may also play a role in their ongoing distress and mental, emotional, and physical harms (van der Kolk, 2015). At its core, trauma is fundamentally a stress response with both psychological and physiological aspects. In this sense, trauma is not about what is wrong with a person; rather, it is an expected response aimed at dealing with events that are overwhelming and that threaten survival.

While trauma was once thought to be only in the mind of the person ("it's all in their head"), we now understand that it is much more complex. Research has demonstrated that trauma affects the mind, the brain, and the body in different and complex ways that are tied to how we think, feel emotions, experience pleasure and pain, and deal with stress. So, while trauma is in the mind, it is also in the body. For this reason, we now think about trauma as an *embodied* experience that is connected to reactions in the brain (van der Kolk, 2015).

Our brains are pre-wired to remember anything that threatens our survival (Wright, 2020). Experiences that are perceived as threatening are imprinted in memory, along with the sights, sounds, feelings, tastes, and smells associated with these experiences. When a person remembers these events or encounters reminders (e.g., someone who looks similar to an abusive partner, being touched in a certain way), the brain responds to the threat as though it is happening in the present. This is referred to as a *trigger*. Imagine, for example, that you experienced food poisoning after eating at a favourite restaurant. You may find that smelling the same dish brings back off-putting memories or that revisiting the same restaurant brings on nausea for no apparent reason. When the experience of trauma is significant, complex, or long-lasting, these triggers can be much more pronounced and less predictable because of their impact on the brain (Lowe, Blachman-Forshay, & Koenen, 2015). In this case, encountering sensations that remind the person of the trauma can trigger panic, intense fear, or outbursts of anger that are out of character for that person. These *automatic* responses are not within the person's control; in some cases, the person may not even be aware of what triggered the reaction, but they must still live with the results.

Trauma changes some important structures in the brain and affects how these structures function as part of a system designed to cope with stress (van der Kolk, 2015; Wright, 2020). The three main structures in the brain that are involved with coping with stress are:

- the *hippocampus*, responsible for responding to threats, regulating mood, storing short-term memories, and making sense of time;

- the *amygdala*, the warning system of the brain that activates fear and imprints emotions onto memories; and
- the *prefrontal cortex*, which is responsible for thinking and cognitive functions (such as problem-solving and decision-making) and self-focused systems (such as one's sense of self and personal values) that are important for social interactions and for reading social cues.

These structures work together in various ways (both positive and negative) to respond to stress. When stress is short-term, structures in the brain are activated that create a *fight or flight* response. We have all experienced the immediate rush of stress hormones that occurs when we experience unexpected stress – our heart rate and breathing increase, we become acutely aware of our surroundings, and our bodies divert blood to our muscles and away from other organs so that we are ready to protect ourselves. When the threat has passed, our bodies return to the pre-threat state. The mechanism that returns the body to a state of balance (or equilibrium) after a threat is referred to as allostasis (McEwen, 2005).

When trauma is complex or ongoing, however, the stress system breaks down and no longer operates in the same way. The brain's alarm system (amygdala) responds to traumatic experiences (threats) by flooding the brain with stress hormones, especially *cortisol*. However, the system that is responsible for signalling that a threat has passed (hippocampus) has been damaged by the chronic exposure to trauma. No longer does the body return to a *pre-threat state*; instead, its stress response remains activated, resulting in a chronic state of arousal (van der Kolk, 2015; Wright, 2020). These stress hormones initially help create balance; however, when they are chronically elevated they can lead to *allostatic overload*, which creates wear and tear on the body and brain (McEwen, 2005). In this state, the body is on high alert and easily triggered, and higher-order thinking, attention, memory, and processing of emotions are affected by the flooding of stress hormones in the brain (Lupien, Juster, Raymond, & Marin, 2018).

Consider a woman in an emergency department who has experienced a sexual assault. When describing her experiences to the sexual assault nurse, she may have difficulty remembering parts of her experience, describe the events out of sequence, or change what she reports. If the nurse is impatient or looks at the woman in a particular way, this may remind her of an abusive parent and further elevate the brain's stress response.

Trauma, Health, and Well-Being

Cortisol supports many important functions in the body; for example, it regulates metabolism, reduces inflammation, and processes negative emotions.

However, high levels of cortisol due to traumatic stress affect all body systems and can lead to short- and long-term health problems (Wright, 2020). There is even evidence that the cells of people who have experienced complex trauma or chronic stress age more quickly, so that their bodies are "older" than their chronological age (Epel & Prather, 2018).

People dealing with chronic stress may exhibit a range of health problems, such as disrupted sleep and fatigue, weight gain, increased blood pressure, headaches, irritability, sexual dysfunction, or intestinal problems (APA, 2013). In both children and adults, research has established links between trauma and major mental health problems, such as post-traumatic stress disorder (PTSD), depression, suicidal ideation, and anxiety (Banyard, Edwards & Kendell-Tackett, 2009; Thomason & Marusak, 2017); and between trauma and greater risk of chronic physical health problems, such as heart disease, cancer, diabetes, and chronic pain associated with a wide range of conditions (e.g., chronic fatigue, arthritis, gastro-intestinal problems, migraines, pelvic pain) (Banyard et al., 2009). Much of the existing trauma research has focused on women because of the prevalence of gender-based violence and the severe impact it has on women (Bacchus, Ranganathan, Watts & Devries, 2018).

Importantly, experiencing trauma in early life and the accumulation of traumatic experiences over the life course together increase the risk of chronic physical and/or mental health problems (Scott-Storey, 2011). For example, stress hormones initially secreted to protect the immune system begin to suppress it, leading to higher risk of infections and resulting in chronic inflammation that affects many different body systems. In the cardiovascular system, for example, these changes place strain on the heart and thicken (or "harden") the arteries and the walls of the heart so that they function less effectively. Under the influence of complex stress, the endocrine system releases glucocorticoids that increase both appetite and insulin resistance (a state that increases the risk of Type 2 diabetes). It is not surprising, then, that many health problems, such as autoimmune disorders, obesity, diabetes, high blood pressure, and stroke, are associated with complex trauma. Risky health behaviours (e.g., substance use, smoking, sexual practices) may be a way of finding relief from the distressing symptoms of trauma and the resulting health problems, including chronic pain. The relationships between trauma, violence, substance use, and pain are complex, making these problems more difficult to manage effectively in many cases. Also, stigma often interferes with efforts to find support and further magnifies the inequities among those who live with the most complex and devastating histories of trauma.

The Social Context of Traumatic Stress

What explains why people can experience the same or similar traumatic events but have different responses to them? Experiences of trauma are complex and are shaped by a multitude of factors. As noted earlier, whether the trauma is a single event that is unlikely to occur again or a chronic, ongoing experience (particularly interpersonal trauma), the timing and accumulation of these experiences both have an impact. Beyond this, the broader context in which trauma occurs profoundly influences the ways in which people experience and respond to any event. An ecological perspective reminds us that people are products of their genetic make-up and their biology and also of the environment in which they live and grow (Harvey, 1996). Local contexts (e.g., family and social relationships, economic situation, neighbourhood safety, access to services) as well as more distant ones (such as public policies, social norms, and historical events) have powerful effects on a person's risk of trauma and their responses to it. Trauma "happens" to people, but to understand the entire picture of trauma, we cannot separate the person from their history and context.

To understand the trauma response of an LGBTQ2I+ youth, for example, we must consider that bullying, harassment, and societal stigma are common experiences. If this young person also faces barriers created by poverty or racism, these additional stressors are likely to both compound the toxic harms of other traumatic experiences and reduce options for seeking help and support. For example, this youth may be (rightly) mistrustful of service providers based on their experiences and more likely to engage in high-risk behaviour (such as substance use) to numb the intolerable pain of complex trauma, because this option is accessible. The effects of social context can also be positive. Having positive and supportive relationships (with an adult or peer) and a sense of community connectedness can help reduce the negative effects of trauma and other toxic stress (Valentine & Shipherd, 2018).

The patriarchal structure of Canadian society partly explains why the types and consequences of traumatic experiences often differ by gender. For example, men in Canada are at greater risk of being murdered, robbed, or assaulted by strangers or acquaintances, while women are more likely to be victims of childhood sexual abuse, rape, criminal harassment, forcible confinement, human trafficking, and intimate partner violence (Allen & McCarthy, 2018). These experiences are linked to differences in gender roles and norms, and to access to power, both at home and in public spaces.

But gender alone does not explain risk of and responses to trauma. For example, intimate partner violence accounts for one quarter of all violent crime reported to police in Canada, 80 per cent of which is a result of male violence perpetrated against a female partner (Burczycka, 2018). Women who have experienced intimate partner violence have poorer mental and physical health than women in the general population (Bacchus et al., 2018) and seek help from family and friends and a wide range of services (e.g., violence against women services, health care, police, social services) (Ford-Gilboe et al., 2015). However, not all women face the same risk of abuse, nor do they experience harms or seek support in the same way, largely because of differing contexts. Those who face the greatest structural barriers (e.g., Indigenous women, women living with a disability and/or on low incomes) are at greatest risk of violence and trauma, and their options for dealing with these issues are also more limited. Furthermore, women who experience multiple forms of trauma across their lifespan (child abuse, sexual assault, intimate partner violence) are more likely to suffer health problems that are cumulative (Davies et al., 2015). Failing to consider the complex, historic and contemporary structural violence experienced by Indigenous people, for example, leads to an utterly inadequate understanding of trauma within Indigenous communities (O'Neil, Fraser, Kitchenham, & McDonald, 2016) (see chapter 3.1).

Two Approaches for Supporting Survivors of Trauma

The question of how to support people who are living with the ongoing impacts of trauma and violence is a critical one that has generated much discussion. This problem has been approached in two ways. *Trauma-specific services* attempt to address the trauma (and the effects of trauma) directly through specialized therapies that are delivered by professionals who have been specially trained in these approaches. For example, there is good evidence that both trauma-focused cognitive behavioural therapy (TF-CBT), a form of talk therapy, and EMDR (eye movement desensitization and reprocessing) reduce PTSD and depression (Lewis, Roberts, Andrew, Starling, & Bisson, 2020; Wilson et al., 2018). Newer approaches, including yoga and meditation, are also being tested and some show promise (Gallegos, Crean, Pigeon, & Heffner, 2017). However, there are long waiting lists for professional services in Canada's publicly funded health care system, with private services available to those who can pay out-of-pocket. Given these access issues, and the inequities built into the system, the benefits of trauma-specific care are out of reach for many.

A second approach, *trauma-informed care (TIC)*, focuses more on creating a culture of safety across services and systems for all people, rather that attempting to identify and address trauma specifically (Harris & Fallot, 2001; Bloom, 2013). TIC grew out of the increasing recognition that trauma is pervasive and has far-reaching impacts, particularly in terms of mental health problems and substance use. Yet systems of care often work in ways that unintentionally re-traumatize people rather than support their healing. While there is significant interest in TIC – and while there are many examples of the positive effects of implementing TIC in a wide range of service settings (Elliott, Bjelajac, Fallot, Markoff, & Reed, 2005; Hales et al., 2019) – some limitations or blind spots have been suggested. Among these, TIC is often taken up in a way that focuses on the individual but pays limited attention to their history and context. As outlined in chapter 1.5, and as discussed in the rest of this volume, trauma- and violence-informed care (TVIC) builds on TIC while also considering these important structural factors.

In summary, not all distressing events are traumatic. Rather, the person's experience of the event(s) determines whether it is traumatic. Furthermore, trauma responses are expected reactions to overwhelming events and can differ from person to person based on factors that include the type of trauma (single event or complex), the person's life history, and the circumstances of the person's life. Having a basic understanding about how trauma impacts on our brains, minds, and bodies can help service providers and administrators be mindful of trauma responses in their daily work and help them design high-quality services that provide effective support to people who have experienced trauma.

KEY MESSAGES AND IMPLICATIONS

- Trauma is a stress response within the brain, the mind, and the body, with potential for serious long-term effects on health, well-being, and life quality. Rather than being a sign of weakness, traumatic stress is an expected response to an event(s) that overwhelms the person's capacity to cope.
- The ability to recognize common "clues" that a person has or is experiencing trauma can radically shift how health and human service providers understand and respond to the significant challenges that people living with effects of trauma and violence face.
- *Trauma awareness* is a foundation for designing and delivering safer, more supportive services across all sectors and a first step in reducing the toll of trauma and violence on individuals, families, and communities.

REFERENCES

Allen, M., & McCarthy, K. (2018). Victims of police-reported violent crime in Canada: National, provincial and territorial fact sheets, 2016. *Statistics Canada*. Retrieved from https://www150.statcan.gc.ca/n1/pub/85-002-x/2018001/article/54960-eng.htm.

American Psychological Association [APA]. (2013). *Diagnostic and statistical manual of mental disorders* (5th ed.). Arlington, VA: APA Publishing.

Bacchus, L.J., Ranganathan, M., Watts, C., & Devries, K. (2018). Recent intimate partner violence against women and health: A systematic review and meta-analysis of cohort studies. *BMJ Open, 8*. https://doi.org/10.1136/bmjopen-2017-019995.

Banyard, V.L., Edwards, V.J., & Kendall-Tackett, K.A. (Eds.). (2009). *Trauma and physical health: Understanding the effects of extreme stress and of psychological harm*. New York, NY: Routledge.

Benjet., C., Bromet, E., Karam, E.G., Kessler, R.C., McLaughlin, K.A., Ruscio, A.M., ... Koenen, K.C. (2016). The epidemiology of traumatic event exposure worldwide: Results from the World Mental Health Survey Consortium. *Psychological Medicine*, 46(2), 327–43. https://doi.org/10.1017/S0033291715001981.

Bloom, S.L. (2013). *Creating sanctuary: Toward the evolution of sane societies*. New York, NY: Routledge.

Bryson, S.A., Gauvin., E., Jamieson, A., Rathgeber, M., Faulkner-Gibson, L., Bell, S., ... Burke, S. (2017). What are effective strategies for implementing trauma-informed care in youth inpatient psychiatric and residential treatment settings? A realist systematic review. *International Journal of Mental Health Systems*, 11, 36. https://doi.org/10.1186/s13033-017-0137-3.

Burczycka, M. (2018). Section 3: Police-reported intimate partner violence. In *Family violence in Canada: A statistical profile, 2016*. Canadian Centre for Justice Statistics, Statistics Canada. Retrieved from https://www150.statcan.gc.ca/n1/pub/85-002-x/2018001/article/54893/03-eng.htm.

Courtois, C.A. (2008). Complex trauma, complex reactions: Assessment and treatment. *Psychological Trauma: Theory, Research, Practice, and Policy*, S(1), 86–100. https://doi.org/10.1037/1942-9681.S.1.86.

Davies, L., Ford-Gilboe, M., Willson, A., Varcoe, C., Wuest, J., Campbell, J., & Scott-Storey, K. (2015). Patterns of cumulative abuse among female survivors of intimate partner violence: Links to women's health and socioeconomic status. *Violence Against Women*, 21(1), 30–48. https://doi.org/10.1177/1077801214564076.

Elliott, D., Bjelajac, P., Fallot, R., Markoff, L., & Reed, B. (2005). Trauma-informed or trauma-denied: Principles for implementation of trauma-informed services for women. *Journal of Community Psychology*, 33, 461–77. https://doi.org/10.1002/jcop.20063.

Epel, E.S., & Prather, A.A. (2018). Stress, telomeres, and psychopathology: Toward a deeper understanding of a triad of early aging. *Annual Review of Clinical Psychology*, 14, 371–97. https://doi.org/10.1146/annurev-clinpsy-032816-045054.

Ford-Gilboe, M., Varcoe, C., Noh, M., Wuest, J., Hammerton, J., Alhalal, E., & Burnett, C. (2015). Patterns and predictors of service use among women who have recently left abusive partners. *Journal of Family Violence*, 30(4), 419–31. https://doi.org/10.1007/s10896-015-9688-8.

Gallegos, A.M., Crean, H.F., Pigeon, W.R., & Heffner, K.L. (2017). Meditation and yoga for post traumatic stress disorder: A meta-analytic review of randomized controlled trials. *Clinical Psychology Review*, 58, 115–24. https://doi.org/10.1016/j.cpr.2017.10.004.

Hales, T., Green, S., Bissonette, S., Warden, A., Diebold, J., Koury, S., & Nochajski, T. (2019). Trauma-informed care outcome study. *Research on Social Work Practice*, 29(5), 529–39. https://doi.org/10.1177/1049731518766618.

Harris, M., & Fallot, R.D. (Eds.). (2001). *New directions for mental health services: Using trauma theory to design service systems*. New York, NY: Jossey-Bass.

Harvey, M.R. (1996). An ecological view of psychological trauma and trauma recovery. *Journal of Trauma Stress, 9*(1), 3–23. https://doi.org/10.1007/BF02116830.

Herman, J.L. (1992). *Trauma and recovery: The aftermath of violence from domestic violence to political terror.* New York, NY: Jossey-Bass.

Lewis, C., Roberts, N.P., Andrew, M., Starling, E., & Bisson, J.I. (2020). Psychological therapies for PTSD in adults: Systematic review and meta-analysis. *European Journal of Psychotraumatology, 11*(1). https://doi.org/10.1080/20008198.2020.1729633

Lowe, S.R., Blachman-Forshay, J., & Koenen, K.C. (2015). Trauma as a public health issue: Epidemiology of trauma and trauma-related disorders. In U. Schnyder & M. Cloitre (Eds.), *Evidence based treatments for trauma-related psychological disorders* (pp. 11–40). Switzerland: Springer. https://doi.org/10.1007/978-3-319-07109-1_2

Lupien, S.J., Juster, R.P., Raymond, C., & Marin, M.F. (2018). The effects of chronic stress on the human brain: From neurotoxicity, to vulnerability, to opportunity. *Frontiers in Neuroendocrinology, 49,* 91–105. https://doi.org/10.1016/j.yfrne.2018.02.001.

McEwen, B.S. (2005). Stressed or stressed out: What is the difference? *Journal of Psychiatry and Neuroscience, 30*(5), 315–18.

Monchalin, L., Marques, O., Reasons, C., & Arora P. (2019). Homicide and Indigenous peoples in North America: A structural analysis. *Aggression and Violent Behavior, 46,* 212–18. https://doi.org/10.1016/j.avb.2019.01.011.

O'Neill, L., Fraser, T., Kitchenham, A., & McDonald, V. (2016). Hidden burdens: A review of intergenerational, historical and complex trauma, implications for indigenous families. *Journal of Child & Adolescent Trauma, 11*(2), 173–86. https://doi.org/10.1007/s40653-016-0117-9.

Scott-Storey, K. (2011). Cumulative abuse: Do things add up? An evaluation of the conceptualization, operationalization, and methodological approaches in the study of the phenomenon of cumulative abuse. *Trauma, Violence, & Abuse, 12*(3),135–50. https://doi.org/10.1177/1524838011404253.

Shonkoff, J.P., Garner, A.S., Seigel, B.S., Dobbins, M.I., Earls, M.F., McGuinn, L., ... Wegner, L.M. (2012). The lifelong effects of early child adversity and toxic stress. *Pediatrics, 129* (1), e232–46. https://doi.org/10.1542/peds.2011-2663.

Thomason, M.E., & Marusak, H.A. (2017). Toward understanding the impact of trauma on the early developing human brain. *Neuroscience, 342,* 55–67. https://doi.org/10.1016/j.neuroscience.2016.02.022.

Valentine, S.E., & Shipherd, J.C. (2018). A systematic review of social stress and mental health among transgender and gender non-conforming people in the United States. *Clinical Psychology Review, 66,* 24–38. https://doi.org/10.1016/j.cpr.2018.03.003.

van Ameringen, M., Mancini, C., Patterson, B., & Boyle, M.H. (2008). Posttraumatic stress disorder in Canada. *CNS Neuroscience & Therapeutics, 14,* 171–81. https://doi.org/10.1111/j.1755-5949.2008.00049.x.

van der Kolk, B. (2015). *The body keeps the score: Brain, mind and body in the healing of trauma*. New York, NY: Penguin.

Wilson, G., Farrell, D., Barron, I., Hutchins, J., Whybrow, D., & Kiernan, M.D. (2018). The use of eye-movement desensitization reprocessing (EMDR) in treating post-traumatic stress disorder – A systematic review. *Frontiers in Psychology, 9*. https://doi.org/10.3389/fpsyg.2018.00923.

Wright, S.E. (2020). *Redefining trauma: Understanding and coping with a cortisoaked brain*. New York, NY: Routledge.

1.2 Integrating Understanding of Structural and Systemic Violence into Trauma- and Violence-Informed Care

COLLEEN VARCOE AND ANNETTE J. BROWNE

A key reason why the authors of this handbook promote the idea of building on "trauma-informed" approaches is that doing so supports specific attention to structural and systemic forms of violence. This chapter focuses on how social and structural arrangements perpetuate violence, differentially affecting some groups more than others. The chapter considers how interpersonal forms of violence intersect with structural forms of violence such as systemic racism and poverty. This understanding sets the foundation for the development of structural competence and structural humility, both of which are fundamental to designing, delivering, and evaluating trauma- and *violence*-informed approaches.

Attention to structural and systemic violence is fundamental to ensuring that health care and social service providers understand people's experiences and needs in context. It also supports efforts to address the conditions of their lives that impair their health and well-being. The term "structural conditions" refers to how societies are structured and organized through policies and practices. In health, social services, justice, education, child welfare, and other systems and sectors, the way things are organized produces an inequitable distribution of the social determinants of health that creates harms for people. Specifically, attending to structural and systemic violence helps providers understand experiences of interpersonal violence in broader contexts that influence health and access to social and health care supports. Developing strategies to mitigate the ongoing harms of structural violence is essential in order to reduce health and social inequities, both locally and globally.

By the end of this chapter, readers will be able to (1) explain the importance of understanding structural and systemic violence, structural competence, and structural humility for the provision of trauma- and violence-informed health care and other human services, (2) explain the relationship between structural and interpersonal violence, and between structural violence and health and well-being, (3) recognize how an understanding of violence as a problem of individuals or of particular "cultures" dominates society in general and health and social care in particular, and identify ways of countering those understandings, and (4) identify ways to integrate understandings of structural violence within organizations, agencies, and individual practices.

Understanding Interpersonal Violence through a Structural Lens

Social responses to interpersonal violence, especially intimate partner violence, are no longer based primarily on the perception that it as an individual problem; such violence is now seen instead as social and systemic. Early understandings of violence as the individual acts of abnormal people have given way to understanding all forms of violence as patterned; yet despite these advances in thinking, individualist and culturalist explanations persist in society and in health and social services (DeKeseredy, 2020; Hunnicutt, 2020; Riemann, 2019). For example, an analysis of nursing textbooks (Price-Glynn & Missari, 2017) found that most of them did not address interpersonal violence and that more than half of those that did, did not take gender-based violence and gender inequities into account, or they provided gender-symmetrical descriptions (i.e., they assumed that people of all genders experience violence in the same way). Those that used asymmetrical lenses (i.e., that assumed that people of different genders and identities experience violence differently) were more likely to contextualize men's violence against women within broader historical and social forces and inequities. It is this latter approach – understanding interpersonal violence in broader contexts – that is required for research, policy, and practice to be effective in relation to violence. Indeed, this understanding is foundational to trauma- and violence-informed care (TVIC).

Explanations of the differential prevalence rates of violence among subpopulations have evolved from earlier "culturalist" explanations to those that consider the social determinants of inequity. Culturalism refers to the process of framing issues (such as intimate partner violence – IPV) as stemming primarily from presumed cultural characteristics or patterns – presumptions often founded on prevailing stigmatizing societal ideas about particular cultural groups, such as rates of violence against women being higher in specific ethnocultural groups (Browne & Varcoe, 2019; Browne, Varcoe, & Wytenbroek, forthcoming; Varcoe, Browne, & Kang-Dhillon, 2019). Culturalism is one means by which misinformation about violence is perpetuated in our societies. For example, in Canada, the higher rates of violence against Indigenous women were at one time often presumed to be somehow related to the "culture" of Indigenous peoples, but increasing attention is now being paid to colonization, racism, and inequity as causative of these differences (Brownridge, 2008; Monchalin, Marques, Reasons, & Arora, 2019; Pedersen, Malcoe, & Pulkingham, 2013; Varcoe, Ford-Gilboe, et al., 2019). This new understanding helps link broad social forces to the violence directed toward Indigenous people in general, and Indigenous women in particular.

1.2 Integrating Understanding of Violence into TVIC

Similarly, in Canada and in other national contexts, while certain racialized groups (i.e., groups identified or described in terms of their presumed "race" or ethnicity) often have been characterized in culturalist and racialized public discourse as particularly violent, increasing attention to the influence of social and contextual factors has shown how violence is patterned, shaped, and understood in the context of historical, social, economic, and linguistic forces. The evolution toward understanding violence as shaped by social determinants has been fuelled by multiple influences, including sequential waves of feminist thinking. Black feminists have offered intersectional analyses as ways of better accounting for the impact of multiple forms of inequity, and this approach can be applied to link structural violence to other forms of violence and to support integrating understanding of structural violence into TVIC.

BOX 1.2.1 "HONOUR KILLING": FROM CULTURALIST TO STRUCTURAL UNDERSTANDINGS OF VIOLENCE

Dr Keith Dormond, a police officer, studied how the idea of honour-related violence (HRV) was understood by organizations such as ethnocultural agencies, shelters, law enforcement services, schools, and mental health providers (Dormond, 2020). He argued that "violence against racialized women that is known as 'honour'-killing or 'honour'-related violence and oppression (HRVO) is typically depicted in dominant media discourses as being the result of the cultures of the victims and perpetrators. Culture is framed as causing HRVO because dominant media discourses in the Western world tend to depict racialized communities through [a lens that frames] them as homogeneously dangerous, uncivilized, and barbaric" (p. iii).

He showed how such service providers have tried to push back against these dominant understandings. These providers found that the most effective strategies accepted the fact that "honour" and "shame" are part of many patterns of violence against women among people from all cultures and social contexts; they also paid attention to the influence of the migration context, as well as to power (specifically, how institutions control access to resources through policy and force). Applying a structural understanding can unseat the idea that "honour-killing" is being justified by notions of honour or of reducing shame (as opposed to being inexcusable violence) and is inherent to racialized communities. Such understanding can reveal how racist lenses can entrench racism and simultaneously excuse violence against women; it can also point to how structural forms of violence (e.g., anti-immigrant and anti-refugee sentiments, as well as policies that exclude certain people from access to health care or employment) create conditions for interpersonal violence.

Structural and Systemic Violence

Structural violence is directly relevant to our understanding of TVIC and our enactment of it. Structural violence provides a lens through which to describe the social arrangements that continue to put people and populations in harm's way; these arrangements are structural because they are embedded in the political and economic organization of our society, and they are violent because they harm people (Farmer, Nizeye, Stulac, & Keshavjee, 2006). Developing an understanding of structural violence is especially helpful for shifting attention away from individualistic framings of racism, stigmatization, discrimination, violence, and trauma. Conversely, when structural violence goes unacknowledged, explanations for how, for example, systemic racism shapes health care often emphasize individual behaviours (e.g., the bad apple in the barrel, the individual provider who may have racist beliefs), cultural characteristics (e.g., it's in "their" culture to be violent toward women), or biologized (e.g., those people are genetically more "prone" to being alcoholic), thus giving the impression that the status quo is somewhat inevitable or "natural" in the sense of not being primarily social or structural in origin (Hansen & Metzl, 2019). So, understanding the relationship between structural violence and interpersonal violence helps us avoid simplistic understandings of (for example) IPV as the consequence of individual pathology or ethnicity. It also draws attention to broader patterns and to the need for changes in public policies and discourses.

The recent events in Canada surrounding the tragic death of Ms Joyce Echaquan ("Joyce Echaquan," 2020), the investigation into emergency department staff playing "games" to guess the blood-alcohol levels of Indigenous patients (Turpel-Lafond, 2020), the decades-long investigation into the death of Mr Brian Sinclair (Brian Sinclair Working Group, 2017; McCallum & Perry, 2018), and the treatment of Ms Ottawa by the RCMP as they investigated the death of her son Colton Boushie (Quenneville, 2021) provide glimpses into the extent to which structural violence, in the form of systemic racism, is enacted and sustained, with lethal impacts. These impacts are entirely relevant in contexts beyond Canada, as recently documented in relation to Aboriginal and Torres Strait Islander peoples in Australia (Cullen et al., 2021; Fisher et al., 2021). Direct care providers need to recognize the context and impact of structural violence and continually orient the practice of TVIC simultaneously (a) toward individuals so as to make them feel as deserving, welcome, and affirmed as possible when they come for services, and (b) toward broader transformations of the structures and systems that sustain violence and inequities. Attending to (b) does not imply acting in "big" ways; actions can be directed toward seemingly small, incremental shifts in how we organize our work or our practices. For example, we can seek ways to acknowledge the racist social context in which we are all steeped, by engaging meaningfully with the people we are serving when we design and deliver services, by making subtle shifts in the language we use in practice settings, both verbally and in documentation, and by seeking ways to acknowledge the history of our local communities.

Structural Violence and TVIC

Understanding people's experiences and needs in context is crucial to TVIC for at least four reasons. First, *people who have experienced trauma and violence often experience shame and guilt and have often been judged, stigmatized, and blamed in many contexts*. When people anticipate judgment and blame, they are deterred from accessing care and services, and this can lead to further judgment and blame for not accessing said care and services. These dynamics are very familiar among people who have been sexually assaulted and/or who are experiencing intimate partner violence. What is less well understood is how these dynamics are exacerbated for people who are experiencing structural violence and inequities. So, to follow the earlier example, Indigenous women who experience violence not only face the blame and judgment associated with experiencing violence but also face racism, and are often stigmatized as irresponsible or as somehow deserving of violence. Because Indigenous-specific racism reflects long-held erroneous assumptions and stereotypes about mental health, indolence, substance use, poor parenting, and violence, Indigenous people simultaneously encounter related stigmas. In much the same way, other racialized groups, people facing poverty and insecure housing, people facing mental health issues, and people using certain stigmatized substances are likely to anticipate and encounter stereotypes related to violence that contribute to feelings of shame and of being dismissed, thus discouraging them from accessing health care and other social services.

Service providers who act on a structural understanding can anticipate what will deter people from services and create an accepting environment that avoids blaming, stigmatizing, or judging those seeking care. For example, saying something like "It is very difficult to make decisions about your safety when your income is at stake" can convey understanding of a person's situation, allay fears of judgment, and acknowledge the layers of complexity influencing the care seeker's decisions. Saying something like "I don't know what your experience with health care has been like, but I am going to do my best to make this one as good as possible" can convey your responsibility and commitment and acknowledge that prior experiences may not have been ideal.

> **BOX 1.2.2 A STRUCTURAL UNDERSTANDING HELPS PROVIDERS TO:**
>
> - anticipate what will deter people from services, allay their fears, and avoid placing blame and passing judgment;
> - recognize structural barriers to health and well-being, focus on supporting access to structural resources, and take a capacity-oriented approach;
> - participate in organizational and systemic policy change to support TVIC;
> - recognize and accept the limits to their capacity to effect change, while valuing their own efforts;
> - broaden their perspectives on the complex, intersecting influences shaping people's decisions, actions, and overall well-being; and
> - contribute to the development of workplaces that create the conditions for TVIC, and the conditions for the well-being of the workforce.

Second, *people who have experienced trauma and violence often face inequitable structural barriers to well-being.* People who face structural economic disadvantages will have difficulty accessing health care and other services due to costs, transportation and child care challenges, lack of paid time off work, and competing demands and priorities related to impaired access to basics such as food and shelter. The impact of structural inequities was laid bare during the COVID-19 pandemic, for example, in the differential impact on low-wage earners and on elderly people who could not afford high-end private care. Also, many Indigenous people face structural barriers to care in the form of race-based policies emanating from the Indian Act (e.g., access only to federally provided health care that is inferior to what is offered to the rest of the population), ongoing racism emanating from long-standing harmful, colonial assumptions, and, for many, financial barriers stemming from policy-enforced exclusion from education, employment, and property ownership (National Inquiry into Missing and Murdered Indigenous Women and Girls, 2019). These structural forms of violence can shape service providers' attitudes and practices, with harmful consequences. The following story, told by an emergency nurse, describes the harm and traumatization that befell all who were involved, including, as we will argue, those who expressed or colluded with such disregard and dismissal: "A young Native Canadian woman was found with her pants down in the park and she was extremely drunk ... There is a strong possibility that she had been assaulted. [The physician] walked into the room ... and in front of the patient and two nurses, he said, 'This is a societal derelict and I am too embarrassed to even call [the sexual assault team] over an issue like this.' He said, 'Put her to bed and let her sober up and then she can go home.'"

1.2 Integrating Understanding of Violence into TVIC 31

Understanding structural violence guides health and social service providers to realize that people's histories and the conditions of their lives often put them at risk for further violence. So, for example, the horrendous histories of colonial practices and racism directed toward Indigenous people, including sexual abuse in residential schools, TB hospitals, mental hospitals, foster homes, and other state institutions, have set the conditions for further abuse, including through substance-use-induced vulnerability and, for many, through poverty and its impact on safe housing, safe neighbourhoods, adequate transportation, and access to services.

Applying TVIC through a structural lens can be affirming and strengthening for all. Taking a capacity-oriented approach, while remaining responsive to how structural inequities and structural violence influence people's health and well-being, is essential to enacting TVIC approaches. When awareness of structural conditions is foregrounded, service providers can acknowledge people's strengths and resourcefulness while simultaneously seeking to understand, attend to, and affirm their capacities. For example, when interviewing a woman who has been sexually assaulted by multiple men, and who is struggling with suicidal thoughts in light of her care for her children, one could focus on her strengths, saying something like, "You have incredible strength for surviving all of that, and being there for your kids." That is an affirming way to enable a positive interaction, thus making it more likely that she will return for follow-up care and help co-develop a plan for next steps. In this way, understanding structural and systemic influences in relation to interpersonal violence can move service providers toward empathy and understanding, instead of judgment or blame. It also directs attention to the importance of structural supports such as housing, transportation, and access to services. But direct service providers cannot facilitate such support on their own.

A third reason why understanding people's experiences and needs in context is imperative for TVIC is that *structural and systemic change is required for TVIC to be operationalized.* Decision-makers in practice, administration, and policy roles need to support the conditions for TVIC. Workplace practices that induce time-pressured interactions (e.g., ten-minute appointments, thirty-minute counselling sessions) can restrict a provider's capacity to engage effectively, to assess wider circumstances, and to marshal structural supports. Signage that conveys blame and judgment makes it more of a challenge to develop the trust necessary for TVIC. Weak links to the community and a lack of access to resources for those served (e.g., transportation, follow-up) contribute to failure to mitigate risks for further trauma and violence.

Fourth, *integrating understanding of structural violence is fundamental to the well-being of the health and social service delivery workforce.* Moral distress is created when practitioners are unable to provide care and services commensurate with their accepted values and standards; this inability stems from the sociopolitical and cultural context of the workplace environment (Varcoe, Pauly,

Webster, & Storch, 2012). Burnout, a psychological response to chronic job stressors, is associated with both moral distress and vicarious trauma (Cieslak et al., 2014; van Mol, Kompanje, Benoit, Bakker, & Nijkamp, 2015). Providers of care for people experiencing violence and trauma are exposed to both individual and structural violence and trauma vicariously (see chapter 1.4); hence, efforts to acknowledge and mitigate structural violence can lessen both moral distress and burnout. Meaningful attention to structural violence supports the development of workplaces that create the conditions for TVIC, which in turn create the conditions for the well-being of the workforce. This, then, calls for organizations and providers to develop *structural competence*. Metzl and Hansen (2014) argue that inequities in health must be understood in relation to the institutions and social conditions that determine health resources; they further maintain that structural competence is the "trained ability" to recognize health issues as "downstream implications of a number of upstream decisions about such matters as health care and food delivery systems, zoning laws, urban and rural infrastructures, medicalization, or even about the very definitions of illness and health" (Metzl & Hansen, 2014, p. 128).

While structural competence is being developed, providers can be overwhelmed by the circumstances of people's lives and by their inability to affect those circumstances. So at the same time, all service providers must be supported as they develop *structural humility*, bearing in mind that systemic change often progresses slowly and requires long-term investment beyond the control of individuals, whether clients or providers, and that collective action is required to follow the lead of patients and communities in developing appropriate, sustainable interventions to address harmful social structures (Hansen & Metzl, 2019; Metzl & Hansen, 2014). Recognizing and accepting the limitations of their ability to effect change can help service providers value their own efforts and deal more effectively with their own feelings of despair.

Developing Structural Competence

Developing structural competence requires two interrelated processes. The first of these involves using "relational consciousness" (Doane & Varcoe, 2021) to pay attention to the relations between structural influences and interpersonal experiences. The second involves acting "upstream" – that is, recognizing these interrelations and asking what can be done at a structural or systemic level to promote well-being. For example, if sexual assault services are not accessible to some people because they are located in a hospital setting distant from communities experiencing high levels of sexual assault, what can be done?

Paying continuous attention to how structural violence shapes people's lives and their experiences of interpersonal violence helps providers understand people's experiences and needs in context; it also supports efforts to address the structural and systemic conditions of people's lives that impede their health and well-being. Paying attention to how policies and practices in health, social services, justice, education, child welfare, and others systems and sectors result in an inequitable distribution of the social determinants of health supports the development of structural competence. For example, children who face barriers to education (many of whom live in rural and remote areas, or in economically disadvantaged areas, and are members of racialized groups) will later face barriers to employment and thus low incomes. Acknowledging these dynamics helps us avoid conveying judgment.

A structural competency lens can help providers move away from individualistic, biological, and cultural explanations for health and social inequities and replace them with a perspective that takes account of harms caused by unjust social arrangements (Hansen & Metzl, 2019). Individualist explanations are rooted in personal responsibility discourse, which attempts to render individuals as blameworthy for their own conditions, circumstances, and poor health. This often justifies paternalistic or punitive policies toward them (Young, 2011). For example, rather than understanding interpersonal violence as a matter of individual "perpetrators" and "victims," with the perpetrators seen as "abnormal," and with that abnormality explained as mental illness or cultural deviance, interpersonal violence is seen as continuous with and an extension of the social context in which it occurs. In other words, violence that is perpetrated at the structural level (e.g., young men with limited economic options recruited to the military, older adults warehoused in long-term care, Indigenous communities dispossessed of land, water, and economic opportunities) is tolerated socially and supports violence at the interpersonal level. Service providers understand that violence is not only always gendered at the interpersonal level; it is also shaped by gender inequities that are built into and sustained by the very structures of our society – from women's economic considerations related to intimate relationships, to policy decisions regarding funding priorities (e.g., military expenditures, pandemic response costs, sexual assault services). And violence, besides always being gendered, is also shaped by racism, classism, ableism, and other differentiating processes at organizational and structural levels. Box 1.2.3 provides strategies to support thinking, and acting, structurally.

BOX 1.2.3 DEEPENING AND USING STRUCTURAL UNDERSTANDING

- Identify structural barriers to health and well-being commonly experienced by those you serve.

- Look for the connections between wider social arrangements and the conditions of people's lives and their experiences (of violence, of trauma, of health and well-being).
- Ask how these connections can be acknowledged in practices and policies (providing support for applications for disability benefits is one commonly used strategy).
- Ask how access to social determinants of health can be increasingly supported.
- Review your workplace. Who will feel most comfortable? What will deter people from care? How can those least likely to feel comfortable be made welcome? How could access be improved?

Kilala Lelum: An Example of Structural Competence and Structural Humility in Action

Kilala Lelum (KL) is an Indigenous-focused and Indigenous Elder–guided health centre that includes a primary health care clinic (https://kilalalelum.ca). A structural lens was used in the design, funding, and delivery of health care at KL with the aim of creating optimal conditions for the provision of TVIC. The people who initiated the development of KL were acutely aware of the structural violence experienced daily by the people who would access care at the clinic, and they were determined to use such a structural lens. Most were staff (administrators, physicians, nurses, Indigenous Elders) who had been serving the community at another clinic in the area. They had a deep understanding of the histories of many of the community members to be served, many of whom were survivors of residential schools and other forms of racialized violence. Moreover, this group was committed to meaningful leadership and input from those who would be accessing care. From the language used, to naming decisions, to budgeting, to hiring decisions and staff training, to the physical layout and social organization, each aspect of the clinic was considered through a structural lens.

The clinic is organized as a cooperative. That structure offers a flatter hierarchy than might be offered through other structures such as a business model, health authority, or not-for-profit organization. The people accessing care can become members of the cooperative – indeed, the staff refer to them as "members," not "clients" or "patients" – in an effort to mitigate the power dynamics common to health care contexts. Financial and other resources are deployed with input from members, always with the conditions of their lives in mind. Most members face extreme financial hardship – hence, all of them prioritize a "full kitchen," and the lead members lobby for funding to support an excellent meal program. Though the clinic is open to the entire community, most of its members are Indigenous and thus have experienced systemic racism (e.g., disproportionate policing and incarceration, state child apprehension) and, consequently, interpersonal violence and racism. Many have lived the consequences of genocidal efforts to eradicate Indigenous identities, cultures, and languages and have been denied access to their traditional lands and cultures. Thus, the clinic works to prioritize Indigenous knowledge, values, and approaches in everything from the design of the space and the art displayed to the recruiting of Indigenous staff (including Elders) to the availability of Indigenous healing practices and ceremonies. For all their good intentions, the clinic, staff, and members face constant challenges: the funding, billing, and accountability mechanisms are built on biomedical models, the members face endless difficulties obtaining safe housing, food, and freedom from violence and racism, and the staff, many of whom have their own histories of trauma and racism, face vicarious trauma. However, trauma- and violence-informed approaches are infused through policies (e.g., no security guards), language used (e.g., welcoming rather than dismissive signage), and practices. A group of providers recently explained that the difference between their approach and the "usual care" encountered in other settings is that "we adore our members."

Conclusion

Social and structural arrangements perpetuate violence, which affects some groups more than others. Interpersonal forms of violence, including sexual assault and partner violence, intersect with structural forms of violence such as systemic racism and poverty. Understanding these dynamics sets the foundation for developing structural competence and structural humility, both of which are fundamental to designing, delivering, and evaluating trauma- and violence-informed approaches. This supports health and social services that attend to the circumstances of people's lives and that support service providers in their efforts to practice in ways that align with professional values and standards.

KEY MESSAGES AND IMPLICATIONS

- Integrating understandings of structural violence within organizations, and in individual practices is feasible, does not necessarily require additional resources, and can bring immediate benefits to people who come for services, and for staff and administrative leaders.

- Finding ways to explicitly attend to the relationship between structural violence and health and well-being will provide the basis for enacting TVIC in the most effective ways possible.

ADDITIONAL RESOURCES

- https://www.thoughtco.com/structural-violence-4174956
- https://online.campbellsville.edu/social-work/structural-violence
- https://equiphealthcare.ca/resources

REFERENCES

Brian Sinclair Working Group. (2017). *Out of sight: A summary of the events leading up to Brian Sinclair's death and the inquest that examined it and the Interim Recommendations of the Brian Sinclair Working Group*. Retrieved from https://libguides.lib.umanitoba.ca/ld.php?content_id=33973085

Browne, A.J., & Varcoe, C. (2019). Cultural and social considerations in health assessment. In A.J. Browne, J. MacDonald-Jenkins, & M. Luctkar-Flude (Eds.), *Physical examination and health assessment* (3rd Canadian ed., pp. 28–45). Toronto, ON: Elsevier.

Browne, A., Varcoe, C., & Wytenbroek, L. (in press). A relational orientation to cultural and social considerations in health assessment. In A.J. Browne, J. MacDonald-Jenkins, & M. Luctkar-Flude (Eds.), *Physical examination and health assessment* (4th Canadian ed.). Toronto, ON: Elsevier.

Brownridge, D.A. (2008). Understanding the elevated risk of partner violence against Aboriginal women: A comparison of two nationally representative surveys of Canada. *Journal of Family Violence, 23*(5), 353–67. https://doi.org/10.1007/s10896-008-9160-0

Cieslak, R., Shoji, K., Douglas, A., Melville, E., Luszczynska, A., & Benight, C.C. (2014). A meta-analysis of the relationship between job burnout and secondary traumatic stress among workers with indirect exposure to trauma. *Psychological Services, 11*(1), 75–86. https://doi.org/10.1037/a0033798

Cullen, P., Mackean, T., Walker, N., Coombes, J., Bennett-Brook, K., Clapham, K., Ivers, R., Hackett, M., Worner, F., & Longbottom, M. (2021). Integrating trauma- and violence-informed care in primary health care settings for First Nations women experiencing violence: A systematic review. *Trauma, Violence & Abuse*, 1524838020985571–1524838020985571. https://doi.org/10.1177/1524838020985571.

DeKeseredy, W.S. (2020). Bringing feminist sociological analyses of patriarchy back to the forefront of the study of woman abuse. *Violence Against Women*. https://doi.org/10.1177/1077801220958485

Doane, G., & Varcoe, C. (2021). *How to nurse: Relational inquiry in action* (2nd ed.). Philadelphia, PA: Lippincott, Williams & Wilkins.

Dormond, K. (2020). *Service providers challenging Orientalism and supporting HRVO victims and perpetrators*. (Doctoral dissertation). University of British Columbia, Vancouver.

Farmer, P.E., Nizeye, B., Stulac, S., & Keshavjee, S. (2006). Structural violence and clinical medicine. *PLoS Medicine, 10*(3), 1686–91. Retrieved from https://doi.org/10.1371/journal.pmed.0030449. https://doi.org/10.1371/journal.pmed.0030449

Fisher, M., Mackean, T., George, E., Friel, S., & Baum, F. (2021). Stakeholder perceptions of policy implementation for Indigenous health and cultural safety: A study of Australia's 'Closing the Gap' policies. *Australian Journal of Public Administration, 80*(2), 239–60. https://doi.org/10.1111/1467-8500.12482.

Hansen, H., & Metzl, J.M. (2019). *Structural competency in mental health and medicine: A case-based approach to treating the social determinants of health*. Switzerland: Springer International Publishing.

Hunnicutt, G. (2020). Commentary on the Special Issue: New ways of thinking theoretically about violence against women and other forms of gender-based violence. *Violence Against Women*. https://doi.org/10.1177/1077801220958484

Joyce Echaquan: Outcry in Canada over treatment of dying indigenous woman. (2020). Retrieved from https://www.bbc.com/news/world-us-canada-54350027

McCallum, M.J.L., & Perry, A. (2018). *Structures of indifference: An Indigenous life and death in a Canadian city*. Winnipeg, MB: University of Manitoba Press.

Metzl, J.M., & Hansen, H. (2014). Structural competency: Theorizing a new medical engagement with stigma and inequality. *Social Science & Medicine, 103*, 126–33. https://doi.org/10.1016/j.socscimed.2013.06.032

Monchalin, L., Marques, O., Reasons, C., & Arora, P. (2019). Homicide and Indigenous peoples in North America: A structural analysis. *Aggression & Violent Behavior, 46*, 212–18. https://doi.org/10.1016/j.avb.2019.01.011

National Inquiry into Missing and Murdered Indigenous Women and Girls. (2019). *Reclaiming power and place: Executive summary of the final report*. Retrieved from https://www.mmiwg-ffada.ca/wp-content/uploads/2019/06/Executive_Summary.pdf

Pedersen, J.S., Malcoe, L.H., & Pulkingham, J. (2013). Explaining aboriginal/non-aboriginal inequalities in postseparation violence against Canadian women: application of a structural violence approach. *Violence Against Women, 19*(8), 1034–58. https://doi.org/10.1177/1077801213499245

Price-Glynn, K., & Missari, S. (2017). Perspectives on violence against women: A study of United States nursing textbooks. *The Journal of Nursing Education, 56*(3), 164–9. https://doi.org/10.3928/01484834-20170222-08

Quenneville, G. (2021, March 22). *RCMP racially discriminated against mother, mishandled witnesses, evidence in Colten Boushie case: Watchdog*. Retrieved from https://www.cbc.ca/news/canada/saskatoon/colten-boushie-rcmp-shooting-complaint-gerald-stanley-1.5934802

Riemann, M. (2019). Problematizing the medicalization of violence: a critical discourse analysis of the "Cure Violence" initiative. *Critical Public Health, 29*(2), 146–55. https://doi.org/10.1080/09581596.2018.1535168

Turpel-Lafond, M.E. (2020). *In plain sight: Addressing Indigenous-specific racism and discrimination in B.C. health care.* Retrieved from https://www.bcchr.ca/sites/default/files/group-opsei/in-plain-sight-full-report.pdf

van Mol, M.M.C., Kompanje, E.J.O., Benoit, D.D., Bakker, J., & Nijkamp, M.D. (2015). The prevalence of compassion fatigue and burnout among healthcare professionals in intensive care units: A systematic review. *PLoS One, 10*(9), 1–22. https://doi.org/10.1371/journal.pone.0136955

Varcoe, C., Browne, A.J., & Kang-Dhillon, B.K. (2019). Culture and cultural safety: Beyond cultural inventories. In C.D. Gregory, L. Raymond-Seniuk, L. Patrick, & T. Stephen (Eds.), *Fundamentals: Perspectives on the art and science of Canadian nursing* (pp. 243–61). Philadelphia, PA: Lippincott.

Varcoe, C., Ford-Gilboe, M., Browne, A.J., Perrin, N., Bungay, V., McKenzie, H., ... Dion Stout, M. (2019). The efficacy of a health promotion intervention for Indigenous women: Reclaiming Our Spirits. *Journal of Interpersonal Violence.* https://doi.org/10.1177/0886260518820818

Varcoe, C., Pauly, B., Webster, G., & Storch, J. (2012). Moral distress: Tensions as springboards for action. *Health Ethics Forum, 24*(1), 51–62. https://doi.org/10.1007/s10730-012-9180-2

Young, I. (2011). *Responsibility for justice.* New York, NY: Oxford University Press. Retrieved from https://oxford.universitypressscholarship.com/view/10.1093/acprof:oso/9780195392388.001.0001/acprof-9780195392388

1.3 Leveraging Implicit Bias Recognition and Management Curricula to Advance Trauma- and Violence-Informed Care

JAVEED SUKHERA

This chapter takes a critical perspective to review the relationship between implicit bias recognition and management (IBRM) curricula and trauma- and violence-informed care (TVIC). Implicit biases can be problematic when they perpetuate prejudicial and discriminatory behaviour that leads to inequities and disparities for stigmatized groups. Promoting awareness of implicit biases and enhancing deliberate efforts to overcome such biases comprise the core ingredients of any bias-related educational activity. The principles of TVIC align with attempts to enhance awareness of implicit bias in many ways. For example, learners can be encouraged to increase their awareness of discrimination as a form of trauma while attempting to manage biases to create safety and reduce harm. Guidance for individual and group education in health contexts is provided, with a focus on how to integrate strategies to embed implicit bias recognition and management curricula in TVIC training and practice. Also, a framework is provided to guide integration.

> **BOX 1.3.1 JIM AND KARL**
>
> 1. Jim is a veteran. When he returned from service he worked in construction. He fell off a roof and had a very serious injury. He was prescribed hydromorphone for the pain. He had suitable pain control and was able to work steadily and maintain safe and stable housing. Unfortunately, there was a mix-up with his pharmacy and he ran out of hydromorphone early. He asked his family doctor for something to fill the gap, and there was a misunderstanding about the prescription. Soon after, the family physician's office informed Jim that the physician was retiring and that their practice was closing. He now had to rely on intravenous hydromorphone bought on the street. After a few months he developed an ulcer on his leg that became infected. He was

> admitted to a hospital ward for surgical debridement and IV antibiotic treatment, with a potential consideration of amputation. He is lying in a room struggling with uncontrolled pain and with strangers in the other three beds.
> 2. Karl has just started working in the same hospital unit. He has recently graduated from nursing school and is looking for full-time employment. He quickly realizes that the unit is frequently understaffed, and he tries to pick up as many shifts as he can. He starts his morning shift and hears about a forty-seven-year-old patient admitted overnight named Jim. The language the team uses to describe Jim includes words like "difficult, rude, drug-seeking, and behavioural." Karl steps out of the nursing station to check on Jim and obtain his vital signs. He walks into the room, and Jim is not there. What happens next?

Bias and Its Impacts on Experiences of Care

Jim and Karl (see box 1.3.1) meet in the context of a system of care that contains multiple types of bias. Bias refers here to an association between certain concepts or categories that can be applied either to thinking or to behaviour. For example, certain health professions can be associated with male or female gender binaries, and certain substances can be associated with acceptable or unacceptable behaviour due to criminal legislation. Bias can be positive or negative. In this chapter, "intergroup" biases related to social categories between different groups are the focus of discussion. For example, Karl may have biases regarding Jim related to substance use, while Jim may have biases against Karl because of his past experiences with other health care workers. Many biases are explicit and are obvious to all involved; many others, though, are more subtle and outside of our awareness.

Implicit biases are associations that form through experiences (Greenwald & Banaji, 1995). These associations are categorizations that our brains use to organize information. Biases can be positive or negative, useful or destructive. For example, some biases related to danger can help individuals respond to threats and stay safe. Affinity bias toward people who share common identities can foster a sense of connection and belonging. Implicit biases can be problematic when they perpetuate prejudicial and discriminatory behaviour that leads to inequities and disparities for stigmatized or marginalized groups.

The research on implicit bias can be traced back to cognitive psychologists who researched thought processes that may be automatic and uncontrolled versus thought processes that are voluntary and under explicit control (Brownstein, Madva, & Gawronski, 2019). First, bias is activated when an individual is categorized as belonging to a specific group. Once a category is assigned, biases become applied outside of awareness and despite best intentions (Chapman, Kaatz, & Carnes, 2013). For example, in Western societies we are encouraged by multiple influences to "size people up" – that is, to categorize them as small, thin, large, obese, and so on.

Research on implicit bias in health care has demonstrated how it influences unequal treatment for groups such as racial minorities, sexual minorities, and individuals with mental illness, substance use disorders, obesity, and lower socio-economic status (Dovidio et al., 2008; Fallin-Bennett, 2015; Green et al., 2007; Haider et al., 2015; Hall et al., 2015; Sabin & Greenwald, 2012; Sabin, Marini, & Nosek, 2012). Such biases can become internalized as those who experience discrimination conform to biases through their own behaviour and interactions (Fallin-Bennett, 2015). Implicit biases may also become embedded in organizations and in society at large, leading to poor outcomes (Dovidio et al., 2008). Given their complexity, implicit biases are a unique form of prejudice and are more challenging to address than other types of inequity (Gaertner & Dovidio, 1986). This is because implicit biases may lead to discrimination even when individuals are well-educated and consciously attempt to behave in equitable and egalitarian ways (Stone & Moskowitz, 2011). Therefore, addressing implicit biases requires a multi-pronged approach that includes attention to how such biases may manifest themselves in individuals as well as in organizations at large (Sukhera, Milne, Teunissen, Lingard, & Watling, 2018a).

Educational interventions are one strategy employed to tackle implicit bias. As with other strategies, education alone may prove unsuccessful, especially when it takes place within a learning environment that has the potential to perpetuate biases already embedded in that environment. For example, a study of medical students found that hearing negative comments from faculty about Black patients can perpetuate negative racial biases despite education efforts that attempt to reduce them (van Ryn et al., 2015).

Consider the different types of biases that may be enacted through the encounter between Jim and Karl. They have never met, but both are sensitized to perceive each other in a biased way based on their past experiences. Previous research shows that when individuals with mental illness or substance use disorders present in acute care settings, they are often implicitly labelled as time-consuming, unpredictable, dangerous, or unfixable, leading health professionals to implicitly avoid them (Sukhera et al., 2017). In the case of Jim and Karl, other staff have already explicitly labelled Jim, so Karl may be primed to apply bias more readily. Both patients and their health professionals experience helplessness and frustration, and repeated cycles of distancing and disconnection erode trust and contribute to poor outcomes.

History of Bias Education for Health Professionals

In Canada, both the health sector and the health education community have been tasked with reducing health disparities and educating health professionals about personal biases. To address the role that health professionals play in perpetuating disparities through cultural or gender-related biases, accreditors for the undergraduate programs of most health care professions include standards related to cultural competence, cultural safety, and bias. For example, the Committee on Accreditation of Canadian Medical Schools (CACMS) Standards states that faculty must ensure that the curriculum prepares medical students to "recognize and appropriately address personal biases (cultural, gender, racial, belief) and how these biases influence clinical decision-making and the care provided to patients" (Committee on Accreditation of Canadian Medical Schools, 2018, p. 13; Liaison Committee on Medical Education, 2008).

In the past, cultural competence has been adopted as a strategy for addressing health disparities and advancing equity. While definitions of cultural competence often vary, mental health researchers originally described it as "a set of congruent behaviours, attitudes, and policies that come together in a system, agency or amongst professionals and enables that system, agency or those professionals to work effectively in cross-cultural situations" (Cross, Bazron, Dennis, & Isaacs, 1989, p. 7). Cultural competence interventions range from increasing minority recruitment to providing language-appropriate health education and provider education on cross-cultural issues (Betancourt, 2003; Cross et al., 1989). Cultural competence training programs seek to improve awareness, knowledge, and skills, leading to changes in behaviour, practice, and patient/professional interactions. Unfortunately, cultural-competence-focused approaches have at times been accused of resorting to stereotypic teaching strategies and of paying too little attention to socio-economic and structural factors related to health (Betancourt & Cervantes, 2009; Betancourt, Green, Carrillo, & Park, 2005; Bourgois, Holmes, Sue, & Quesada, 2017; Metzl & Hansen, 2014). In recent years, a collection of approaches, including implicit bias recognition and management (IBRM), have taken steps toward fostering "critical consciousness." Those steps include developing curricula that enhance awareness and communication skills and promote feedback-seeking (Kumagai & Lypson, 2009) while addressing the intersecting forms of discrimination within organizations (Byrne & Tanesini, 2015; Carnes et al., 2015; Gonzalez, Kim, & Marantz, 2014; Teal et al., 2010; van Ryn et al., 2015).

The earliest interventions related to biases included "de-biasing" strategies in the context of clinical decision-making and diagnostic errors (Mamede et al., 2012; Norman, 2009; Norman & Eva, 2010; Norman et al., 2014; Sibbald & de Bruin, 2012). Strategies such as checklists (Ely, Graber, & Croskerry, 2011), counter-stereotype thinking, meta-cognitive training, and mindful practice training were also considered relevant. An example of such strategies is the use of checklists to ensure that certain biases do not lead health professionals to overlook atypical clinical presentations for certain populations. To take another example, mindful practice training could help health professionals practise individuating those seeking health services so as to see them as more than stereotypes. Researchers have come to recognize that promoting awareness of implicit biases and enhancing conscious efforts to overcome such biases are the core ingredients of any bias-related educational activity (Mamede et al., 2010). Educational interventions related to implicit bias may include delivering the Implicit Association Test (IAT) as a measure of bias and then utilizing the IAT as a trigger for self-reflection (Teal et al., 2010). Additional techniques include enhancing perspective-taking and empathy (Burgess, van Ryn, Dovidio, & Saha, 2007), identifying common identities, and emphasizing counter-stereotypes (Stone & Moskowitz, 2011). An example of such techniques would involve intentionally reflecting on one's biases and then consciously imagining the opposite stereotype associated with a group. Practising counter-stereotypic thinking has the potential to decrease the likelihood of activating biased thinking and behaviour. Several authors have also suggested that any education relating to implicit bias should normalize bias and emphasize that the removal of all bias is impossible (Sukhera & Watling, 2018). Instead of considering the idea of ending or eliminating bias, IBRM should emphasize the responsibility to acknowledge the adverse impact of bias and to overcome these impacts (Carnes et al., 2015).

State of Research on IBRM

In general, research on IBRM has found that teaching and learning about biases is a complex process that taps into ambivalent and nuanced attitudes, making it more challenging than other learning (Gaertner & Dovidio, 1986). Also, the topic of bias can provoke sensitive reactions, defensiveness, and strong emotions within both learners and teachers (Sukhera, Milne, Teunissen, Lingard, & Watling, 2018a; Sukhera, Wodzinski, Teunissen, Lingard, & Watling, 2018). In our earlier work, our team established a conceptual framework (figure 1.3.1) related to implicit bias recognition and management informed by transformative learning theory (Sukhera, Watling, & Gonzalez, 2020).

Individual Level: Feedback for Individuals Evokes Emotions and Defensiveness

Research on feedback in health professions education poses a challenge to teaching and learning about implicit bias. For example, previous research on feedback intervention theory (FIT) suggests that because feedback directed at the self may threaten identity and distract from learning, it is best avoided

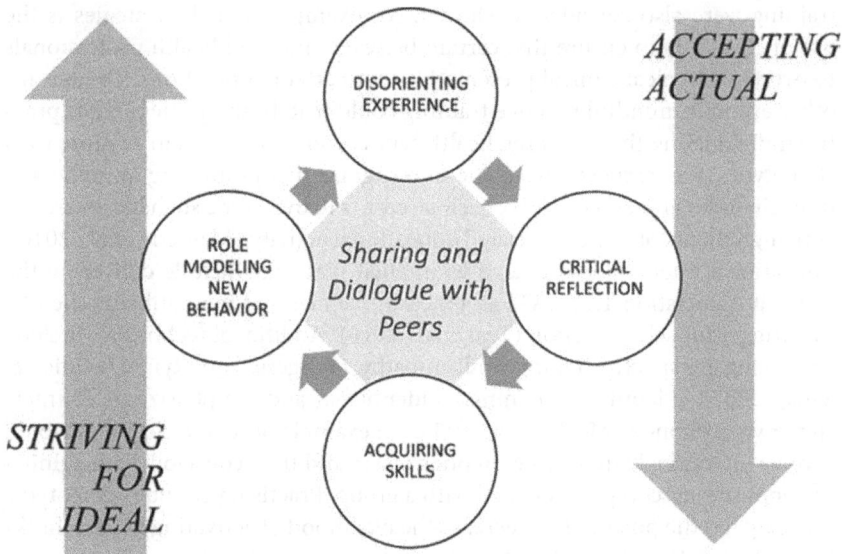

Figure 1.3.1 A visual depiction of how the elements of transformative learning theory align with those of implicit bias recognition and management curricula.
From "Implicit bias in health professions: From recognition to transformation," by J. Sukhera, C.J. Watling, and C. Gonzalez, 2020, *Academic Medicine: Journal of the Association of American Medical Colleges, 95*(5), p. 718. Copyright 2020 by the Association of American Medical Colleges. Reprinted with permission.

(Kluger & DeNisi, 1996). However, feedback about bias involves a circumstance where identity and behaviour are so linked that feedback cannot but approach the self. Our previous research on implicit bias-related feedback underscores that certain types of feedback are particularly difficult to navigate for both providers and receivers of feedback. During our initial studies, we explored how participants process and integrate feedback about their implicit biases. We found that providing implicit-bias-related feedback is a stressful experience that may trigger intense emotions (Sukhera, Milne, et al., 2018a). We also found that once feedback is received, the resulting emotions had a significant impact on the learner. Our participants described emotional reactions to bias-related feedback and sought reconciliation (Sukhera, Milne, et al., 2018b). Overall, feedback about our biases results in a situation where there is no way to avoid approaching feedback related to the self.

The approaches to reconciling self-related feedback that may evoke an emotional response are largely underexplored in health professions education research. Several studies on feedback in the health professions highlight the importance of facilitated feedback conversations (Boerboom et al., 2011;

Branch & Paranjape, 2002; Eva et al., 2012; Sargeant, 2015; Sargeant et al., 2015; Sargeant, Mann, van der Vleuten, & Metsemakers, 2009; Sargeant et al., 2011; Telio, Ajjawi, & Regehr, 2015; Watling, Driessen, van der Vleuten, & Lingard, 2012). For example, Sargeant and colleagues (2015) propose a model that suggests that reflective performance feedback can be facilitated through developing a relationship, and exploring the recipient's reaction as well as the content of feedback data as a means to coach toward performance change. Sargeant and colleagues' (2015) model acknowledges the importance of asking non-judgmental questions and exploring emotional reactions while focusing on a few specific opportunities for feedback data. However, if this model is applied to feedback about bias, it may not be sufficient to address the emotional nature of such conversations.

Feedback related to our biases thus represents a unique form of feedback, and this poses a challenge to traditional advice regarding effective feedback provision. We found that when discussing sensitive topics such as implicit biases, participants experienced challenging emotions yet described their experience as positive. Bias-related feedback was an example of feedback about the self that was still perceived as actionable (Sukhera et al., 2019). This finding is a paradox that furthers the need to explore how bias-related feedback is processed, integrated, and reconciled. In particular, the role of emotions merits further research.

Another reason why bias-related feedback is unique relates to how feedback and identity intersect. Categorizing others and making inferences about their identity is nearly impossible unless we activate our own beliefs about which groups and social identities we identify with. In our previous research, we also found that discussing sensitive topics such as implicit bias evokes identity tensions for health professionals. Therefore, professional identity may play an influential role in how bias-related feedback is processed and integrated.

Organizational Level – The Influence of Context: Where Feedback and Identity Intersect

Research on feedback context also suggests that participants appraise the usefulness of feedback in culturally specific ways. For example, how individuals interpret the credibility and constructiveness of feedback information may constrain or enable the provision of meaningful feedback (Watling, Driessen, van der Vleuten, Vanstone, & Lingard, 2013). In a study of coaching, researchers compared how feedback is exchanged between music students and medical students. This work illuminated potential vulnerabilities in medicine's learning culture, which overemphasizes competence and performance over practice and growth (Watling et al., 2013; Fuller, 2002). Context also influences how teachers can coach learners toward behaviour change. In a study of different professions with a shared philosophy of coaching, enactments of core aspects of coaching such as engagement, reflection, and growth were influenced by how the coaching role was positioned in the learning context. Compared to other professions, the cultures within the health professions may make it more challenging to embrace failure and demonstrate vulnerability (Watling et al., 2013).

In our own research on bias-related feedback, we also found that how individuals interpret the credibility and constructiveness of feedback information may constrain or enable the actionable steps a learner takes once feedback has been processed, interpreted, and integrated in a meaningful way (Sukhera, 2018). As a result of our research, we recognize that the norms and factors that comprise "culture" do not exist in a vacuum. Professional context is shaped by deliberate organizational and policy decisions, which means that it can be reshaped. Therefore, the influence of organizational context, culture, and policy on the processing and integration of bias-related feedback is an important component of IBRM.

Health Systems Level: Disruption and Dissonance within the Workplace

While most educational interventions focus on individual biases, several authors also emphasize the need to consider how implicit bias functions within organizations and institutions and how sociocultural factors may sustain or inhibit bias mitigation targeted at an individual level (Burgess et al., 2007; Fallin-Bennett, 2015; van Ryn et al., 2015). Overall, research suggests that clinical learning environments may both perpetuate and increase biases. For example, the CHANGES study conducted over four years across forty-nine medical schools in the United States found that factors such as hearing negative comments from faculty may predict increases in negative implicit biases (van Ryn et al., 2015). In addition, little research thus far has identified how interventions to reduce implicit bias may produce change. A 2018 review found only two studies of interventions to reduce implicit bias, and only one of the two demonstrated a decrease in implicit biases as measured by the IAT (Maina, Belton, Ginzberg, Singh, & Johnson, 2018).

In our previous work, we found that bringing implicit biases into conscious awareness for learners is a more intricate process than the educational strategies currently described in the health professions education literature. Biases are developed over time, and many become ingrained, automatic, and difficult to access. Therefore, brief educational interventions alone cannot advance meaningful and sustainable change within individuals and learning environments. Our findings suggest that teaching and learning about implicit bias may be positioned as a form of iterative, continuous, yet transformative reflective practice. The constant, iterative nature of feedback, reflection, and action is familiar to audiences from several disciplines that seek improvement processes.

Described in other terms, promotion of continuous recognition and management of implicit biases may align with a "way of being" that is shared, modelled, and internalized through relationships between teachers and learners. This concept also applies to those who may consider themselves informal teachers or role models.

Shared Humanity Framework

To translate the products of our initial IBRM research into practice, we engaged in a participatory process with youth with lived experience of bias related to mental health/substance use and health professions learners to co-design an IBRM training model. This model is described as the shared humanity framework and is available publicly at http://sharedhumanity.ca. The model has three pillars: trust, power, and humanity. The main findings of the initial work emphasized that educational interventions that focus on the relationships between patients and health professionals can foster humanizing labels and promote empathy and engagement (Sukhera, 2018). We developed a training program that sought to facilitate awareness of implicit bias, promote self-reflection, increase knowledge about the adverse impact of bias, enhance communication skills, and promote perspective-taking. We conducted both a longitudinal evaluation of our initial curriculum (Sukhera et al., 2019) and a research study to explore how implicit bias training influences workplace learning (Sukhera, 2018). We also conducted several studies exploring how health professionals process and integrate implicit bias feedback. This research contributed to the framework outlined in figure 1.3.1 (Sukhera et al., 2020).

To translate this knowledge, we began to adapt our curricular framework by convening a diverse group of participants, including medical/nursing students and youth with lived experience of mental illness. Through several co-design activities, including focus groups, we co-constructed the Shared Humanity digital framework for implicit stigma reduction. Although our initial intention was to design an anti-bias intervention targeted toward health professionals, the co-design process led us to focus on the relational aspects of bias. While previous research emphasizes that bias is enacted through a social process that involves a differential power dynamic between patient and health professionals (Hall et al., 2015; Sabin, Marini, & Nosek, 2012), our further research led us to appreciate that the social process that perpetuates implicit bias is bidirectional.

If applied to the example earlier in this chapter, a patient with lived experience of substance use may act more defensively when they perceive the health system as inherently biased (Sabin et al., 2012), resulting in strained social interactions that perpetuate bias in both implicit and explicit ways. Anticipating negative judgment, Jim might express hostility and defensiveness on first meeting Karl, contributing to strain that both must negotiate. This idea resonates with previous research on implicit bias that emphasizes the concept of a common in-group identity (Fuller, 2002). The common in-group identity theory suggests that bias may be reduced if members of non-stigmatized groups are reminded to regard themselves as sharing the common humanity of those who are stigmatized, and vice versa (Green et al., 2007). Therefore, we shifted our focus from educating health professionals to educating both health professionals and patients. The Shared Humanity framework is novel in that it targets bias reduction at both health professionals who exhibit bias and vulnerable individuals with lived experience of prejudice and discrimination, who may implicitly label health professionals as inherently biased. The framework is designed to make ourselves aware of the biases we exhibit toward one another, and toward ourselves.

Case Example

A medical unit in an acute care hospital is struggling with a large number of patients who are admitted for conditions related to injection drug use. Approaching this challenge using the model described earlier and illustrated in figure 1.3.1 would involve the key steps of feedback, critical reflection, goal-setting, and explicit role-modelling. These steps would need to include discussion and sharing as well as balancing striving for the ideal with accepting the actual. These steps could be applied in a clinical teaching context, in a colleague-to-colleague relationship, or in a formal classroom. For example, Karl could be guided by a mentor or preceptor or could be taking a course on a range of topics such as ethics, health communication, substance use, or even infection control.

Step 1: Shared Trust

After starting with knowledge about what trust is, how it manifests, and processes that can enhance or erode trust, learners are introduced to the concept of implicit bias and how it gets in the way of trust. Examples include a nurse who may automatically assume that someone admitted for infection control who has a history of drug use "chooses" addiction, or a colleague who may have biases about someone else who works in health care because of their profession and scope of practice. After providing examples that illustrate the impact of implicit biases, learners develop skills to cultivate feedback from patients and are encouraged to foster continuous self-improvement.

Regarding the encounter between Karl and Jim, building shared trust would involve Karl recognizing that any behaviour that is labelled as problematic or disruptive within a highly structured hospital setting may relate to past experiences of mistrust. Karl would be encouraged as a nurse to validate any negative past experiences and seek genuine feedback from Jim on how Karl can practise more effectively in the future.

Step 2: Shared Power

The next step involves the concept of shared power, where health professionals work on reducing and reconciling power differentials by learning about how these can erode trust. They also develop skills to reduce perceptions of power differentials and foster shared decision-making. When considering how power influences our case example, Karl would be encouraged to ensure that Jim has access to all the information that Karl has about his care, and to be honest and transparent about his role on the team and what he needs from Jim in order to be able to ensure that Jim's medical care is optimal. Similarly, Jim could be encouraged to better understand Karl's role in the system and the limits of Karl's influence and authority. Both Karl and Jim will then be able to relate to each other's vulnerability and shared powerlessness in some areas, while feeling empowered and enhancing each other's agency in other areas.

Step 3: Shared Humanity

Sharing one another's humanity is at the heart of the shared humanity framework. In this step, the focus is on decreasing bias between patients and health professionals while inviting all parties to be comfortable with sharing their authentic selves. Sharing humanity involves learning about how biases can be internalized while developing skills to engage in self-disclosure and fostering self-compassion and self-forgiveness. For Karl, this involves recognizing the vicarious trauma that may be inherent to his job while recognizing the structural determinants that may contribute to compassion fatigue. By being more comfortable sharing his authentic self with Jim, Karl is inviting Jim to feel safer and more comfortable being vulnerable in the interaction.

Bias Recognition and Management and TVIC

In this chapter, we make the case that IBRM is fundamental to the practice of TVIC. This is because TVIC demands recognition and management of biases regarding what is perceived as trauma, who/what is perceived as violent, and why. In particular, addressing biases related to race, class, gender, and ability may promote a shift away from polarizing cycles of blame and shame toward a collective sense of shared responsibility for action. As noted earlier, the emotional nature of IBRM also aligns with TVIC's emphasis on understanding how trauma can manifest itself through emotions and behaviours that can be productive or counterproductive for healing and reconciliation.

Trauma-informed approaches generally refer to a philosophical or cultural stance that integrates understanding and awareness of trauma with service delivery (Hopper, Bassuk, & Olivet, 2010). Such definitions are complemented by inclusion of the word violence, suggested by the term trauma- and *violence*-informed care. This approach to service delivery integrates an understanding both of trauma and of trauma's impact on individual development and present functioning (Elliott, Bjelajac, Fallot, Markoff, & Reed, 2005), as well as of social-structural conditions that themselves cause harm (including racism and other forms of discrimination – see chapters 1.2 and 1.5). The United States Substance Abuse and Mental Health Services Administration describes organizations that adopt T(V)IC as organizations that are "based on an understanding of the vulnerabilities or triggers of trauma survivors that traditional service delivery approaches may exacerbate, so that these resources and programs can be more supportive and avoid re-traumatization" (Substance Abuse and Mental Health Services Administration, 2014, p. 2).

There are several parallels between IBRM and TVIC. Both require a cultural and systemic shift. Our research on IBRM highlights the shift away from "doing" the work of reflecting on and managing biases toward "being" an individual who role-models an iterative way of practice. Similarly, TVIC challenges organizations to shift from asking those seeking services, "What's wrong with you," to considering "What's happened and is still happening to you?" and "What in social arrangements and practices sustains harm?" All three emphasize how power differentials between service professionals and service users exist within a sacred space that can be co-created to foster trust, healing, and connection. Both IBRM and TVIC prioritize safety and trust while recognizing that these have implications for structural biases at organizational and societal levels. The relationship between secondary or vicarious trauma and both TVIC and IBRM is an important aspect of how the two approaches intersect. Both approaches recognize the range of emotional and cognitive reactions that may accompany work to address trauma and inequity. A more detailed description of secondary or vicarious trauma is found in chapter 1.4 of this handbook.

During our initial research on IBRM, we were struck by the range of emotional reactions from health professionals when they were provided with feedback about their biases (Sukhera, 2018). It was clear that there was something about our culture that encouraged health professionals to compartmentalize their identity as a form of self-protection. They struggled to reconcile that they could have biases because they felt that professionals were not "allowed" to have biases. Yet they acknowledged their vulnerable human identity. Through subsequent research, we learned that reconciling these identity tensions requires framing IBRM interventions as an activity in which individuals can strive to be an idealized version of themselves while accepting and embracing that they have inherent shortcomings, vulnerabilities, and flaws. We built our shared humanity framework around these principles and regularly emphasize the importance of cultivating self-compassion and self-forgiveness as a mechanism to advance equity.

Similarly, TVIC emphasizes the importance of considering secondary trauma. Secondary trauma refers to a process whereby a service professional's

Table 1.3.1 Comparing features of TVIC and IBRM

	Individual	Structural
TVIC	• Build awareness and consider trauma a risk factor • Emphasize safety and trust • Adapt language • Find, acknowledge, and build on strengths	• Develop policy • Create inclusive culture • Allow time and flexibility • Foster meaningful engagement between service providers and service users
IBRM	• Cultivate bias awareness through feedback • Critical reflection on implications of biases for service delivery • Explicit behavioural change • Sharing and discussing vulnerabilities openly with peers	• Critically reflect on structural biases within organizations • Speak up about changing organizational norms to improve equity • Co-design policy solutions with people with lived and living experience
BOTH	• Address vicarious trauma • Foster self-compassion and self-forgiveness • Sharing and validation with peers	• Address vicarious trauma • Consider workload and workplace stress • Provide opportunities for peer support and connection

Note: IBRM = implicit bias recognition and management; TVIC = trauma- and violence-informed care

inner experience may be adversely impacted through empathic engagement (see chapter 1.4). The residue from these experiences may accumulate over time, resulting in significant psychological distress and symptoms (Motta, 2008). Risk factors include high care load demands, lack of supervision, lack of support, and difficulty recognizing and meeting one's own needs (Motta, 2008). Symptoms of secondary trauma may include hypervigilance, hopelessness, difficulty with embracing complexity, anger, cynicism, and guilt (American Academy of Pediatrics, 2014).

TVIC also emphasizes the need to create emotional and physical safety while fostering opportunities for choice and connection. By explicitly acknowledging secondary traumatic stress, staff are able to recognize the very human and personal ways in which trauma can manifest itself; this helps them foster connection and empathic engagement. Supportive relationships are also key to advancing both IBRM and TVIC. We found that enacting the idea of *striving while accepting* required supportive relationships between teachers and learners (Sukhera, 2018). TVIC also emphasizes creating time and space for meaningful engagement within organizations while encouraging service providers to provide choice, actively listen, and foster shared decision-making with service users. Table 1.3.1 provides examples of how both approaches are aligned.

Conclusion

IBRM curricula provide a framework for addressing and managing the adverse impacts of harmful biases on the care of stigmatized and vulnerable populations. We have found through our research on IBRM that there may be unintended consequences of bias training that trigger negative and defensive emotional reactions. Our work has found that for IBRM to be effective, it must be designed in contextually specific ways that honour personal and professional identity while cultivating a sense of shared humanity. We also learned about the importance of sharing and support among peers to reinforce change through IBRM curricula. Lastly, we found that any singular bias training interventions were unlikely to produce meaningful change unless they were implemented on a regular basis and framed as a critically reflexive way of being, rather than a box that one can check.

KEY MESSAGES AND IMPLICATIONS

- There are many parallels between IBRM and TVIC. Both approaches require considering secondary trauma and how trauma and structural violence may influence the process of advancing equity.
- By recognizing and naming the importance of self-compassion and self-forgiveness as a part of one's journey toward justice, both approaches emphasize a shared common humanity among and between service providers and service users.

ADDITIONAL RESOURCES

- The Shared Humanity Project: http://www.sharedhumanity.ca

REFERENCES

American Academy of Pediatrics. (2014). Protecting physician wellness: Working with children affected by traumatic events. Retrieved from https://www.aap.org/en-us/advocacy-and-policy/aap-health-initiatives/healthy-foster-care-america/Pages/Trauma-Guide.aspx

Betancourt, J.R. (2003). Cross-cultural medical education: Conceptual approaches and frameworks for evaluation. *Academic Medicine: Journal of the Association of American Medical Colleges, 78*(6), 560–9. https://doi.org/10.1097/00001888-200306000-00004

Betancourt, J.R., & Cervantes, M.C. (2009). Cross-cultural medical education in the United States: Key principles and experiences. *The Kaohsiung Journal of Medical Sciences, 25*(9), 471–8. https://doi.org/10.1016/S1607-551X(09)70553-4

1.3 Leveraging Implicit Bias Recognition 53

Betancourt, J.R., Green, A.R., Carrillo, J.E., & Park, E.R. (2005). Cultural competence and health care disparities: Key perspectives and trends. *Health Affairs (Project Hope)*, 24(2), 499–505. https://doi.org/10.1377/hlthaff.24.2.499

Boerboom, T.B., Jaarsma, D., Dolmans, D.H., Scherpbier, A.J., Mastenbroek, N.J., & Van Beukelen, P. (2011). Peer group reflection helps clinical teachers to critically reflect on their teaching. *Medical Teacher*, 33(11), e615–e623. https://doi.org/10.3109/0142159X.2011.610840

Bourgois, P., Holmes, S.M., Sue, K., & Quesada, J. (2017). Structural vulnerability: Operationalizing the concept to address health disparities in clinical care. *Academic Medicine: Journal of the Association of American Medical Colleges*, 92(3), 299–307. https://doi.org/10.1097/ACM.0000000000001294.

Branch Jr., W.T., & Paranjape, A. (2002). Feedback and reflection: Teaching methods for clinical settings. *Academic Medicine: Journal of the Association of American Medical Colleges*, 77(12 Pt 1), 1185–8. https://doi.org/10.1097/00001888-200212000-00005

Brownstein, M., Madva, A., & Gawronski, B. (2019). What do implicit measures measure? *Wiley Interdisciplinary Reviews: Cognitive Science*, 10(5), e1501. https://doi.org/10.1002/wcs.1501

Burgess, D., van Ryn, M., Dovidio, J., & Saha, S. (2007). Reducing racial bias among health care providers: Lessons from social-cognitive psychology. *Journal of General Internal Medicine*, 22(6), 882–7. https://doi.org/10.1007/s11606-007-0160-1

Byrne, A., & Tanesini, A. (2015). Instilling new habits: Addressing implicit bias in healthcare professionals. *Advances in Health Sciences Education: Theory and Practice*, 20(5), 1255–62. https://doi.org/10.1007/s10459-015-9600-6

Carnes, M., Devine, P.G., Baier Manwell, L., Byars-Winston, A., Fine, E., Ford, C.E., ... Sheridan, J. (2015). The effect of an intervention to break the gender bias habit for faculty at one institution: A cluster randomized, controlled trial. *Academic Medicine: Journal of the Association of American Medical Colleges*, 90(2), 221–30. https://doi.org/10.1097/ACM.0000000000000552

Chapman, E.N., Kaatz, A., & Carnes, M. (2013). Physicians and implicit bias: How doctors may unwittingly perpetuate health care disparities. *Journal of General Internal Medicine*, 28(11), 1504–10. https://doi.org/10.1007/s11606-013-2441-1

Committee on Accreditation of Canadian Medical Schools. (2018). *Standards for accreditation of medical education programs leading to the M.D. degree*. Retrieved from https://cacms-cafmc.ca/sites/default/files/documents/CACMS_Standards_and_Elements_AY_2020-2021.pdf

Cooper, L.A., Roter, D.L., Carson, K.A., Beach, M.C., Sabin, J.A., Greenwald, A.G., & Inui, T.S. (2012). The associations of clinicians' implicit attitudes about race with medical visit communication and patient ratings of interpersonal care. *American Journal of Public Health*, 102(5), 979–87. https://doi.org/10.2105/AJPH.2011.300558

Cross, T.L., Bazron, B.J., Dennis, K.W., & Isaacs, M.R. (1989). *Towards a culturally competent system of care: A monograph on effective services for minority children who are severely emotionally disturbed*. Bethesda, MD: National Institute of Mental Health.

Dovidio, J.F., Penner, L.A., Albrecht, T.L., Norton, W.E., Gaertner, S.L., & Shelton, J.N. (2008). Disparities and distrust: The implications of psychological processes for understanding racial disparities in health and health care. *Social Science & Medicine*, *67*(3), 478–86. https://doi.org/10.1016/j.socscimed.2008.03.019

Elliott, D.E., Bjelajac, P., Fallot, R.D., Markoff, L.S., & Reed, B.G. (2005). Trauma-informed or trauma-denied: Principles and implementation of trauma-informed services for women. *Journal of Community Psychology*, *33*(4), 461–77. https://doi.org/10.1002/jcop.20063

Ely, J.W., Graber, M.L., & Croskerry, P. (2011). Checklists to reduce diagnostic errors. *Academic Medicine: Journal of the Association of American Medical Colleges*, *86*(3), 307–13. https://doi.org/10.1097/ACM.0b013e31820824cd

Eva, K.W., Armson, H., Holmboe, E., Lockyer, J., Loney, E., Mann, K., & Sargeant, J. (2012). Factors influencing responsiveness to feedback: On the interplay between fear, confidence, and reasoning processes. *Advances in Health Sciences Education: Theory and Practice*, *17*(1), 15–26. https://doi.org/10.1007/s10459-011-9290-7

Fallin-Bennett, K. (2015). Implicit bias against sexual minorities in medicine: Cycles of professional influence and the role of the hidden curriculum. *Academic Medicine: Journal of the Association of American Medical Colleges*, *90*(5), 549–52. https://doi.org/10.1097/ACM.0000000000000662

Fuller, K. (2002). Eradicating essentialism from cultural competency education. *Academic Medicine: Journal of the Association of American Medical Colleges*, *77*(3), 198–201. https://doi.org/10.1097/00001888-200203000-00004

Gaertner, S.L., & Dovidio, J.F. (1986). The aversive form of racism. In J.F. Dovidio & S. L. Gaertner (Eds.), Prejudice, discrimination, and racism (pp. 61–89). Cambridge, MA: Academic Press.

Gonzalez, C.M., Kim, M.Y., & Marantz, P.R. (2014). Implicit bias and its relation to health disparities: A teaching program and survey of medical students. *Teaching and Learning in Medicine*, *26*(1), 64–71. https://doi.org/10.1080/10401334.2013.857341

Green, A.R., Carney, D.R., Pallin, D.J., Ngo, L.H., Raymond, K.L., Iezzoni, L.I., & Banaji, M.R. (2007). Implicit bias among physicians and its prediction of thrombolysis decisions for black and white patients. *Journal of General Internal Medicine*, *22*(9), 1231–8. https://doi.org/10.1007/s11606-007-0258-5

Greenwald, A.G., & Banaji, M.R. (1995). Implicit social cognition: attitudes, self-esteem, and stereotypes. *Psychological Review*, *102*(1), 4–27. https://doi.org/10.1037/0033-295x.102.1.4

Haider, A.H., Schneider, E.B., Sriram, N., Scott, V.K., Swoboda, S.M., Zogg, C.K., … Cooper, L.A. (2015). Unconscious race and class biases among registered nurses: Vignette-based study using implicit association testing. *Journal of the American College of Surgeons*, *220*(6), 1077–86. https://doi.org/10.1016/j.jamcollsurg.2015.01.065

Hall, W.J., Chapman, M.V., Lee, K.M., Merino, Y.M., Thomas, T.W., Payne, B.K., … Coyne-Beasley, T. (2015). Implicit racial/ethnic bias among health care professionals and its influence on health care outcomes: A systematic review. *American Journal of Public Health, 105*(12), e60–e76. https://doi.org/10.2105/AJPH.2015.302903

Hopper, E.K., Bassuk, E.L., & Olivet, J. (2010). Shelter from the storm: Trauma-informed care in homelessness services settings. *The Open Health Services and Policy Journal, 3*(1), 80–100.

Institute of Medicine. (2003). *Unequal treatment: Confronting racial and ethnic disparities in health care*. Washington, DC: National Academies Press. https://doi.org/10.17226/12875

Kluger, A.N., & DeNisi, A. (1996). The effects of feedback interventions on performance: A historical review, a meta-analysis, and a preliminary feedback intervention theory. *Psychological Bulletin, 119*(2), 254–84. https://doi.org/10.1037/0033-2909.119.2.254

Kumagai, A.K., & Lypson, M.L. (2009). Beyond cultural competence: Critical consciousness, social justice, and multicultural education. *Academic Medicine: Journal of the Association of American Medical Colleges, 84*(6), 782–7. https://doi.org/10.1097/ACM.0b013e3181a42398

Liaison Committee on Medical Education. (2008). Functions and structure of a medical school: Standards for accreditation of medical education programs leading to the MD degree. Retrieved from https://med.fsu.edu/sites/default/files/userFiles/file/FacultyDevelopment_Functions_and_Structure_of_a_Medical_School.pdf

Maina, I.W., Belton, T.D., Ginzberg, S., Singh, A., & Johnson, T.J. (2018). A decade of studying implicit racial/ethnic bias in healthcare providers using the implicit association test. *Social Science & Medicine, 199*, 219–29. https://doi.org/10.1016/j.socscimed.2017.05.009

Mamede, S., Schmidt, H.G., Rikers, R.M., Custers, E.J., Splinter, T.A., & van Saase, J. L. (2010). Conscious thought beats deliberation without attention in diagnostic decision-making: At least when you are an expert. *Psychological Research, 74*(6), 586–92. https://doi.org/10.1007/s00426-010-0281-8

Mamede, S., van Gog, T., Moura, A.S., de Faria, R.M., Peixoto, J.M., Rikers, R.M., & Schmidt, H.G. (2012). Reflection as a strategy to foster medical students' acquisition of diagnostic competence. *Medical Education, 46*(5), 464–72. https://doi.org/10.1111/j.1365-2923.2012.04217.x

Metzl, J.M., & Hansen, H. (2014). Structural competency: Theorizing a new medical engagement with stigma and inequality. *Social Science & Medicine (1982), 103*, 126–33. https://doi.org/10.1016/j.socscimed.2013.06.032

Motta, R.W. (2008). Secondary trauma. *International Journal of Emergency Mental Health, 10*(4), 291–8. PMID:19278145.

Norman, G. (2009). Dual processing and diagnostic errors. *Advances in Health Sciences Education: Theory and Practice, 14*(S1), 37–49. https://doi.org/10.1007/s10459-009-9179-x

Norman, G.R., & Eva, K.W. (2010). Diagnostic error and clinical reasoning. *Medical Education, 44*(1), 94–100. https://doi.org/10.1111/j.1365-2923.2009.03507.x

Norman, G., Sherbino, J., Dore, K., Wood, T., Young, M., Gaissmaier, W., ... Monteiro, S. (2014). The etiology of diagnostic errors: A controlled trial of system 1 versus system 2 reasoning. *Academic Medicine: Journal of the Association of American Medical Colleges, 89*(2), 277–84. https://doi.org/10.1097/ACM.0000000000000105

Sabin, J.A., & Greenwald, A.G. (2012). The influence of implicit bias on treatment recommendations for 4 common pediatric conditions: Pain, urinary tract infection, attention deficit hyperactivity disorder, and asthma. *American Journal of Public Health, 102*(5), 988–95. https://doi.org/10.2105/AJPH.2011.300621

Sabin, J.A., Marini, M., & Nosek, B.A. (2012). Implicit and explicit anti-fat bias among a large sample of medical doctors by BMI, race/ethnicity and gender. *PloS One, 7*(11), e48448. https://doi.org/10.1371/journal.pone.0048448

Sargeant, J. (2015). Reflecting upon multisource feedback as "assessment for learning." *Perspectives on Medical Education, 4*(2), 55–6. https://doi.org/10.1007/s40037-015-0175-y

Sargeant, J., Lockyer, J., Mann, K., Holmboe, E., Silver, I., Armson, H., ... Power, M. (2015). Facilitated reflective performance feedback: Developing an evidence- and theory-based model that builds relationship, explores reactions and content, and coaches for performance change (R2C2). *Academic Medicine: Journal of the Association of American Medical Colleges, 90*(12), 1698–706. https://doi.org/10.1097/ACM.0000000000000809

Sargeant, J.M., Mann, K.V., van der Vleuten, C.P., & Metsemakers, J.F. (2009). Reflection: A link between receiving and using assessment feedback. *Advances in Health Sciences Education: Theory and Practice, 14*(3), 399–410. https://doi.org/10.1007/s10459-008-9124-4

Sargeant, J., McNaughton, E., Mercer, S., Murphy, D., Sullivan, P., & Bruce, D.A. (2011). Providing feedback: Exploring a model (emotion, content, outcomes) for facilitating multisource feedback. *Medical Teacher, 33*(9), 744–9. https://doi.org/10.3109/0142159x.2011.577287

Sibbald, M., & de Bruin, A.B. (2012). Feasibility of self-reflection as a tool to balance clinical reasoning strategies. *Advances in Health Sciences Education: Theory and Practice, 17*(3), 419–29. https://doi.org/10.1007/s10459-011-9320-5

Stone, J., & Moskowitz, G.B. (2011). Non-conscious bias in medical decision making: What can be done to reduce it? *Medical Education, 45*(8), 768–76. https://doi.org/10.1111/j.1365-2923.2011.04026.x

Substance Abuse and Mental Health Services Administration. (2014). *SAMHSA's concept of trauma and guidance for a trauma-informed approach.* Retrieved from https://ncsacw.samhsa.gov/userfiles/files/SAMHSA_Trauma.pdf

Sukhera, J. (2018). *Bias in the mirror: Exploring implicit bias in health professions education.* Maastricht, The Netherlands: Datawyse/Universitaire Pers Maastricht.

Sukhera, J., Miller, K., Milne, A., Scerbo, C., Lim, R., Cooper, A., & Watling, C. (2017). Labelling of mental illness in a paediatric emergency department and its implications for stigma reduction education. *Perspectives on Medical Education, 6*(3), 165–72. https://doi.org/10.1007%2Fs40037-017-0333-5

Sukhera, J., Milne, A., Teunissen, P.W., Lingard, L., & Watling, C. (2018a). Adaptive reinventing: Implicit bias and the co-construction of social change. *Advances in Health Sciences Education, 23*(3), 587–99. https://doi.org/10.1007/s10459-018-9816-3

Sukhera, J., Milne, A., Teunissen, P.W., Lingard, L., & Watling, C. (2018b). The actual versus idealized self: Exploring responses to feedback about implicit bias in health professionals. *Academic Medicine: Journal of the Association of American Medical Colleges, 93*(4), 623–9. https://doi.org/10.1097/ACM.0000000000002006

Sukhera, J., & Watling, C. (2018). A framework for integrating implicit bias recognition into health professions education. *Academic Medicine: Journal of the Association of American Medical Colleges, 93*(1), 35–40. https://doi.org/10.1097/ACM.0000000000001819

Sukhera, J., Watling, C.J., & Gonzalez, C.M. (2020). Implicit bias in health professions: From recognition to transformation. *Academic Medicine, 95*(5), 717–23. https://doi.org/10.1097/acm.0000000000003173

Sukhera, J., Wodzinski, M., Milne, A., Teunissen, P.W., Lingard, L., & Watling, C. (2019). Implicit bias and the feedback paradox: Exploring how health professionals engage with feedback while questioning its credibility. *Academic Medicine, 94*(8), 1204–10. https://doi.org/10.1097/acm.0000000000002782

Sukhera, J., Wodzinski, M., Teunissen, P. W., Lingard, L., & Watling, C. (2018). Striving while accepting: Exploring the relationship between identity and implicit bias recognition and management. *Academic Medicine: Journal of the Association of American Medical Colleges, 93*, S82–S88. https://doi.org/10.1097/ACM.0000000000002382

Teal, C.R., Shada, R.E., Gill, A.C., Thompson, B.M., Frugé, E., Villarreal, G.B., & Haidet, P. (2010). When best intentions aren't enough: Helping medical students develop strategies for managing bias about patients. *Journal of General Internal Medicine, 25*(S2), S115–S118. https://doi.org/10.1007/s11606-009-1243-y

Telio, S., Ajjawi, R., & Regehr, G. (2015). The "educational alliance" as a framework for reconceptualizing feedback in medical education. *Academic Medicine: Journal of the Association of American Medical Colleges, 90*(5), 609–14. https://doi.org/10.1097/acm.0000000000000560

van Ryn, M., Hardeman, R., Phelan, S.M., Burgess, D.J., Dovidio, J.F., Herrin, J., ... Przedworski, J.M. (2015). Medical school experiences associated with change in implicit racial bias among 3547 students: A medical student CHANGES study report. *Journal of General Internal Medicine, 30*(12), 1748–56. https://doi.org/10.1007/s11606-015-3447-7

Watling, C., Driessen, E., van der Vleuten, C.P., & Lingard, L. (2012). Learning from clinical work: The roles of learning cues and credibility judgements. *Medical Education, 46*(2), 192–200. https://doi.org/10.1111/j.1365-2923.2011.04126.x

Watling, C., Driessen, E., van der Vleuten, C.P., Vanstone, M., & Lingard, L. (2013). Beyond individualism: Professional culture and its influence on feedback. *Medical Education, 47*(6), 585–94. https://doi.org/10.1111/medu.12150

1.4 Vicarious Trauma, Moral Distress, and Compassion Fatigue/Burnout through a Structural Lens

COLLEEN VARCOE

Working with people who have experienced and/or are currently experiencing trauma and violence can be hard on service providers; it also can be rewarding and fulfilling. A key principle of trauma- and violence-informed care (TVIC) is to ensure the well-being and safety of all, including service and care providers. Throughout this handbook, the authors contend that the "V" in TVIC must be at the core of our efforts to provide effective support for the well-being of people using services because it draws our attention to ongoing *interpersonal* violence as well as to *structural* violence. In this chapter, we argue that such attention is also key to supporting the well-being of service providers. Most service providers are well aware of the potential for vicarious trauma, moral distress, and compassion fatigue/burnout when working with people who have experienced violence, and there have been numerous calls for "self-care" and other individual strategies; however, unless they pay attention to structural violence and inequities, these strategies can leave responsibility for harmful dynamics with individual providers, when such dynamics are well beyond their control. This chapter uses a relational approach (Doane & Varcoe, 2021) to offer a structural analysis of the impact of providing service to people experiencing trauma and violence with the aim of supporting action toward the well-being of providers. Organizational, personal, and interpersonal strategies to prevent and deal with vicarious trauma, moral distress, and compassion fatigue/burnout are offered, with an emphasis on structural competence and humility as underlying approaches.

By the end of the chapter, the reader will be able to (1) define vicarious trauma, compassion fatigue/burnout, and moral distress from relational and structural perspectives, (2) explain how a structural analysis of the impact of working with people experiencing trauma and violence places responsibility for the well-being of service providers on workplace cultures and co-worker interactions and on social systems, not just the individual workers themselves, (3) discuss the usefulness of a structural analysis of each concept to their own work setting, and (4) plan how to use structural competence and humility as key strategies in their own work settings to prevent, reduce, and mitigate vicarious trauma, compassion fatigue/burnout, and moral distress.

A Relational and Structural Approach

A relational approach, as used in this chapter, is not just about relationships between people. Rather, the chapter draws on a relational approach based on pragmatism, a philosophy that views knowledge as useful to the extent that it "works" and thus encourages examination of how contextual conditions influence knowledge and practices, as well as of Indigenous world views that consider "how all things are interrelated" (Doane & Varcoe, 2021). This approach means thinking about how people influence one another and how people and contexts influence each other reciprocally. For example, in relation to trauma- and violence-informed approaches, how do staffing levels, workloads, and turnover influence the capacity of service providers? And how do a few key people modelling person-first language influence the culture of respect for people? Considering how all things are interrelated requires analysis at the intrapersonal (what is going on within the person), interpersonal (what is going on between people), and contextual (what is going on within organizations and systems) levels. Such a relational approach draws attention to the dynamic, reciprocal, and ever-changing nature of people and their worlds, with the result that people are seen as both influencing and being influenced by their contexts and one another. Applied to TVIC, this means that each interaction (between service providers and service users, among service providers, and within organizations and wider systems) is influential and can be harnessed toward the well-being of all, including the organizations themselves. So, for example, at the intrapersonal level, implicit bias (see chapter 1.3) is not located solely in the individual, but rather is influenced by wider social discourses. An implicit bias toward associating certain groups with higher levels of violence is shaped by exposure to such ideas. This is powerful because, with that awareness, individuals can more readily recognize, limit their exposure to, and counter such influences. Consider, for example, the impact of the various responses of the advertising industry to #Black Lives Matter (e.g., Stewart, 2020). To what extent might increasing public exposure to positive images of Black people mitigate the harmful stereotypes that have been propagated, such as those that link Black people to violence? What is the potential impact on you and on the public of the portrayals of Black Lives Matter marches as violent? Considering the broader contextual influences that shape biases helps us develop critical literacy about and beyond public media (see chapter 3.3).

At the interpersonal level, each individual is understood as having influence in every interaction and thus the potential to promote the well-being of both the self and others. Relationships among people are understood as always imbued with power and as reciprocal and situated in their context(s). For example, when the person with whom you are working addresses you with anger or aggression, your response is crucial; and, given that service providers are generally positioned to withhold or provide service, that response will involve an enactment of power. At the contextual level, people and their organizations are understood as shaped by, and as having influence on, wider social, political, and economic systems. Thus, the organizations within which TVIC services are offered can be understood in their broad contexts. For example, Lavoie and colleagues have shown that organizations that serve people who are marginalized by structural inequities are themselves marginalized organizations (Lavoie, Boulton, & Dwyer, 2010; Lavoie, Varcoe, Wathen, & Browne, 2018). Such organizations often depend on the willingness of staff to forgo benefits and wages that are commensurate with their qualifications and that they would receive elsewhere. Consider, for example, how anti-violence services in Canada are funded and what this says about how they are valued in Canadian society. Consider, as well, how the underfunding of violence services may be contributing to unsupportive workplaces such as through high workloads, low pay, the lack of employee assistance programs, and challenges attracting and retaining the most qualified staff. A relational approach supports a structural analysis that is helpful for understanding the impact of providing services to people experiencing trauma and violence, as well as the concepts of vicarious trauma, compassion fatigue/burnout, and moral distress.

Key Concepts

Vicarious trauma. Vicarious trauma or secondary traumatic stress and compassion fatigue/burnout are concepts that identify the harms experienced by those working with people who have experienced trauma, with compassion fatigue/burnout being applied to the impact of work stressors more widely. Vicarious trauma refers to the negative changes experienced by those working with survivors of violence and trauma due to the repetitive invasion of others' trauma experiences (Tabor, 2011). Vicarious trauma manifests itself in much the same way as primary trauma (i.e., trauma directly experienced); its impacts include repeated and unwanted thoughts, difficulty sleeping, and feelings of disconnection from others. People working with those who have experienced trauma and violence are always at risk of vicarious trauma. For example, staff at the settlement agency described in chapters 2.6, 3.5, and 4.1 of this handbook wanted to implement TVIC because of the rising numbers, complexity, and trauma needs of newly arrived refugees and the impact that vicarious trauma was having on staff and volunteers (Javan, 2022). Staff were listening daily to horrendous experiences and observing the impact of those experiences on the people with whom they were working.

More recently, the concepts of "vicarious resilience" and "vicarious post-traumatic growth" have been used to draw attention to the positive impacts of such work. The notion of trauma resilience has been applied to service providers, with vicarious resilience being defined as "the positive impact on and personal growth of therapists resulting from exposure to their clients' resilience" (Hernandez-Wolfe, 2018, p. 9). Similarly, building on the notion of post-traumatic growth, "the positive changes people report as they struggle with the aftermath of highly stressful and potentially traumatic events" (Tedeschi, Cann, Taku, Senol-Durak, & Calhoun, 2017, p. 11), research has found that those who experience vicarious trauma also may experience post-traumatic growth (Gueta, Cohen-Leibovich, & Ronel, 2021; McNeillie & Rose, 2021).

A trauma- and violence-informed approach as conceptualized in this handbook aims to support the well-being of both staff and clients, recognizing that providing support to those who have experienced violence and trauma necessitates thinking about the suffering they have endured and, to some extent, experiencing the suffering in a secondary way. Such an approach recognizes that organizations must make an effort to mitigate negative impacts as a means to support healthy workplaces and workers.

Burnout/compassion fatigue. Burnout is a psychological response to chronic job stressors (Laschinger & Smith, 2013). Such job stressors can include vicarious trauma, racism, and moral distress. Burnout is associated with compassion fatigue and is the final, cumulative result of prolonged exposure to workplace stress. Peters (2018) examined the use of the term compassion fatigue across psychology, social work, and nursing, defining it as "a preventable state of holistic exhaustion that manifests as a physical decline in energy and endurance, an emotional decline in empathetic ability and emotional exhaustion, and a spiritual decline as one feels hopeless or helpless to recover that results from chronic exposure to others' suffering, compassion, high stress exposure, and high occupational use of self in the absence of boundary setting and self-care measures" (p. 470). Neville and Cole (2013) write that compassion fatigue is a newer concept that some claim encompasses both burnout and the secondary stress from thinking about the suffering of those to whom care is being provided. They also note that others claim that compassion fatigue (CF) should replace burnout as a more accurate term for the experience. However, others argue that these two are unique concepts. A recent concept analysis concluded that "while burnout is an accumulation of stress related to work environment, CF is depletion of compassion resulting from exposure to suffering and trauma" (Henson, 2020, p. 81). By contrast, compassion satisfaction is a sense of gratification derived from caring for those who are suffering (Baqeas, Davis, & Copnell, 2021; Xie et al., 2021). The key point is that people working with those who have experienced trauma and violence will experience stress and that the more stressful their work and workplaces are, the greater the potential impact of that stress. Minimizing negative impacts starts with normalizing these dynamics as expected and requiring attention, rather than merely expecting service providers to "toughen up" or "cope."

Moral distress. Moral distress is identified as one workplace stressor that contributes to compassion fatigue/burnout. Much of the extensive work on moral distress has stemmed from Jameton's (1984) definition of moral distress in nursing practice as "when one knows the right thing to do but institutional constraints make it nearly impossible to pursue the right course of action" (p. 6). Importantly, this definition points toward the context of practice. However, the definition (a) places responsibility for "knowing the right thing to do" on individuals, leaving open diverse and conflicting opinions, (b) implies that the "right course of action" is an individual choice, (c) does not account for pursuing the "right course of action" having little or no impact, and (d) does not point toward the larger sociopolitical context (Varcoe, Pauly, Webster, & Storch, 2012).

Analysing the impact of this definition and related ideas based on theoretical work and empirical data, the alternative we proposed was to define moral distress as "the experience of being seriously compromised as a moral agent in practicing in accordance with accepted professional values and standards ... a relational experience shaped by multiple contexts, including the socio-political and cultural context of the workplace environment" (Varcoe et al., 2012, p. 59). We argued that such a relational definition recast moral distress as a highly political concept that is inherently about power and differences in power, and we pointed to the need to address structures and systemic issues in order to lessen moral distress. Figure 1.4.1 presents these key concepts in relation to one another.

Scope and Nature of the Issues

The interrelated phenomena of vicarious trauma, compassion fatigue/burnout, and moral distress have been shown to be widely experienced by diverse human service workers, including first responders (Greinacher, Derezza-Greeven, Herzog, & Nikendei, 2019), those working in the homelessness sector (Lemieux-Cumberlege & Taylor, 2019), child protection workers (Molnar et al., 2020) and health care workers, including nurses (López-López et al., 2019), physicians (Rotenstein et al., 2018), and others. The dimensions and impacts of working with people who have experienced or are experiencing violence and trauma have been studied extensively and include significant mental and emotional impacts on individual workers, as well as negative impacts on workplace environments and indeed on organizations and entire professions as people leave jobs and their chosen vocations. The impacts of moral distress are similar,

1.4 Vicarious Trauma, Moral Distress, and Compassion Fatigue/Burnout

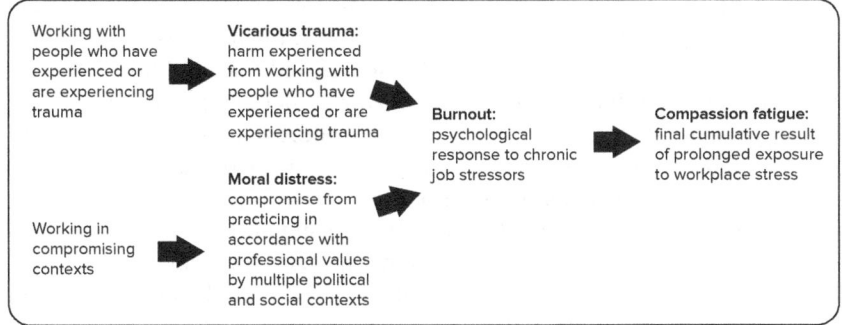

Figure 1.4.1 Interrelated concepts of vicarious trauma, compassion fatigue/burnout, and moral distress. Copyright 2021, the author.

and it is likely that working with people who have experienced or are experiencing violence and trauma in unsupportive and morally constraining workplaces is a toxic combination.

Toward a Structural Analysis

Repeatedly in the literature and in common understandings, the problems of vicarious trauma, compassion fatigue/burnout, and moral distress are located in the individual worker. Furthermore, responsibility (or worse, blame) for the problem is assigned primarily to individual workers. For example, note that in the previously cited definition of compassion fatigue, it is said to occur "in the absence of boundary setting and self-care measures." The language that is used does not routinely point to upstream causes, with terms such as "trauma overload" or "trauma burden" or "toxic and distressing workplaces." Similarly, the positive language of "compassion satisfaction" and "vicarious resilience" often points to the characteristics of individual workers, risking the implication that the answer to the problem is also located in individuals. Repeatedly, the solutions offered are aimed primarily at the individual worker. Most strategies related to vicarious trauma and compassion fatigue are at the level of the individual and focus on self-care strategies (see for example, Fiore, 2021; Grabbe, Higgins, Baird, & Pfeiffer, 2021; Hallam et al., 2021). For example, in a systematic review of emotional distress among health care professionals in a hospital intensive care unit (ICU) that emphasized the prevalence of burnout and compassion fatigue, strategies identified were those that encouraged health care providers to "cope," perhaps through "different intensivist work schedules, educational programs on coping with emotional distress, improving communication skills, and relaxation methods" (van Mol, Kompanje, Benoit, Bakker, & Nijkamp, 2015).

Yet in studies of these dynamics, the protective and exacerbating factors repeatedly point not only to the characteristics and behaviours of individual workers but also to the collective work cultures and the conditions of work. For example, Levin, Putney, Crimmins, and McGrath (2021) found that greater employee belief that their organizations were addressing issues of stress and trauma predicted lower levels of secondary traumatic stress and burnout and higher levels of compassion satisfaction, indicating a need to strengthen organizational efforts to address stress and trauma and promote health and wellness. A recent study of physicians found that greater institutional support was associated with lower burnout and secondary stress and higher compassion satisfaction (Doolittle, 2021). Rather than being left to "sink or swim," service providers need collective action and institutional support.

Vicarious Trauma, Compassion Fatigue/Burnout, Moral Distress, and TVIC: Structural Responses

TVIC, as understood in this handbook, provides direction for structural understanding of these phenomena and for implementing structural responses. First, and most importantly, because the "V" draws attention to structural violence, TVIC requires the creation of organizational conditions and cultures that create capacity for TVIC and for the well-being of providers. Second, to address structural violence, organizations need to develop policies and processes that take the context of service users into account; this will buffer providers from vicarious trauma, compassion fatigue/burnout, and moral distress.

Developing Structural Competence

The concept of structural competence was first developed within medical education (Metzl & Hansen, 2014; Metzl & Roberts, 2014) but is also useful for developing structural responses in the provision of TVIC in diverse contexts. Metzl and Hansen (2014) conceptualized structural competence as beginning with an "awareness of forces that influence health outcomes at levels above individual interactions" (p. 127); this idea has since been extended to promote wider understanding of social inequities and the social determinants of health (Hansen & Metzl, 2019) and applied in the context of responding to interpersonal violence (Mackenzie, Gannon, Stanley, Cosgrove, & Feder, 2019).

The core structural competencies identified by Metzl and Hansen (box 1.4.1) can be used to develop the capacity of both individuals and organizations to provide TVIC, as well as to prevent and mitigate vicarious trauma, compassion fatigue/burnout, and moral distress. Recognizing how economic, physical, and sociopolitical forces shape service interactions will be a lesser or greater challenge depending on the organization at hand. Organizations that already embrace a mandate for equity and social justice are often structured based on such understanding, providing services based on the recognition that those served are variously grappling with poverty, racism, housing instability, and so on. Organizations that have not embraced such a mandate (surgical units in hospitals, for example) are structured in ways that make such considerations more challenging to imagine or put into action. Recognizing these dynamics can help service providers avoid taking responsibility for organizational challenges, and provide direction for change.

BOX 1.4.1 CORE STRUCTURAL COMPETENCIES FOR INDIVIDUALS AND ORGANIZATIONS

1. Recognize the economic, physical, and sociopolitical forces that shape interactions in service provision.
2. Develop a language of structure, including the language of inequities and privilege.
3. Rearticulate individual service users' presentations in structural terms.
4. Observe, imagine, and implement structural interventions.
5. Develop structural humility.

Note. Adapted from "Structural competency: Theorizing a new medical engagement with stigma and inequality," by Metzl, J. M., & Hansen, H., 2014, *Social Science & Medicine*, *103*, 126–133, doi:10.1016/j.socscimed.2013.06.032.

Organizations and providers that recognize structural forces are better able to name and acknowledge barriers to service and well-being for themselves and for those served and to avoid blaming providers or clients for circumstances that are beyond their control. For example, greeting a client who is late for an appointment with "I am guessing you ran into difficulties getting here" sets a different tone than "You're late." Calling a co-worker "burned out" contributes to one culture; saying "They have got a lot on their plate" contributes to a different culture. Javan (2022) offers an excellent example of the power of structural understanding. The managers at a settlement agency studied by Javan shifted their understanding of the anger and frustration shown by clients who were rejecting offered housing (because it was not near family members) as a reflection of their need to prioritize their safety within very limited housing options.

Language always matters. From how service users are described, to the names of programs and organizations, a structural understanding can draw attention to, and disrupt, patterns of power and privilege. For example, Kilala

Lelum, an Indigenous health centre in Vancouver (chapter 1.2), refers to, and treats, those coming for service as "members" rather than "clients," "patients," or the array of diagnostic and other labels they experience in other contexts. The impact of this has been profound on members, staff, and other service organizations; "member" conveys respect and disrupts the usual power dynamics. Setting up respectful relationships between providers and those they are serving fosters better work environments and working relationships. Contrast this with the dominant approaches in health care, which use security guards, bars, and threats of force in an effort to mitigate violence.

However, undoing individualistic and decontextualized understandings of the issues people face requires shifting more than language; it also requires that we understand power dynamics and create new understandings. For example, in research in primary care clinics, our team observed that as the clinics integrated TVIC, they shifted the ways they talked about patients (Browne et al., 2016). Thus, when introducing people at clinical conferences, instead of saying "63-year-old Indigenous woman with a history of drug use, HIV positive," staff started at a different place: "63-year-old woman from [Nation], residential school survivor, living at [shelter] who has been struggling with ..." Leading with the structural conditions created a different starting place for service, and doing so in relation to all people served underscored the patterns of structural violence experienced by the whole community and thus the structural solutions that were required.

Developing and implementing *structural* interventions requires "swimming against the tide." Efforts to improve services and to mitigate vicarious trauma, compassion fatigue/burnout, and moral distress are typically aimed at individual providers, who are advised to "set boundaries" and engage in "self-care." While these are important, the conditions of work also require attention. The resources required to provide services to people with histories or present experiences of interpersonal and structural violence are high, yet ironically, such services are often the most marginalized. Staff need adequate salaries and benefits, including sick time and counselling support; they also need reasonable and manageable workloads and a workplace culture that is trauma- and violence-informed.

The fifth competency, structural humility, is crucial. The ability to recognize the limitations of structural competency can help service providers and organizations come to grips with the fact that structural violence and inequity are pervasive and beyond any individual or organization to resolve. In a program of research on an intervention (iHEAL) supporting women who have experienced violence, nurses repeatedly have been overwhelmed by the conditions of women's lives and have experienced moral distress at the impact of policies, services (or the lack of them), and the way women are treated as they try to access support (Varcoe et al., 2019). Recognizing that each contribution matters, but no one contribution is enough, can position service providers in such a way that they can keep working without becoming overwhelmed.

Action at All Levels

Vicarious trauma, compassion fatigue/burnout, and moral distress cannot be prevented, nor can the impacts be mitigated, by individuals working on their own. Drawing on structural competence can help individuals (intrapersonally) to frame their work in ways that recognize the limitations of individuals and organizations, in this way decreasing blame (including self-blame), vicarious trauma, and moral distress. However, such stances need to be shared within the workplace culture. Opportunities are needed to develop and share a supportive workplace philosophy and to debrief and plan together (interpersonally) both with other providers and with those served. Feedback mechanisms and opportunities for dialogue between providers and those served will build trust and serve as a meaningful basis for structural improvements. Actions at the level of organizations are required to create these conditions.

Conclusion

A TVIC approach to "safety for all" includes caring for the carers, which means having an explicit awareness of the forms of harm reviewed in this chapter that can affect individual workers and the organizational culture. Knowing about, and being able to name and effectively respond to, vicarious trauma, compassion fatigue/burnout, and moral distress, and destigmatizing these expected consequences of the work, will require a shift toward more structurally competent workplaces in which individuals are supported in their work. This is a win–win–win, as a healthier workforce provides better care, services users are more satisfied and well, and organizations are more likely to retain highly qualified personnel – all aspects of core system goals articulated in most quality improvement efforts. Caring for carers is not only the right thing to do but also the most efficient and effective thing to do.

KEY MESSAGES AND IMPLICATIONS

- People who work in health and social service settings are working with a high proportion of people who have experienced trauma and violence, and this places them at risk for experiencing trauma by thinking about and seeing the impact of those experiences.
- Health and social service settings are often operating with resources inadequate to the demands of the work, thus creating more stressful environments and increasing

the risk for moral distress (i.e., being unable to practise in a way that aligns with professional values).
- Stressful working circumstances and inadequate social and organizational resources coupled with serving people who have experienced violence and trauma create risk for secondary (vicarious) trauma, moral distress, compassion fatigue, and burnout.
- Understanding the structural forces that affect both workers and clients, and understanding that every interaction has an impact on others and on organizations, sets a foundation for optimizing work cultures.

ADDITIONAL RESOURCES

- EQUIP-GTV Vicarious Trauma Tool: https://equiphealthcare.ca/files/2019/12/EQUIP-GTV-Tool-Vicarious-Trauma-Nov-25-2019.pdf

REFERENCES

Baqeas, M.H., Davis, J., & Copnell, B. (2021). Compassion fatigue and compassion satisfaction among palliative care health providers: A scoping review. *BMC Palliative Care*, *20*(1), 1–13. https://doi.org/10.1186/s12904-021-00784-5

Browne, A.J., Varcoe, C., Lavoie, J., Smye, V.L., Wong, S., Krause, M., . . . Fridkin, A. (2016). Enhancing health care equity with Indigenous populations: Evidence-based strategies from an ethnographic study. *BMC Health Services Research*, *16*(544), 1–17. https://doi.org/10.1186/s12913-016-1707-9

Doane, G., & Varcoe, C. (2021). *How to nurse: Relational inquiry in action* (2nd ed.). Philadelphia, PA: Lippincott, Williams & Wilkins.

Doolittle, B.R. (2021). Association of burnout with emotional coping strategies, friendship, and institutional support among internal medicine physicians. *Journal of Clinical Psychology in Medical Settings*, *28*(2), 361–7. https://doi.org/10.1007/s10880-020-09724-6

Fiore, J. (2021). Randomized pilot study exploring an online pre-composed receptive music experience and a mindfulness-based intervention for hospice workers' stress and professional quality of life. *Arts in Psychotherapy*, *74*. https://doi.org/10.1016/j.aip.2021.101797

Grabbe, L., Higgins, M.K., Baird, M., & Pfeiffer, K.M. (2021). Impact of a resiliency training to support the mental well-being of front-line workers: Brief report of a quasi-experimental study of the community resiliency model. *Medical Care*, *59*(7), 616–21. https://doi.org/10.1097/MLR.0000000000001535

Greinacher, A., Derezza-Greeven, C., Herzog, W., & Nikendei, C. (2019). Secondary traumatization in first responders: A systematic review. *European Journal of Psychotraumatology*, *10*(1). https://doi.org/10.1080/20008198.2018.1562840

Gueta, K., Cohen-Leibovich, Y., & Ronel, N. (2021). "Even crap can be fertilizer": The experience of volunteering at sexual assault crisis centers for women survivors of

1.4 Vicarious Trauma, Moral Distress, and Compassion Fatigue/Burnout 69

sexual assault. *Feminism & Psychology, 31*(2), 270–90. https://doi.org/10.1177 /0959353520955141

Hallam, K.T., Leigh, D., Davis, C., Castle, N., Sharples, J., & Collett, J.D. (2021). Self-care agency and self-care practice in youth workers reduces burnout risk and improves compassion satisfaction. *Drug and Alcohol Review, 40*(5), 847–55. https:// doi.org/10.1111/dar.13209

Hansen, H., & Metzl, J.M. (2019). *Structural competency in mental health and medicine: A case-based approach to treating the social determinants of health.* Switzerland: Springer International Publishing.

Henson, J.S. (2020). Burnout or compassion fatigue: A comparison of concepts. *MEDSURG Nursing, 29*(2), 77–95. Retrieved from https://www.proquest.com /docview/2388933

Hernandez-Wolfe, P. (2018). Vicarious resilience: A comprehensive review. *Resiliencia vicaria: una revisión comprensiva*, 9–17. https://doi.org/10.7440/res66.2018.02

Jameton, A. (1984). *Nursing practice: The ethical issues.* Englewood Cliffs, NJ: Prentice Hall.

Javan, T. (2022). Organizational implementation of trauma- and violence-informed care. Doctoral dissertation. Western University. https://ir.lib.uwo.ca/etd/8411/

Laschinger, H.K.S., & Smith, L.M. (2013). The influence of authentic leadership and empowerment on new-graduate nurses' perceptions of interprofessional collaboration. *Journal of Nursing Administration, 43*(1), 24–9. https://doi.org/10 .1097/NNA.0b013e318278606-

Lavoie, J., Boulton, A., & Dwyer, J. (2010). Analysing contractual environments: Lessons from Indigenous health in Canada, Australia, and New Zealand. *Public Administration, 88*(3), 665–79. https://doi.org/10.1111/j.1467-9299.2009 .01784.x

Lavoie, J., Varcoe, C., Wathen, C.N., & Browne, A.J. (2018). Sentinels of inequity: Examining policy requirements for equity-oriented primary healthcare. *BMC Health Services Research, 18*(705). https://doi.org/10.1186/s12913-018-3501-3

Lemieux-Cumberlege, A., & Taylor, E.P. (2019). An exploratory study on the factors affecting the mental health and well-being of frontline workers in homeless services. *Health & Social Care in the Community, 27*(4), e367–e378. https://doi.org/10.1111 /hsc.12738

Levin, A.P., Putney, H., Crimmins, D., & McGrath, J.G. (2021). Secondary traumatic stress, burnout, compassion satisfaction, and perceived organizational trauma readiness in forensic science professionals. *Journal of Forensic Sciences.* https:// doi.org/10.1111/1556-4029.14747

López-López, I.M., Gómez-Urquiza, J.L., Cañadas, G.R., De la Fuente, E.I., Albendín-García, L., & Cañadas-De la Fuente, G.A. (2019). Prevalence of burnout in mental health nurses and related factors: a systematic review and meta-analysis. *International Journal of Mental Health Nursing, 28*(5), 1035–44. https://doi.org /10.1111/inm.12606

Mackenzie, M., Gannon, M., Stanley, N., Cosgrove, K., & Feder, G. (2019). "You certainly don't go back to the doctor once you've been told, 'I'll never understand women like you'": Seeking candidacy and structural competency in the dynamics of domestic abuse disclosure. *Sociology of Health & Illness, 41*(6), 1159–74. https://doi.org/10.1111/1467-9566.12893

McNeillie, N., & Rose, J. (2021). Vicarious trauma in therapists: A meta-ethnographic review. *Behavioural & Cognitive Psychotherapy, 49*(4), 426–40. https://doi.org/10.1017/S1352465820000776

Metzl, J.M., & Hansen, H. (2014). Structural competency: Theorizing a new medical engagement with stigma and inequality. *Social Science & Medicine, 103*, 126–33. https://doi.org/10.1016/j.socscimed.2013.06.032

Metzl, J.M., & Roberts, D.E. (2014). Structural competency meets structural racism: race, politics, and the structure of medical knowledge. *The Virtual Mentor: VM, 16*(9), 674–90. https://journalofethics.ama-assn.org/article/structural-competency-meets-structural-racism-race-politics-and-structure-medical-knowledge/2014-09

Molnar, B.E., Meeker, S.A., Manners, K., Tieszen, L., Kalergis, K., Fine, J.E., . . . Wells, M.K. (2020). Vicarious traumatization among child welfare and child protection professionals: A systematic review. *Child Abuse & Neglect, 110*. https://doi.org/10.1016/j.chiabu.2020.104679

Neville, K., & Cole, D.A. (2013). The relationships among health promotion behaviors, compassion fatigue, burnout, and compassion satisfaction in nurses practicing in a community medical center. *Journal of Nursing Administration, 43*(6), 348–54.

Peters, E. (2018). Compassion fatigue in nursing: A concept analysis. *Nursing Forum, 53*(4), 466–80. https://doi.org/10.1111/nuf.12274

Rotenstein, L.S., Torre, M., Ramos, M.A., Rosales, R.C., Guille, C., Sen, S., & Mata, D.A. (2018). Prevalence of burnout among physicians: A systematic review. *JAMA, 320*(11), 1131–50. https://doi.org/10.1001/jama.2018.12777

Stewart, R. (2020, July 13). Black Lives Matter: What have advertising's biggest agencies promised? *The Drum*. Retrieved from https://www.thedrum.com/news/2020/07/13/black-lives-matter-what-have-advertisings-biggest-agencies-promised

Tabor, P.D. (2011). Vicarious traumatization: concept analysis. *Journal of Forensic Nursing, 7*(4), 203–8. https://doi.org/10.1111/j.1939-3938.2011.01115.x

Tedeschi, R.G., Cann, A., Taku, K., Senol-Durak, E., & Calhoun, L.G. (2017). The Posttraumatic Growth Inventory: A revision integrating existential and spiritual change. *Journal of Traumatic Stress, 30*(1), 11–18. https://doi.org/10.1002/jts.22155

van Mol, M.M.C., Kompanje, E.J.O., Benoit, D.D., Bakker, J., & Nijkamp, M.D. (2015). The prevalence of compassion fatigue and burnout among healthcare professionals in intensive care units: A systematic review. *Plos One, 10*(9), 1–22. https://doi.org/10.1371/journal.pone.0136955

Varcoe, C., Ford-Gilboe, M., Browne, A.J., Perrin, N., Bungay, V., McKenzie, H., . . . Dion Stout, M. (2019). The efficacy of a health Promotion intervention for

Indigenous women: Reclaiming Our Spirits. *Journal of Interpersonal Violence.* https://doi.org/10.1177/0886260518820818

Varcoe, C., Pauly, B., Webster, G., & Storch, J. (2012). Moral distress: Tensions as springboards for action. *Health Ethics Forum, 24*(1), 51–62.

Xie, W., Chen, L., Feng, F., Okoli, C.T.C., Tang, P., Zeng, L., ... Wang, J. (2021). The prevalence of compassion satisfaction and compassion fatigue among nurses: A systematic review and meta-analysis. *International Journal of Nursing Studies, 120.* https://doi.org/10.1016/j.ijnurstu.2021.103973

1.5 The Principles of Trauma- and Violence-Informed Care

NADINE WATHEN AND COLLEEN VARCOE

Exposure to trauma and violence has long-term effects, whether the experiences are ongoing or in the past. When providers, organizations, and systems that serve survivors lack understanding of the complex and lasting impacts of trauma and violence, they miss opportunities to provide effective services and risk causing further harm.

This chapter formally introduces the concept of trauma- and violence-informed care (TVIC), defining and articulating the "V" (see also chapter 1.2) and situating TVIC as a structural approach to addressing the significant prevalence and impacts of trauma and violence. It then outlines the four principles of TVIC: understand trauma, violence, and its impacts on people's lives and behaviour; create emotionally and physically safe environments for all clients and providers; foster opportunities for choice, collaboration, and connection; and use a strengths-based and capacity-building approach to support clients. "Maria's Story" is used throughout as a case example to demonstrate what TVIC can look like in practice.

> **BOX 1.5.1 MARIA'S STORY – PART 1**
> **HER FIRST VISIT TO YOU**
> Maria is a single mother with four children under age ten. She's visiting you today with her son, who is exhibiting post-traumatic stress symptoms as a result of having been exposed to his father's abuse of Maria. Maria is being harassed by her ex-partner, who ignores restraining orders that he not contact her or the children. He has threatened to call child protection services, and she is afraid he will use the fact that their son is unwell as evidence of her "bad parenting."

1.5 The Principles of Trauma- and Violence-Informed Care

From Trauma-Informed to Trauma- and *Violence*-Informed

Work from the US Substance Abuse and Mental Health Administration specific to women, violence, and substance use helped establish the concept of "trauma-informed care" (or practice) (TIC/P). TIC/P aims to create safety for people seeking care by understanding the effects of trauma and its close links to health and behaviour. Unlike trauma-specific care, it is not about eliciting or treating people's trauma histories but about creating safe spaces that limit the potential for further harm for all people (Covington, 2008; Dechief & Abbott, 2012; Elliot, Bjelajac, Fallot, Markoff, & Reed, 2005; Hopper, Bassuk, & Oliver, 2010; Savage, Quiros, Dodd, & Bonavota, 2007; Strand, Popescu, Abramovitz, & Richards, 2015). While such safety helps create the conditions for disclosures of trauma, disclosure is not the goal.

Trauma- and violence-informed care (TVIC) expands the concept of TIC to account for the intersecting impacts of systemic and interpersonal violence and structural inequities – including stigma, discrimination, and bias – on a person's life (Elliot et al., 2005; Ponic, Varcoe, & Smutylo, 2016). These concepts were reviewed in previous chapters. This shift is important as it emphasizes both past and ongoing violence and their traumatic impacts and focuses on a person's experiences of previous and current violence, so that problems are seen as residing both in a person's psychological state (Williams & Paul, 2008) and in their social circumstances. Thus, TVIC explicitly positions experiences of violence and trauma, and their sequelae, as strongly linked to social/structural determinants of health – a fact supported by epidemiological data. Socially contextualized information about trauma shifts the focus away from perceived individual flaws in a person's "personality" or "character" and instead situates traumatized people's coping within the range of normal and typical human responses to trauma imposed from external sources (Haskell & Randall, 2009).

Viewed this way, responses to trauma and violence, including substance use and poor mental health, are predictable consequences of highly threatening events and experiences. This is especially the case when stigma, inequities, and system-induced trauma are present. Specifying "violence" in TVIC points toward violence as often ongoing. Because trauma refers both to events and to responses to them (Covington, 2008, chapter 1.1), there is a risk that providers will focus on past traumatic events without recognizing that any person may be experiencing multiple forms of ongoing structural and interpersonal violence.

Provider knowledge and skill are key to creating safety in any service encounter; this includes addressing the traumatic effects of harmful institutional practices such as any form of discrimination. Organizational leadership and operationalized strategies to support shifts in practice are essential to create the conditions for providers to practise in a trauma- and violence-informed way. TVIC strives to make practices and policies safe, especially by preventing further harm. These practices and policies can help individual providers in any context to more safely, equitably, and effectively interact with those seeking care who have experienced, or are still experiencing, trauma and violence, regardless of whether the individual has disclosed such experiences. Emerging research shows that providing care in these ways is better both for those seeking care *and* for those providing it (Browne et al., 2018; Ford-Gilboe et al., 2018) and depends on key organizational factors (Lavoie, Varcoe, Wathen, Ford-Gilboe, & Browne, 2018).

BOX 1.5.2 WHAT'S THE DIFFERENCE?

The main differences between TIC and TVIC are that TVIC brings an explicit focus to:

- broad structural and social conditions, to avoid seeing trauma as happening only "in people's minds";
- ongoing violence, to avoid seeing trauma only as something that happened in the past;
- institutional and systemic violence, including policies and practices that perpetuate harm (system-induced trauma) because they are designed to satisfy the needs of the system rather than those of the person; and
- the responsibility of organizations and providers, supported by resources, policies, and systems, to shift services at the point of care, so that people do not have to work around services to get what they need.

Below we outline the principles of TVIC, specifically considering stigma, discrimination, implicit bias, and cultural safety, while integrating the considerations from the previous chapter on vicarious trauma – that is, "caring for the carers."

Principles of TVIC

Figure 1.5.1 outlines examples of the four TVIC principles as developed and tested in our previous and ongoing work (Ponic et al., 2016; Wathen & Varcoe, 2019):

1. Understand trauma and violence (including structural and systemic violence) and their impacts on the lives and behaviours of people, including those providing care.
2. Create emotionally, culturally, and physically safe environments for service users and providers.

1.5 The Principles of Trauma- and Violence-Informed Care

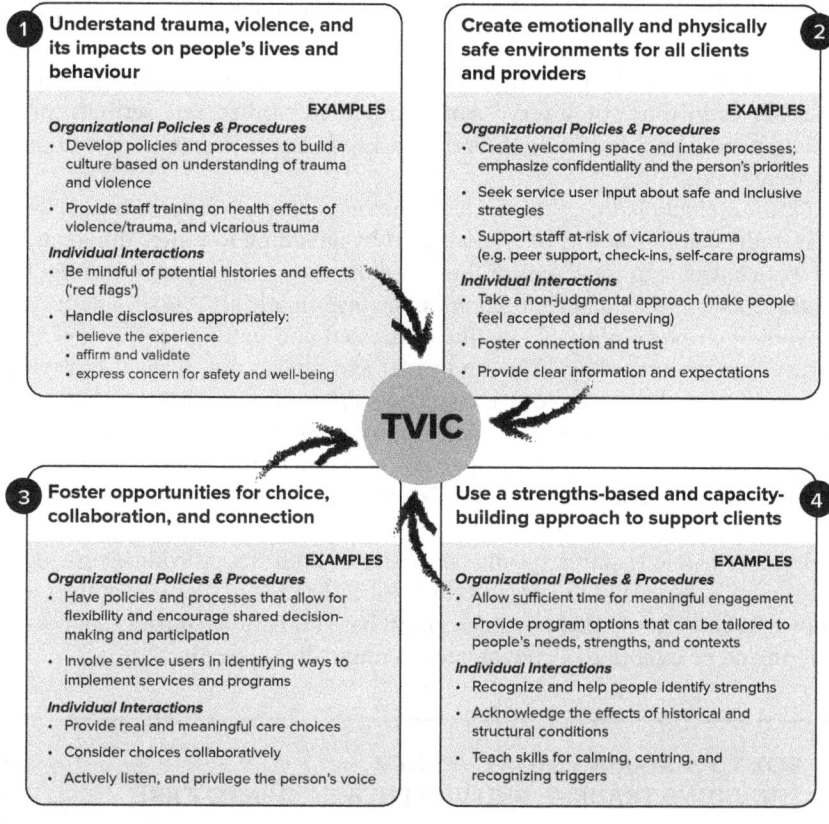

Figure 1.5.1 Principles of trauma- and violence-informed care. Copyright 2021, the authors.

3. Foster opportunities for choice, collaboration, and connection.
4. Provide strengths-based and capacity-building ways to support service users.

These principles work together. Because of the prevalence of multiple forms of trauma and violence, including but not limited to interpersonal violence (e.g., child maltreatment, the exposure of children to intimate partner violence, intimate partner violence, sexual assault, and elder abuse) and structural violence (e.g., racism, war, poverty, homelessness), it is safest to assume that any person seeking service may have been exposed to trauma and violence. *Knowing the pervasiveness, and understanding that the effects may be far-reaching and long-lasting,* leads providers to approach every person with mindfulness of that potential history or ongoing experience.

Knowing the specific key impacts of trauma and violence on attitudes (e.g., distrust), behaviours (e.g., substance use), and health problems (e.g., chronic pain, sleeplessness) helps providers anticipate how the impacts may manifest themselves in those they serve. For example, in cardiac care settings, providers would be mindful of the relationship between systemic racism and hypertension.

Creating emotionally, culturally, and physically safe environments begins with that understanding and is operationalized by attending to power differentials so that control is in the hands of those seeking care. *Creating opportunities for choice, collaboration, and connection* can involve simple actions such as asking ("Would you be comfortable getting undressed and putting on this gown?") rather than commanding ("Get undressed and put on this gown"). Fostering connection can be as simple as recognizing a person's experience ("That must be difficult"). Similarly, *taking a strengths-based and capacity-building approach* can be as simple as recognizing a person's efforts and intentions ("It sounds as though you have really tried…" or "Can you tell me about what's worked for you in the past?").

Each principle requires specific strategies at both the individual provider/staff member level and the organizational/unit/team level. Some examples are shown in figure 1.5.1. These strategies must have both leadership and staff-level buy-in and be intentionally integrated and mutually supportive.

BOX 1.5.3 MARIA'S STORY – PART 2
PROVIDING TRAUMA- AND VIOLENCE-INFORMED CARE

Considering the experiences of Maria and her children (and likely others in your practice), there are strategies you can put in place to provide care in a trauma- and violence-informed way. The following are considerations for any setting:

1 Prepare your space:
- Do you have signs and wayfinding in multiple locally spoken languages?
- Do your art and pictures of people fully reflect the diversity of those served?
- Are your intake procedures and reception area set up to make it easy for people to check in and wait comfortably? Is the latter welcoming for children?
- Do you have conditions for private and confidential conversation?

2 Ask yourself:
- What's happened and is still happening to Maria and her children?
- How is this impacting them?

3 Ask Maria:
- How has she kept herself and the children safe – what works and doesn't work?
- What are her preferences for next steps? What's realistic and feasible for her?

> - What supports does she have, and what else would she need to follow an agreed-upon plan?
> 4 Acknowledge:
>   - The difficulty of the situation.
>   - Maria's efforts and successes to date.

What This Means for Service Providers

Trauma- and violence-informed, stigma-aware, and culturally safe service is about more than access to care; it also considers social and political conditions that shape people's health, including what care is offered and how it is provided, with a focus on improving the well-being of those who face the greatest disadvantage and risk of poor health. It means:

- *being aware* of how immediate and more subtle factors, including previous and ongoing exposure to various types of violence, shape people's real-life experiences;
- *being open* to consider how our practices and policies may unintentionally harm people, especially those experiencing social exclusion and discrimination, and changing these policies and practices; and
- working in ways that are *respectful and inclusive* of peoples' diverse histories and contexts and placing the responsibility for emotional, physical, and cultural safety in the care encounter on the provider and setting, with particular emphasis on racism and other forms of discrimination.

BOX 1.5.4 MARIA'S STORY – PART 3
NEXT STEPS

As you work with Maria and help her consider next steps for her and her son, the following are helpful to consider:

- What are the larger circumstances of the lives of Maria and her children? How is this impacting them? Without violating boundaries, can you convey that you relate to Maria's situation in some way?
- What's going on in Maria's life and how is this affecting her and the children, including what is realistic and feasible for her?
- What else is required in the face of these circumstances? Acknowledge any broader challenges she faces.

- Are you familiar with local services that could support Maria and the children? Do you have information and referral materials about these services that are likely to be relevant for Maria and her son?
- Are you able to make a "warm referral" to help Maria connect to these services?

Having learned that Maria arrived in Canada less than a year ago but hadn't accessed any newcomer resources, you used the end of the visit to call a colleague you know at the local settlement agency and learned that they would subsidize trauma-focused therapy for Maria's son. They also suggested a service specializing in newcomer women, which included on-site child care for her other children. To address the ongoing violence and harassment from her ex-partner, you suggested that Maria contact the outreach line for the local domestic violence service. While not ready to do so now, Maria took the information and agreed that creating a safety plan would be an important next step. You documented this action in your notes so you could follow-up at her next visit.

Connecting the Dots: Intersections between TVIC and Health Equity

Approaches to addressing trauma and violence in health care are rapidly evolving from a narrow focus on "interventions" for individual "victims" to a broader understanding of trauma and violence as pervasive social problems embedded in social and structural inequities. We're starting to understand that the effectiveness of interventions to prevent poor outcomes can be limited by the broader circumstances of people's lives. The capacity of providers to respond to experiences of trauma and violence is reduced when they do not take these circumstances into account and are not supported by their organizations to practise in a trauma- and violence-informed way, and when we fail to acknowledge and mediate the harm that caregivers themselves may experience as they do this difficult work.

BOX 1.5.5 MARIA'S STORY – PART 4
SELF-CHECK

You feel good about how things are going for Maria. In the process of working with her, you realize that though there has been an influx of newcomers from her country, there is no information about violence services in her first language. Maria's English is very good; even so, you draw this gap to the attention of the head of a community organization that can address it. However, hearing her story has been difficult for you, because of how often you see trauma and violence in the lives of those you serve, and also because of your own experiences of violence in a previous relationship. You take a few extra minutes for yourself and go for a brief walk, then schedule a debriefing session with a colleague. You also look up services available through your Employee Assistance Plan. It may be time to talk to someone.

Conclusion

In sum, interventions to prevent and mitigate the effects of trauma and violence must include an understanding of the circumstances of people's lives. Similarly, interventions to promote equity in health and social care must attend to all forms of violence. Interpersonal, including gender-based, violence should be understood within broad social circumstances, along with other forms of systemic violence and inequity. Finally, structural forms of violence filter down to everyday experiences, including interactions with health and social services – this is where organizations and individual providers can have the most impact on client experiences and outcomes (Browne, Varcoe, Ford-Gilboe, & Wathen, 2015; Browne et al., 2016; Farmer, 2003; Whitehead & Dahlgren, 2006).

KEY MESSAGES AND IMPLICATIONS

- The "V" in TVIC expands our understanding of the range of experiences that cause harm, focusing on the historical and ongoing conditions of people's lives as well as their individual experiences of trauma and violence.
- A structural understanding of trauma and violence, and their impacts, requires a structural response. TVIC, with its focus on organizational and individual practices, is such a response; it is also a key component in equity-oriented care.
- The four principles of TVIC are simple and highly tailorable to different practice and organizational contexts; each can be applied at both the individual level (where providers interact with service users) and, crucially, at the organization level, where policies and protocols set the conditions for practice.

ADDITIONAL RESOURCES

- TVIC Tool: https://gtvincubator.uwo.ca/wp-content/uploads/2021/05/GTV-EQUIP-Tool-TVIC-Spring2021.pdf
- TVIC principles (1-page graphic): https://gtvincubator.uwo.ca/wp-content/uploads/2019/07/EQUIP_GTV_TVIC_principles.pdf
- TVIC Backgrounder (6 pages): https://gtvincubator.uwo.ca/wp-content/uploads/2020/05/TVIC_Backgrounder_Fall2019r.pdf

REFERENCES

Browne, A.J., Varcoe, C.M., Ford-Gilboe, M., & Wathen, C.N. (2015). EQUIP Healthcare: An overview of a multi-component intervention to enhance equity-oriented care in primary health care settings. *International Journal for Equity in Health, 14*,152. https://doi.org/10.1186/s12939-015-0271-y

Browne, A.J., Varcoe, C., Ford-Gilboe, M., Wathen, C.N., Smye, V., Jackson, B.E., et al. (2018). Disruption as opportunity: impacts of an organizational-level health equity intervention in primary care clinics. *International Journal for Equity in Health, 17*(1),154. https://doi.org/10.1186/s12939-018-0820-2

Browne, A.J., Varcoe, C., Lavoie, J., Smye, V.L., Wong, S., Krause, M., . . . Fridkin, A. (2016). Enhancing health care equity with Indigenous populations: Evidence-based strategies from an ethnographic study. *BMC Health Services Research, 16*(544), 1–17. https://doi.org/10.1186/s12913-016-1707-9

Covington, S. (2008). Women and addiction: A trauma-informed approach. *Journal of Psychoactive Drugs, S5*, 377–85. https://doi.org/10.1080/02791072.2008.10400665

Dechief, L., & Abbott, J. (2012). Breaking out of the mould: Creating trauma-informed anti-violence services and housing for women and their children. In N. Poole & L. Greaves (Eds.), *Becoming trauma-informed* (pp. 329–38). Toronto, ON: Centre for Addiction and Mental Health.

Elliot, D.E., Bjelajac P., Fallot, R.D., Markoff, L.S., & Reed, B.G. (2005). Trauma-informed or trauma-denied: Principles and implementation of trauma-informed services for women. *Journal of Community Psychology, 33*(4), 461–77.

Farmer, P. (2003). *Pathologies of power: Health, human rights, and the new war on the poor*. Berkeley, CA: University of California Press.

Ford-Gilboe, M., Wathen, C.N., Varcoe, C., Herbert, C., Jackson, B.E., Lavoie, J., . . . Browne, A.J. for the EQUIP Research Program. (2018). How equity-oriented health care affects health: Key mechanisms and implications for primary health care practice and policy. *Milbank Quarterly, 96*(4), 635–71. https://doi.org/10.1111/1468-0009.12349

Haskell, L., & Randall, M. (2009). Disrupted attachments: A social context complex trauma framework and the lives of Aboriginal peoples in Canada. *Journal of Aboriginal Health, 5*(3), 48–99. Retrieved from https://papers.ssrn.com/sol3/papers.cfm?abstract_id=1569034

Hopper, E.K., Bassuk E.L., & Oliver J. (2010). Shelter from the storm: Trauma-informed care in homelessness services settings. *The Open Health Services and Policy Journal, 3*, 80–100. https://doi.org/10.2174/1874924001003010080

Lavoie, J., Varcoe, C., Wathen, C.N., Ford-Gilboe, M., & Browne, A.J. (2018). Sentinels of inequity: Examining policy requirements for equity-oriented primary healthcare. *BMC Health Services Research, 18*, 705. https://doi.org/10.1186/s12913-018-3501-3

Ponic, P., Varcoe, C., & Smutylo, T. (2016). Trauma- (and violence-) informed approaches to supporting victims of violence: Policy and practice considerations.

Victims of Crime Research Digest, 9. Department of Justice (DOJ); Canada. Retrieved from http://www.justice.gc.ca/eng/rp-pr/cj-jp/victim/rd9-rr9/p2.html

Savage, L., Quiros, A., Dodd, S., & Bonavota, D. (2007). Building trauma-informed practice: Appreciating the impact of trauma in the lives of women with substance abuse and mental health problems. *Journal of Social Work Practice in the Addictions,* 7(1-2), 91-116. https://doi.org/10.1300/J160v07n01_06

Strand, V., Popescu, M., Abramovitz, R., & Richards, S. (2015). Building agency capacity for trauma-informed evidence-based practice and field instruction. *Journal of Evidence-Informed Social Work, 13*(2), 179-97. https://doi.org/10.1080/23761407.2015.1014124

Wathen, C.N., & Varcoe, C. (2019). *Trauma- & violence-informed care: Prioritizing safety for survivors of gender-based violence.* Retrieved from https://gtvincubator.uwo.ca/wp-content/uploads/sites/22/2020/05/TVIC_Backgrounder_Fall2019r.pdf

Whitehead, M., & Dahlgren, G. (2006). Levelling up (part 1): A discussion paper on concepts and principles for tackling social inequities in health. University of Liverpool: WHO Collaborating Centre for Policy Research on Social Determinants of Health. Retrieved from http://www. who.int/social_determinants/resources/leveling_up_part1.pdf

Williams, J., & Paul, J. (2008). *Informed gender practice: Mental health acute care that works for women.* London, England: National Institute for Mental Health in England. Retrieved from https://webarchive.nationalarchives.gov.uk/20110512085546/http://www.nmhdu.org.uk/silo/files/informedgenderpractice.pdf

SECTION TWO

TVIC Implementation Case Studies

This section provides practice-based case studies of TVIC education and implementation in a range of health, social service, criminal justice, and educational settings. The contributors, who have expertise leading these activities, provide specific practice- and policy-ready advice on processes, outcomes, and lessons learned. The chapters pay attention to system, organization, and individual levels of intervention and reflect on the TVIC principles and core concepts, with specific examples on engaging service users in a TVIC approach and how to support staff well-being and safety.

2.1 Taking Organizational-Level Action: Creating a Context for Implementing TVIC in Health Care Settings

ANNETTE J. BROWNE AND COLLEEN VARCOE

Drawing on research and practice experiences, this chapter highlights strategies for implementing TVIC that are applicable in a range of settings and organizations. We focus on the organizational-level[1] considerations, supports, and resources needed to successfully deliver TVIC in health care, recognizing that these may also apply to non–health service settings. We pay particular attention to how to create supportive organizational contexts, and we point to the kinds of shifts in organizational dynamics and culture required to support uptake of TVIC. Using examples from research involving primary health care clinics and emergency departments, we highlight considerations and recommendations for health care providers, program leaders, and managers and administrators regarding implementation of TVIC.

TVIC is increasingly recognized as a highly relevant and universally applicable approach to providing care in all settings. In our health equity intervention research known as EQUIP Health Care, we have been experimenting with ways to enhance capacity to implement TVIC in a range of health care settings. Our understanding of TVIC, aligned with chapter 1.5,

- is based on understanding the effects of interpersonal (e.g., child maltreatment, intimate partner violence) and structural (e.g., poverty, racism) forms of violence as intersecting, with compounding impacts on health;
- recognizes that people disadvantaged by systemic inequities often experience multiple forms of violence that have ongoing traumatic impacts;
- shifts emphasis from client disclosure of violence experiences to care providers creating a safe environment for disclosure (or not), including for those most traumatized;
- counters the tendency to locate "the problem" of trauma primarily in the psyche of those experiencing violence by emphasizing social and structural conditions as causes of trauma;

- creates a safer environment for all, including staff, by developing a plan to address vicarious trauma; and
- requires certain organizational conditions and strategies to be effectively enacted.

Learning about TVIC can be accomplished through TVIC education and training; however, as we discuss in this chapter, training is only one component of implementation; that is, training may be necessary but is not enough for the meaningful organizational cultural changes required. Also needed are shifts in policies and interprofessional practices to support successful implementation of TVIC. In this chapter, we highlight the importance of acting at the organizational level to create the conditions for TVIC. Drawing on two diverse health care contexts, the primary health care (PHC) sector and emergency departments (EDs), we orient readers to the importance of organizational change processes, which include policies and resources to support the enactment of TVIC. We offer practical examples of how to implement and operationalize TVIC, and we highlight strategies and guidance relevant to a wide range of settings and sectors – for example, maternity units, mental health settings, and acute care units. By the end of this chapter, the reader will be able to:

- describe organizational factors that support TVIC as a key dimension of equity-oriented health care; and
- identify strategies for implementing TVIC at the point of care, as well as the organizational contexts that can support implementation.

Creating a Context for Implementing TVIC: Two Case Examples

In this section, we provide an overview of what we have learned about implementation of TVIC from EQUIP Health Care. The intervention studies we describe below were based on earlier work. Most importantly, we studied the delivery of PHC at two urban Indigenous health clinics serving Indigenous and non-Indigenous people who face structural inequities and discrimination (Browne, Varcoe, & Fridkin, 2011; Browne et al., 2016; Browne et al., 2012; Wong et al., 2014). Our goal was to learn how care was being delivered in alignment with equity-oriented and social justice goals, which we came to refer to as "equity-oriented health care" (EOHC). Because of the high levels of structural and interpersonal violence experienced by people accessing care at the clinics, health care providers were highly attuned to the impact of trauma and violence (both structural and interpersonal). This led us to identify TVIC as one of the three key dimensions of EOHC; figure 2.1.1) and as necessarily intersecting with cultural safety[2]/anti-racism and harm reduction strategies (Browne et al., 2018).

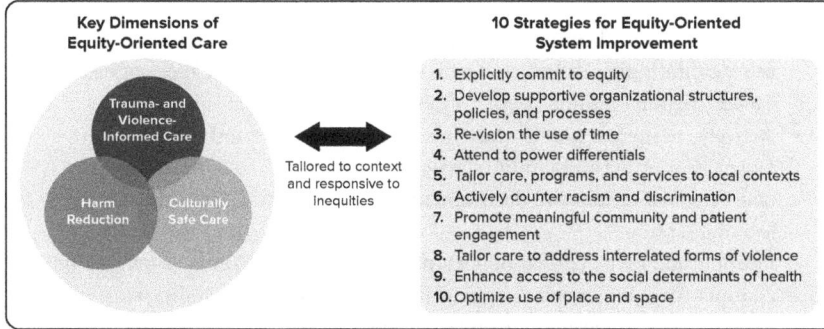

Figure 2.1.1 Key dimensions and strategies for equity-oriented health care. Copyright 2021 by the authors. See https://equiphealthcare.ca/files/2020/10/EQUIP-Equity-System-Improvement-Policy-Brief-Spring2020.pdf.

As also shown in figure 2.1.1, we identified strategies the clinics were deploying to create conditions at the organizational level to make EOHC possible. Importantly, because the key dimensions of EOHC are interrelated, these conditions are necessary to TVIC and, as shown in box 2.1.1, can be seen as specific to TVIC.

We used the evidence from our research to develop a complex, multicomponent health equity intervention that would enhance capacity for organizational change in support of health equity. We studied its effectiveness in PHC; currently, we are studying an adaptation of the intervention in the context of EDs.

BOX 2.1.1 WHAT IS REQUIRED FOR ORGANIZATIONS TO ENACT TVIC

- Commit to TVIC (in strategic plans, mission statements, etc.).
- Create structures, policies, and procedures that support the principles of TVIC (e.g., non-invasive intake procedures; optimizing service recipients' safety and privacy).
- Be flexible in using time as a way to give control and choice to service recipients (e.g., enough time is scheduled for people to tell their histories, with care processes that prevent the need for people to repeat their histories, such as occurs during ten-minute appointments with different providers).
- Flatten the organizational hierarchy, as well as hierarchical interprofessional relationships, to support control and choice by service recipients; allocate time for staff to rest and debrief regularly.

- Tailor care to local communities and populations served, coordinating with other community services, and with attention to the specific types of historical and ongoing trauma commonly experienced by service users.
- Actively counteract racism and discrimination, understood as forms of violence; examine and modify signage, intake forms, and spoken language; take claims of racism and discrimination seriously and address them, regardless of intention.
- Promote and invite regular opportunities for meaningful engagement of local communities and service recipients in service planning, including with regard to how to safely and meaningfully engage people who are experiencing the impacts of trauma and violence.
- Address structural and interpersonal violence as experienced by people in their daily lives and in health care; approach historical and structural violence such as systemic racism and poverty as something beyond individual control that requires collective action.
- Increase access to social determinants of health for service recipients (e.g., supports for housing, income, food security); that is, care interactions should support access to resources that prevent or mitigate the harms of violence, such as affordable, safe housing, and income above the poverty line.
- Enhance the physical places and spaces where care is provided to create safe and respectful environments that welcome and accept diverse groups of people.

Primary Health Care Settings

In our health equity intervention research known as EQUIP-PHC, we partnered with four PHC clinics across two provinces in Canada with the explicit goal of integrating equity-oriented health care, including TVIC, into their organizational practices and policies (Browne, Varcoe, Ford-Gilboe, & Wathen, 2015). Standardized education on TVIC was provided, though also tailored to be optimally relevant to each clinic's unique context. The *education* involved workshop-style face-to-face sessions with all staff and clinic leaders (including receptionists, nurses, physicians, social workers, and administrators). The *organizational integration and tailoring* discussions involved all staff participating in building on the education sessions to design organizational changes unique to the context and needs of each clinic. Importantly, the education, integration, and tailoring drew on data derived from the clinics themselves – specifically, the levels of trauma symptoms, depressive symptoms, and chronic pain experienced by the people accessing care at each clinic. Cases pertinent to the clinics' actual patients were featured so that staff could work through the process of applying TVIC principles and discuss the value-add of using a TVI lens.

As staff gained more awareness of the implications of integrating TVIC into their contexts, they brought to the surface organizational issues particular to their clinic. For example, at one clinic during interprofessional team meetings, staff identified the need to shift the usual ways of discussing challenging cases – to contextualize the broader historical and economic conditions shaping patients' health issues (Browne et al., 2018). This required staff to truncate the "air time" given to physicians and nurse practitioners, who tended to focus on the biomedical aspects of treatment, and to invite and encourage input from other team members, including receptionists, outreach workers, and social workers (Levine, Varcoe, & Browne, 2020). These kinds of changes in team meetings and staff dynamics signalled an organizational shift that supported the uptake of TVIC as a lens for understanding how best to respond to patients' needs. The following lessons learned in these PHC clinics offer insights about how to support efforts to implement TVIC in any health care setting; they are also relevant to other sectors.

The unique context of each setting needs to be assessed. The characteristics and histories of the populations served, including the forms of structural and interpersonal violence commonly experienced, the resources available, and the unique features of each setting, need to be thought through. Although each of the clinics knew that those they served had such experiences, considering specific experiences was essential to the implementation of strategies. For example, one clinic newly serving high numbers of newcomers to Canada who were fleeing war and genocide needed to implement strategies to address the vicarious trauma being experienced by staff.

TVIC education is one component of creating an organizational context to support implementation, must be interprofessional, and should include "organizational integration and tailoring" opportunities to take learning to action in specific settings. Findings from EQUIP-PHC showed that staff who participated in TVIC education, including organizational integration and tailoring discussions, reported an overall increase in confidence related to TVIC (Browne et al., 2018). The interprofessional discussions focused on the practicalities of providing TVIC, as well as the organizational policies and point-of-care shifts required. For example, discussing the health effects of trauma and violence uncovered how both individual practices and organizational policies impact patients; this helped staff become more aware of the need to be responsive to high rates of trauma. During integration and tailoring discussions, we provided opportunities for staff to respond to data compiled by our research team that illustrated the extent to which patients were impacted by trauma, PTSD, depression, and chronic pain. Through these discussions, staff and clinic leaders identified priorities based on their specific patients and communities. Involving all levels of staff in TVIC education and integration and tailoring – including people who might not previously have been included in staff-wide education, such as receptionists and medical office assistants (MOAs) who work at the front desk to register patients, make referrals, and manage the waiting room environment – was key to the initiatives undertaken. Through interprofessional group discussions, staff generated ideas about how to implement low-cost changes in their clinics to enhance people's sense of safety, comfort and ease when coming for care.

As the harms of structural and interpersonal violence increasingly were discussed, the need became apparent for viable and sustainable ways to support staff experiencing vicarious or secondary trauma stemming from their work with populations who experience high levels of trauma and violence (Browne et al., 2018) (see chapter 1.4). This prompted leaders and staff to prioritize processes for working together on previously unacknowledged trauma that many were experiencing, focusing their TVIC integration and tailoring activities on team-based strategies and supports to better address vicarious trauma.

Incremental, low-cost shifts in organizational policies and practices are feasible to implement in support of TVIC. Changes (see table 2.1.1) aligned with the principles of TVIC do not need to be expensive or time-consuming; adequate staffing ratios and resources to support staff are, however, prerequisites. Many of the strategies were aimed at helping people feel safe and comfortable, avoiding judgmental and stigmatizing language, and greeting people in an accepting way and promptly when they called or came to the health care setting. This could simply mean providing water or coffee in waiting rooms. In one clinic, one of the MOAs explained how learning about TVIC affected how staff responded to people via phone and in person: "Before it was like, I know I've got to get all this stuff done before I go… but then I realize I'm going well wait a minute, if I'm just spewing something back or I'm not making eye contact, you know, I'm causing that person trauma" (Levine et al., 2020, p. 4).

Another example that stood out for us was that nursing staff at one clinic, in collaboration with MOAs, initiated reconsideration of a policy that required people seeking same-day appointments to line up on a busy street to wait for the clinic doors to open. Staff identified how this policy exacerbated patients' experiences of feeling stigmatized and negatively judged. At times, they were harassed by people walking by. As one MOA put it, "That is structural violence!" Working with clinic leaders, the MOAs and nursing staff instituted an organizational change so as to permit the clinic to open its doors early enough to enable people to wait indoors for their appointments.

Applying a TVIC lens to reconsider how the policy environment of a clinic, department, or organization impacts people can be especially powerful. For example, at one clinic, staff prioritized changes to the services offered, including care for people experiencing chronic pain. A physician explained how focusing on the links among trauma, chronic pain, and substance use shifted approaches to caring for people experiencing chronic pain: "Just think about the context where all this stuff is coming up and let's talk to [the client] about some of those traumatic, painful, violent, abusive things that happened to her" (Levine et al., 2020, p. 4). Taking a TVIC perspective prompted staff to offer a chronic pain group and promote access to services such as physiotherapy, group counselling, and mindfulness.

The process of deciding how to implement TVIC in organizations is as important as the delivery. Many staff found the interprofessional organizational integration and tailoring conversations more impactful than the didactic TVIC training, which some found to be redundant with their prior training. The interprofessional discussions enabled complex, open conversations across professions, which allowed for the consolidation of learning and consideration of how TVIC could work in practice (Levine et al., 2020). These conversations provided staff with the opportunity to learn together, to learn about one another's perspectives on violence and trauma in their practices, and to engage in an unprecedented level of collaborative action. Indeed, in one clinic, staff from diverse roles noted that prior to EQUIP they had never all met together. In another clinic, a mental health counsellor recounted: "I think it, it just helped, it more brought us together because when the whole team is using the [TVIC] skills and learning the skills ... We just do a better job and we feel like we're doing a better job and working more as a team" (Levine et al., 2020, p. 5).

In sum, in EQUIP PHC, we demonstrated that engaging in interprofessional discussions about the principles of TVIC and how to enact it in practice within the organization, when supported with education, led to powerful innovations that positively impacted both staff and patients. We showed that EOHC, with TVIC as a key dimension, predicted better health outcomes, including reduced disabling chronic pain, lower depressive symptoms, lower trauma symptoms, and better quality of life (Ford-Gilboe et al., 2018). However, we also concluded that the sites needed to be better prepared for the disruption that often followed from intentionally working across power dynamics, that support for direct care staff to be more involved was needed, and that the education offered needed to be more fully aligned with staff learning needs. We would build on these lessons when partnering with emergency departments.

Emergency Departments

Building on the experiences and insights gained from the PHC study, we are now adapting the EQUIP intervention and assessing its uptake and impact in the unique context of emergency departments (EDs). In the study known as EQUIP-ED (Varcoe et al., 2019), we are studying the impact of engaging with the intervention components focused on TVIC, cultural safety, and harm reduction at three geographically and demographically diverse EDs in one Canadian province. In the context of EDs, the adaptions focus on supporting direct care providers to have greater ownership in implementing the intervention, delivering it more intensely over a shorter time frame, and preparing staff and leadership for inevitable disruptions in knowledge, attitudes, and practices. The goal is to strengthen intervention uptake and, ideally, impact.

Using the concept of front-line ownership (Kaufman, McCready, & Powess, 2017; Zimmerman et al., 2013), ED staff were invited to form a working group (WG). The WG was supported in their efforts to assess their organization and identify and implement priorities. We offered the WG a Health Equity Workbook to guide this process, as well as access to online modules[3] that focused on TVIC. The WG was encouraged to undertake assessment strategies, which included (a) reviewing a "context profile" that described key features of the populations served, (b) reviewing data from patient and staff surveys we conducted, and (c) undertaking activities such a SWOT (strengths, weaknesses, opportunities, threats) analysis and an "equity walk-through." The "equity walk-through," based on the notion of a "trauma walk-through," encompasses attention to what might be traumatizing when encountering practices in *any* setting. As shown in the brief instructions in box 2.1.2, it directs attention broadly.

WG members conducted walk-throughs first on their own and then with representatives of groups for whom they wanted to improve care, such as people with lived experience of substance use, those with stigmatizing health conditions, and people assumed to be Indigenous. These walk-throughs helped illuminate the relevance of TVIC to care in EDs. For example, in one ED, WG members were alarmed at the state of patient washrooms and signage about drug use and sought to develop strategies for counteracting the stigma and discrimination that many people encounter when seeking health care.

BOX 2.1.2 ABBREVIATED INSTRUCTIONS FOR AN EQUITY WALK-THROUGH

This exercise will help staff "walk through" the physical and social spaces where they provide care or services to clients. It will prompt staff to consider the extent to which these environments are likely to feel welcoming, culturally and emotionally safe, and reduce harm for everyone, but especially for those who are most likely to feel unwelcome and unsafe. The space can be anywhere you provide care or services to clients (e.g., in an office, a clinic, a community centre, a home setting, an acute care or a hospital setting).

In this activity, we ask you to put yourself in your clients' "shoes" and imagine what it might be like for them to be in this physical and social space. Be sure to

> think through equity from the perspective of key demographics that your organization is aiming to serve, for instance Indigenous people or LGBTQ2+ peoples. Pay particular attention to things in this environment that might create feelings of discomfort, stigma or feeling unsafe. If you find it helpful, you can think about a specific client or group of clients.
>
> Copyright 2021 by the authors. See https://equiphealthcare.ca/resources/toolkit/equity-walk-through.

To date, the uptake of the intervention has been variable among our three partner EDs, not because of a lack of commitment to enhancing capacity for equity-oriented care, but rather because of organizational and institutional influences shaping uptake. Our further lessons are as follows (see also table 2.1.1).

Mandatory education can provide important opportunities for interprofessional discussions. While in the two (of three) settings in which WGs were formed they began as intraprofessional, in one setting, physicians were never involved, and in both settings, ongoing involvement was primarily by nurses. Furthermore, because the WGs were not "educational" in intent, and because there was no "required" education, the discussions were not grounded in particular TVIC content or principles, and there was no way of assessing the knowledge level of participants. We now suggest that there may be benefit to setting minimum standards for TVIC education that can be delivered to all staff.

The unique contextual features of each setting influence the level of involvement. Our plan had been to engage executive- and management-level leadership while supporting direct care providers to lead the change processes independently. Executive-level administrators in all three partner EDs fully and unconditionally supported involvement with EQUIP. However, at all three sites, significant turnover at this level resulted in the need to repeatedly engage and orient new leaders. Furthermore, the scope of mid-level managers frequently changed, affecting their ability to participate and/or to support WG members as they navigated the institutional context of the hospital/setting, despite their expressed interest. Similarly, working conditions influenced the involvement of staff in WGs. The one ED in which there was no WG engagement had extremely high turnover of direct care staff and a significantly widening scope for the manager. Each ED had a unique culture and a seemingly characteristic stance toward change, ranging from weary resignation in the face of constant change to resistance to what was seen as constant top-down imposition of change. We now recommend that the management-level staff be engaged more fully in leading change and that they partner with staff WGs, first assessing the features that will shape the extent to which TVIC will be taken up.

In summary, what we have learned is that, regardless of the intentions or expressed enthusiasm of front-line staff and leadership regarding the value and aims of TVIC and its related health equity components, implementation is a complex and context-dependent process. We have learned that making organizational adaptations to support the delivery of TVIC requires input from all levels of staff, ongoing interprofessional discussions aimed at disrupting the status quo, and thinking creatively "outside the box" to forge new ways of enacting the fundamentals of TVIC. Regardless of the type of setting in which you work, it will be essential to assess your particular workplace context – including strengths, weakness, opportunities, and threats that will inevitably arise – especially when attempting to scale up TVIC and related equity-oriented approaches in any given organization/agency (See chapter 4.2 for an Action Kit to guide change).

Organizational-Level Recommendations to Create a Context for Implementing TVIC

Based on our studies of PHC and ED settings, we offer the following recommendations for optimizing uptake of TVIC that may be useful in other settings:

1. Balance working with formal leaders and engaging point-of-care staff; up-front work with leadership is essential to optimize the effectiveness of working with staff.
2. Gather information about the organizational context prior to engaging point-of-care staff so that they begin with a comprehensive analysis of the organizational strengths, weaknesses, opportunities, and threats within their own setting with respect to implementing TVIC.
3. Maximize "front-line" engagement of point-of-care staff and integrate common and predictable clinical cases and scenarios that draw attention to organizational considerations, in learning activities related to TVIC.
4. Balance front-line ownership with minimum required structured learning activities oriented toward organizational change. TVIC education, inclusive of integration and tailoring activities, should be flexible and provide clear guidelines for how it may benefit individual staff practices and organizational/workplace culture. The goals of TVIC curriculum should be explicitly oriented toward organizational change as well as to individual clinical skill-building and perspective shifts.
5. Given the known intersections among trauma, violence, chronic pain, and substance use, find ways to review patient health status data through a TVIC lens on an ongoing basis, such as by building data collection into routine

2.1 Taking Organizational-Level Action

Table 2.1.1 Examples of TVIC-specific actions in EQUIP implementations

Action/principle (P)	Impact
Primary health care clinics	
➢ Created opportunities for staff to review clinic-level client data on key health and social outcomes, compared to local, regional, and national population (P1).	✓ Increased understanding of level of health and social inequities experienced by patients; prioritized and targeted interventions accordingly.
➢ MOAs changed their phrasing and tone on phone calls from patients, minimized putting people on hold, offered brief explanations for why appointment times may have been delayed, etc. (P2, 3).	✓ People do not feel dismissed or demeaned when calling for appointments or to make inquiries; they are acknowledged and given agency in these decisions.
➢ Provided place and space for people to wait as the clinic opened for the day, including water, coffee (P2).	✓ People need not wait in the cold/wet and/or face harassment on the street; they feel safe, calm, and supported as they wait to be seen, leading to better interactions with providers and a better experience overall.
➢ Learned about local populations and aligned policies to serve their needs. Ensured adequate training to support application of policies to promote safety and choice and to build on client strengths (All Ps).	✓ Policies, resources, and practices that support TVIC, reduce stigma, and improve support and well-being for staff and clients.
Emergency departments	
➢ Created and provided opportunities for staff to review "context profiles" and SWOT analysis (P1).	✓ Staff are aware of who they serve and their needs, in social and community context (structural lens); they participate in identifying areas for improvement.
➢ Provided "walk-through" exercises with staff to prompt awareness and discussion regarding how people experience the setting (P1, 2).	✓ Increased empathy and awareness of how people experience the setting, leading to spaces and interactions that are safer and not dehumanizing.
➢ Improved signage in washrooms re: safe supplies, safe drug use, needle disposal (P2, 3).	✓ Language demonstrates respect by not judging or stigmatizing re: substance use; provides choice for using as safely as possible.
➢ Oriented staff to how experiences of racism and discrimination impact peoples' expectations of care (P1, 2).	✓ Conveys intent to reduce/eliminate the judgment people might anticipate.

Note: MOA = medical office assistant

clinical processes. For example, ask to what extent the populations served experience intersecting issues related to chronic pain, trauma, mental health, violence, and substance use. Consider using short clinical assessments for chronic pain, and train staff on using them in a non-judgmental way.
6. Build in mechanisms to routinely and actively seek input from clients to ensure that care addresses their needs and is perceived as safe and respectful. For example, the equity walk-through can be done with a small number of patient representatives to tap into their perspectives of what may be needed to enhance safety while avoiding retraumatizing people.
7. Develop organizational policies and procedures to support staff (and leadership) to deal effectively with the secondary/vicarious traumas that can arise in the process of drawing attention to and addressing issues of trauma and violence.

Conclusion

Engaging in an iterative process of learning, developing materials, trying them out with each study setting, and revising them across the two studies, we have developed a suite of practice-ready tools, workshop outlines, and strategies for implementing TVIC in diverse settings. We have featured examples of these tools in text boxes; they are further fleshed out in the Additional Resources section (see below). We provide further details and an Action Kit to guide organizational change in chapter 4.2.

Our research in the primary care context shows that confidence levels to deliver TVIC can increase with staff education and integration and that patient experiences of care can be positively impacted when TVIC is embedded as part of broader equity-oriented organization approaches (Browne et al., 2018; Ford-Gilboe et al., 2018; Levine et al., 2020). Ongoing research is needed, and is under way, to extend our understanding of the organizational conditions required to optimally support uptake of TVIC in rapidly changing health care environments.

NOTES

1 The terms "organization" and "organizational-level" are inclusive of institutions, agencies, departments, or units. In the health care sector, these include community health settings, primary health care clinics, mental health outpatient departments, substance use treatment units, maternity units, hospital emergency and other departments, physician or Nurse Practitioner practices, etc.
2 In the EQUIP research program, cultural safety is taken up as an explicit antiracism strategy, which intersects directly with TVIC (Browne et al., 2021).
3 https://equiphealthcare.ca/equipping-for-equity-online-modules

KEY MESSAGES AND IMPLICATIONS

- A TVIC approach demands organizational culture change.
- Education is necessary but not sufficient; TVIC education must include integration and tailoring at the organizational level to create the conditions for supporting individual practice change.
- Interprofessional collaboration is needed to support implementation of TVIC.
- Administrative and leadership support is required to support implementation of TVIC by point of care staff.
- A combination of capitalizing on staff motivation, and setting standards, is required.

ADDITIONAL RESOURCES

- Principles of TVIC: https://gtvincubator.uwo.ca/resources
- Trauma- and Violence-Informed Care (TVIC): A Tool for Health & Social Service Organizations and Providers: https://equiphealthcare.ca/toolkit/trauma-and-violence-informed-care
- Equity Walk Through: https://equiphealthcare.ca/toolkit/equity-walk-through
- Addressing Vicarious Trauma: https://equiphealthcare.ca/resources/toolkit/preventing-recognizing-and-addressing-vicarious-trauma/
- Organizational Implementation Tools, including SOAR analysis using an equity lens: https://equiphealthcare.ca/resources/toolkit/organization-tools

REFERENCES

Browne, A.J., Varcoe, C., Ford-Gilboe, M., & Wathen, C.N., on behalf of the EQUIP Research Team. (2015). EQUIP Healthcare: An overview of a multi-component intervention to enhance equity-oriented care in primary health care settings. *International Journal for Equity in Health*, *14*, 152. https://doi.org/10.1186/s12939-015-0271-y

Browne, A.J., Varcoe, C., Ford-Gilboe, M., Wathen, C.N., Smye, V., Jackson, B.E., . . . Blanchet Garneau, A. (2018). Disruption as opportunity: Impacts of an organizational health equity intervention in primary care clinics. *International Journal for Equity in Health*, *17*(1), 154. https://doi.org/10.1186/s12939-018-0820-2

Browne, A.J., Varcoe, C., & Fridkin, A. (2011). Addressing trauma, violence, and pain: Research on health services for women at the intersections of history and economics. In O. Hankivsky (Ed.), *Health inequities in Canada: Intersectional frameworks and practices* (pp. 295–311). Vancouver, BC: UBC Press.

Browne, A.J., Varcoe, C., Lavoie, J., Smye, V., Wong, S., Krause, M., . . . Fridkin, A. (2016). Enhancing health care equity with Indigenous populations: Evidence-based strategies from an ethnographic study. *BMC Health Services Research*, *16*(544). https://doi.org/10.1186/s12913-016-1707-9

Browne, A.J., Varcoe, C., & Ward, C. (2021). San'yas Indigenous cultural safety training as an educational intervention: Promoting anti-racism and equity in health systems, policies, and practices. *International Indigenous Policy Journal, 12*(3). https://doi.org/10.18584/iipj.2021.12.3.8204

Browne, A.J., Varcoe, C., Wong, S.T., Smye, V.L., Lavoie, J.G., Littlejohn, D., . . . Lennox, S. (2012). Closing the health equity gap: Evidence-based strategies for primary health care organizations. *International Journal for Equity in Health, 11*(59), 1–15. https://doi.org/10.1186/1475-9276-11-59

Ford-Gilboe, M., Wathen, C.N., Varcoe, C., Herbert, C., Jackson, B.E., Lavoie, J.G., . . . Browne, A.J. (2018). How equity-oriented health care affects health: Key mechanisms and implications for primary health care practice and policy. *Milbank Quarterly, 96*(4), 635–71. https://doi.org/10.1111/1468-0009.12349

Kaufman, A.J., McCready, J., & Powess, J. (2017). Impact of a multifaceted antimicrobial stewardship program: A front-line ownership-driven quality improvement project in a large urban emergency department. *Canadian Journal of Emergency Medicine, 19*(6), 441–9. https://doi.org/10.1017/cem.2017.11

Levine, S., Varcoe, C., & Browne, A.J. (2020). "We went as a team closer to the truth": Impacts of interprofessional education on trauma- and violence- informed care for staff in primary care settings. *Journal of Interprofessional Care*, 1–9. https://doi.org/10.1080/13561820.2019.1708871

Varcoe, C., Bungay, V., Browne, A.J., Wilson, E., Wathen, C.N., Kolar, K., . . . Price, E.R. (2019). EQUIP Emergency: Study protocol for an organizational intervention to promote equity in health care. *BMC Health Services Research, 19*(1), 687. https://doi.org/https://doi.org/10.1186/s12913-019-4494-2

Wong, S.T., Browne, A.J., Varcoe, C., Lavoie, J., Smye, V.L., Fridkin, A., . . . Tu, D. (2014). Development of health equity indicators in primary health care organizations using a modified Delphi. *PLoS One, 9*(12). https://doi.org/10.1371/journal.pone.0114563

Zimmerman, B., Reason, P., Rykert, L., Gitterman, L., Christian, J., & Gardam, M. (2013). Front-line ownership: Generating a cure mindset for patient safety. *Healthcare Papers, 13*(1), 7–22. https://doi.org/10.12927/hcpap.2013.23299

2.2 Trauma- and Violence-Informed Mental Health Interventions: Our Work with Indigenous Men

VICTORIA SMYE, VIVIANE JOSEWSKI, PAUL GROSS,
ILORADANON EFIMOFF, LYANA PATRICK, AND SANDY LAMBERT

Mental health care remains chronically underfunded in Canada (Moroz, Moroz, & D'Angelo, 2020); in 2016, more than 7.5 million Canadians reported a mental health condition and over 20 per cent indicated that their service needs were not being met (Mental Health Commission of Canada, n.d.). Mental health services, when available, are fragmented and often rely on precarious funding, including corporate fundraising such as Bell's "Let's Talk" (Bell, n.d.; Johnson, 2017), to fill the major funding gaps that exist. Youth mental health services, for example, are woefully inadequate, with up to 75 per cent of young people with mental health issues not receiving required services (Centre for Addiction and Mental Health, n.d.). Even when available, most youth-specific services end at age eighteen, meaning that young people must then be "transferred" to the adult system, a transition during which many are lost from service due to wait times and other factors (Centre for Addiction and Mental Health, 2018). Concurrently, Canada has seen the rates of suicide among young people grow (Statistics Canada, 2019), especially among Indigenous youth (Kumar & Tjepkema, 2019).

Similarly, despite evidence of disproportionate health inequality and inequity associated with health service and support access, men's health issues have been largely glossed over by Canadian health authorities and other decision-making bodies, and little is known about men's distinct health experiences and their health and social support needs. In addition, men whose lives are shaped by structural social and health inequities, especially those living with histories of mental health and substance use issues and trauma, access care less frequently and often only seek treatment late in the illness process, when medical conditions and symptoms are severe (Evans, Frank, Oliffe, & Gregory, 2001; Oliffe & Phillips, 2008). For example, men are three times more likely than women to die by suicide (Public Health Agency of Canada, 2019); these high rates of suicide are thought to be due at least in part to inadequate diagnosis and treatment of men's mental health issues (Oliffe et al., 2010; Wide, Mok,

McKenna, & Ogrodniczuk, 2011). Goldenberg (2014) has asserted that conformity to dominant ideas about masculinity that emphasize male independence and fearlessness may further delay access to treatment – a concern that is especially pressing for older men (Tannenbaum & Frank, 2011). Indigenous men and youth are at an even higher risk for suicide (Center for Mental Health and Addictions, n.d.; Kumar & Tjepkema, 2019).

Particularly salient are the findings related to the multiple forms of trauma/violence experienced by Indigenous men and the need to identify and address their distinct needs. This chapter therefore explores intervention work specific to Indigenous men's health and mental well-being as a way to think about how trauma- and violence-informed care (TVIC), tailored to intersecting underserved contexts, can contribute to more empowering and effective care. Our starting point is the accounts of Indigenous men in our studies, who highlight the ways in which their lives have been shaped by racism, loss of cultural identity, and early childhood trauma and violence (e.g., Gross et al., 2016; Smye, Browne, Varcoe, & Josewski, 2011). Numerous studies have established the connections between trauma and mental health issues such as post-traumatic stress disorder (PTSD), substance use, depression, and suicide (Anda et al., 2006; Green et al., 2016; Katz & Gurtovenko, 2015) alongside numerous other health conditions (see also chapter 1.1).

The men in our studies often perceived culturally informed health and social supports, such as men's groups, as the only safe spaces available, but such spaces were consistently identified as lacking. Indigenous men's experiences need to be understood in the context of ongoing neocolonial processes and practices (including forms of structural violence) that continue to shape their health and well-being. Interventions/programs to assist Indigenous men need to be tailored so that they align with the unique social, historical, and political factors influencing their health and well-being.

Drawing on research and program development experiences, in this chapter we provide strategies for implementing TVIC in health care and social support contexts and for supporting those using substances. We focus on serving the groups and individuals most marginalized in these contexts and on addressing and countering the racism, stigma, and discrimination they face. To highlight implementation considerations, we use examples from the field, such as the Indigenous Men's Health Narratives study and the DUDES Club. This chapter adds to the current body of knowledge by providing practical strategies for implementing TVIC in health care and aligned social support contexts (e.g., housing, policing, child welfare).

By the end of this chapter, the reader will (1) understand how the key elements of TVIC can be applied in health and social support contexts, including as this relates to the challenges to its implementation (e.g., societal norms regarding masculinity), (2) be able to explore the strategies/tools for implementing a TVIC approach, such as the creation of a safe, welcoming physical and socio-emotional environment and workplace/organization, and (3) know how to practice/employ counter-narratives to racism and discrimination in a health care and social support context.

Case Examples: The Indigenous Men's Health Narratives Study and the DUDES Club

In response to the lack of knowledge regarding the unique experiences of Indigenous men and the challenges they face in their efforts to heal from past and current trauma, our research team met with other researchers and members of local agencies and the community in a "think tank" format over an eighteen-month period. Informed by this dialogue as well as by critical theoretical perspectives and an Indigenous relational lens, we designed a community participatory ethnographic study to explore Indigenous men's narratives of well-being so as to develop an understanding of what constitutes appropriate, culturally safe health and social services and supports for men as they worked to move forward with their lives in the face of multiple health and other challenges. In a three-year Canadian Institutes of Health Research (CIHR)–funded ethnographic study (2013–16) titled "Indigenous Men's Health Narratives: Reclaiming Our Lives," we conducted focus groups, individual interviews, participant observation, photovoice, and videography with men whose health had been shaped by multiple forms of social and structural inequity. We identified positive connection with other men as vital to the ability of men to move forward in their lives. Especially salient were the findings related to the multiple forms of trauma/violence experienced by Indigenous men and the need to identify and address their distinct needs.

The men in this study highlighted the ways in which their lives had been shaped by racism, early childhood trauma and violence, and loss of cultural identity. Many of them lived with mental health issues, substance use issues, chronic illness, and homelessness or near homelessness and could obtain access to needed health and social systems and supports only through the justice system. Services for men living this reality were consistently described as lacking by the men in our study. Echoing these men, Indigenous women who had participated in a previous study exploring the women's experiences of leaving and/or staying with and abusive partner (Smye et al., 2021; see chapter 3.1) described how existing services and supports excluded men even though trauma and violence are not women-specific issues but include men, families, and communities. As one of the women who had lived with an abusive partner for many years noted, "men also suffer the burden of history" (Smye et al., 2021, p. 1598). Many of the Indigenous men in our study derived particular benefits from joining the DUDES Club, founded in Vancouver's Downtown Eastside (DTES) in 2010.

Since 2017, the DUDES Club has been expanding into northern BC. With the help of a partnership between the Canadian Men's Health Foundation (which funded DUDES Club activities from 2017 to 2020) and the First Nations Health Authority, it has grown to include forty partner sites in BC and two sites nationally (Efimoff et al., 2021; Gross et al., 2016). The men who access the DUDES Club often carry with them intergenerational trauma related to the loss of or damage to their land, culture, family, language, and identity. The DUDES Club is a proven model for Indigenous men's wellness promotion that builds solidarity and brotherhood, enabling men to regain a sense of pride and purpose in their lives while developing more effective partnerships with health care providers (Efimoff et al., 2021; Gross et al., 2016).

Project/Intervention/Activity

The Indigenous Men's Health Narratives study and the DUDES Club serve as two case examples of TVIC integration and implementation. In the Indigenous Men's Health Narratives study, the photovoice aspect of the larger research study became a centrepiece of our project early on. We gave ten men cameras to take photographs of their neighbourhood (the Vancouver DTES). The goal in this was to enable them to record their life journeys and capture aspects of their day-to-day lives that held personal significance or meaning in their recovery process. The men then met to share their chosen photos and the narratives attached to them and co-created further stories together. Eight of the men continued with the photovoice element of the study to co-create a video titled *A Thousand Words* (Smye et al., 2016). In the photovoice and videography element of the larger research study, we injected an explicit and pronounced participatory element into the research process. Drawing on a strengths-based, people-centred, non-judgmental, and anti-racist approach, over an eighteen-month period we engaged with the men to co-create wellness narratives. Photovoice transformed the research process, and at the same time, the photovoice process itself became transformed; the participating men morphed into researchers of their own experiences and began to make powerful connections to one another and to aspects of themselves that they wanted to explore through ongoing collective activities around the photos and their stories, including public presentations of their photos and narratives. All of the men involved in this aspect of the research project also were members of the DUDES Club – the name stands for Dudes United Defending Equality and Solidarity.

In response to the glaring need for services for men, a group of men, led by an outreach worker to whom this piece is dedicated (Richard Johnson) and a primary care physician (one of the co-authors, Paul Gross), launched the DUDES Club, a brotherhood for mental wellness. The DUDES Club meetings in Vancouver are held every two weeks at a drop-in space at the Kílala Lelum

Health Centre, where men feel safe and other successful peer-support programs operate. On average, the club hosts fifty to sixty men per meeting, with a core of volunteers who direct the activities that reflect the project's vision. Volunteers receive modest compensation for their work, which can include cooking, serving, cleaning, facilitating activities, and planning meetings. Because a large percentage of the members are Indigenous, the club strives to create cultural safety (see chapter 3.1) by including Indigenous perspectives. This includes medicine wheel teachings and regular participation by Elders; it also involves bringing in health care professionals who provide a culturally safe context for Indigenous peoples. The DUDES Club also attends to systems and services more broadly. For example, until funding cuts were made, the DUDES Club partnered with the BC Provincial Health Services Authority, which manages health care in the province's correctional facilities; two to three groups met weekly at the Prince George Regional Correctional Centre. The purpose of these groups was to reduce recidivism and help men make a more sustainable transition to the community upon their release. This also involved supporting men in their efforts to re-engage with family in a healthy way. This meant finding strategies for breaking the cycle of violence, including domestic violence.

A hot meal is provided at each DUDES Club meeting, and after the meal, a health care worker (usually a physician, but occasionally a nurse or social worker) facilitates an interactive health discussion where men have the opportunity to ask questions about their health and to improve their health literacy and peer support skills. Men are encouraged to explore emerging notions of masculinity in an attempt to destigmatize health-seeking behaviours and decolonize masculinity (Efimoff et al., 2021; Gross et al., in press). The DUDES Club represents an important paradigm shift in health care services, for it has created a safe place where men can proactively address their health needs in a non-threatening, inclusive environment. The health care providers involved with DUDES practise the principles of TVIC; they offer cultural safety, genuine connections, and support to help men navigate the health care system. The program is community-driven and emphasizes the importance of peer champions. The DUDES club serves as a safe entry point into primary health care for many of the men.

Tailoring TVIC in Mental Health Settings

Adapting and Applying TVIC and TVIC Principles

The Indigenous Men's Health Narratives study and, later on, the photovoice element of the project were conducted with an understanding that any man could have a history of trauma stemming from the intersection of interpersonal and structural violence and that such violence could well be ongoing (i.e., be an everyday reality for many men). Every day, for example, many of the men faced the reality of inadequate and/or unsafe housing as well as racism and discrimination (i.e., structural violence). So it was essential to begin the project by spending time building understanding, safety, and trust (principles 1 and 2). Thus, we spent many months in the field in those sites where we recruited the men into the study (e.g., the DUDES Club and other local agencies) and became actively involved in the activities in those settings.

Over the course of the project, we took a pointedly non-judgmental approach (principle 3). For example, though there were several men struggling with substance use issues, we welcomed *all* men to all photovoice and videography planning sessions, regardless of this. There was an expectation among the men they would be respectful of one another, whether or not they were using substances, but there were a couple of challenging moments in this regard. Even so, respectful engagement was the priority, and we assisted one another in navigating those challenges and supporting the men to remain engaged. The starting place for all photovoice sessions was *where the men were at* on that day; that is, they helped set the agenda. We also made sure to always have food at our sessions; several of the men were hungry and living on or near the street.

Another essential element of the photovoice sessions was that the project built on the strengths of *all* of the men involved (principle 4). For example, one of the men had a background as a photographer; another had strong links to community housing resources, which he shared with the other men in the group; another was strongly linked with community food resources and another to volunteer opportunities that provided meaningful experiences for several of the men. These attributes and linkages, as well as others, supported all of the men to connect in positive ways with one another and the project. As we neared the end of the project, the men helped one another vision for the future and engage with new educational activities to enhance their lives based on this experience. Vancouver's DTES is one of the poorest postal codes in Canada (Krausz & Jang, 2015), but it also is home to these men, and a place where they are connected with history, services, supports, and brotherhood – a place where they found meaning and hope, captured in the video "A Thousand Words" (see Smye et al., 2016, and below, a link to the video).

The DUDES Club works in a context of historical colonialism and the resulting displacement from traditional land and destruction of culture, language, and healthy roles for men in society. Many men are experiencing well-being regardless, but for others, this displacement has led to structural inequities related to poverty, social marginalization, lateral violence, intergenerational trauma, cycles of violence, and addictions. The DUDES Club also recognizes a historical context of patriarchy, which has defined inequitable and unsustainable gender roles that all too often result in women and certain groups of men being marginalized in society (DUDES Club, n.d).

Within DUDES Clubs the hierarchy of the Western medical model is flattened (Efimoff et al., 2021). The health care providers who are involved prioritize cultural safety and humility, genuine connections, and support to help men navigate the health care system. Men are able to begin to drop some of their armour as they build a sense of safety and trust (Efimoff et al., 2021). All initiatives are community-driven and highlight the importance of peer champions. Executive decisions are made "by us, about us, and for us."

Practical Strategies/Guidance for Individual Practitioners and Organizations

Building on the findings described in the previous section, in this section we outline specific strategies for individual service providers and organizations to follow when implementing a TVIC approach in mental health and related services. These strategies are based on the research findings and our experience in the field, including relevant forms of knowledge emerging from EQUIP Health Care (chapter 2.1) and associated research on equity-oriented approaches more broadly. The EQUIP Primary Health Care (PHC) study examined the impact of an organization-level intervention to enhance capacity in equity-oriented health care (Browne, Varcoe, Ford-Gilboe, & Wathen, 2015; Browne et al., 2018; and see chapter 2.1) to better serve people who are socially and economically marginalized.

Create a Person-Centred Environment

Our studies point to the importance of creating an environment in which mechanisms for routinely and actively seeking input from men are integrated to ensure that all aspects of care address their needs and are perceived as safe and respectful. For example, in the photovoice element of the Indigenous Men's Health Narratives study we partnered with the men to brainstorm the knowledge mobilization activities related to the findings of photovoice. The outcome of this effort was the creation of a video and photo presentations, and both products were owned and utilized by the investigative team and the research participants (Smye et al., 2016; DUDES Club, n.d.). The men who volunteer and are supported to provide leadership at the DUDES Club direct decisions regarding the ongoing development of activities related to the club. In addition, the survey designed for the program evaluation of the DUDES Club was developed with critical input from a community advisory team made up of DUDES Club members, providers, community members, and Elders. This team was crucial in guiding how the research team theorized the possible linkages among the program's activity inputs, outputs, and outcomes (Gross et al., 2016).

Create a Strengths-Focused Environment

Beginning with a strengths-based orientation toward services and care has been a key element of our research, including with DUDES programs, and there are a number of ways in which we have incorporated this approach. In the Indigenous Men's Health Narratives project, rather than focusing on the less positive elements of their lives, we drew on the men's experience and knowledge of what worked to assist them in moving forward. For example, the experiences, skills, and abilities they could use to assist both themselves and others were emphasized – cooking skills and volunteer activities in which they were engaged, the spiritual dimensions of their lives, employment opportunities, and so on. The DUDES Club also draws on the unique skills and abilities men bring to the group – barber skills, physical fitness, safety skills, housing knowledge, and so on. This does not mean that men are not assisted in identifying and addressing the challenges/barriers they face in their daily lives – rather, they address such challenges through a strengths-based approach that highlights and builds on what they already know and do while also helping them cultivate new skills. However, the issues the men raise in their lives are addressed as they themselves raise them and in accordance with a plan co-created with them.

TVIC also draws attention to the structural elements of an organization that require redress. The creation of a welcoming environment is important to creating safety and trust. The physical space needs to convey inclusivity. For example, we found in the Indigenous Men's Health Narratives study that men very much appreciated the positive meeting space we were able to access part way through the photovoice element of the work – a safe, clean educational space that offered other resources to the men. As the study drew to a close, this organization invited the men to meet in this space beyond the boundaries of the study. It also hosted a presentation space for the men to display their photos.

Invest in TVIC Training and an Anti-racism/Anti-oppression Stance

Health care teams are often ill-prepared to care for clients impacted by trauma and violence. A trauma- and violence-informed approach requires that all members of the health care team incorporate an understanding of trauma and violence into their work; for this, interprofessional education and collaboration are key (Levine, Varcoe, & Browne, 2021). In the EQUIP PHC study, interprofessional TVIC education sessions were provided for PHC staff. This included components on cultural safety, equity-oriented care, and organizational integration and tailoring – staff had an opportunity to engage in discussion and learn from one another. As Levine and colleagues (2021) report, staff across professions in the EQUIP study identified this as the most valuable experience of the entire intervention: "For some, shifts in awareness, knowledge and confidence – whether modest or profound – were the main impacts of the TVIC sessions. For others, these shifts led to a changed perspective, or 'looking through a TVIC lens'–which in turn had impacts on multiple levels in their practices" (pp. 48–9). Staff also noted the need for TVIC tools to assist them in engaging with TVIC approaches. TVIC has been designed with explicit attention to required organizational shifts; thus, Levine and colleagues (2021) note that sessions could be strengthened with the addition of concrete "take-aways" for practitioners to assist them with this understanding. Practitioners in this study, especially those who were already familiar with TVIC concepts, were hungry for concrete TVIC tools and advice from clinical mentors experienced in TVIC, and this led the research team to develop a series of publicly available online modules and resources for interprofessional staff members, organizational leaders, and policy-makers (see chapter 2.1).

Support for Interprofessional Collaboration

One strength of the DUDES Club is its interprofessional dimension. For example, the health talks (on topics requested by the men) are provided by physicians across specialty areas as well as nurses, social workers, and other professionals. In addition, the men can access a number of different professionals – for example, a therapist or an Elder. The services need to reflect the diverse needs of the men accessing them and need to be offered in a timely manner.

Lessons Learned

Over the duration of the Indigenous Men's Health Narratives study, it became clear that understanding the unique experiences of men is key to providing TVIC in men's health and social services. Also, interventions informed through a TVIC lens need to be developed at individual *and* structural levels, since men's health and well-being have both been shaped by the intersection of ongoing interpersonal and structural violence. For example, in our study we found that (1) complex trauma and violence, *including structural violence,* is an ongoing lived experience associated with colonial and neocolonial processes and practices, ongoing racism, and discrimination and "life on the street," (2) stigma and discrimination associated with living with mental illness and substance use is normalized and pervasive, and (3) health and healing are found in myriad ways but *safe connections* to other men have been life-changing for many – for example, through the DUDES club – in terms of connections to new job opportunities, housing, health information, and the like.

TVIC: A Paradigm Shift

In keeping with the findings of Levine and colleagues (2021), our experience illustrates how TVIC concepts can challenge the dominant paradigms of biomedicine and individualism. A biomedical paradigm and associated practice models can create a barrier to practitioners' efforts to take action to address structural violence. For example, in the photovoice element of our study, some men took photographs of, and shared stories about, the horrendous living conditions (e.g., infestations of bed bugs and rats) they had endured prior to finding suitable housing, and some men continued to live in those conditions at the time of the study (figure 2.2.1). Clean and safe housing (figure 2.2.2) supports health and well-being; thus, advocacy for safe housing is an important element of the work. They also spoke of the lack of safety they experienced as they aged; sometimes they were preyed upon by younger men both on the street and in single room occupancy (SRO) units, where men shared bathrooms and security was often non-existent or compromised. Aging also intersected with living with chronic disease to make physical work more difficult and finding employment more challenging (most men in our study were living with multiple comorbid conditions).

Education regarding TVIC needs to stress that TVIC amounts to a paradigm shift and requires interventions at both individual and structural levels. A TVIC approach requires that the social determinants of health be addressed – for

Figure 2.2.1 Housing conditions – single room occupancy (SRO). Copyright, the authors.

Figure 2.2.2 Housing conditions – second-level housing. Copyright, the authors.

example, the men in our study were often hungry and underhoused, and most lived in poverty. They also endured racism and discrimination at multiple levels on a daily basis. TVIC-informed interventions should strive to address such individual and structural challenges.

Future Collection of TVIC Data

The Indigenous Men's Health Narratives study and the DUDES Club survey results (Gross et al., 2016; Efimoff et al., 2021) suggest that connectedness to other men is central to supporting men's health and well-being. Future research- or practice- based efforts at TVIC will need to incorporate strategies to collect or use existing data to advocate for, sustain, and evaluate trauma- and violence-informed changes. Many practices already collect data on chronic pain and substance use, which could be used as proxy measures for trauma (Levine et al., 2021). Future efforts to support interdisciplinary uptake of TVIC approaches should look to access and use these data as indicators of quality TVIC (Levine et al., 2021).

Conclusion

Although many Indigenous men are enjoying well-being, the burden of history has severely impacted the health and life quality of many others. Our collective work suggests that it is vitally important to draw on the unique experiences of men in the development of policies, programs, and services for them. Our research and the DUDES Club program also point to TVIC approaches as fundamental to the successful establishment of safety and trust, as well as to address inequity. In addition, the techniques we employed – for example, the use of photo-based narratives in our research – show incredible promise as a means to engage men in discussion of their experiences collectively – indeed, it proved to be a powerful venue for creating positive connections with other men. During our earlier photovoice experience in our research with women (Smye et al., 2021), one of our participants shared that her male partner wondered why men do not have an opportunity to engage with this kind of experience. This theme emerged again during the "think tank" meetings that led to the CIHR grant proposal and the Indigenous Men's Health Narratives study. Ultimately, and as also demonstrated through the DUDES Club, positive connections with other men can serve as an important avenue toward improved health/well-being (Efimoff et al., 2021; Gross et al., 2016), with the establishment of safety and trust as a key starting point.

In addition, the men who participated in the Indigenous Men's Health Narratives study also were actively engaged in disrupting socially constructed gender norms (e.g., norms about masculinity). For example, the men in the photovoice aspect of the study were helping one of the participants to work toward regaining access to his child, whom he had lost to state care, by supporting him in his attempt to address substance use. The men in this study also were creating ties to the other men, whom they now considered "family." Notions of family need to be understood by practitioners as defined by the men. Traditional norms regarding "family" simply may not fit. As one of the participants in our study said, "Then I ended up at the Dudes Club, it's a men's club, right? You know, men are supposed to be strong and tough, be the protectors and bring in the money and stuff like that but down here it's not like that. This place helped me change my life because of the brotherhood there, I really, really feel good about that."

Lastly, TVIC draws our immediate attention as practitioners to social and structural inequity. Fundamentally, an anti-racism/anti-oppression stance and access to healthy food, safe and comfortable living conditions, and educational and employment opportunities were vital supports for health/wellness for the men in our study. The social determinants of health were recognized as important, and supports were put in place to support the men to achieve across these domains. As one participant eloquently put it, "The environment that you live in can have so much of an influence on the way you live your life. If you have to share the bathroom, and the hallways are all dirty, and you've got this cramped little room, you're not going to feel too good about your life. It puts you into a depression. But if you've got a nice space, you just feel great because it's good."

KEY MESSAGES AND IMPLICATIONS

- It is vitally important to draw on the unique experiences of men when developing policies, programs, and services for them, with particular attention to gender norms and other social-structural barriers to change.
- Photo-based narratives have important potential to collectively engage men in discussion of their experiences, creating positive connections among men and between men and potential supports.
- TVIC is a key paradigm shift for supporting mental well-being. Its attention to anti-racism/anti-oppression, coupled with practical ways to access social determinants of health, such as healthy food, safe and comfortable housing and educational and employment opportunities, is paramount to supporting health and wellness of those facing structural inequities.

DEDICATION

We dedicate this chapter to the late Mr Richard Johnson, the late Mr Henry Charles, and Paul. Mr Richard Johnson co-founded the DUDES Club and was an outreach worker for the Positive Outlook Program at the Vancouver Native Health Society. He laid the strong foundation on which the DUDES Club was built. Henry Charles was the DUDES Club Elder from 2011 to 2017 and joined the spirit world in late January 2017. He was a source of comfort, culture, humour, and knowledge for all members. Paul was a participant in the Indigenous Men's Health Narratives study (including photovoice) and a long-standing and committed member of the DUDES Club who died suddenly in 2018.

ADDITIONAL RESOURCES

- DUDES Club: https://dudesclub.ca
- *A Thousand Words* –a Photovoice Project Exploring Men's Health and Well-Being (20 min. video): https://www.youtube.com/watch?app=desktop&v=Mi9IZJkBprk

REFERENCES

Anda, R.F., Felitti, V.J., Bremner, J.D., Walker, J.D., Whitfield, C., Perry, B.D., ... Giles, W.H. (2006). The enduring effects of abuse and related adverse experiences in childhood – a convergence of evidence from neurobiology and epidemiology. *European Archives of Psychiatry and Clinical Neuroscience, 256*(3), 174–86. https://doi.org/10.1007/s00406-005-0624-4

Bell. (n.d.). Bell let's talk. https://letstalk.bell.ca/en/

Browne, A., Varcoe, C., Ford-Gilboe, M., & Wathen, C., on behalf of the EQUIP Research Team. (2015). EQUIP healthcare: An overview of a multi-component intervention to enhance equity-oriented care in primary health care settings. *International Journal for Equity in Health, 14*(152), 443–54. https://doi.org/10.1186/s12939-015-0271-y

Browne, A.J., Varcoe, C., Ford-Gilboe, M., Wathen, C. N., Smye, V., Jackson, B.E., ... Blanchet Garneau, A. (2018). Disruption as opportunity: Impacts of an organizational health equity intervention in primary care clinics. *International Journal for Equity in Health, 17*(1), 154. https://doi.org/10.1186/s12939-018-0820

Centre for Addiction and Mental Health. (n.d.). *The crisis is real*. Retrieved from https://www.camh.ca/en/driving-change/the-crisis-is-real

Centre for Addiction and Mental Health (2018, November 27). Closing the gap between youth and adult care. *Brain Buzz Newsletter*. https://www.camh.ca/en/camh-news-and-stories/closing-the-gap-between-youth-and-adult-care

DUDES Club. (n.d.). About. https://dudesclub.ca/about

Efimoff, I., Patrick, L., Josewski, V., Gross, P., Lambert, S., & Smye, V. (2021). The power of connections: How a novel Canadian men's wellness program is improving the health and well-being of Indigenous and non-Indigenous men. *International Indigenous Policy Journal, 12*(2). Retrieved from https://10.18584/iipj.2021.12.2.10896

Evans, J., Frank, B., Oliffe, J.L., & Gregory, D. (2001). Health, illness, men and masculinities (HIMM): A theoretical framework for understanding men and their health. *Journal of Men's Health, 8*(1), 7–15.

Goldenberg, S.L. (2014). Status of men's health in Canada. *Canadian Urological Association Journal, 8*(7–8), S142–S144. https://doi.org/10.5489/cuaj.2308

Green, B.L., Dass-Brailsford, P., Hurtado de Mendoza, A., Mete, M., Lynch, S.M., DeHart, D.D. ... Belknap, J. (2016). Trauma experiences and mental health among incarcerated women. *Psychological Trauma: Theory, Research, Practice, and Policy, 8*(4), 455–63. https://doi.org/10.1037/tra0000113.

Gross, P., Efimoff, I., Patrick, L., Josewski, V., Hau, K., Smye, V. & Lambert, S. (2016). The DUDES Club: A brotherhood for men's health. *Canadian Family Physician, 62*(6), e311–e318.

Gross, P., Efimoff, I.H., Josewski, V., Cohn, F., Lambert, S., Everstz, T., & Oliffe, J. (in press). Where are our men? How the DUDES Club has supported Indigenous men in British Columbia, Canada to seek a path of healing and wellness. In J. Smith, D. Watkins & D. Griffith (Eds.), Health promotion for adolescent boys & men of color: Global strategies for advancing research, policy, and practice in context. Switzerland: Springer International Publishing.

Johnson, E. (2017, November 25). Bell's "Let's Talk" campaign rings hollow for employees suffering panic attacks, vomiting, and anxiety. CBC News. https://www.cbc.ca/news/health/bell-employees-stressed-by-sales-targets-1.4418876

Katz, L.F., & Gurtovenko, K. (2015). Posttraumatic stress and emotion regulation in survivors of intimate partner violence. *Journal of Family Psychology, 29*(4), 528–36. https://doi.org/10.1037/fam0000128

Krausz, M., & Jang, K. (2015). Lessons from the creation of Canada's poorest postal code. *The Lancet Psychiatry, 2*, e5. https://doi.org/10.1016/S2215-0366(15)00045-0

Kumar, M.B., & Tjepkema, M. (2019). Suicide among First Nations people, Métis and Inuit (2011–2016): Findings from the 2011 Canadian Census Health and Environment Cohort (CanCHEC). Retrieved from https://www150.statcan.gc.ca/n1/pub/99-011-x/99-011-x2019001-eng.htm

Levine, S., Varcoe, C., & Browne, A.J. (2021) "We went as a team closer to the truth": Impacts of interprofessional education on trauma- and violence-informed care for staff in primary care settings, *Journal of Interprofessional Care, 35*(1), 46–54. https://doi.org/10.1080/13561820.2019.1708871

Mental Health Commission of Canada (n.d.). *Strengthening the case for investing – Backgrounder*. Retrieved from https://www.mentalhealthcommission.ca/English/case-for-investing-backgrounder

Moroz, N., Moroz, I., & D'Angelo, M.S. (2020). Mental health services in Canada: Barriers and cost-effective solutions to increase access. *Healthcare Management Forum, 33*(6), 282–7. https://doi.org/10.1177/0840470420933911

Oliffe, J.L., Ogrodniczuk, J.S., Bottorff, J.L., Johnson, J.L., & Hoyak, K. (2010). "You feel like you can't live anymore": Suicide from the perspectives of men who experience depression. *Social Science & Medicine, 74*(4), 506–14. https://doi.org/10.1016/j.socscimed.2010.03.05

Oliffe, J.L., & Phillips, M.J. (2008). Men, depression and masculinities: A review and recommendations. *Journal of Men's Health, 5*(3), 194–202. https://doi.org/10.1016/j.jomh.2008.03.016

Public Health Agency of Canada (2019). *Suicide in Canada: Key statistics*. https://www.canada.ca/content/dam/phac-aspc/documents/services/publications/healthy-living/suicide-canada-key-statistics-infographic/pub-eng.pdf

Smye, V., Browne, A., Gross, P., Johnson, R., Littlejohn, D., Mussell, W., ... Azak, E. (2016.) *A thousand words* by J. Topham (Producer). Aboriginal Men's Health Narratives – Reclaiming our Lives. Retrieved from https://www.youtube.com/watch?v=ZG2pL68uHqg&t=2s (10 min. version) and https://www.youtube.com/watch?v=Mi9IZJkBprk (20 min. version)

Smye, V., Browne, A., Gross, P., Johnson, R., Littlejohn, D., Mussell, W., ... Azak, E. (2014.) *In their words (The DUDES Club)*, by L. Wright (Producer). Three Bridges Films. Funded by the Canadian Institutes of Health Research (CIHR). Aboriginal Men's Health Narratives – Reclaiming our Lives. Retrieved from https://vimeo.com/85651263

Smye, V., Browne, A.J., Varcoe, C., & Josewski, V. (2011). Harm reduction, methadone maintenance treatment and the root causes of health and social inequities: An intersectional lens in the Canadian context. *Harm Reduction Journal, 8*(17), 1–12. https://doi.org/10.1186/1477-7517-8-17

Smye, V., Varcoe, C., Browne, A.J., Dion Stout, M., Josewski, V., Ford-Gilboe, M., & Keith, B. (2021). Violence at the intersections of women's lives in an urban context:

Indigenous women's experiences of leaving and/or staying with an abusive partner. *Violence Against Women, 27*(10), 1586–607. https://doi.org/10.1177 /1077801220947183

Statistics Canada. (2019). *Deaths and age-specific mortality rates, by selected grouped causes.* Retrieved from https://www150.statcan.gc.ca/t1/tbl1/en/cv.action?pid =1310039201#timeframe

Tannenbaum, C., & Frank, B. (2011). Masculinity and health in late life men. *American Journal of Men's Health, 5*(3), 243–54. https://doi.org/10.1177/1557988310384609

Wide, J., Mok, H., McKenna, M., & Ogrodniczuk, J.S. (2011). Effect of gender socialization on the presentation of depression among men: A pilot study. *Canadian Family Physician, 57,* e74–e78. Retrieved from https://www.ncbi.nlm.nih.gov/pmc /articles/PMC3038836/

2.3 Population Health and Trauma- and Violence-Informed Approaches: A Leadership Role for Public Health

SUSAN M. JACK, HEATHER LOKKO, AND NADINE WATHEN

Increased and sustained recognition of trauma – in particular, interpersonal and structural violence – as a public health issue is critical, given the pervasiveness of these experiences and their associated health effects. The World Health Organization (WHO) measured the prevalence and correlates of mental health issues in twenty-four countries (Kessler & Üstün, 2008). These surveys included assessment of twenty-nine unique types of trauma, grouped into seven categories: (1) war, (2) physical violence, (3) intimate partner violence (IPV) or sexual violence, (4) accidents, (5) unexpected or traumatic loss of a loved one, (6) traumas, and (7) other. Across countries, the majority (70.4%) of all respondents reported at least one lifetime experience of at least one trauma, with 30.5 per cent reporting four or more different traumatic experiences (Benjet et al., 2016). Often these events occur in childhood: it is estimated that in North America, 23.4 per cent of individuals experience at least one adverse childhood experience (ACE), with 35 per cent of individuals experiencing two or more ACEs (Bellis, Hughes, Ford, Rodriquez, Sethi, & Passmore, 2019). Furthermore, since March 2020, when the WHO declared COVID-19 to be a pandemic, that infectious disease has been experienced globally as a collective health, social, and economic trauma. The short- and long-term health effects associated with trauma are well-documented (see chapter 1.1), contributing to our understanding that individuals who experience trauma are at greater risk for poor mental health, injuries, and chronic health conditions, including cardiovascular disease and diabetes (e.g., Hughes et al., 2017; Shonkoff & Garner, 2012). Given the ubiquity of trauma across populations, and the substantive economic, social, and health burdens, applying a public health approach to address trauma would seem a natural imperative. Yet few public health frameworks outline recommendations for action to identify trauma, or interpersonal or structural violence, as risk indicators contributing to the conditions underlying preventable communicable or chronic health conditions. For example, Cancer Care Ontario does not do so, nor does Public Health Ontario (Cancer

Care Ontario & Ontario Agency for Health Protection and Promotion, 2012; Public Health Agency of Canada [PHAC], 2013).

The role of public health is to develop and implement programs and services, engage in collective action, and inform healthy public policies that prevent injury, illness, or disease and that promote and protect the health of individuals, families, groups, communities, and society as a whole. The core functions of public health include health protection, health surveillance, population health assessments, emergency preparedness and response, disease and injury prevention, and health promotion (Canadian Public Health Association [CPHA], 2019). To influence population health, public health must also focus on understanding, reporting on, and reducing health inequities and creating greater health and social equity throughout the population. To do this, public health organizations and providers must understand and integrate concepts such as the social determinants of health, proportionate universalism, authentic engagement, power-sharing, cultural safety, anti-oppression, and trauma- and violence-informed approaches into policy, planning, and practice.

The intersections of these mandates, and the need for trauma- and violence-informed and equity-specific public health responses, have been made very clear during the COVID-19 pandemic. Heightened awareness of public health's response to that pandemic has created opportunities to refocus attention on other pervasive yet poorly addressed epidemics that continue to negatively impact public health, including violence against women, substance use with harmful effects, the toxic drug overdose crisis, and racism. The confluence of a highly contagious and mutating infectious disease with severe social, health, and economic impacts is being experienced as a collective trauma, but one that is unevenly distributed across communities and populations. Given that it is the purview of public health organizations to focus on upstream preventive strategies, the present moment is an opportunity for public health to provide leadership in the implementation of trauma- and violence-informed approaches within population health responses, not only to minimize these disproportionate harms to mental and physical health but also to restructure health and social systems to make them resilient to future crises.

A Call to Action for Public Health

Public health decision-making and action is influenced by multiple factors, including research evidence, available resources, public health mandates, local population health needs, and context. The latter encompasses the values, beliefs, and will of individuals and local communities (National Collaborating Centre for Methods and Tools, n.d.). Adding to this complexity, while many public health actions are conducted by invitation and with consent, public health does play a role in enacting and enforcing legislation (e.g., school immunizations; health inspections of restaurants, tattoo parlours, and spas; vaping/tobacco control; and, during COVID-19, mask use in public spaces, physical distancing, sanitizing, and other precautions). In this complex context of decision-making, we present key calls to action for public health, aligning them with four trauma-and violence-informed care (TVIC) principles. These four TVIC principles, adapted for public health, are:

1. Build awareness and knowledge of the impacts of trauma and of strategies that can be implemented at multiple levels and across sectors to mitigate its impacts, reduce risk, and promote population health.
2. Modify public health approaches to apply a trauma- and violence-informed lens, focusing on safe interactions and experiences for all involved.
3. Connect and collaborate with internal and external partners to work toward the primary and secondary prevention of trauma in the community and to become a trauma-informed organization.
4. Prioritize efforts at informing healthy public policy that will prevent trauma by reducing risk factors and increasing protective factors, to create strong and healthy communities.

1. Build awareness and knowledge of the impacts of trauma and of strategies that can be implemented at multiple levels and across sectors to mitigate its impacts, reduce risk, and promote population health

Critical elements of action within this recommendation include assessing and reporting on the population health impacts of individual and collective trauma and associated risk and protective factors, as well as on inequities related to trauma and violence among population groups. While there is a growing awareness of the prevalence and associated health impacts of trauma and violence, we still need to increase recognition of these as a public health issue, including our understanding of the individual and collective signs, symptoms, and impacts and how to develop and implement public health strategies to reduce risk and promote population health. For example, by sharing trauma-related data and highlighting evidence-informed interventions with community partners and stakeholders, public health practitioners can shift attitudes toward trauma and violence and support engagement among community members, service providers, and decision-makers across various sectors. Increasing knowledge about the negative impacts of individual and collective trauma on health, and associated cost/benefit analyses, supports trauma- and violence-informed approaches and, subsequently, the allocation of resources toward multilevel, multisectoral preventive interventions. In this way, awareness and understanding of trauma and violence and its impacts (principle 1) can underpin public health action to prevent trauma (which in turn can promote health and prevent illness, injury, and disease), thus addressing health inequities.

Perhaps even more important for public health is increased awareness and knowledge of the risk and protective factors related to trauma and violence experienced by individuals and communities. This knowledge will drive public health organizations to prioritize this critical public health issue and provide resources for developing and implementing comprehensive population health interventions aimed at preventing trauma and violence from occurring in the first place. Table 2.3.1 uses the steps outlined by Public Health Ontario (2018) to illustrate population health approaches for the primary prevention of trauma and violence. As public health organizations are responsible for reporting publicly on community and population health status, this awareness and knowledge can also inform the work and priorities of other health, community, and municipal partners.

2. Modify public health approaches to apply a trauma- and violence-informed lens, focusing on safe interactions and experiences for all involved

Typically, public health agencies encompass a diverse range of programs and divisions, such as chronic disease and injury prevention, environmental health, healthy growth and development, sexual health, and communicable diseases. The specialized nature of public health programing therefore requires that tailored and program-specific approaches to TVIC implementation be developed and integrated for sustainability. When a "safety first" approach is embedded in organizational practice, community and system interactions, and program development, services will be culturally safe and prioritize the emotional and physical safety of both service recipients and providers (principle 2). For many public health agencies, the first step in creating a workplace culture that prioritizes safety and well-being will be to complete an organizational assessment. Multiple tools are available to assess an organization's implementation of T(V)IC principles (e.g., British Columbia Centre of Excellence for Women's Health, 2013; Manitoba Trauma Informed Education & Resource Centre, 2021); several of these recommend conducting a trauma review as a starting point. When planning a trauma review, it is important to welcome and include service providers and recipients, administrators, volunteers, and support staff to participate and share their experiences.

Trauma-informed reviews (Brown, Harris, & Fallot, 2013) provide organizations with information about (1) how service recipients perceive and experience their programs and services, (2) structures, practices, processes, or activities that may trigger a trauma response or inadvertently result in retraumatization of service recipients or vicarious trauma for service providers, and (3) strategies or policies to improve system processes. Engaging public health

2.3 Population Health and TVI Approaches

Table 2.3.1 Steps to guide development and implementation of population health approaches for the primary prevention of trauma and violence

1. Select and define the type(s) of trauma or violence that are perceived to be of significance and importance to the local community or population.
   - External trauma – e.g., gun violence, suicidal loss, homicide/femicide, extreme poverty.
   - Interpersonal violence – e.g., child maltreatment, intimate partner violence, sexual assault.
   - Systemic violence – e.g., racism, sexism.
2. Conduct a situational assessment to guide effective decision-making (PHO, 2018).
   - Research evidence – e.g., use high-quality literature to understand what is known about risk and protective factors, health impacts, priority populations, and effective interventions that fit within the public health mandate.
   - Community health issues – e.g., gather information on local prevalence and incidence, risk and protective factors, health impacts, population group disparities, and existing community resources and strengths.
   - Community/political preferences – e.g., assess the current political, organizational, community, and social climate, as well as the needs and interests of the community.
   - Resources – e.g., identify existing financial, human, and other resources.
3. Identify the overall goals and outcome objectives of intended public health action to prevent interpersonal and systemic trauma and violence, as well as target audiences for public health action.
4. Choose and invest in strategies and actions that are likely to reach intended audiences and realize intended outcomes.
   - Strategies and actions at the individual, family, group, community, population, or system level should focus on:
     - mitigating, reducing, and eliminating risk factors; and
     - leveraging, enhancing, and increasing protective factors.
   - Strategies and actions may include engaging in collective action initiatives, informing healthy public policy, engaging in education and skill-building initiatives, and offering programs and services at the individual, family, group, or community level.
5. Identify meaningful indicators as to which data can be gathered, analysed, and used to inform evaluation and future planning and implementation efforts.

administrators, staff, service providers, and service recipients in a joint review of a specific public health program or service provides an opportunity to (1) identify potential organizational practices that result in harm or retraumatization and (2) create an action plan to prioritize the safety of both service recipients and providers. When conducting a trauma-informed review within a public health organization, two overarching questions guide this activity: (1) To what extent do the organization's program-specific communication materials, activities, and settings prioritize the emotional, physical, and cultural safety of service recipients, service providers, support staff, administration, and volunteers? And (2) how can the program's services be modified to ensure that these types of safety are prioritized within all physical or virtual encounters, as well as verbal/written communications, between the organization and the service recipients and providers? Examples of specific actions that public health organizations may wish to attend to in their local trauma-informed review are provided in table 2.3.2.

3. Connect and collaborate with internal and external partners to work toward the primary and secondary prevention of trauma in the community and to become a trauma- and violence-informed organization

The National Collaborating Centre for Determinants of Health (2013) identifies partnering with other sectors to reduce health inequities as a key role for public health. At local and regional levels, public health personnel collaborate regularly with representatives from a range of organizations across sectors to address the health, social, education, economic, and legal needs of community members. Public health relies on effective and authentic partnerships to achieve many of its population health goals; trauma prevention and TVIC approaches are no exception.

The primary prevention of individual and collective trauma and creating and sustaining a TVIC community both require long-term commitment with broad and diverse engagement. Use of the Collective Impact Framework can lead to meaningful community change (Tamarack Institute, n.d.). To be most effective, five core conditions need to be met: (1) a common agenda must be developed and used to guide the collective work; (2) processes and indicators for shared measurement need to be agreed on and implemented to better understand collective progress; (3) stakeholders have to identify and implement mutually reinforcing activities; (4) participants need to engage in transparent and continuous communications; and (5) backbone support must be available to enable collective action efforts to move forward in a timely and effective manner (Tamarack Institute, n.d). The role public health plays within the collective impact framework should be responsive to the local context. In addition to committing to being an active participant aligned with the core conditions, the public health sector can provide evidence and data to understand the current community reality, monitor trends, and identify evidence-informed approaches to addressing the issue; provide backbone support to collective impact initiatives that align with community needs and the public health mandate; and provide leadership for the identification of indicators, information-gathering processes, and data analysis and reporting to facilitate shared measurement. Weaver (2017) wisely observes that "authentic community change moves at the speed of trust" (p. 1). Understanding the importance of trust, committing the time required to build trust, consistently demonstrating behaviours and

Table 2.3.2 Trauma-informed review: Areas of assessment

Goal	Focused areas of assessment: Service recipients	Focused areas of assessment: Service providers and staff/volunteers
Ensure that service recipients and all staff and volunteers feel welcome when contacting and engaging with public health programs and services	• Initial (e.g., intake line, website) contact with program is welcoming, respectful, and engaging. • Physical and virtual program spaces are welcoming, and potential triggers are identified and removed wherever possible. • Accessibility issues are identified and addressed. • Information about service/program location, goals, and logistics (e.g., parking, how to contact provider upon arrival) are clearly communicated, with reminders sent. • Program/service signage is clearly visible and provides clear direction for next steps. • Community members are engaged as consultants, staff, peer support, or volunteers to provide input and make connections between service recipients and providers. • Flexible options are available for contacting agency or service providers (e.g., phone, web, text messaging). • Flexibility to reschedule missed or cancelled appointments without any punitive actions. • Reminders for booked appointments or the day/time when a new program (e.g., parenting group, food handler course) starts. Include detailed information about program location, logistics, goals, activities, and "what to expect" upon arrival.	• New staff/volunteers/service providers are individually welcomed and greeted on the first day and introductions to and connections with colleagues are facilitated throughout onboarding processes. • Provide a detailed written overview of orientation activities (e.g., checklist of activities to complete), with adequate support and mentorship throughout the orientation period. • Provide information on key contacts to respond to administrative, human resource, or clinical queries.

(Continued)

Table 2.3.2 Trauma-informed review: Areas of assessment *(Continued)*

Goal	Focused areas of assessment: Service recipients	Focused areas of assessment: Service providers and staff/volunteers
Prioritize physical safety	• Adequate physical space is available to ensure privacy and confidentiality during intake or receipt of one-on-one services. • If security personnel are required (e.g., at congregate settings for mass vaccination clinics), they are trained to engage with service recipients using TVIC approaches. • Service providers are trained to determine the safety of the community/home environment for the client and themselves prior to assessing or responding to sensitive client issues such as intimate partner violence, substance use, or mental health concerns.	• Make policies and training available for maximizing personal safety when providing services in the community, workplaces, or home settings. • Cell phones and data plans are supplied by the organization. • Policies are implemented with respect to workplace violence, domestic violence, and sexual harassment. • Requirements (or policies) to work from home assess employee safety within the home and capacity to establish a safe, confidential workspace. • Workspaces with a door/walls are available for providers using telehealth to provide public health services/programing.
Prioritize emotional safety	• Information is available or provided that has clear explanations about procedures/services to be received as well as information about what comes next. • Individuals are treated with respect and in a way that makes them feel valued and heard. • If security personnel are required, consideration is given to attire that will prioritize emotional safety. • During assessments, individuals are not asked potentially retraumatizing questions repeatedly by different service providers, and if trauma of any kind is disclosed, details are not requested by the service provider unless critical to the assessment/intervention.	• Formal and informal opportunities for peer support/debriefing and strengthening social networks within the workplace are available. • High-quality reflective supervision is available. • Employee wellness, including self-care, is supported through organizational policy and practices. • Employee assistance programs are available. • All employee interactions, within and between various levels, are mutually respectful, workplace harassment is not tolerated, and measures are in place to facilitate safe reporting of harassment.

(Continued)

2.3 Population Health and TVI Approaches 123

Table 2.3.2 Trauma-informed review: Areas of assessment *(Continued)*

Goal	Focused areas of assessment: Service recipients	Focused areas of assessment: Service providers and staff/volunteers
Ensure that service providers and program/service components create a safe and inclusive environment	• Services and service information is available in common local languages, and/or via professional interpretation. • Service settings are welcoming for all (i.e., they include acknowledgment of local communities via art, multilingual signage, etc. • Employees engage in education and skill-building opportunities in areas such as cultural humility and safety, anti-racism, anti-oppression, dis/ability inclusion, 2SLGBTQ+ (e.g., positive space training), with accountability to apply learnings in their practice	• Hiring and volunteer selection reflect local communities. • Onboarding emphasizes local history and current community challenges and opportunities. • Organizations hire external consultant to periodically conduct an internal equity, diversity, and inclusion assessment. • All employees are held accountable for creating a positive and inclusive work environment.

Note: Based on the Trauma Review Exercise developed by EQUIP Health Care and the GTV Incubator (see Additional Resources)

practices that build trust, acknowledging actions taken that break trust, and taking steps to restore trust when needed are all critical to the success of collective impact initiatives. Building and sustaining trust is especially paramount when addressing individual and collective trauma; unless trust is established within and among community members, organizations, and leadership, engaging in effective and productive collective action is not possible, and the vision of creating a TVIC community cannot be realized. Box 2.3.1 provides examples of efforts to embed TVIC in a community, and a country.

BOX 2.3.1 TVIC AT THE COMMUNITY LEVEL AND BEYOND

Case 1: London, Ontario. Driven in part by the work of the Gender, Trauma, and Violence Knowledge Incubator (www.GTVIncubator.uwo.ca) and by the reality of London's deeply embedded and interrelated problems with lack of affordable housing, substance use, trafficking, and other forms of violence against women and girls, and acknowledging the success of several existing collaborative initiatives, several organizations in London joined together to begin envisioning how TVIC approaches could be more effectively and comprehensively embedded broadly across organizations and sectors (many of the examples in this volume derive from this work). The goal is for people to receive seamless, safe, person-centred, trauma- and violence-informed services regardless of where they go, with the knowledge among providers that referrals will be to other organizations and services practising in this way. However, the approach, somewhat stalled (but made more relevant than ever) by the COVID-19 pandemic, requires a jump-start. As outlined above, public health can serve as a catalyst for this work, based on evolving learnings from application of the Collective Impact approach (e.g., the elimination of homelessness in Medicine Hat, Alberta) (Cabaj & Weaver, 2016)].

Case 2: Scotland. The Government of Scotland, through the National Health Service–Education for Scotland, has committed to developing and supporting a trauma-informed national health workforce. The National Trauma Training Programme (NTTP), through its online portal (https://transformingpsychologicaltrauma.scot), supports organizational leaders as well as "local champions" in transforming the entire Scottish health sector so that it takes a trauma-informed approach. Resources continue to emerge, and evaluation is planned. This whole-country strategy has significant potential to improve individual experiences of care across the health sector, as well as to shift health and social outcomes.

Given its extensive engagement in collaboration and partnership, public health is ideally situated to demonstrate leadership in supporting the establishment of trauma- and violence-informed organizations. Strategies for how professionals can directly implement TVIC principles in the care, education, and services they provide to individuals or groups have been outlined in several chapters of this book. However, these practices can only be sustained when organizations align their strategic plans with TVIC principles and commit resources to fostering a culture that prioritizes the health and well-being of both service recipients and the workforce (Center for Substance Abuse Treatment, 2014).

In alignment with the first area of action outlined above, public health can support internal and external organizational stakeholders at all levels in their efforts to recognize and understand that trauma and experiences of violence are common among both service recipients and providers, and that histories of trauma and the associated presence of traumatic stress, post-traumatic stress disorder (PTSD), and other health effects influence one's capacity to engage with services, as well as to recognize and acknowledge that for some, the services offered through the organization may be harmful and retraumatizing (Trauma Informed Oregon, 2018b). Organizations also have a responsibility to reflect on and examine how the sectors or systems they represent (or are aligned with) may have been (and still are) part of systems of oppression.

The next step involves assessing the organization's readiness and commitment to adopt TVIC principles, implementing training initiatives, and conducting a thorough review and revision of policies and practices. An organization that is trauma-responsive is focused on collecting and analysing data to understand staff's, service providers', and service recipients' experiences of trauma and to identify opportunities where TVIC can be implemented at both service and organizational levels. During this phase, work plans to review and revise existing policies, practices, and the working/service environment are developed and implemented. During the development of these work plans, the role of community residents in creating change cannot be overlooked. Those in traditional positions of power (e.g., government agencies, researchers, service providers, enforcement agencies) must create space for community members to provide leadership in designing and implementing plans for change and take steps to support their success in these leadership roles. There must be equitable participation and accountability among stakeholders, and organizations must leverage their own positions of power to benefit historically marginalized communities (Falkenburger, Arena, & Wolin, 2018).

An organization that ultimately makes claims to be "trauma-informed" is then able to provide evidence that recommended changes to policy, practices, and the environment have been adopted and initiated and become "institutionalized," with plans for ongoing evaluations to identify where further changes or modifications are required (Trauma Informed Oregon, 2018b). In table 2.3.3, suggested actions for public health leaders seeking a pathway to initiate the adoption and implementation of a trauma- and violence-informed approach within their organization are outlined, using the steps proposed by Trauma Informed Oregon (2018b). Public health can lead by example – by committing to and actively pursuing steps to becoming a trauma- and violence-informed organization – and, in so doing, can encourage and support other organizations within their community to do the same as they work together to create a trauma- and violence-informed community.

4. Prioritize efforts at informing healthy public policy that will prevent trauma by reducing risk factors and increasing protective factors, to create strong and healthy communities

Public health has embraced the "health in all policies" approach, which calls for an intentional and systematic consideration of the health and social implications of policies across all government sectors, in recognition that the socio-economic and environmental determinants of health and wellness are often outside the scope of influence of the health sector (Tonelli, Tang, & Forest,

Table 2.3.3 Process for becoming a trauma- and violence-informed organization

Action	Guidance
• Identify champions in the organization who understand and are advocates for adopting a trauma- and violence-informed approach to care and service delivery.	Often a TVIC "champion" will emerge, for example, a public health leader (staff or management) who demonstrates trauma awareness and who sees the potential for applying these principles within public health practice or policies.
• Develop a work group to lead the process of transforming the organization from "trauma and violence aware" to one that is "trauma- and violence-informed," guided by TVIC principles to inform decision-making and communications.	A TVIC work group in a public health organization should include individuals who reflect diversity in roles and responsibilities, e.g., • TVIC content experts, • representatives from different levels of leadership and staff, • practitioners/providers (e.g., from sexual health, family health, harm reduction, environmental health, or chronic disease prevention programs), • educators and instructional designers, and • individuals with lived experience of trauma or current/past recipients of public health services. Establish meeting processes that reflect TVIC principles to guide communication and decision-making within the group.
• Select and then complete an organizational assessment tool to serve as a guideline for identifying opportunities within the organization regarding where to focus TVIC implementation efforts.	Examples of organizational assessment tools: • Trauma Informed Care Screening Tool (Trauma Informed Oregon, 2018a) • Organizational Self-Assessment (Manitoba Trauma Informed Education & Resource Centre, 2021) • EQUIP Health Care: Rate Your Organization (http://EQUIPHealthcare.ca) • Creating Cultures of Trauma-Informed Care: A Self-Assessment and Planning Protocol (Fallot & Harris, 2009)
• Define how the TVIC principles will be operationalized within the organization and develop a list of goals that will guide the implementation of this work within the organization.	To guide the implementation of their Trauma-Informed Systems (TIS) Initiative, the project work group from the San Francisco Department of Public Health articulated the following central aims (Loomis et al., 2019, p. 253): 1. All staff, even those not providing direct services, must be educated on a core set of TIS values. 2. These values, including addressing bias and discrimination, must be practised across the organization, not just within service delivery. 3. An organization must assess and regularly evaluate their implementation of these values. 4. A collaborative process must be used to embed these values within the system. 5. Both staff and the community served must benefit from these values.

(Continued)

Table 2.3.3 Process for becoming a trauma- and violence-informed organization *(Continued)*

Action	Guidance
• Conduct an environmental scan of staff, service providers, and recipients to understand (1) their experiences of trauma, interpersonal violence, and structural violence (including racism); and (2) their needs with respect to TVIC implementation.	An environmental scan may include surveys of and interviews with service providers and staff to: • assess competence and confidence in understanding and responding to trauma; • measure experiences of trauma, compassion fatigue/stress, burnout or moral distress, or vicarious trauma; and • explore and identify education and practice needs related to TVIC implementation. Surveys and interviews of clients, community partners, or service recipients to: • measure perceptions of trauma-informed care received, e.g., through use of the TIC Grade Trauma-Informed Care Client Evaluation (Boucher et al., 2020; see also chapter 4.5); and • explore their experiences of care/services received through public health or community-partner agencies.
• Develop (or locate, e.g., see chapter 4.3) a foundational TVIC curriculum to provide basic information about trauma and violence, associated health effects, and TVIC principles to all service providers, volunteers, staff, and individuals within management or leadership positions.	Suggested core content: • Overview of the definitions, prevalence, and health effects associated with trauma, including experiences of interpersonal or structural violence. • Introduction to NEAR science (neuroscience, epigenetics, ACES, and resilience). • Introduction and review of TVIC principles, discussion of importance, application, and implementation of principles in practice and policy. • Discussion of the importance of workforce wellness, including identification of where vicarious trauma, secondary stress, and burnout, as well as vicarious resilience and compassion satisfaction, occur within the workplace.
• Develop and implement a sustainable training plan to deliver the foundational TVIC curriculum to all current and future staff, volunteers, and students.	• Identify who within the organization is required to complete the TVIC training and to what degree (we recommend that all staff, volunteers, community partners, and managers complete all relevant training). • Discuss if TVIC training is required or voluntary. • Develop structure for TVIC training, including format of educational delivery (e.g., online modules, in-person workshops, multi-modal sessions); single or multiple sessions; individual, team-based, or group learning activities.

(Continued)

Table 2.3.3 Process for becoming a trauma- and violence-informed organization *(Continued)*

Action	Guidance
• Develop tailored approaches for implementing TVIC principles within different public health programs or divisions.	Within public health, different programs and divisions, due to their unique functions (e.g., health promotion, injury and disease prevention, health protection), will need to tailor how the TVIC principles are operationalized and implemented within standard operating procedures, policies, and practices, e.g.: • Development of practice guidance, with examples on how to implement TVIC in direct service provision. • Opportunities to engage service recipients or community partners in co-design or co-production of services and programs.
• Develop evaluation or quality assurance plans to monitor implementation of TVIC in practice.	Public health agency or partner organization to identify the type of data required to evaluate or monitor whether public services/care is TVI, and whether the implementation of these principles is improving the experiences and outcomes of individuals, families, organizations, or communities served. This may include: • assessing changes in service users' experiences of services or programs; • assessment or monitoring of rates of specific forms of trauma (e.g., child maltreatment, intimate partner violence, gun violence, racism) among program clients or communities served; and • evaluation of implementation of TVIC initiatives within the public health agency or partner agency (e.g., evaluation of training).

2020). This approach acknowledges the complexity of improving health and health equity, as well as the need for a broad range of comprehensive interventions to realize positive population impact. Tonelli and colleagues (2020) posit that a national Canadian plan for "health in all policies" would enhance efforts to reduce non-communicable diseases, promote mental health, and address health inequities experienced by Indigenous people. While this is true, the evidence pointing to the role of trauma and structural and interpersonal violence in contributing to poor health outcomes across populations elucidates the wisdom of ensuring that policies are also assessed through a trauma- and violence-informed lens. Bowen and Murshid (2016) observe that where the literature on trauma-informed practice discusses the importance of policy intervention, it usually refers to policy exclusively at the institutional level. They recommend that, in addition to taking an organizational perspective on policies, trauma-informed principles (and by extension TVIC principles) be used as a framework for analysing social policy, not universally, but with particular policies most likely to address trauma- and violence-linked social issues, such as substance use, mental health, chronic disease, and homelessness. They go further, adding that, in addition to taking an approach that recognizes the universal experience of trauma, "trauma-informed social policy should ... address [trauma's] specific sociopolitical and economic roots as well as its disproportionate impacts among marginalized populations" (Bowen & Murshid, 2016, p. 224). This goal aligns with and proposes a concrete approach to fulfilling public health's mandate to reduce health inequities.

One of the four research and action priorities recommended by Tebes and colleagues (2019) is to adopt trauma-informed policies aimed at preventing trauma exposure across an individual's lifespan and promoting resilient communities. Policies must both strengthen protective factors and mitigate risk factors for individual, structural, and collective trauma, and the effects of these policies must be "felt" by individuals and communities in various contexts (such as schools or workplaces) – that is, changes in policies must "pull through" to the service interface, be experienced by individuals and families in their communities at large, shape government policies and practices, and ultimately lead to positive effects on health and social outcomes. For trauma- and violence-informed change, policies must prevent and mitigate adverse childhood and adverse community experiences – the "pair of ACEs" (Kain & White, 2018). Kain and White (2018, para 3) clarify that "without addressing both historical traumas, and generational trauma, ACEs awareness about an individuals' history with developmental trauma, will not be enough. Too many children and communities are rooted in and shaded by the multiple branches of adversity." As we have seen since early 2020, the COVID-19 pandemic has layered a new form of community-level trauma on top of the existing pair of ACEs and pervasive health inequities (Sonu, Marvin, & Moore, 2021). A trauma- and violence-informed policy framework can contribute to recognizing structural violence, reducing inequities, changing social and economic realities, and creating systems that confront and prevent trauma, besides promoting resiliency at all levels.

Shifting to TVIC in the Post-COVID-19 Environment

In addition to making visible pre-existing health and social inequities (Sonu et al., 2021) the COVID-19 pandemic has demonstrated that capacity, resources, and tools exist at the national, provincial, and local levels of public health to rapidly collect, assess, and disseminate information about COVID-19 cases, as well as to conduct and communicate modelling to anticipate next steps, including how to address inequities in specific groups by, for example, prioritizing vaccine distribution among those most in need. Table 2.3.4 uses the standard

Table 2.3.4 Lessons learned from COVID-19: Public health leadership to orient services and systems to TVIC

A trauma- and violence-informed public health population-level response to COVID-19	Trauma- and violence-informed public health example: COVID-19 vaccination clinics
PRINCIPLE 1: Build awareness and knowledge of the impacts of trauma and of strategies that can be implemented at multiple levels and across sectors to mitigate its impacts, reduce risk, and promote population health.	
• Collect and report on case data according to equity indicators (gender, ethnic identity, ability, income, housing, etc.). • Integrate equity indicators into modelling for all facets of surveillance and response. • Consult with communities regarding how to represent these data (avoid stigmatizing language, etc.). • Gather information to better understand the implications of public health measures on those who are experiencing or who have experienced trauma. • Monitor changes in incidence of trauma-inducing (e.g., intimate partner violence, child abuse) or trauma-responsive (e.g., substance misuse) behaviours at a population level throughout the pandemic/public health measures.	• Be mindful that historical experiences of medical racism, distrust of health systems, and fear or past negative/painful experiences with medical procedures may underpin expressions of vaccine hesitancy. • Be mindful of behaviours that may indicate fear/anxiety (e.g., pulling chair away from vaccinator, express they are "nervous"); greet individual warmly. Reassure them by saying, "I'm going to spend a few minutes asking you some questions about your health, then I am not going to surprise you with the needle. I will tell you what I am going to do and ask your permission before we proceed." • Prior to administering vaccine, ask, "Is there anything that has happened in your past that makes it difficult for you to be immunized (or to have a needle)? Is there anything we can do to make this easier for you?"
PRINCIPLE 2: Modify public health approaches to apply a trauma- and violence-informed lens, focusing on safe interactions and experiences for all involved.	
• Ensure availability of on-site or virtual interpreters, especially for specialized clinics for prioritized groups, including essential and migrant workers; provide written health information in multiple languages. • When planning mass or mobile vaccination clinics, consult with equity-seeking groups and those with lived experience (including staff) to ensure that TVIC approaches are considered and incorporated wherever possible in the structures, processes, and environment of the clinics.	• Appointment booking: provide clear information about location, parking, check-in procedures, special considerations for PPE and physical distancing, what to wear (e.g., short sleeves), any restrictions on who can accompany client and/or what they can/cannot bring to appointment. • In public immunization sites (e.g., arenas) have private spaces available for individuals who may experience discomfort/anxiety being immunized in public.

(Continued)

2.3 Population Health and TVI Approaches   131

Table 2.3.4 Lessons learned from COVID-19: Public health leadership to orient services and systems to TVIC (*Continued*)

A trauma- and violence-informed public health population-level response to COVID-19	Trauma- and violence-informed public health example: COVID-19 vaccination clinics
• Acknowledge and use the expertise of all relevant local organizations, civil society groups/NGOs, and community advocates, to create a safe and respectful forum for knowledge-sharing and service-planning. • Provide education and screening questions to case investigators to be integrated into case management work (e.g., when advising self-isolation, ask, "Do you have a safe place to self-isolate for 14 days? Will self-isolation prevent you from accessing food or other basic necessities?"). • Ensure that leaders, staff, security, and volunteers at vaccine clinics are representative of the community members accessing immunization services (e.g., visible minority, Indigenous). • Ensure that evaluation questions effectively capture meaningful feedback to inform current and future integration of trauma- and violence-informed approaches. • Identify credible community leaders who can safely share information about their experiences being tested and/or vaccinated as well as information on how to access services.	• Prior to administering the vaccine, provide a brief yet detailed description of what the individual can expect next (e.g., "I am going wipe your skin with an alcohol swab, it may feel cold. I will then administer the vaccine, which will take less than ten seconds, and will put a band-aid on.") • Obtain consent to touch the individual's arm and to proceed with immunization. • Be mindful that for some individuals, receiving the vaccine in a supine (laying down) position may increase feelings of vulnerability. • For individuals, especially children, who are experiencing anxiety or distress, strategies to employ include humour, distraction, or relaxation techniques such as deep breathing or "pretending" to blow bubbles. • Confidentially communicate concerns re: post-vaccine reactions (e.g., including fainting, need to wait thirty minutes because of history of anaphylactic reactions with past vaccines) between vaccinator and staff in recovery area; this could include escorting individual to the recovery area and verbally communicating concerns to recovery staff, having individuals sit in a specific (non-labelled) space in the recovery area, or writing a note on the health information sheet. • Throughout the clinic space, have clear signage providing clear direction to the next step of the vaccination process. Ensure that all staff (e.g., greeters, intake clerks, security, vaccinators) can clearly explain their role as well as direct individuals to the next step in the process.

(*Continued*)

Table 2.3.4 Lessons learned from COVID-19: Public health leadership to orient services and systems to TVIC (*Continued*)

A trauma- and violence-informed public health population-level response to COVID-19	Trauma- and violence-informed public health example: COVID-19 vaccination clinics
PRINCIPLE 3: Connect and collaborate with internal and external partners to work towards the primary and secondary prevention of trauma in the community and to become a trauma-informed organization.	
• Identify and collaborate with community partners to plan and implement services in neighbourhoods or communities that have been disproportionately impacted by COVID-19 or in areas where priority populations live, work, or go to school. • Consult with priority populations to understand how to engage effectively with them, reduce barriers to COVID-19 testing and vaccine information and access, and increase testing/vaccine uptake. • In communication/social media strategies, build trust by addressing community concerns about COVID-19, providing information about how testing and vaccines work (including effectiveness and side effects) in a non-judgmental manner. • Be transparent in communicating information, and acknowledge what is unknown, uncertain, or even changing information related to the vaccine. • Collaborate with community partners to provide basic necessities for people in self-isolation where needed. • Look for opportunities for shared measurement between community partners.	• Introduce self with name, title (e.g., public health nurse, greeter, pharmacist), and role (e.g., administer the vaccine). • Where possible, offer the client "choice" e.g., choice of arm to receive vaccine. • Engage various community partners in vaccination efforts, and leverage their strengths and resources to ensure that they are included and valued as key community players. • In collaborative clinic planning and implementation, facilitate shared decision-making and/or shared leadership with community partners where possible. • Recognize that community partners come to the table with various contexts and resources and expect equitable rather than equal participation. • Ensure that leadership, staff, and volunteers from all community partner organizations are provided with sufficient breaks and vacation time, in spite of urgent and overwhelming workload demands. • Ensure that equity-seeking groups that are working or volunteering at the vaccination clinics are provided with appropriate and commensurate compensation. • Ensure that community partners involved in vaccination clinic work receive recognition for their contributions.

(*Continued*)

Table 2.3.4 Lessons learned from COVID-19: Public health leadership to orient services and systems to TVIC (*Continued*)

A trauma- and violence-informed public health population-level response to COVID-19	Trauma- and violence-informed public health example: COVID-19 vaccination clinics
• Collectively identify COVID-19 response and recovery priorities and optimize each community partner's mandate, resources, and role within those priorities, in an effort to maximize positive community outcomes. • Consider identifying and training local community members to serve as advocates for their communities.	
PRINCIPLE 4: Prioritize efforts at informing healthy public policy that will prevent trauma by reducing risk factors and increasing protective factors to create strong and healthy communities	
• Collect data to identify COVID-19-related inequities that can be used to inform health public policy. • Advocate for the province to mandate health units to gather ethnic/racial identity and SES data for all COVID-19 cases. • Work to influence decision-makers to implement policies that will reduce COVID-19 risk factors (e.g., reduce the number of people working 2–3 minimum-wage jobs, increasing their exposure to COVID-19, by providing a basic guaranteed income); also, enhance protective factors (mandate that employers provide work time for employees to get vaccinated). • Advocate for decision-makers to consider potential unintended negative consequences for those experiencing or who have experienced trauma and identify and implement mitigating factors when determining which population-level public health measures will be put in place.	• Develop and implement a policy to ensure that all leaders, staff, and volunteers at vaccination clinics are educated on TVI-PH. • Create and hold individuals accountable to an immunization clinic "code of conduct" for all leaders, staff, and volunteers at immunization clinics. • Recommend that a trauma review checklist be completed, with any identified concerns sufficiently addressed, prior to the launch of a vaccination clinic.

accepted principles for implementing TVIC approaches to present specific ways that, via lessons learned through pandemic response, public health can not only (re)orient itself to TVIC but also take a leadership role in moving entire communities (and beyond) to TVIC as a means to reduce health and social inequities.

Conclusion

It is likely that many public health practitioners are unaware of the connection between individual and community trauma and population health. Public health can play a key role in assessing and reporting on trauma and its population health impacts, in order to build TVIC knowledge within public health and other sectors (e.g., health care, social services, education). This knowledge can inspire other organizations to embrace TVIC approaches and lead to the establishment of a trauma- and violence-informed service system. Public health must commit to integrating the TVIC principles into all their organizations' practices and policies and to modifying its programs and policies to ensure that people feel safe and that optimal outcomes are achieved.

KEY MESSAGES AND IMPLICATIONS

- Public health is well-positioned to lead or actively engage in collective efforts with various partners to plan and implement strategies intended to reduce risk factors and enhance protective factors, with the ultimate goal of preventing individual, structural, and collective trauma from occurring.
- Public health can support decision-makers in understanding the value of reducing trauma and violence at all levels; the potential upstream impact this could have on population health, through trauma- and violence-informed public policy, is significant.
- This vision will require shifts in thinking and practice, sustained comprehensive effort, and commitment of resources to realize a transformation to a society in which trauma is the exception rather than the norm, and to a reality where experiences of trauma and violence are no longer significant contributors to poor and inequitable health outcomes.

ADDITIONAL RESOURCES

- Trauma Review/Walkthrough: https://gtvincubator.uwo.ca/resources
- Scotland's National Trauma Training Programme: https://transformingpsychologicaltrauma.scot

- EQUIP Health Care Organizational readiness Tools: https://equiphealthcare.ca/equip-my-organization
- Public Health Nursing Practice, Research, and Education Program (PHN-PREP) TVIC Tools: https://phnprep.ca/resource-hub

REFERENCES

Bellis, M.A., Hughes, K., Ford, K., Rodriquez, G.F., Sethi, D., & Passmore, J. (2019). Life course health consequences and associated annual costs of adverse childhood experiences across Europe and North America: A systematic review and meta-analysis. *The Lancet Public Health*, 4(10), E517–E528. https://doi.org/10.1016/S2468-2667(19)30145-8

Benjet, C., Bromet, E., Karam, E.G., Kessler, R.C., McLaughlin, K.A., Ruscio, A.M., … Koenen, K.C. (2016). The epidemiology of traumatic event exposure worldwide: Results from the World Mental Health Survey Consortium. *Psychological Medicine*, 46(2), 327–43. https://doi.org/10.1017/s0033291715001981

Boucher, N., Darling-Fisher, C.S., Sinko, L., Beck, D., Granner, J., & Seng, J. (2020). Psychometric evaluation of the TIC Grade, a self-report measure to assess youth perceptions of the quality of trauma-informed care they received. *Journal of the American Psychiatric Nurses Association*. doi:10.1177/1078390320953896

Bowen, E.A., & Murshid, N.S. (2016). Trauma-informed social policy: A conceptual framework for policy analysis and advocacy. *American Journal of Public Health*, 106(2), 223–9. https://doi.org/10.2105/AJPH.2015.302970

British Columbia Centre of Excellence for Women's Health. (2013). *Trauma-informed practice guide*. Retrieved from https://bccewh.bc.ca/wp-content/uploads/2012/05/2013_TIP-Guide.pdf

Brown, V.B., Harris, M., & Fallot, R. (2013). Moving toward trauma-informed practice in addiction treatment: A collaborative model of agency assessment. *Journal of Psychoactive Drugs*, 45(5), 386–93.

Cabaj, M., & Weaver, L. (2016). *Collective impact 3.0: An evolving framework for community change*. Retrieved from https://cdn2.hubspot.net/hubfs/316071/Events/CCI/2016_CCI_Toronto/CCI_Publications/Collective_Impact_3.0_FINAL_PDF.pdf

Canadian Public Health Association (CPHA). (2019). *Public health in the context of health system renewal in Canada: Position Statement*. Retrieved from https://www.cpha.ca/public-health-context-health-system-renewal-canada

Cancer Care Ontario & Ontario Agency for Health Protection and Promotion (Public Health Ontario). (2012). *Taking action to prevent chronic disease: Recommendations for a healthier Ontario*. Toronto, ON: Queen's Printer for Ontario. Retrieved from https://www.publichealthontario.ca/-/media/documents/T/2012/taking-action-chronic-diseases.pdf?la=en

Center for Substance Abuse Treatment. (2014). Chapter 2: Building a trauma-informed workforce. In *Trauma-informed care in behavioral health services* (pp. 33–58). Rockville, MD: Substance Abuse and Mental Health Services Administration. Retrieved from https://www.ncbi.nlm.nih.gov/books/NBK207194/

Falkenburger, E., Arena, O., & Wolin, J. (2018). Trauma-informed community building and engagement. *Tamarack Institute for Community Engagement*. Retrieved from https://www.tamarackcommunity.ca/collectiveimpact

Fallot, R.D., & Harris, M. (2009). Creating cultures of trauma-informed care: A self-assessment and planning protocol. Washington, DC: Community Connections. Retrieved from https://traumainformedoregon.org/wp-content/uploads/2014/10/CCTIC-A-Self-Assessment-and-Planning-Protocol.pdf

Hughes, K., Bellis, M.A., Hardcastle, K.A., Sethi, D., Butchart, A., Mikton, C., ... Dunne, M.P. (2017). The effect of multiple adverse childhood experiences on health: A systematic review and meta-analysis. *Lancet Public Health*, 2(8), e356–e66. https://doi.org/10.1016/S2468-2667(17)30118-4

Kain, L., & White, C.C. (2018). Be the spark: Igniting trauma-informed change within our communities. *PACES Connect*. Retrieved from https://www.pacesconnection.com/g/ACE-nashville/blog/be-the-spark-igniting-trauma-informed-change-within-our-communities

Kessler, R.S., & Üstün, T.B. (Eds.). (2008). *The WHO World Mental Health Survey: Global perspectives on the epidemiology of mental disorders*. New York, NY: Cambridge University Press.

Loomis, B., Epstein, K., Dauria, E.F., & Dolce, L. (2019). Implementing a trauma-informed public health system in San Francisco, California. *Health Education and Behavior*, 46(2), 251–9. https://doi.org/10.1177/1090198118806942

Manitoba Trauma Informed Education & Resource Centre. (2021). *Organizational Self-Assessment*. Retrieved from https://trauma-informed.ca/trauma-informed-organizationssystems/organizational-self-assessment/

National Collaborating Centre for Determinants of Health. (2013). Let's talk: Public health roles for improving health equity. National Collaborating Centre for Determinants of Health, St Francis Xavier University. Retrieved from https://nccdh.ca/resources/entry/lets-talk-public-health-roles

National Collaborating Centre for Methods and Tools. (n.d.). *Evidence-informed decision making: A model for evidence-informed decision making in public health*. Retrieved from https://www.nccmt.ca/uploads/media/media/0001/02/5da8cf329a940bdd81a956a1984f05456c4a7910.pdf

Public Health Agency of Canada. (2013). *Preventing chronic disease strategic plan: 2013–2016*. Retrieved from https://epe.lac-bac.gc.ca/100/201/301/weekly_checklist/2014/internet/w14-10-U-E.html/collections/collection_2014/aspc-phac/HP35-39-2013-eng.pdf

Public Health Ontario. (2018). *Planning health promotion programs: introductory workbook* (5th ed.). Toronto, ON: Queen's Printer for Ontario.

Shonkoff, J.P., & Garner, A.S. (2012). The lifelong effects of early childhood adversity and toxic stress. *Pediatrics, 129*, e232–e246.

Sonu, S., Marvin, D., & Moore, C. (2021). The intersection and dynamics between COVID-19, health disparities, and adverse childhood experiences: "Intersection/dynamics between COVID-19, health disparities, and ACEs." *Journal of Child & Adolescent Trauma*, 1–10. https://doi.org/10.1007/s40653-021-00363-z

Tamarack Institute. (n.d.). *Collective impact*. Retrieved from https://www.tamarackcommunity.ca/collectiveimpact

Tebes, J.K., Champine, R.B., Matlin, S.L., & Strambler, M.J. (2019). Population health and trauma-informed practice: Implications for programs, systems, and policies. *American Journal of Community Psychology, 64*(3–4), 494–508. https://doi.org/10.1002/ajcp.12382

Tonelli, M., Tang, K.C., & Forest, P.G. (2020). Canada needs a "Health in All Policies" action plan now. *CMAJ, 192*(3), E61–E67. https://doi.org/10.1503/cmaj.190517

Trauma Informed Oregon. (2018a). Trauma Informed Care Screening Tool. Retrieved from https://traumainformedoregon.org/roadmap-trauma-informed-care/screening-tool/

Trauma Informed Oregon. (2018b). Trauma-informed care workgroup meeting guidelines. Retrieved from https://traumainformedoregon.org/wp-content/uploads/2016/01/Trauma-Informed-Care-Workgroup-Meeting-Guidelines.pdf

Weaver, L. (2017). Turf, trust, co-creation, and collective impact. *Tamarack Institute*. Retrieved from https://www.tamarackcommunity.ca/library/turf-trust-co-creation-collective-impact

2.4 The Trauma- and Violence-Informed Classroom, K–12

SUSAN RODGER, KATHY HIBBERT, MATTHEW SEREDA, AND JACQUELINE SPECHT

Drawing on research and practice experiences, this chapter presents critical issues and provides strategies to implement TVIC in kindergarten to Grade 12 (K–12) educational settings. These insights are then considered in terms of how they might inform teacher education, with a focus on serving teachers and the most marginalized learners/classrooms/schools. Examples from the field will be used to highlight implementation considerations.

TVIC can be and has been applied in both K–12 schools and professional teacher education settings. Using TVIC highlights critical issues including the relative "invisibility" of structural violence (i.e., the ways that we have excluded it from conversations and practice in education) and the challenges and opportunities inherent in encouraging uptake by teachers in schools. As with all crises, the COVID-19 pandemic and recent civil unrest have amplified the violence and vulnerability experienced by many students. Crises also expose the reality that interpersonal and structural violence are both always present in the lives of students and teachers.

A TVIC approach seeks to create safe, inclusive, and equitable environments for students and teachers. In this way, it is viewed as a responsive strategy for enhancing student engagement and availability for learning. Much like culturally relevant and responsive pedagogy (Ladson-Billings, 1995), TVIC encourages educators to build their instructional and assessment strategies in ways that allow students to see themselves reflected in their learning.

As educators prepare the optimal learning environment, considerations of their students' identities and lived experiences inform their ability to promote student achievement and well-being. Acknowledging the role that violence (both interpersonal and structural) can play in learning provokes questions about what may be relevant for students and their families and what supports or resources may be needed to create learning experiences that promote engagement and success. Prioritizing the lived experiences of students is central to creating a safe and inclusive learning environment and mitigates the risk that instructional and assessment strategies may be biased or inadvertently triggering/harmful to students who have experienced trauma and/or violence.

We are a group of psychologists and educators; three of us work in a Faculty of Education and one works in our partner school board. We contend that TVIC provides an important standard of care in teaching: it guides conversations in ways that provide entry into what can be difficult topics, helps us establish and respect boundaries, uses language that is respectful and inclusive, and guides care encounters between students and teachers to build safe and supportive learning environments. Its underlying principles guide classroom teachers' entry into conversations about issues such as racism *in this moment*, with particular attention to ensuring the safety of students – something identified as a gap in the "best practice" literature. Thus, by the end of this chapter, readers will understand the principles of TVIC as they apply to K–12 education; value the experiences of all people and the ways in which experiences of interpersonal and structural violence appear in schools (for students and teachers); know the language to use and how to address structural violence in the classroom and school with respect to relationships, pedagogy, and curriculum materials; and feel prepared with some strategies to notice, support, and build on strengths.

Case Examples

Case 1: Global Read Aloud

Every year, school districts around the world participate in the Global Read Aloud initiative, which is celebrated as an opportunity for students to form global connections to texts selected to shine a light on contemporary issues. As part of this initiative, a positive example of TVIC in action may be explored.

Choosing to participate in the Global Read Aloud initiative, a Grade 6 teacher chose the text "Indian No More" by Charlene McManis and Traci Sorell to read aloud with students. Understanding that the text contains examples of racism and discrimination toward Indigenous peoples, as well as racist language toward Black individuals, the teacher reached out to colleagues at the board level to request assistance with the instruction of these difficult topics. Consultations engaging board staff, the teacher, and Indigenous and Black educators led the teacher to take a TVIC and cultural safety approach to the text.

The approach. The approach required an orientation to the language that was used in the text, as well as a social, historical, and political contextualization of the language for the students. Prior to reading the text aloud, the teacher took the time to set parameters: he explained to the class that racist language, including the "n" word, would not be spoken out loud at any point in the reading of the text. He explained his reasons for this decision, highlighting the historic and present harm this word has caused to Black individuals and communities. He also sent a letter home to parents and guardians explaining his decision and inviting parent feedback.

By adopting this approach, the teacher accomplished several significant pedagogical turns:

- Prioritized the safety of Indigenous and Black students.
- Demonstrated sensitivity to the ways in which racism and violence can manifest themselves in classrooms where a TVIC approach is not implemented.
- Modelled the need to critically assess the language, context, and political-historical and social power of a text.
- Demonstrated respectful engagement of communities, including members of marginalized communities potentially affected, but also families who are learning along with us.
- Engaged in a meaningful discussion through difficult topics, rather than avoiding them due to the potential risks.

Case 2: Maya's Journey as an ESL Student through the "System"

Consider the following scenario – a common occurrence at schools across Canada:

Thursday morning, a knock on Ms Moddares's door was the entry point to a whole new educational opportunity for Maya, a Grade 3 student who had recently settled into the community from Syria. Maya gripped her father's hand tightly as he and the principal explained that she was experiencing a difficult transition, having fled her home country, resettling, and sadly, starting a new life without her mother and older brother.

Ms Moddares found Maya a desk and introduced her to the rest of the class. She placed her desk in a group of students that she was confident would welcome her and help her navigate this new classroom and its expectations. Over the next week, Ms Moddares conducted different assessments to try to get a grasp of what the starting point for Maya might be. It quickly became clear that she spoke no English. The school did not have a large population of English as a Second Language learners, so the only support available was a consultant at the Board of Education, who served all schools in the district.

Ms Moddares found an Arabic-speaking graduate student at a nearby university and worked with her to create dual-language books out of the small readings available in the class. She also helped create a basic list of vocabulary that enabled Maya to learn the English words and the rest of the class to learn the Arabic words. Despite efforts like these, academic progress for Maya was slow. At midterm, the principal requested a psychoeducational assessment. As they were unable to conduct a first-language assessment, it was conducted in English. The principal was especially concerned about the quality of her past education in Syria and how long it may have been since she had been in school. This information was not available from Maya's father, nor were records available.

Since it was impossible to conduct the assessment fully, and therefore to identify any specific processing deficits, the result of the assessment was mixed. To access resources, Ms Moddares carefully completed the referral for IPRC (Identification, Placement, and Review Committee) with the resource teacher, identifying all of the things that Maya was unable to do that would be expected for a girl her age. The assessment, and thus the programing that was recommended, put Maya fully three years behind her peers. The IPRC committee "placed" Maya in a special education program. This placement meant that Maya worked with a special education teacher in her school twice a week for forty minutes. One of those days, the teacher came into Maya's classroom and worked with her at her desk. The second day, Maya went to a resource room and worked with other children learning basic rote memorization of a new alphabet and numerical system.

The approach. Consider the approach in Case 2. Ms Moddares, the principal, and the special education team are all caring individuals. They work to make sure that Maya is physically safe and comfortable, but with limited resources. Their overriding fear is that she has fallen behind and that she will continue to fall further behind. They assume that her prior schooling was substandard. They largely overlook the emotional trauma she has experienced in favour of filling out referrals to secure additional resources to ensure that she is "assessed, tracked, and then programmed." The system requires that a history be taken and that strengths be listed. However, the resource teacher knows that to compete for limited resources, she must work hard to build a case that identifies significant deficits. The special education system in and of itself is traumatizing in that students are othered because they are assumed to be less capable of learning than their peers. The system perpetuates the myth that students who have learning issues need something different and special rather than a teacher who believes that all students belong as well as the skill set to teach in universal ways and the confidence to do so. The special education system provides an education based on presumed deficits, rather than one that focuses on the strengths and competencies that should be promoted in all learners. Because knowledge about her prior schooling is unavailable, and because it is not possible to assess her in her first language, an assessment is conducted by an English-speaking assessor, using English testing materials. There is no discussion about whether Maya's lack of progress may be related to the trauma of leaving her home, the likely violence that she has experienced and witnessed, and the unexplained absence of her mother and older brother.

It is not sufficient that the professionals in Maya's case are caring and well-intended. It is critical to ensure that all educators grow their understanding of the significant role that trauma and violence have on learning and how to take a more effective approach in these circumstances.

TVIC in K–12 Schools

As we have illustrated through the cases, taking a TVIC approach shifts the focus: it is a proactive approach to considerations of trauma and violence rather than a reactive approach to harm. It requires educators to think actively in advance about structural bias, systemic barriers, and the barriers likely to exist in schools. It provides a set of considerations that map a way through the difficult conversations that students and educators must engage with if learning is to be meaningful.

TVIC and the Education of Teachers

An effective way to influence thinking at a system level is through the Initial Teacher Education (ITE) program. In Ontario, Canada, the ITE program is comprised of four terms, with equal time allocated to coursework and practica. Roles and responsibilities for teachers are guided by the Ontario College of Teachers' (OCT) Standards for the Profession and Ethical Standards (Ontario College of Teachers, 1999). The TVIC approach aligns with the Ethical Standard of Care: "The ethical standard of Care includes compassion, acceptance, interest, and insight for developing students' potential. Members express their commitment to students' well-being and learning through positive influence, professional judgment, and empathy in practice." The OCT standards establish what is expected of teacher candidates as they move from the university class to the K–12 classroom. To reinforce our collaborative efforts, a reciprocal relationship between universities and school boards is critical as we plan and design learning experiences for the next generation of teachers (Sharma, 2018).

One of the central tenets of TVIC is that institutional support is needed; it is not something that can be satisfactorily practised by individuals within systems that fail to change. A TVIC approach is most successful when the model has been universally adopted and schools, communities, and universities work together. This collaborative approach ensures a seamless transition to responsibilities and expectations for teacher candidates (Essex, Alexiadou, & Zwozdiak-Myers, 2019) as they move from one classroom context to another. Investment in preparing in-service teachers to understand the TVIC approach has taken on new urgency now that Ontario is moving once again to "destream" students in secondary schools. Streaming requires students to choose whether they will enter an "applied" or "academic" programmatic stream when they begin secondary school. The concept has been contentious: attempts to destream

Ontario's schools were initiated in the early 1990s by a social democratic government only to be reversed when a conservative party came to power a year later. Research has consistently shown that streaming disproportionately affects the rates of graduation and progression to post-secondary education for Black students, students living in poverty, and those with disabilities (Herbert, 2017; Kinnon, 2016). Investing in the preparation of our future generation of teachers, alongside investment in continuing teacher education for in-service teachers, will "ready" the profession to implement TVIC and consider issues such as streaming from this more structural lens.

Adapting and Applying TVIC and TVIC Principles

The TVIC approach engages critical reflection and questioning skills to challenge traditional ways of thinking; it also invites people to examine their own implicit biases, assumptions, and world views and provides a gentle "on-ramp" to develop and share new ways of thinking, feeling, and doing in service to clients, students, patients, and colleagues.

Part of the work of an initial teacher education program involves inculcating those being trained with the norms of the profession through implicit and explicit messages. The TVIC principles offer those of us working in ITE some tangible guidance when developing program outlines and syllabi, which traditionally detail disciplinary or pedagogical priorities. Prioritizing a student's assets allows us to view our students in terms of what they are able to do confidently. It also helps educators think about how to build a pedagogical program that relies on fostering strong collaborative institutional support to create safe and welcoming communities, school-based teams, and a shared understanding of how critical the learning environment – which all of us contribute to creating – is for students who may have experienced trauma and/or violence.

In the context of both the preparation of teacher candidates for inclusive classrooms and professional development for in-service teachers, TVIC can be successfully adopted as a framework that provides a way to learn about and create anti-oppressive classrooms at the same time as it encourages personal and professional growth (Rodger et al., 2020). The four principles of TVIC are provided below, with examples of how these are enacted, as outlined in the two case studies in terms of relationships. Two key domains identified in prior research as central to promoting TVIC in K–12 education are (a) developing and leveraging strong and positive relationships with students and families through an understanding of power and agency, and (b) grasping the relationship between pedagogy, teaching materials, and outcomes on the one hand (Rodger et al., 2020) and strong relationships between schools and communities on the other:

Principle 1. Build awareness and understanding of trauma and violence, including structural violence:
- Understand the impact of interpersonal and structural violence on healthy development and learning for students.
- Consider trauma from an equity/inclusion perspective, which aligns with the professional standards for teachers.
- Cultural humility – assume that students in our classrooms will have experienced trauma and violence, and teach to the most vulnerable person in the room (even if we don't know who that is) (Hook et al., 2013).

Principle 2. Emphasize safety and trust, building healthy relationships:
- Adopt the stance of cultural safety, and understand that language matters.
- Model respect for self and others.

Principle 3. Foster opportunities for choice, collaboration, and connection:
- Employ a universal design for a learning approach that serves all learners.
- Involve students in the planning of their learning and assessment through collaborative decision-making and choice.

Principle 4. Use a strengths-based and capacity-building approach to support students:
- Acknowledge the effects of historical and social conditions.
- Work from students' strengths while supporting skill development.
- Maintain high expectations for all students.

In the two tables below (tables 2.4.1 and 2.4.2), we have applied the TVIC principles to our case studies as an illustration.

The design of effective and meaningful initial teacher education requires that we make explicit choices, acknowledging the slippages between the intended, enacted, and null curriculum (what we plan to do, what we actually do, and what gets left out). There are many, sometimes competing, components to building a TVIC-oriented teacher education program:

- Disciplinary traditions (defining the role and scope of practice; interrogating practices just because "this is the way we have always done it").
- Continual improvement:
  o Professional accreditation requirements (staying current with legislation and preparation to participate in qualifying examinations).
  o Higher education quality council outcomes and review cycles.
- Cultural relevance and the context in which professional education was developed and continues to operate (often, within the dominant culture) (Ladson-Billings, 1995).
- Collective responsibility – that is, doing what is needed, for the right reason, at the right time (Hibbert, 2012).

Table 2.4.1 TVIC principles applied to Case 1: Global read aloud

Principles→	1: Build trauma and violence awareness and understanding	2: Emphasize safety and trust and building relationships	3: Foster opportunities for choice, collaboration, and connection	4: Use a strengths-based and capacity-building approach to support students
Developing and leveraging strong positive relationships with an understanding of power and agency.	• Provide guidance and explain to the class that racist language, including the "n" word, would not be spoken out loud at any point in the reading of the text.	• Through words and actions, show an understanding of the teacher's responsibilities for the safety of students and families.	• Letter home to families sharing the plan and inviting feedback.	• In preparing students for learning, the teacher demonstrates their confidence that the students will engage, learn, and be part of a community of learners, supporting one another.
The relationship between pedagogy, teaching materials, and outcomes.	• Be aware of the power of language and its relationship to experiences of violence.	• Acknowledge the power of the teacher and system in selecting this book.	• Reach out to other teachers and, at the board level, request assistance with difficult topics.	• Teacher provides context and highlights the historic and present harm this language has caused to Black individuals and communities.

Ultimately, we seek to prepare teachers who bring professional agency to their curriculum-making (Ott & Hibbert, 2021), who recognize the ways in which all of the policies, material resources and conditions, and current and past learning environments work together to shape the experiences of students – including the trajectory of those experiences, depending on the path we lay out for them.

Practical Strategies/Guidance for Individual Practitioners and System Leaders

Within systems, leaders and even individual teachers have multiple opportunities every day to think differently about their approach to teaching and decision-making. Sometimes provocation is needed to disrupt taken-for-granted

Table 2.4.2 TVIC principles applied to Case 2: Maya's journey through the system

Principles →	1: Build trauma and violence awareness and understanding	2: Emphasize safety and trust and building relationships	3: Foster opportunities for choice, collaboration, and connection	4: Use a strengths-based and capacity building approach to support students
Developing and leveraging strong positive relationships with an understanding of power and agency.	<ul><li>Help teachers better understand students' "out of school" lives (Ministry of Education, 2009).</li><li>Focus first on providing a safe and healing community</li><li>Build trust and compassion, and allow friendships to form.</li></ul>	<ul><li>Through words and actions, understand the responsibilities of the teacher for the safety of students and families.</li><li>Find ways to celebrate Maya's culturally bound knowledge and skills within the classroom, to demonstrate the value she brings.</li><li>Work with community resources to ensure that support for appropriate health/nutrition/ hygiene/clothing needs are met.</li></ul>	<ul><li>Leverage Arabic-speaking community members and/or technologies to learn more about Maya's past learning experiences in Syria.</li><li>Assess strengths not dependent on English (e.g., music, arts, athletics, technologies).</li><li>Employ non-verbal partnering pedagogies to ensure inclusion</li></ul>	<ul><li>Develop a program that allows the student to lead with and through their strengths and begin supporting skills alongside those opportunities to grow, developing a sense of security and confidence.</li><li>Ensure that teachers recognize that differentiating instruction to accommodate language needs also supports socioemotional development (Cummins & Early, 2015).</li></ul>
The relationship between pedagogy, teaching materials, and outcomes.	<ul><li>Be aware of the power of language and the relationship to experiences of violence.</li></ul>	<ul><li>Acknowledge the power of the system in directing the course of Maya's educational pathways.</li><li>Acknowledge that English-language proficiency takes 5–7 years, so plan from that timeline, not from the "normal" timeline of English first-language students.</li></ul>	<ul><li>Seek support at the system level, and where that is limited, seek support through the community (local) or more broadly through the online community.</li></ul>	<ul><li>Teacher provides context and highlights the harm a lack of knowledge of ESL strategies and supports have caused to individuals and communities.</li></ul>

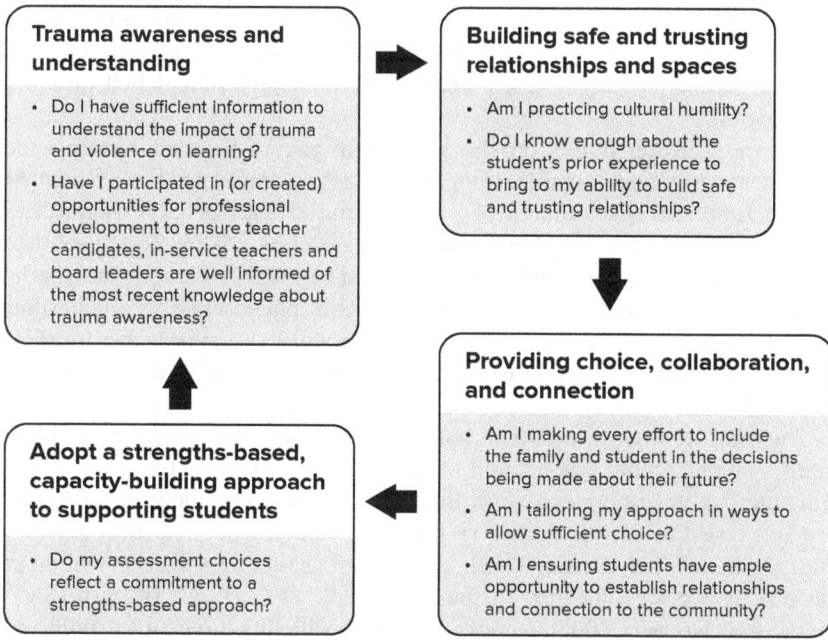

Figure 2.4.1 Example of a trauma- and violence-informed care heuristic. Copyright, the authors.

policies that may have been designed in the absence of better information. Policy change often lags behind practice needs. At such times, it is helpful to adopt a heuristic (figure 2.4.1) that allows professionals seeking to improve the educational experience of students to expand their options in ways that best serve the students.

Lessons Learned

The cases presented in this chapter offer several outcomes to guide us when applying TVIC approaches to our own classrooms and schools. First, it is important to provide professional learning to all members of the school system so that they have a common language and a shared appreciation and commitment. Teachers who have learned that a TVIC approach is expected within their school will know there are colleagues who can support them in their desire to use, for example, the Read Aloud book even though it contains hurtful and violent language. They will know that the very lesson of not using the n-word emphasizes safety and trust for students who would be traumatized by that word, thus building awareness and understanding in those who would not experience such trauma. In Case 2, we saw that a prioritization of the system's need to access resources to support the student may have unintentionally resulted in the application of pathologizing practices that too often lead to deficit-oriented pedagogies.

Our next lesson builds on the knowledge gained through system-wide approaches to professional learning. Our teacher candidates have benefited greatly from the development of a shared understanding between faculties of education and boards of education (Rodger et al., 2020). To consolidate that understanding, we developed and offered workshops for associate teachers (those who teach new teachers in practicum placements) in our partner boards. Associate teachers were then able to model TVIC approaches for their teacher candidates. Ongoing evaluation of the impacts of these strategies is required.

The third lesson gestures to an issue we encounter across education. Politicians, parents, school leaders, and teachers are often looking for a "quick fix." This may be in response to work intensification and the adoption of ministry and board initiatives that carry multiple requirements and minimal support (Williamson & Myhill, 2008). The pace of change and the sheer number of initiatives place educators in the passive role of "receivers of knowledge" (Hibbert & Iannacci, 2005), who try to keep up with little time for learning and self-reflection, with the result that they want to be told what to do. These are reasons why TVIC approaches must be seen as a way of *being* rather than as an *approach to teaching*. The principles and strategies learned and demonstrated will go beyond individual encounters and classrooms and, holistically and cohesively, change the teaching and learning culture for all.

Change can be difficult. When introducing a TVIC approach it will be necessary to demonstrate that the model helps us move away from a system that may work for *some* students toward a system designed to support *all* students. We will also need to take note of the need to strengthen teacher agency (Priestley, Edwards, Priestley & Miller, 2012) and to support their ability to create safe and inclusive environments for all students. What is most important for the classroom teacher is support for these changes. Our message to teachers must be that "this work is difficult, and we are all in it together for the betterment of our society."

School leaders must also ensure that they create a safe and supportive environment for teachers to do this work in their classroom communities. Teachers need visible and material support that demonstrates a shared commitment to the value of TVIC. We can never know what people have experienced and what background they bring – nor do we need to know all of these details to provide a safe experience for students and for teachers. We must strive to build healthy relationships and trust in our teachers if we are to bring that to the youth in our schools.

2.4 The Trauma- and Violence-Informed Classroom, K–12   149

Conclusion

We acknowledge the emotional labour and moral distress faced by teachers within the classroom. As the COVID-19 lockdown began, for example, teachers knew which students would be hungry, unsafe, or otherwise not supported in their learning at home. It was overwhelming for them to have this knowledge at the same time as they worked tirelessly to ensure that their students learned. Here are some important ways to build towards the future with TVIC in schools:

- Individual teachers will require material and environmental organizational/professional supports if they are to be successful in applying TVIC in the classroom.
- School systems may not be responsive to educators' own experiences with trauma and violence, so educator / staff well-being also needs to be a consideration when addressing a systems approach to TVIC (see chapter 4.4).
- Specific strategies on a path to trauma- and violence-informed schools and classrooms include both professional development opportunities for educators to learn about TVIC and how it affects their practice, but also, updates to policies that acknowledge and promote TVIC in K-12 education. Those policies must be accompanied by appropriate supports and resources to implement and sustain TVIC at every level.

KEY MESSAGES AND IMPLICATIONS

- A TVIC approach to education holds promise for healing not only the trauma and violence that our learners bring to the classroom, but also the trauma and violence experienced by teachers, who too often bear the brunt of political blaming and shaming for all student achievement in ways that deflect attention away from failures to address broad and costly societal issues, such as poverty.
- As we return to a "post-pandemic" educational reality, the need to attend to trauma and violence will have only grown. Now is the time to deeply understand that there can be no optimal learning if the conditions outlined in the TVIC approach are not first addressed.
- It is time for healing and restoring, and forging new, healthier, TVIC-based learning pathways.

ADDITIONAL RESOURCES

- Link to GTV Ed specific tools: https://gtvincubator.uwo.ca/resources
- ACEs video: https://youtu.be/W-8jTTIsJ7Q

REFERENCES

Cummins, J., & Early, M. (2015). *Big ideas for expanding minds: Teaching English language learners across the curriculum.* Don Mills, ON: Pearson Canada Inc.

Essex, J., Alexiadou, N., & Zwozdiak-Myers, P. (2019). Understanding inclusion in teacher education – a view from student teachers in England. *International Journal of Inclusive Education.* https://doi.org/10.1080/13603116.2019.1614232

Herbert, C. (2017). Viewing the Toronto education system through an anti-racist framework: The systematic oppression of Black youth in Toronto based on geography, race, and class. In A. Ayan & A. N. Obeyesekere (Eds.), *New framings on anti-racism and resistance* (pp. 143–59). Leidem, the Netherlands: Brill.

Hibbert, K. (2012). Cultivating capacity: Learning & diversity in professional education. In A. Pitman & A. Kinsella (Eds.), *Phronesis as professional knowledge* (pp. 731–8). Rotterdam, the Netherlands: Sense Publishing.

Hibbert, K., & Iannacci, L. (2005). From dissemination to discernment: The commodification of literacy instruction and the fostering of "good teacher consumerism." *Reading Teacher, 58*(8), 716–27. Retrieved from http://www.jstor.org/stable/20204299

Hook, J.N., Davis, D.E., Owen, J., Worthington Jr., E.L., & Utsey, S.O. (2013). Cultural humility: Measuring openness to culturally diverse clients. *Journal of Counseling Psychology, 60*(3), 353–66. https://doi.org/10.1037/a0032595

Kinnon, E. (2016). *(In)equity and academic streaming in Ontario: Effects on students and teachers and how to overcome these* (Master's thesis, University of Toronto, Toronto, Canada). Retrieved from https://tspace.library.utoronto.ca/handle/1807/72216

Ladson-Billings, G. (1995). Toward a theory of culturally relevant pedagogy. *American Educational Research Journal, 32*(3), 465–91. http://dx.doi.org/10.3102/00028312032003465

Ministry of Education (2009). *Students from refugee backgrounds: A guide for teachers and schools.* Ministry of Education, British Columbia. Retrieved from https://www2.gov.bc.ca/assets/gov/education/administration/kindergarten-to-grade-12/diverse-student-needs/students-from-refugee-backgrounds-guide.pdf

Ontario College of Teachers. (1999). *Standards of practice for the teaching profession.* Toronto: Ontario College of Teachers. Retrieved from https://www.oct.ca/public/professional-standards/ethical-standards

Ott, M., & Hibbert, K. (2021). Designing assessment for professional agency. In J. Nickel & M. Jacobsenn (Eds.), *Preparing teachers as curriculum designers* (pp. 21–55). Canadian Association of Teacher Education (CATE) Polygraph. Retrieved from https://prism.ucalgary.ca/bitstream/handle/1880/113294/Preparing-Teachers-as-Curriculum-Designers_ebook_FINAL.pdf?sequence=1&isAllowed=y

Priestley, M., Edwards, R., Priestley, A., & Miller, K. (2012). Teacher agency in curriculum making: Agents of change and spaces for manoeuvre. *Curriculum Inquiry, 42*(2), 191–214. https://doi.org/10.1111/j.1467-873X.2012.00588.x

Rodger, S., Bird, R., Hibbert, K., Johnson, A.M., Specht, J., & Wathen, C.N. (2020). Initial teacher education and trauma and violence informed care in the classroom: Preliminary results from an online teacher education course. *Psychology in the Schools, 57*, 1798–814. https://doi.org/10.1002/pits.22373

Sharma, U. (2018). Preparing to teach in inclusive classrooms. *Oxford Research Encyclopedia of Education*, 1–22. https://doi.org/10.1093/acrefore/9780190264093.013.113

Williamson J., & Myhill, M. (2008) Under "constant bombardment": Work intensification and the teachers' role. In D. Johnson & R. Maclean (Eds.), *Teaching: Professionalization, development, and leadership* (pp. 25–43). Dordrecht, the Netherlands: Springer. https://doi.org/10.1007/978-1-4020-8186-6_3

2.5 Developing and Implementing Trauma- and Violence-Informed Physical Activity Programing

FRANCINE DARROCH, GABRIELA GONZALEZ MONTANER,
JESSICA WEBB, MICHELLE PAQUETTE, AND COLLEEN VARCOE

This chapter maps out how concepts of trauma- and violence-informed care have been adopted in the realm of physical activity and health promotion. Drawing on research and program development experiences, we provide key lessons learned in developing and implementing trauma- and violence-informed physical activity (TVIPA) programing with and for pregnant and parenting women facing complex systemic challenges related to health, housing, poverty, and barriers to accessing existing health and/or social services. We suggest how these lessons may be useful for a range of organizations seeking to integrate or enhance physical activity in their programing.

Physical activity has been identified as a key public health priority to help prevent chronic disease and promote overall positive health (Kohl et al., 2012). Physical activity is defined as including all muscular movement with an increase in energy expenditure (World Health Organization, n.d.), whereas leisure-time physical activity (i.e., behaviour consciously aimed at improving physical fitness) is typically considered sport and exercise (Steinbach & Graf, 2008). The literature suggests engaging in regular physical activity can improve mental health as well as decrease depression, anxiety, sleep disturbances, and other health conditions associated with post-traumatic stress disorder (PTSD) (Babson et al., 2015; Goldstein et al., 2018). This may be of particular importance to people who have experienced high levels of trauma and violence, in that physical activity may be a useful adjunct to usual care (e.g., talk therapy, medications) to improve health outcomes for individuals with PTSD or for those who do not have diagnoses (or who do not actually align with the notion of PTSD). Despite the widely accepted benefits of physical activity for populations affected by trauma, inequities in access and uptake of physical activity remain (Clark et al., 2014; Frisby et al., 2007).

TVIPA (box 2.5.1) is an approach to programing adapted from trauma- and violence-informed care (TVIC) as developed and evaluated in primary health care (see chapter 2.1). Browne and colleagues (2012) described TVIC as "recognizing that most people affected by systemic inequities and structural violence have experienced, and often continue to experience, varying forms of violence with traumatic impact. Such care consists of respectful empowerment practices informed by understanding the pervasiveness and effects of trauma and violence" (p. 5). Wathen and Varcoe (2019) build on trauma-informed care, in which providers create a safe environment for clients based on understanding the impact of trauma on health and behaviours with the goal of preventing further victimization. Importantly, and as articulated in chapter 1.2, TVIC draws explicit attention to *structural violence*, that is, the ways societies are organized to harm some people, such as through absolute and relative poverty, systemic racism, and other forms of systemic discrimination, exclusion, and disadvantage.

Conventional physical activity programs seldom account for social and structural inequities. Thus, a TVIPA approach calls for physical activity providers to understand and account for the intersecting effects of systemic, structural, and interpersonal violence. Based on a scoping review of existing trauma-informed approaches to movement, the following tenets were identified as central to this approach: safety, communication, modifications/adaptations, instructor attributes (training in a trauma-informed approach specific to the discipline, e.g., yoga), and mindful awareness exercises (Darroch et al., 2020). However, this review noted a paucity of research on the use of trauma-informed approaches outside of yoga (Darroch et al., 2020). There have been calls to increase the uptake of TVI approaches to physical activity (Darroch et al., 2020; Ponic et al., 2014). Despite this, TVIPA is not yet well-developed conceptually, and there has been limited empirical research examining its effectiveness. Furthermore, little is known about how to enhance the provision of physical activity and address inequities for populations affected by violence and trauma. In particular, there is no literature at all outlining how to do so in the context of structural violence. So we have drawn on the principles of TVIC to co-develop and implement TVIPA programing with/for pregnant and parenting women facing high levels of disadvantage, with the goal of extending understanding of how to do so effectively.

BOX 2.5.1 TRAUMA- AND VIOLENCE-INFORMED PHYSICAL ACTIVITY

Trauma- and violence-informed physical activity (TVIPA) is an approach that considers and accounts for the intersecting effects of systemic, structural, and interpersonal violence in the development, implementation, and delivery of physical activity programs. It is crucial to create safe, appropriate, appealing, and effective methods to engage all individuals in physical activity to ensure equitable access to the benefits of exercise. Anyone can benefit from a TVIPA program; however, physical activity programs that are not trauma- and violence-informed risk excluding people who have experienced trauma and structural forms of violence. TVIPA enables an equitable, accessible, and person-centred approach to physical activity; this is a change with the potential to improve physical health, mental well-being, and social connections for people experiencing numerous barriers to physical activity.

Case Example: Taking Steps: Warrior Women's Wellness

Research that led to the development of Taking Steps: Warrior Women's Wellness (Taking Steps) was initiated in 2016 in response to inequities in access to and uptake of physical activity (Clark et al., 2014; Frisby et al., 2007) and community need. The Downtown Eastside of Vancouver (DTES), home to approximately 18,000 people, has been identified as the lowest-income neighbourhood in Canada (Campbell et al., 2009). Residents experience high rates of precarious housing, poverty, racism, substance use, communicable disease, and mental illness compared to Vancouver's general population (Linden et al., 2013; McNeil et al., 2014; Miewald & Ostry, 2014). This community is often stigmatized and pathologized by researchers, enforcement agencies, media, and the general public. Often unnoticed is the resilience, innovation, and cross-community solidarity and mobilization of people and organizations to impact change. Most residents of the DTES are adults; 38 per cent of them live within a family structure, and single parents lead 24 per cent of those families (City of Vancouver, 2013). This has resulted in multiple barriers to positive physical activity engagement for pregnant and parenting women living in the DTES (Darroch et al., 2022). TVIPA programing was identified as a means to cultivate appropriate, accessible, and desirable physical activity programs and resources. Through community-based participatory research (CBPR), intersectionality theory, and application of the four principles of TVIC to program development, design, and implementation, Taking Steps was developed to serve as a TVIPA program for pregnant and parenting women who live in or access services in the DTES. The program was co-created with (and for) pregnant and parenting women facing complex challenges related to health, housing, poverty, and barriers to accessing existing health and social services.

CBPR is a collaborative approach to research that aims to equitably involve all partners in the research process. Central to CBPR is engaging the strengths of all those involved while collaborating with community members to identify and address an important issue (Minkler & Wallerstein, 2003). In the Taking

2.5 Developing and Implementing TVI Physical Activity Programing   155

Figure 2.5.1 CBPR-specific process. Copyright 2021, the authors.

Steps project, this meant that women were central to the research process as well as program development. In addition, we took an intersectional approach to understand how women's identities, and choices, were formed by the overlap of various social factors, including poverty, ability, race, and gender (Crenshaw, 1991). Key aims of this work were to honour the lived experience and knowledge of women, commit to genuine collaboration in every aspect of the research and program development process, co-produce knowledge, and take action to directly support women to be physically active (including addressing individual, organizational, and structural barriers). We engaged in a very successful process that might serve as a model for a broad range of organizations seeking to implement such programing with or without a research or evaluation component (see figure 2.5.1).

As a first step, we assessed community needs in three ways: an environmental scan, focus groups with women in the community, and interviews with service providers working in the neighbourhood. Through this process we also formed a community advisory board consisting of six community members, three service providers (at what would become our host site), and two researchers. The initial needs assessment revealed that women living in the DTES wanted to access physical activity programing but were experiencing barriers, such as cost, lack of child care, equipment, and clothing, discrimination, mental health problems, lack of women-only spaces, and general safety concerns. Addressing the barriers identified by the advisory board was central to the conceptualization and development of the program. Women on the board steered the development of Taking Steps by providing preliminary and ongoing consultation and guidance for all aspects of research and program development. The environmental scan identified organizations, community spaces, and classes in the community that aligned with our work, and this led to various collaborations, including access to weight training, kickboxing, hip hop classes, yoga, and hiking outings following the pilot program.

After assessment of community needs and consultations with the advisory board, we hosted focus groups with community members to help us conceptualize what a trauma- and violence-informed approach to physical activity could look like. Community members identified barriers to physical activity and ways to overcome them, and this guided the conceptualization of an appropriate physical activity program. Women in the focus groups identified several key considerations for TVIPA programming, including these: train all staff in TVIPA, be mindful of the potential histories of all clients, learn skills for preventing and recognizing triggers, make the space welcoming for all members of the community, provide clear information and expectations, encourage shared planning and decision-making, involve staff and clients in identifying strategies, services, and programs, and respond in non-judgmental ways. Women expressed interest in trialing a walking group, emphasizing the importance of an activity that was accessible for a broad group and inclusive of children. After focus groups and advisory board consultation, we piloted a weekly walking program.

The walking group met once a week on Friday mornings at a well-used community space that offered women and children breakfast and coffee. From there, the group walked one of three predictable routes, which allowed participants to anticipate path and length. Of critical importance to women was knowing what to expect, especially given the complexity of the DTES and their potential experiences of trauma, substance use, and local supports.

After four months of pilot programming and monthly advisory board meetings, we integrated the feedback and scaled up programing by engaging partner organizations and instructors interested in hosting classes; many of them were interested in providing TVIPA but had little or no experience working in a trauma-informed context. Under the guidance of the community advisory board, we created a TVI training session appropriate for a broad audience, to support organizations and instructors as they enhanced their resources, services, and programing for individuals who might access their organizations or classes. During the training sessions we focused on individual-level strategies as well as on organizational structures and policies to build trauma and violence awareness into the programing. Specifically, we wanted to ensure a basic level of preparedness for leading programing with women. Training included (a) a brief overview of trauma and its psychosocial impacts on individuals, (b) the connection between physical activity and trauma, (c) how Taking

Table 2.5.1 Principles of TVIPA as co-defined by the community

1. Trauma awareness • Build trauma and violence awareness into the culture of your organization. • Ensure that structures and policies reflect the culture. • TVIPA training for staff. • Use supportive language. • Recognize that there is no "one size fits all" approach. • Be mindful of the potential histories of all clients. • Learn skills for preventing and recognizing triggers.	2. Emphasis on safety • Make the space welcoming. • Provide confidential areas to discuss free or sliding scale rates. • Offer gender neutral restrooms. • Private changeroom options. • Establish safety protocols for clients and staff. • Provide clear information and expectations. • Ensure awareness of boundaries. • Use supportive language. • Use accessible verbal and written language. • Take a non-judgmental approach. • Use adaptable and alternative techniques.
3. Foster choice and collaboration • Provide clear information and expectations. • Maintain awareness of boundaries. • Use supportive language. • Use accessible verbal and written language. • Take a non-judgmental approach. • Use adaptable and alternative techniques. • Provide non-judgmental responses. • Provide options for the session. • Actively listen. • Provide positive feedback. • Support decision-making.	4. Strengths-based and capacity-building approach • Allow sufficient time for meaningful engagement. • Present program options that can be tailored to individual needs, strengths, and contexts. • Provide staff with ongoing opportunities for skill and knowledge development. • Help clients identify strengths. • Acknowledge the effects of historical and structural conditions. • Encourage personal decision-making. • Give motivating constructive feedback.

Steps was implemented, and (d) the principles of TVIPA, as defined by the women involved in the program and aligned with the four TVIC principles (table 2.5.1).

The final iteration of Taking Steps had two days a week of programing: walking on one day, and on the other, engagement in month-long introductions to various physical activities available in the community such as yoga, boxing, soccer, hiking, strength training, self-defence, aqua-aerobics, hip hop, and powwow dance classes. Women received two bus tickets each time they participated and a $10 gift card for every three times they attended the program;

children could attend the activities, and/or free child-minding was provided on-site.

Taking Steps provided programing to more than one hundred women and seventy-five children over two years, with women participating more than six hundred times. Despite the complexity of their lives and the precarious nature of their housing, women sustained their involvement, with attendance ranging from two to seventy-five sessions. Every community or academic presentation and publication included at least one each of a community member, a community partner, and a researcher. The women also participated in a documentary about their experiences and in the development of a toolkit to support TVIPA, and in a photovoice project (see Resources, below).

Taking Steps included an optional research component in which fifty-six women took part (baseline, three-month, six-month, and one-year assessments, which included completion of a questionnaire and a semi-structured interview). This sample of women was closely representative of the broader Taking Steps group: 60 per cent identified as Indigenous; 47.3 per cent reported being in a relationship with a partner; and 65.5 per cent lived in public social or supportive housing. The vast majority of participants (93%) reported experiences of discrimination and stigma in their daily lives and expressed that these experiences, along with histories and ongoing experiences of trauma and/or violence, were significant barriers to physical activity.

Lessons Learned

In this section, readers will reflect on the considerations needed in the process of co-creating and developing TVIPA programing and on how our approach might be adapted to related programing. We outline specific lessons learned based on our research findings and experience in the field.

System Level: Stigma, Unstable Funding, and Access Inequity

The systems in which physical activity programs or resources are offered are typically not designed to respond to the needs of individuals who have experienced trauma or are experiencing ongoing violence. The ways in which cultures, policies, and practices influence the conditions in which TVIPA programing is offered must be considered and addressed at the systems level.

Through our research and program implementation, we learned a great deal from partners in the field who have worked in the DTES community to create accessible physical activity opportunities for community members. Partners cited a lack of funding available for recreation focused on women living

2.5 Developing and Implementing TVI Physical Activity Programing

in poverty; social justice organizations must prioritize funds for housing and food and, ultimately, for keeping people alive. Thus, women who live on lower incomes and face other barriers are disproportionately restricted from physical activity. Physical activity is often perceived as "leisure"; despite interest from the community, it is rarely identified as a priority for this population by policy-makers or organizations attempting to address competing social determinants of health.

In line with challenges of access to consistent and reliable funding, there has been a recent shift toward funding organizations committed to innovative and short-term pilot programs; while this approach certainly has advantages, some smaller community organizations must struggle to secure funding for ongoing core operational costs. This reflects the lack of political will and/or commitment to allocating resources to create equitable opportunities for physical activity. The scarcity of programming available to pregnant and parenting women reflects the political choices being made and the historical inequities these women face. Service providers described a lack of funding to implement and maintain programs for their clients. Such funding decisions further perpetuate inequities.

While there are existing policies and programs in place to support physical activity, they often do not account for individuals experiencing the greatest number of barriers. The women in our program had access to Vancouver's Leisure Access Program, which offers basic recreation programs and services for low-income residents at reduced cost (City of Vancouver, n.d). However, the participants in our program noted that the reduced rates were still a challenge for people living on fixed incomes or in shelters. As one mother noted, "even $1.25 can be too much to pay some days." Moreover, women had limited knowledge of existing leisure access programs and other community services. Sustained efforts must be made to ensure that people are aware of these programs and supported to process often complicated applications.

Despite the indisputable evidence of the benefits of physical activity (Babson et al., 2015; Goldstein et al., 2018), especially for pregnant and parenting women (Mottola et al., 2019), there remains a dearth of physical activity programs in the DTES and other low-income communities. Because provision of physical activity is often not connected across systems of care (such as health care and community-based services and supports), we identified a need for health/social services organizations/providers to develop partnerships with physical activity organizations and ensure effective referrals and supports to address inequities in access for specific populations (box 2.5.2). The success of effective TVIPA programs hinges on securing adequate funding, collaboration across systems, and buy-in from community partners and organizations.

> **BOX 2.5.2 WHAT IS REQUIRED?**
>
> - Women-only, private, gender-neutral spaces, with child care.
> - Staff who are flexible, as well as gentle but encouraging, who use "no touch," and who do self-care and debriefing.
> - Access to comprehensive supports, including appropriate workout clothing and equipment.
> - Strength-based approaches that foster relationships and social connections.

Organizational Level: Safety, Skills, and Supports

Based on the tenets of our participatory approach, we sought to work with organizations that were already offering services for DTES community members. These organizations were doing great work; even so, some significant changes were required to better meet the needs of the pregnant and parenting women in our study. Based on these experiences, we recommend that the following program aspects be considered:

Women's privacy, safety, and space. Women-only, private, gender-neutral, with child care. Our participants identified that a women's-only space was necessary for them to feel comfortable moving their bodies and trying new things. Said one Taking Steps participant: "It's a safe environment, and because it's no guys allowed also, so a lot of women, like I know for myself like I used to work the sex trade ... so coming here I don't have to worry about that."

Organizations should consider offering privacy screens or women's-only hours. Also, in the spirit of our intersectional framework, where feasible, we encouraged organizations to transform their change areas and washroom configurations to be more gender-neutral and offer private areas for changing. Third, because child care was identified as a significant barrier to engaging in physical activity, we prioritized ensuring appropriate child care for our participants. Based on the design of our program and the needs of our participants, we had to be very flexible as to where child care happened. Often it was as simple as providing a few blankets and playmats to the side of the room for younger children. To accommodate older children in the physical activity, we suggest making any necessary changes to turn adult-oriented settings into child-friendly spaces. In sum, organizations should consider ways that their physical space can be more flexible to meet the complex needs of groups experiencing trauma and marginalization. Said one Taking Steps participant: "Women who have gone through trauma, addiction, things like that – I think there is a lot of self-confidence issues ... I mean when it comes down to your body, your parenting, you feel like you are constantly being watched or judged. That internal feeling is always there, it's hard to get over, so [Taking Steps] being inclusive of those women and letting them know there is no judgment, no shame, no blame – if you want to come work out – you work out."

Staff skills and attributes. Flexible, gentle but encouraging, using "no touch," doing self-care and debriefing. The participants in our study led very complex lives that dictated their schedules and availability. For us to meet this need, we encouraged the facilitators and organizations to be as flexible as possible with people coming late or leaving early. We learned that the women really appreciated that they did not need to feel shame or guilt about coming in late. For many of the women, this was their first time exercising as a group after many years, so a gentle but encouraging approach was necessary. The participants also stated that they felt more comfortable when the instructors offered a variety of modifications for each exercise. We assert that physical assists should not be used in TVIPA; said another way, we encourage organizations to implement a "no touch" policy in physical activity programing. Emerson (2015) has argued that simply asking for consent to touch does not disrupt the power dynamics between practitioners and participants. We extend this to addressing power dynamics with physical activity practitioners and participants – an iterative and ongoing process. Finally, because this work is new and offers some unique challenges, we encourage organizations to support their staff by offering opportunities for self-care and for them to debrief after each session.

Comprehensive supports. For those, like the women in our study, who experience poverty, houselessness, and food insecurity, participation in physical activity can be bolstered by some simple supports. In our earliest focus groups, participants identified that access to appropriate workout clothing and equipment (e.g., running shoes, socks, tank tops, bathing suits) was a major barrier to their participation. Based on these findings, we recommend that organizations address these barriers by providing workout essentials for participants or having some extra equipment and clothing available onsite, as well as offering healthy snacks, coffee, and water.

Individual Level: Strength-Based and Social Connection

In addition to the organizational changes needed to support TVIPA, there are some skills that we recommend individual facilitators also consider. Throughout the development of Taking Steps we heard feedback from participants in our study, as well as the facilitators who worked with us, that highlighted the importance of relationships in TVIPA. The development of trusting relationships between the facilitators and the participants was one reason why Taking Steps was so successful. Our facilitators took the time to get to know the participants and their children by name, congratulated them each time they joined in, and acknowledged their growth and development within the activity.

We also encourage individual facilitators to "check in" with themselves and engage in self-reflexivity to ensure that they are using a strength-based approach and not perpetuating rhetoric associated with weight loss and restrictions and pushing outside of one's comfort zone. Almost all of our participants identified that their primary motivation for participating in our programs was to socialize with their peers. So it is worthwhile emphasizing social connection and creating time for women to engage in discussions prior to or post the physical activity session.

Conclusion

The purpose of Taking Steps was to assess the feasibility and acceptability of a community-created TVIPA program for pregnant and parenting women. While there are a number of considerations in co-creating, implementing, and sustaining TVIPA, our research demonstrated that TVIPA is both acceptable to community members and feasible from an organizational and research perspective. Despite the complex individual, organizational, and systemic barriers pregnant and parenting women accessing services or living in the DTES face, they overwhelmingly reported wanting to engage in physical activity programing. Moreover, women also wanted to be involved in all aspects of decision-making in the development and implementation of their physical activity programs.

TVIPA programing facilitates increased participation and accessibility while reducing barriers. Participants indicated various ways in which TVIPA programing addressed barriers – the provision of child care, free services, and a safe space for women to be with their peers was imperative for women to feel comfortable when trying new activities and exploring the neighbourhood. The program's focus on women's unique needs and contexts increased their physical activity levels.

Through this work, we have confirmed that TVIPA programing is feasible and desirable for women; however, consistent organizational support is required for continued success. Having trusted staff co-lead and participate in the programing is essential for gaining participants' trust and developing their confidence. This is crucial to ease introductions to new physical activity. Our efforts focused on addressing the social determinants of inequities in physical activity, supporting organizations to offer trauma- and violence-informed programs, and providing individual and organizational training to enhance existing physical activity programs. We believe that integrating practices that account for social and structural inequities is key to developing accessible programs. Said one Taking Steps service provider: "It is not so simple to say 'go work out' – so much of physical activity rhetoric is about being disciplined, pulling yourself up by your bootstraps, that doesn't account for all the circumstance women have dealt with. A TVIPA approach creates opportunities for people to engage in physical activity safely, and on their own terms."

KEY MESSAGES AND IMPLICATIONS

- While anyone can benefit from a TVIPA program, those that are not TVI risk excluding people who have experienced trauma – that is, the majority of the Canadian and global population.
- TVIPA enables an equitable, accessible, and person-centred approach to physical activity; this is a change with the potential to improve physical health, mental well-being, and social connections for people experiencing numerous barriers to physical activity.

ADDITIONAL RESOURCES

- TVIPA Toolkit: https://equiphealthcare.ca/projects/tvipa
- Photovoice project report: https://carleton.ca/healthequity/wp-content/uploads/TakingStepsPhotovoiceBook.pdf

REFERENCES

Babson, K.A., Heinz, A.J., Ramirez, G., Puckett, M., Irons, J.G., Bonn-Miller, M.O., & Woodward, S.H. (2015). The interactive role of exercise and sleep on veteran recovery from symptoms of PTSD. *Mental Health and Physical Activity, 8,* 15–20. https://doi.org/10.1016/j.mhpa.2014.12.002

Browne, A.J., Varcoe, C.M., Wong, S.T., Smye, V.L., Lavoie, J., Littlejohn, D., ... Lennox, S. (2012). Closing the health equity gap: Evidence-based strategies for primary health care organizations. *International Journal for Equity in Health, 11,* 59. https://doi.org/10.1186/1475-9276-11-59

Campbell, L., Boyd, N., & Culbert, L., & Canadian Publishers Collection-non-CRKN. (2009). *A thousand dreams: Vancouver's Downtown Eastside and the fight for its future.* Vancouver, BC: Greystone Books.

City of Vancouver. (2013). *Downtown Eastside Local Area Profile, 2013.* Vancouver. Retrieved from https://vancouver.ca/files/cov/profile-dtes-local-area-2013.pdf

City of Vancouver. (n.d.). *Leisure Access Program.* Retrieved from https://vancouver.ca/parks-recreation-culture/leisure-access-card.aspx

Clark, C.J., Lewis-Dmello, A., Anders, D., Parsons, A., Nguyen-Feng, V., Henn, L., & Emerson, D. (2014). Trauma-sensitive yoga as an adjunct mental health treatment in group therapy for survivors of domestic violence: A feasibility study. *Complementary Therapies in Clinical Practice, 20*(3), 152–8. https://doi.org/10.1016/j.ctcp.2014.04.003

Crenshaw, K. (1991). Mapping the margins: Intersectionality, identity politics, and violence against women of color. *Stanford Law Review, 43*(6), 1241-99. https://doi.org/10.2307/1229039

Darroch, F.E., Roett, C., Varcoe, C., Oliffe, J.L., & Montaner, G.G. (2020). Trauma-informed approaches to physical activity: A scoping study. *Complementary Therapies in Clinical Practice, 41.* https://doi.org/10.1016/j.ctcp.2020.101224

Darroch, F.E., Varcoe, C., Hillsburg, H., Neville, C., Webb, J. & Roberts, C. (2022). Supportive movement: Tackling barriers to physical activity for pregnant and parenting women who have experienced trauma. *Canadian Journal of Community Mental Health, 41*(1), 18-34. https://doi.org/10.7870/cjcmh-2022-002

Emerson, D. (2015). *Trauma-sensitive yoga in therapy: Bringing the body into treatment.* New York, NY: W.W. Norton & Company.

Frisby, W., Reid, C., & Ponic, P. (2007). Levelling the playing field: Promoting the health of poor women through a community development approach to recreation. In P. White & K. Young (Eds.), *Sport and Gender in Canada* (pp. 121-36). Don Mills, ON: Oxford University Press.

Goldstein, L A., Mehling, W.E., Metzler, T.J., Cohen, B.E., Barnes, D.E., Choucroun, G.J., Silver, A., Talbot, L.S., Maguen, S., Hlavin, J.A., Chesney, M.A., & Neylan, T.C. (2018). Veterans Group Exercise: A randomized pilot trial of an Integrative Exercise program for veterans with posttraumatic stress. *Journal of Affective Disorders, 227,* 345-52. https://doi.org/10.1016/j.jad.2017.11.002

Kohl 3rd, H.W., Craig, C.L., Lambert, E.V., Inoue, S., Alkandari, J.R., Leetongin, G., ... & Lancet Physical Activity Series Working Group. (2012). The pandemic of physical inactivity: Global action for public health. *The Lancet, 380*(9838), 294-305. https://doi.org/10.1016/s0140-6736(12)60898-8

Linden, I.A., Mar, M.Y., Werker, G.R., Jang, K., & Krausz, M. (2013). Research on a vulnerable neighborhood – the Vancouver Downtown Eastside from 2001 to 2011. *Journal of Urban Health, 90*(3), 559-73. https://doi.org/10.1007/s11524-012-9771-x

McNeil, R., Shannon, K., Shaver, L., Kerr, T., & Small, W. (2014). Negotiating place and gendered violence in Canada's largest open drug scene. *International Journal of Drug Policy, 25*(3), 608-15. https://doi.org/10.1016/j.drugpo.2013.11.006

Miewald, C., & Ostry, A. (2014). A warm meal and a bed: Intersections of housing and food security in Vancouver's Downtown Eastside. *Housing Studies, 29*(6), 709-29. https://doi.org/10.1080/02673037.2014.920769

Minkler, M., & Wallerstein, N. (2003). Part one: Introduction to community-based participatory research. In N. Wallerstein, B. Duran, J.G. Oetzel, & M. Minkler (Eds.), *Community-based participatory research for health* (pp. 5-24). San Francisco, CA: Jossey-Bass.

Mottola, M.F., Davenport, M.H., Ruchat, S., Davies, G.A., Poitras, V.J., Gray, C.E., ... Zehr, L. et al. (2019). Canadian guideline for physical activity throughout pregnancy. *British Journal of Sports Medicine, 52*(1), 1339-46. https://doi.org/10.1136/bjsports-2018-100056

Ponic, P., Greaves, L., Pederson, A., & Young, L. (2014). Power and empowerment in health promotion for women. In L. Greaves, A. Pederson, & N. Poole (Eds.), *Making it better: Gender-transformative health promotion* (pp. 42–57). Toronto, ON: Canadian Scholars' Press.

Steinbach, D., & Graf, C. (2008). Leisure time physical activity and sedentariness. *Encyclopedia of Public Health*, 849–51. https://doi.org/10.1007/978-1-4020-5614-7_1968

Wathen, C.N. & Varcoe, C. (2019). *Trauma- & violence-informed care: Prioritizing safety for survivors of gender-based violence*. London, Ontario, Canada. Retrieved from https://gtvincubator.uwo.ca/wp-content/uploads/sites/22/2020/05/TVIC_Backgrounder_Fall2019r.pdf

World Health Organization. (no date). *Physical activity*. Retrieved from https://www.who.int/dietphysicalactivity/pa/en/

2.6 Becoming Trauma- and Violence- Informed in Policing

MARGARET MACPHERSON, SUSAN MACPHAIL, AND TANAZ JAVAN

It is an intense time of change for police services in Canada. Increased public scrutiny facilitated by social media has put policing on trial in recent years. Although there are marked differences between the two countries, the denunciation of policing in the United States after the murder of George Floyd quickly found resonance in Canada, where there were similar calls for significant reform and defunding. Despite the widespread criticism levelled at police, the public still expects them to maintain law and order. The turbulence in 2020 came on the heels of forty years of economic austerity policies that eroded the social safety net while simultaneously increasing income inequality. The results have been rises in poverty rates, homelessness, gang and gun violence, and family violence, as well as a toxic drug overdose crisis. These are the difficult social conditions that police now face every day.

A TVIC Approach to Mitigating Operational Stress

Police officers experience trauma and violence routinely. A 2015 Finnish study found that over the course of their careers, officers will experience as many as nine hundred potentially traumatic events. That creates the conditions for significant operational and organizational stress (Andersen, Konstantinos, Koskelainen, & Nyman, 2015). Compared to civilians, police are more at risk for post-traumatic stress injury (PTSI) symptoms, as well as health-related issues such as hypertension and cardiovascular disease, and are more likely to smoke and consume alcohol. Policing also sees higher rates of marital breakdown, domestic violence, charges of sexual harassment, and suicide. Policing is ideally situated to benefit from trauma- and violence-informed (TVI) approaches.

Despite pressure for institutional change in recent years, police officers experiencing the impacts of trauma and violence still struggle under a traditional style of policing that resists vulnerability, interpreted as weakness, in a "don't ask, don't tell" hyper-masculine environment that makes it difficult for them to seek support or even acknowledge that they need it. These are deeply entrenched social norms in policing culture. In response to myriad internal and external pressures, many police organizations are attempting to transform themselves from strict paramilitary operations that sharply delineate "right" from "wrong" into flatter structures that can hold competing tensions and acknowledge the blurring of lines that is inherent in the human condition.

In this chapter, we examine the journey of an urban police service to adapt and implement TVI principles as a strategy to bring about change in the organization so as to better support police members. Note that prior to the project, the organization had been taking steps to address operational stress by instituting better supports for members through police-specific training and by bolstering available supports. As we will discuss, a TVI framework can consolidate seemingly separate change efforts under a broad umbrella, thus generating momentum and support for a more widely shared vision.

One Police Service's Efforts to Become TVI

The journey for this police service began in 2010 with amended legislation under Ontario's Occupational Health and Safety Act (OHSA) that explicitly included domestic violence (DV) as a form of workplace violence and required employers to protect workers.[1] While there are few Canadian statistics specific to the policing profession, we know that domestic violence is a serious issue in every Canadian workplace (Wathen, MacGregor, & MacQuarrie, 2015) and that domestic violence, family breakdown, and suicide are all too common in policing (MacQuarrie, Saxton, Olszowy, Jaffe, & Singer, 2020). The police service we discuss in this chapter felt that it had met the OHSA legislation's requirements but also recognized that more was needed to address the issue effectively among its members. The organization had suffered a domestic homicide/suicide of two of its members a decade earlier that was still impacting the organization. Expertise was sought from the Centre for Research and Education on Violence Against Women and Children (CREVAWC) to provide training on workplace domestic violence. The first session with senior leaders in 2017 revealed that police services face unique challenges.

CREVAWC training sets an overarching goal for employers to address domestic violence as early as possible. Workers need training to be able to recognize warning signs and to know how to respond safely and effectively. In policing, it is difficult to talk about what may be happening at home because admitting to domestic violence brings an automatic criminal charge. In this context, warning signs signal criminality. While important and necessary, the policy is a barrier to help-seeking for everyone involved. Victims want the violence to stop but not to necessarily end their partner's career. Officers who rely heavily on one another for safety and support may observe a "code of silence" that emphasizes secrecy and discourages reporting of misconduct or concerns, and the officer committing the violence has few visible "off-ramps" that do not carry significant career implications (MacQuarrie et al., 2020, p. 191). For a trauma- and violence-informed (TVI) intervention to be effective, a different strategy would be needed for this police service.

CREVAWC and police leaders discussed the merits of moving upstream to focus more broadly on building capacity within the membership to recognize warning signs earlier, before it escalated to domestic violence. This upstream approach was initially conceived as a way to talk about domestic violence without talking about it directly. As a member of the Gender, Trauma, and Violence Knowledge Incubator at Western University, CREVAWC proposed an innovative project to adapt and implement TVIC principles and strategies to a police service. The police leaders agreed, and a three-year project was designed and submitted to the federal government for funding. As far as we know, this was the first police service in Ontario to adopt TVIC as a strategy for linking to workplace domestic violence by focusing upstream on the health and well-being of its members.[2] The move to place the issue of domestic violence within the purview of trauma and violence is significant in and of itself and requires further unpacking. Using a TVI approach in a workplace to address domestic violence is not a straightforward exercise.

TVIC and Officer-Involved Domestic Violence

Popular opinion still holds that domestic violence (DV) is an individual issue that requires strict accountability for the few "bad apples" through punishment and social exclusion. There is little incentive to view the issue as anything more than deviant behaviour by bad individuals, mostly men, who will never change. In male-dominated professions, the employer is more likely to be dealing with the perpetrator due to the gendered nature of domestic violence, in which women are most often the victims (Burczycka, 2019).[3] There is evidence of increased DV perpetration in policing and military professions (Bostock & Daley, 2007). Although there is very little Canadian research, US studies have found markedly higher rates of DV among police than in the general population (Blumenstein, Fridell, & Jones, 2012; Garvey, 2015).

Applied universally, TVI contends that every behaviour has a reason. Can this include the perpetration of violence in intimate relationships? For police officers who give their lives to public service in taking the "bad guys" off the street, a TVI approach represents a way to reclaim members who engage in criminal behaviour and possibly to reconcile the internal contradictions that are inevitable when people are reduced to a binary of "good and bad." It bears repeating that trauma does not excuse or explain criminal acts or behaviour. Accountability for individual behaviour is non-negotiable. But if the goal is to

2.6 Becoming Trauma- and Violence-Informed in Policing

create a pathway within a police service for a member who is at risk of perpetrating domestic violence to be able to seek help early and to reduce their risk for future violence, then the path must provide genuine opportunity and support for the possibility of real change. A way back to the community for violent offenders must be constructed. Research has found that the majority of domestic violence offenders can change their behaviour with support, treatment, and accountability (Scott, Heslop, Kelly, & Wiggins, 2013). Through a TVIC lens, this is a meaningful and fundamental shift that has allowed police advisers on the project to speak about officers who had been charged or fired with compassion born from the shared experience of collective trauma. We should not underestimate the power of a trauma- and violence-informed narrative to open hearts and minds to the possibility of change and redemption.

Many of the risk factors associated with DV perpetration in the general population are embedded in police culture and police work. They can be broken down into three clusters:

- Attitudes and behaviours instilled as part of police training.
- The masculine and authoritarian nature of traditional police culture.
- Officers' work stress and resulting mental health injuries and burnout.
(Johnson, Todd, & Subranmanian, 2005; Oehme, Prost, & Saunders, 2016)

The confluence of patriarchal attitudes steeped in top-down, traditional command-and-control police hierarchies operating within a continual high-stress environment is baked into police culture. Some have wondered whether the culture in policing and paramilitary organizations in general reinforces violence against women (MacQuarrie et al., 2020, p. 188). At the same time, it is important to acknowledge that the majority of police officers are not violent with their partners. The point to be made here is that the individual behaviour of domestic violence offenders is both a *factor* and an *outcome* of the environment and the social milieu. Individuals are responsible for their actions, but abusive and violent behaviour is not generated in a vacuum. For this reason, interventions should include individual, environmental, and societal components. Introducing TVIC as a potential intervention for DV begins with placing it in a larger context that includes consideration of relationships as well as community and societal influences as intervention points.

The World Health Organization contends that an ecological framework is needed to acknowledge social conditions and structures that contribute to all social issues, including interpersonal violence (World Health Organization, 2021; see also chapter 4.4). Changing how we regard perpetrators of domestic violence is a steep hill to climb in the public domain, especially for organizations that are mandated to draw clean lines between good and bad guys. Moreover, there is incredible resistance in the community to viewing domestic violence offenders who are police officers as anything but individual and criminal and as too often protected by their police service. When looking at domestic violence through a TVI lens, care must be taken not to rationalize misogyny.

The Project

The Department of Justice funded the project for two years. The police service went through a series of significant leadership changes that delayed the start of the project, including the appointment of a new Chief of Police. As a result, there were stops and starts as reorganization under new leadership took place and advisory group members changed. Despite the changes, the commitment to the project by the new chief was clear: a senior leader remained assigned to the project team throughout. The importance of ongoing support from senior leadership was key to the project's survival. Later, the COVID-19 pandemic halted the project for six months. Despite the challenges, the project has already generated important insights and tools. The funder granted a project extension to allow training for all members to be completed. The conclusion of this project will not be the end of the road for the police service, as becoming TVI is an ongoing journey. At best, the project approach has facilitated first steps in phase one of an implementation model. The project elements included an advisory committee, the design and production of online and in-person curricula, the establishment of an internal police implementation team, and ongoing process evaluation. The advisory committee is comprised of three leaders from the police service and a CREVAWC team that includes a mental health professional, a former police officer, a researcher, an evaluator, and CREVAWC project management staff. The daily pressures of policing and competing priorities even before the pandemic made the first months of the project challenging, and efforts were made to set and keep meetings despite the turnover in advisory members. Given that we were working in the white-water environment of policing, it was important to be able to communicate the core aspects of the TVI project quickly and clearly and to focus on tasks that moved the project along.[4]

In the early months, discussions focused on training processes and products as the most tangible and easily understood components of the project. The long thread of the implementation process and what it actually takes for any organization to embed TVI principles into institutional memory was more difficult to hold. If the police service wanted the project to result in more than just one-off training, responsibility for planning ongoing implementation had to be made a priority. The original workplan provided a timeline that included launching the implementation team early in the project. The police advisory lead identified a new committee that was being formed to address mental health and wellness as the group that would also be tapped for ongoing implementation and accountability. It was unclear when and how to engage the committee. The lead suggested that the committee was not yet established enough to take on the role. In fact, the role and responsibility for ongoing implementation was still emerging in the final months of the project.

Lessons Learned

As noted, an early lesson learned was to let go of strict timelines and expectations by the CREVAWC team so as to allow the project to unfold in a more organic way – one that aligned with the schedules and priorities of the police advisers. It is one thing to design a project with deliverables and a workplan and another to work out the process in the real world. TVI projects require a lot of flexibility and room to manoeuvre between budget lines. As discussed in chapter 4.1, the Active Implementation Frameworks provide an evidence-based approach that recognizes the nature of iterative work.

The CREVAWC team met more often to do as much of the legwork as possible so that time with the police advisers could be focused and task-oriented, aimed along a point-to-point navigation path in developing the training products, implementation strategies, and evaluation processes. It was decided early in the project that a climate survey would provide a baseline regarding TVI awareness across the service, allowing assessment of change over time. As CREVAWC learned more about the steps the police service had been taking in recent years to better support members, it became apparent that the organizational project to become "trauma-informed" was well under way. The critical V – "Violence" – of TVI is the essential element in a serious change agenda needed to push organizations to think consciously and critically and to look beyond the individual. Becoming TVI entails ongoing examination and exposure regarding the ways that harm is embedded in daily operations, and then taking steps to mitigate the harm. That said, many of the investments over the prior five years in training, resources, and personnel align with TVI principles. These have included hiring a staff psychologist and a wellness coordinator, launching a mental health and well-being committee, convening an annual conference with a focus on mental health, offering various trainings that build skills such as Crucial Conversations, launching an anti-stigma campaign, developing peer support, and establishing a reintegration program that trains officers to support peers in making choices about how to return to work safely after an operational stress leave. These are mitigation investments; however, it was when they were shown to be aligned under TVI that the dots connected regarding TVI's potential to support system change. This was an important moment for the project, because the context shifted from TVI as a "new" initiative to TVI as a tool to support the vision of police leaders and as a language that affirmed the path the organization was already on. Looking back at past initiatives through a TVI lens for the climate survey generated a sense of momentum and of ground already gained. Anecdotally, CREVAWC advisers heard back from police members, who noted how much the organizational culture had been changing for the better in recent years. When asked "what" had changed, descriptions were vague – it was hard to know what had changed or how change was happening. In any event, the introduction of TVI principles proved to be both useful and timely.

Perhaps the most important element of the project was the production of ten video scenarios for the training. The scenarios provided an opportunity to illustrate the TVI principles in action and then to make a direct connection to organizational commitment by pointing to different ways the police service was putting resources, training, policies, and procedures into place to better support members. Developing the storylines and scripts occupied the team for several months. During the early project planning phase, police advisers had identified three specific aspects of police culture that they wanted to address: (1) show no weakness, (2) don't ask – don't tell, and (3) gender inequality and sexism. The scenarios were written to highlight these cultural challenges through characters who were struggling in different ways at work and at home. In each story, the protagonist is experiencing a variety of yet unrecognized impacts that can be attributed to untreated trauma and violence. It is clear in each case that without intervention, they are headed down a bad path. Colleagues and supervisors who witness behaviour and events model the TVI principles through supportive responses that demonstrate understanding of trauma and violence, take steps to create emotional and physical safety, make connection, and point to potential supports while communicating a "can do" strengths-based belief in the character's ability to make life-affirming choices. Colleagues are not trying to solve the problem but rather to identify with the troubled character while pointing out the specific concern, persisting even when met with resistance. The selection and development of compelling stories with believable interactions and dialogue served as the focal point for the project; it was made possible through a dynamic scene-by-scene development process with police advisers. The situations included a character who was engaging in domestic violence at home and having issues at work. The scenarios were produced using professional actors and crews in a television studio to ensure high production values. Luckily, the production was scheduled for the end of January 2020, just a few weeks ahead of the first pandemic lockdown.

The curriculum was developed around selected scenarios to anchor TVI concepts and research in relatable stories.[5] Video messages endorsing the training were recorded and posted to the service's intranet from the chief, the Police Board chair, and the Police Association president to convey their commitment to becoming TVI as a police service. Prior to the launch of the member training, the project advisory committee presented an overview of the workshop to senior police leaders and to the mental health and wellness committee to introduce TVI principles and to provide opportunities for input. One leader commented that "show no weakness" was a persistent norm in police culture, one that led to harsh judgment of colleagues struggling in the ways dramatized in the scenarios. Another voiced concern that the scenarios painted a too rosy picture that might be received cynically. The concerns highlighted for the advisory team the importance of setting realistic goals for the training in terms of what was wanted from members, and of being clear that the dramatizations put out a vision for what was possible rather than what currently existed. In identifying the difference between the goal and the current state, members across the organization would be encouraged to provide feedback on barriers.

Because of the pandemic, the training was postponed; then, when the second wave began, it had to be adapted to an online environment. Police leaders committed themselves to putting every member, including senior leaders, through the initial training over a twenty-four-week period in two-and-a-half hour sessions. In this way, complex change projects were broken down into a few "doable" actions that were consistent and generalized across the population. The learning objectives for the all-member training included:

- being aware of, and recognizing, warning signs attributable to trauma and violence impacts, for self and in colleagues;
- being aware of available resources and supports, with encouragement to seek help;
- learning how to respond to support colleagues; and
- understanding how organizational policies and procedures interface with individual experiences in the scenarios.

At the organizational level, becoming TVI requires critical reflection and continued focus on using TVI principles to guide decision-making. It also involves establishing policies and procedures that support the learning objectives. Engaging everyone in the organization in the change process is what separates the active implementation process from a single training. Throughout the workshops, participants were encouraged to relate their experiences to specific practices, leadership, policies, and procedures as a means to bring awareness to the often invisible impacts of structural violence. Participants have commented that there is power in being able to name what is happening both personally and organizationally.

The training was launched in January 2021. All police members had participated by June 2021. The mix of sworn officers, civilian staff, and leaders created a flat training environment, supporting the idea that the impacts of trauma and violence do not recognize rank. Concerns about whether people would participate when sitting in a room with a superintendent were quickly alleviated. The scenarios are proving to be powerful tools that fuel discussion and thought. Focused questions are used to encourage dialogue in small breakout groups; these are followed by debriefing with the group as a whole. Participants are asked to use the chat and reaction features throughout the online session to make it as interactive as possible. Whether participants engage in the discussions or not, the content is intended to stimulate reflection about the impacts of trauma and violence on a personal level and in relation to colleagues.

The workshops were evaluated against the learning objectives. Evaluations showed that the workshops were well-received and that the learning objectives were met for the majority of participants. Anecdotally, members of the TVI implementation team reported a shift in the organization that they attributed to the training. They described the shift as greater openness and increased conversations taking place about the impact of trauma on themselves and their colleagues.

Themes arising from the training propelled discussion with the police advisers in a way that crystallized the "active" implementation process. For example, in the very first session, a comment was made by a front-line officer that sergeants are transferred frequently in the organization, creating a barrier to building the kinds of relationships that foster connection and open communication. Whatever the rationale behind the original decision to rotate leaders often, the unintended consequence of creating a barrier to bonding may not have been considered. TVI principles may eventually put an entirely new frame around decision-making criteria. That single comment stimulated rich discussion about the importance of creating a robust feedback loop with well-articulated communication pathways. How can members provide feedback when they have an insight or idea about how the organization is functioning? How can that information be taken up and factored into decision-making? How do members know they are being heard? What already exists in the organization to gather input? Can it be strengthened? This is only one example from the first session. The questions help generate reflection and prompt more careful consideration about how to stimulate and deepen engagement at all levels of the organization. Genuine engagement can be a strong counterweight to cynicism and alienation.

Discussions generated in the training and themes that emerged from the climate survey are helping inform the development of the phase two project. A significant focus will be the development of a long-term (ten-year) evaluation design so that the organization can demonstrate, with metrics, change over time. As well, phase two will expand to look at the relationship with the community to explore how interaction with the public can benefit from the application of TVI principles. A mindfulness program will be piloted to support staff in dealing with burnout from the pandemic, and communication tools will be added to keep the initiative in front of people. The police service has recently launched a new Member Care Division to hold a focus on the health and well-being of staff. This is a significant change for the organization at a time when leaders are being challenged to protect staff from high demands for police services in the community while they face complex and relentless pressure from the pandemic. This division will be responsible for the ongoing implementation of TVI approaches. As such, the TVI project is undergoing another time of great change during which the need to persist in looking forward is the only constant. At the time of this writing, ongoing support from senior leadership has been given for phase two.

Conclusion

Becoming TVI requires enlisting all members to contribute to the change process through reflection and to provide input and ideas. It is important to acknowledge the gaps and challenges that follow from structural violence and to create a variety of opportunities for people to talk about their experiences, good and bad. A strong feedback loop takes input from all areas within the organization so as to foment action. The proof of leadership commitment is in how the organization invites, acknowledges, and responds to constructive critique from within. There is always a gap between what is wanted and what *is*. As leaders act concretely to reduce harm, confidence in the process grows.

Active implementation involves building the road as you walk it. By seeking out and valuing input from members in demonstrable ways, a different future is created. The steps taken in recent years have already changed the structure of the organization in ways that members recognize. Several participants in the workshops, often newer officers, have described the problematic behaviour depicted in the scenes as "old school," as if it no longer exists. These comments confirm that change is happening. A police service with a long tradition of strictly top-down command-and-control leadership can transform itself to be both hierarchal and flat. The role for CREVAWC advisers is to pay attention to the themes emerging from the training and to continue to bring them forward and follow where they lead.

Next steps for the current advisory committee will include developing a living chart to track themes along the journey. As any anthropologist will tell you, when venturing into new territory, if you don't keep track of the path taken, you won't know how you arrived at a destination, and you won't be able to tell others how to get there. By the end of the project, there will be a map of where the organization has been and directions for the next phase regarding where to focus attention moving forward. One of the most significant challenges still ahead is the hand-off from the advisory group to a dedicated committee that will have the authority and mandate to hold the TVI focus for the organization over time. Policing is a high-pressure, fast-paced environment. Becoming TVI is slow work. It is like building a muscle. It takes time, practice, persistence, and the long vision of committed leaders.

NOTES

1 The 2010 amendments to the *OHSA* in Ontario were groundbreaking in that they were the first legislation in the world to identify domestic violence as a workplace hazard. This is one example of how legislation can be a catalyst for significant systemic change.
2 Whether there are long-term implications for preventing domestic violence through a trauma- and violence-informed approach is a future research question well beyond the scope of this chapter.
3 Women in Canada are more likely than men to experience intimate partner violence. According to 2018 police-reported data, women accounted for almost 8 in 10 victims (79%) of intimate partner violence.
4 The advisory refers to a TVI approach instead of TVIC because "care" is not as relevant to a police service.
5 It was decided the domestic violence scene will be used later in an issue-specific online training that references Occupational Health and Safety requirements.

KEY MESSAGES AND IMPLICATIONS

- TVIC can be adapted to support culture change in police services.
- A TVI approach can support police services in responding to external pressure to develop greater sensitivity and awareness of structural violence and systemic issues in dealing with the public.
- Teaching police members to recognize the warning signs of untreated trauma impacts that can result in operational stress and problems at home is a path to earlier intervention.

REFERENCES

Andersen, J., Konstantinos P., Koskelainen, M., & Nyman, M. (2015). Knowledge and training regarding the link between trauma and health: A national survey of Finnish police officers. *The Journal of Police Emergency Response*, 5(2). https://doi.org/10.1177/2158244015580380

Blumenstein, L., Fridell, L., & Jones, S. (2012). The link between traditional police subculture and police intimate partner violence. *Policing: An International Journal of Police Strategies & Management*, 35(1), 147–64. https://doi.org/10.1108/13639511211215496

Bostock, D.J., & Daley, J.G. (2007). Lifetime and current sexual assault and harassment victimization rates of active-duty United States Air Force women. *Violence Against Women*, 13(9), 927–44. https://doi.org/10.1177/1077801207305232.

Burczycka, M. (2019). Section 2: Police-reported intimate partner violence in Canada, 2018. In *Family violence in Canada: A statistical profile, 2018*. Canadian Centre for Justice Statistics, Statistics Canada. Retrieved from https://www150.statcan.gc.ca/n1/pub/85-002-x/2019001/article/00018/02-eng.htm

Garvey, T. (2015). The highly trained batterer: Prevention, investigation, and prosecution of officer-involved domestic violence. *Strategies, 14,* 1–12. Retrieved from https://aequitasresource.org/wp-content/uploads/2018/09/Strategies-The-Highly-Trained-Batterer-14.pdf

Johnson, L., Todd, M., & Subranmanian, G. (2005). Violence in police families: Work-family spillover. *Journal of Family Violence, 20*(1), 3–12. https://doi.org/10.1007/s10896-005-1504-4

MacQuarrie, B., Saxton, M., Olszowy, L., Jaffe, P., & Singer, V. (2020). Domestic homicides in police and military: Understanding the risks enhanced by trauma and culture. In P. Jaffe, K. Scott, & A. Straatman (Eds.), *Preventing domestic homicides: Lessons learned from tragedies* (pp. 187–207). Cambridge, UK: Elsevier Academic Press.

Oehme, K., Prost, S., & Saunders, D. (2016). Police responses to cases of officer-involved domestic violence: The effects of a brief web-based training. *Policing: A Journal of Policy and Practice, 10*(4), 391–407. https://doi.org/10.1093/police/paw039

Scott, K., Heslop, L., Kelly, T., & Wiggins, K. (2013). Intervening to prevent repeat offending among moderate- to high-risk domestic violence offenders: A second-responder program for men. *International Journal of Offender Therapy and Comparative Criminology, 59*(3), 273–94. https://doi.org/10.1177/0306624X13513709

Wathen C. N., MacGregor, J. C. D., & MacQuarrie, B. J. (2015). The impact of domestic violence in the workplace: results from a pan-Canadian survey. *Journal of Occupational and Environmental Medicine, 57*(7): e65–71. http://journals.lww.com/joem/Fulltext/2015/07000/The_Impact_of_Domestic_Violence_in_the_Workplace_.19.aspx

World Health Organization. (2021). The Ecological Framework. *Violence Prevention Alliance*. Retrieved from: https://www.who.int/violenceprevention/approach/ecology/en/

SECTION THREE

Cutting across Contexts

This section discusses how TVIC has been enacted in culturally safe, contextually tailored, person-centred ways. Using a case study approach, authors share lessons learned in adapting, integrating, and applying TVIC principles in various contexts. Explicit links are made between TVIC and cultural safety by exploring its integration into services for Indigenous peoples and for migrants. At a slightly different level, this section discusses taking a TVIC approach to understanding and enhancing communications.

3.1 Cultural Safety and Trauma- and Violence-Informed Care: Integrated Services for Indigenous Peoples

VICTORIA SMYE, BILL HILL, COLLEEN VARCOE, ANNETTE J. BROWNE, CHANTEL ANTONE, LISA JACKSON, AND LLOY WYLIE

In this chapter, we present considerations for the enactment of trauma- and violence- informed care (TVIC) in culturally safe, contextually tailored, person-centred ways by employing two case exemplars and a reflection from projects and research involving Indigenous peoples regarding their experiences with the health care sector. Cultural safety is conceptualized as integral to TVIC for both Indigenous and non-Indigenous peoples (Browne et al., 2018; Ford-Gilboe et al., 2018) and as having the potential to move practice and policies beyond notions of cultural sensitivity to more actively address inequitable power relations, discrimination, racism (Browne et al., 2016; Wylie & McConkey, 2019), and the ongoing impacts of historical injustices on health and well-being (Browne, Varcoe, & Ward, 2021).

Indigenous peoples often have negative experiences with health care and social service supports, with serious consequences to health and well-being (Kitching et al., 2020; McLane, Bill, & Barnabe, 2021; Phillips-Beck et al., 2020). This burden of history has been ever-present in all our research. Employing two cases, we will present lessons learned from our research and project work to suggest tangible means to support culturally safe, trauma- and violence-informed services and systems. We provide strategies for building safe and effective linkages within and between hospital and community-based sectors in the provision of services and care for Indigenous and other peoples.

By the end of this chapter, the reader will be able to (1) understand the linkage between cultural safety and TVIC, (2) consider the unique features of culturally safe care with regard to health care and social service sector support involving Indigenous people in Canada, (3) reflect on those aspects of relationship-building and engagement that might be applied in workplaces/organizations, and (4) consider the application of locally tailored solutions for the enactment of TVIC in culturally safe ways within their organizations and across systems of care.

Why Cultural Safety

Originally developed by Māori nurses in Aotearoa/New Zealand (NZ) in response to the glaring health inequities experienced by Māori (the Indigenous people of NZ) compared to non-Māori (Papps & Ramsden, 1996; Polaschek, 1998; Ramsden, 1993, 2000), cultural safety is an approach to understanding health and providing health care that attends to the historical and ongoing impacts of colonialism and inequitable power relations, discrimination, and racism (Varcoe, Browne, & Kang-Dhillon, 2019).

Early in the history of cultural safety applications in Canada, Dyck and Kearns (1995) and Lynam and Young (2000) convincingly asserted its transportability to a research context and, in particular, to the researcher/participant encounter as a means of ensuring that the "dignity and historical context of individuals is recognized" (Dyck & Kearns, 1995, p. 144). Since that time, many researchers in Canada have been applying the concept to examine health care involving a number of groups marginalized by inequity, including Indigenous peoples (e.g., more recently, Berg et al., 2019; Browne & Varcoe, 2019; Firestone, Syrette, Jourdain, Recollet, & Smylie, 2019; Gerlach, Browne, & Greenwood 2017; Greenwood, Lindsay, & Loewen, 2017; McCall, Mollison, Browne, Parker, & Pauly, 2017; Pauly, McCall, Browne, Parker, & Mollison, 2015; Urbanoski et al., 2020).

In addition, after the release of the document titled *Cultural Competency and Safety: A Guide for Health Care Administrators, Providers and Educators* (National Aboriginal Health Organization, 2008), and as a reflection of a commitment to cultural safety in Canada, a number of interdisciplinary collaborations focused on the development of educational tools, webinars, and competencies associated with cultural safety (e.g., Aboriginal Nurses Association of Canada, 2009; Baba, 2013). Also, San'yas, the Indigenous Cultural Safety (ICS) Training Program delivered by the Provincial Health Services Authority of British Columbia, was developed and launched (see https://sanyas.ca/); this was later adapted for use in Ontario (see https://sanyas.ca/core-training/ontario) and Manitoba (see https://sanyas.ca/core-training/manitoba). Rooted in critical anti-racist pedagogy, San'yas is a facilitated online educational intervention that aims to (a) build the knowledge, self-awareness, and skills of participants so that they work more safely and effectively with Indigenous peoples, and (b) support broader organizational and systemic change (Browne et al., 2021; Ward, Morton Ninomiya, & Firestone, 2021). Since its inception more than a decade ago, thousands of health care professionals across Canada have received ICS training.

There are a number of differences between the Canadian and New Zealand contexts, but in both countries, the consequences of colonization and neocolonialism, structural violence, and racism cross geographical and political boundaries continue with extremely deleterious effects on health and well-being. It is in this context that cultural safety can be used as a concept for examining the health and social relations practices that are shaped by dominant organizational, institutional, and structural conditions. As a moral and political discourse and an anti-racist stance (Smye & Browne, 2002), cultural safety was intended to transform the health care system by drawing attention to how power operates in health care contexts as a means to transform the health system (Greenwood, 2019) – that is, it is concerned with power relations between health care professionals and clients in the context of the health systems and structures – it is a relational concept.

It is well-known that the social determinants of health play a significant role in health status, yet for many, rising inequities in these determinants, along with weak access to health services for people marginalized by inequity – including many Indigenous people – is leading to increasingly poor health (e.g., Kitching et al., 2020). Health equity interventions can be implemented at multiple levels, including within health services (Greenwood, 2019; Wyatt, Laderman, Botwinick, Mate, & Whittington, 2016). EQUIP Health Care (www.equiphealthcare.ca) has shown that equity-oriented health care, conceptualized as being comprised of three *intersecting* key dimensions – cultural safety, trauma- and violence-informed care (TVIC), and harm reduction – is associated with better health outcomes, including better quality of life, less chronic pain, and fewer depressive and post-traumatic stress symptoms over time (Browne et al., 2018; Ford-Gilboe et al., 2018).

In response to the unique features associated with health inequities experienced by First Nations, Métis, and Inuit in Canada, Downey (2020) has put forward the concept of IND-equity. Situated within a self-determining, rights-based perspective, this model draws attention to the impacts of colonialism, neocolonialism, and racism on the health and well-being of First Nations, Métis, and Inuit and the need to address the social, political, and historical determinants of Indigenous people's health (e.g., structural violence) in a culturally safe (Downey, 2020, p. 99) and trauma- and violence-informed way.

We offer the following case examples from our collective work to illustrate the interoperability of TVIC and cultural safety strategies, to support the argument that truly trauma- and violence-informed approaches *must* be culturally safe. We end with a reflection from colleagues who have been doing the work to shift services toward cultural safety and humility.

Case Descriptions

Indigenous Pathways to Mental Wellness: Biigajiiskaan *(Victoria Smye & Bill Hill, on behalf of the Biigajiiskaan team)*

Under the co-leadership of a community agency in London, Ontario, Atlohsa Family Healing Services, and an acute care hospital, St Joseph's Health Care

London (St Joseph's Parkwood), a regional Indigenous pathway to Mental Wellness titled Biigajiiskaan has been created to redesign a system of care around the needs of Indigenous people experiencing serious mental illness, including people who face substance use stigma. The Biigajiiskaan program is creating Indigenous-informed pathways that combine Elder-guided approaches to health and well-being and Indigenous healing practices and knowledges with current hospital-based mental health care practices. "Biigajiiskaan" is an Ojibway concept that alludes to how a broken or rotting tree stump feeds new life. It acknowledges the importance of all living things working together in harmony for the greater good.

The development of Biigajiiskaan is informed by a Two-Eyed Seeing approach, a perspective put forward by Mi'kmaq Elder Albert Marshall. Two-Eyed Seeing is a guiding principle found in Mi'kmaq Knowledge known as "Etuaptmumk," whereby two knowledges are brought together. Two-Eyed Seeing refers to learning to see from one eye with the strengths of Indigenous knowledges and ways of knowing, and from the other eye with the strengths of Western knowledges and ways of knowing, and learning to use both these eyes together for the benefit of all (Ermine, Sinclair, & Jeffrey, 2004; Hogue & Bartlett, 2014). Biigajiiskaan also is guided by the notion of culture as care and healing and by the Thunderbird Partnership Foundation's First Nations Mental Wellness Continuum Framework (Health Canada, 2015); Indigenous practices, such as healing circles, ceremony, smudging, and drumming circles are integrated alongside Western approaches to mental health care. By providing culturally safe and accessible mental health care to Indigenous peoples through an Indigenous lens, the Biigajiiskaan program aims to create connections with and beyond Western notions of mental wellness and to seek ways to support community through relationships with the self, the land, and all of creation. By dismantling the barriers of long-standing distrust and bridging Indigenous and Western modalities, Atlohsa Family Healing Services and St Joseph's Health Care London have been able to transform the mental wellness design and service delivery model.

The Biigajiiskaan program model recognizes ongoing systemic racism as well as the institutional trauma caused by residential schools and Indian hospitals and their impact. The model serves as a recognition of the assault on Indigenous identity, knowledge, and culture and the importance of these for shaping health and well-being moving forward. The program aims to create a more positive experience for Indigenous people within the health care system by reinstating the importance of Indigenous healing practices. The overall aim of the partnership activities has been to create enhanced, culturally safe and trauma- and violence-informed care practices and spaces that will result in equitable and timely access to care for Indigenous peoples, who currently are not well-served by the mental health system. The program has three main developmental foci.

(1) Okwari: Kowa, which translates into "the great bear," is an in-hospital healing space available to all clients within St Joseph's Hospital (in particular, Parkwood Mental Health). (2) A mobile outreach team, grounded in an "Elder-guided treatment" approach, is guided by an Elder who communicates/connects with Elders in all the other communities around London-Middlesex (a rural/urban area in the province of Ontario). There is also an outreach team that includes an Indigenous helper (Shkaabewis) program lead, a clinical documentation coach/administrator, a social worker, a psychiatrist, a substance use specialist, and a registered practical nurse (RPN). This team works within the hospital units as well as in the community, including on reserve. The mobile outreach team provides services and also supports the creation of safe "pathways" between the hospital and the community, and between clients and service providers. (3) An urban-based healing lodge has been approved to be created on land at the hospital site. The lodge will be accessible to clients in both the hospital and the community. Land-based healing practices will be central to services provided at the lodge. Bill Hill, Ro'nikonkatste (Standing Strong Spirit), is the program lead, and team engagement is largely supported in circle in the Okwari:Kowa space (figure 3.1.1).

Reclaiming Our Spirits *(Colleen Varcoe and Annette J. Browne)*

Reclaiming Our Spirits (ROS) is a health promotion intervention designed for Indigenous women who have experienced intimate partner violence (IPV). Building on a theory-based health promotion intervention (iHEAL) that showed promising results in feasibility studies (e.g., Wuest et al., 2015), ROS was developed using a series of related approaches, including (a) guidance from Indigenous women with research expertise specific to IPV and Indigenous women's experiences, (b) interviews with Elders living in the study setting, and (c) articulation of an Indigenous lens, including using Cree (one of the largest Indigenous language groups in North America) concepts to identify key aspects. For the latter, Madeleine Dion Stout built on her previous work (Dion Stout, 2012) in describing the harms Indigenous women experience and the possibilities for healing in Cree, which better captured the complexity of Indigenous women's experiences of colonization and violence than could be done in English. From this direction, the intervention was modified. First, ten principles specific to ROS were developed: being Aboriginal is a strength; identity is a priority; history is the present; diversity is valued; women-led; culture and tradition; women in historical and cultural context; healthy interventionist; sustainability; and cultural safety. For more detailed information regarding the development of these principles, see Varcoe and colleagues (2017, table 1, pp. 239–40). From these principles, other innovations were developed, including an Elder-led circle. Pilot testing with Indigenous women led to improvement in most measures of health between pre- and

Figure 3.1.1 Okwari: Kowa space, Parkwood, London, Ontario. Copyright by Bill Hill.

post-intervention (Varcoe et al., 2017). Women found the pilot intervention acceptable and helpful but also offered valuable suggestions for improvement. The intervention was revised based on input from the women, nurses, and Elders. Improvements included having more structure within the circle and providing nurses with stronger knowledge of Indigenous women's experiences and community health. This version was then offered to 152 Indigenous women. These women experienced significant improvements in all measures of health, which were sustained six months after the program ended (Varcoe et al., 2019).

In the fall of 2020, an Indigenous primary care clinic in Vancouver, BC, began offering ROS to women, and this work is ongoing. Importantly, preliminary results of a randomized controlled trial of iHEAL, completed in 2021, showed significant improvements in women's health and well-being (Ford-Gilboe et al., forthcoming). A number of different dimensions of health and well-being in iHEAL were measured using self-report tools, including these: quality of life (QOL Scale), symptoms of depression (CESD-R) and post-traumatic stress (PCL-C), women's personal agency (Personal Agency Scale), confidence/self-efficacy (developed for iHEAL), and chronic pain disability.

Trauma- and Violence-Informed Care as Integral to Our Work

Trauma- and violence-informed care was integral to the presented cases in several ways. Most obviously, in Biigajiiskaan and ROS, the providers and Elders were enacting trauma- and violence-informed approaches in their engagements with people and teams and within their communities. Perhaps less obviously, the design of the Biigajiiskaan program and the ROS intervention, and the processes of program development and research, respectively, were necessarily trauma- and violence-informed. The entire Biigajiiskaan program design and ROS intervention are, of course, built on an understanding of the pervasiveness and impacts of violence – in the case of the Biigajiiskaan program, on interpersonal, systemic, and structural violence, and in the case of the ROS intervention, specifically on the disproportionately high levels of violence against Indigenous women in Canada. All of these forms of violence stem from racism and colonialism (Brownridge, 2008; Daoud, Smylie, Urquia, Allan, & O'Campo, 2013; Pedersen, Malcoe, & Pulkington, 2013; Smye et al., 2021). This understanding of violence and its origins demanded that program development and research be guided by Indigenous people at every step.

In the Biigajiiskaan program, this is reflected in the use of the findings of the ongoing formative program evaluation (three phases) to inform the development and shaping of the program; the narratives and survey information from Elders, Knowledge Keepers, thought leaders, providers, and persons who access services continue to provide important information. For example, "culture as healing" has been a consistently expressed element of importance in the creation of mental health services. Thus, the Okwari:Kowa space is a central feature of the program – it was the first element of the Biigajiiskaan program put in place at both institutional sites, St Joseph Health Care London and the London Health Sciences Centre. Land-based healing is an arm now being developed. In addition, the Native Mental Wellness Assessment Tool, which has been incorporated at the Atlohsa site, has informed how we evaluate the overall program.

In the ROS intervention, the integration of trauma- and violence-informed care and cultural safety was enacted through (a) taking guidance from Elders and Knowledge Keepers at the outset of the design and throughout, and (b) taking guidance from the women not only in terms of their work with nurses and Elders, but also in the design and modification of the intervention. Combined with the TVIC principle of fostering collaboration, choice, and control, this meant that "everything" was "optional" for the women. As is required research practice, women chose whether and how to participate, but all research personnel redoubled their efforts to ensure that each moment was fully voluntary. Women chose whether and how to work with their assigned nurse or Elder, and they changed nurses and circles as needed. They chose whether and how to answer questions on surveys, and they provided directions for modifying those surveys. Both research and the intervention activities had to be conducted in emotionally and physically safe spaces. Creating such spaces required thinking about "who," "where," "when," "what," and "how" with regard to locally determined protocols. For example, when we were unable to conduct the research in the clinic with which we had initially partnered, we moved to a new setting. Although it was within six blocks of the former setting, it was outside the community in which the women felt comfortable. Thus, we sought a new setting – a place called the "Learning Exchange," which offered a range of community programs that would not be associated with mental health, substance use, or violence programing. To take another example, we learned to be very careful about "what" was discussed, particularly in circles; thus, we carefully navigated the grief associated with Mother's Day, given that the state had apprehended most of the women's children as part of the genocidal colonial project in Canada (McKenzie, Varcoe, Browne, & Day, 2016). Finally, we infused a strengths-based approach throughout, acknowledging the women's strength and survival in every aspect; to follow the example, that women were able to survive the pain and grief of their children being taken was greatly honoured.

This work has led to the enhancement of the iHEAL intervention overall. First, we took the ten principles from ROS along with our original ten iHEAL principles and collapsed them down to five principles to guide our work: safety first, woman-led, health promotion as a priority, strengths-based, and positioning for the future. Most importantly, our experience with women in ROS moved us beyond "woman-centred" (which often still privileged provider perspectives) to "woman-led" as integral to enacting the principles of TVIC.

Tailoring TVIC in Culturally Safe, Contextually Tailored, and Person-Centred Ways

Common to the cases presented in this chapter is the commitment to Indigenous- and/or women-led (e.g., ROS) services and supports along with relational engagement underpinned by mutual respect and trust, and reciprocity. This includes joint accountabilities and priority planning, reflected in policies and protocols that can support sustainable change in health care. In addition, Indigenous identity – that is, ancestry, history, culture, and tradition – is seen as a strength and as an essential starting place to support meaningful improvements, paying attention to how diversity of Indigenous identity and experience shapes local solutions.

In this chapter's cases, anti-Indigenous racism, stigma, discrimination, and other forms of violence endemic in our systems of care have been and continue to be determinants of health (Greenwood, de Leeuw, & Lindsay, 2018) and continue as barriers to building trust and positive relational engagement.

Disrupting the status quo (Browne et al., 2018; Browne et al., 2016) is viewed as essential to achieve improvements in health and well-being.

Practical Strategies/Guidance for Organizations

In this section we offer specific strategies/guidance for Indigenous program development and the enactment of culturally safe, contextually tailored TVIC approaches. We also provide a brief reflection that synthesizes one person's journey toward embedding cultural safety and humility in practice (see box 3.1.1).

Seeking and Strengthening Partnerships and Creating Safe Spaces

Informed by the findings of our previous research (e.g., Browne et al., 2018; Ford-Gilboe et al., 2018) and by phase one of the evaluation of Biigajiiskaan, our teams have become acutely aware of the importance of strong, meaningful partnerships with Indigenous and non-Indigenous agencies and institutions. A key element in building the Biigajiiskaan program to date has been the work of the project lead and team to establish new partnerships and strengthen existing ones – for example, this activity has resulted in a recent alliance with another large health care institution, London Health Sciences Centre (LHSC), and the opening of a new Indigenous sacred space within that setting. This initiative was led by the project lead of Biigjiiskaan and Atlohsa through senior leadership connections at both LHSC and St Joseph's Health Care London (SJHC).

In addition, during the Biigajiiskaan program development it became clear that creating culturally safe, trauma- and violence-informed spaces within institutional settings required ongoing awareness of and education about Biigajiiskaan and its importance across institutions – it could not simply be tucked away somewhere but needed to be central to achieve its goal (https://www.lhsc.on.ca/patients-visitors/indigenous-healing-space). The ROS intervention also points to the imperative of safe space; as noted earlier, long-standing partnerships and networking in the local community built on mutual trust and respect resulted in the opening of the Indigenous primary care clinic, where ROS was welcomed and offered. The space is accessible to the women and located within their area of comfort. So far, this has had a positive impact on women's health and well-being.

Relational Engagement

Our research experiences point to the importance of relational engagement guided by TVIC principles and cultural safety across health and social service sectors. This includes relational engagement not only with Indigenous peoples and communities, but also with and across health care providers, who need to be given appropriate supports to ensure the congruence of practice with culturally safe, contextually tailored, person-centred TVIC. Safe relational engagement also has meant addressing program and interpersonal issues through ongoing education and dialogue within the circle in both the Biigajiiskaan program and ROS intervention. Successful engagement begins in accordance with local protocols – for example, with smudging and tobacco (Biigajiiskaan). Working through difference can be a challenging and satisfying process.

Indigenous- and Women-Led

Biigajiiskaan is an Indigenous-led program. In phase one of the Biigajiiskaan program evaluation/research, the narratives of the stakeholders (Elders, Knowledge Keepers, providers, and persons accessing services) were integrated into the ongoing development of Indigenous pathways, and this is ongoing. The phase one findings highlighted the following central themes/needs: culture as healing, decolonizing practice, equity-oriented care, seamless pathways, and people-centred care. In addition, support was expressed for an Indigenous Governance Circle to oversee the program's development.

The positive findings of the ROS study strongly suggest that the intervention's success has been in large part due to the meaningful engagement with the women, including the Elders and Knowledge Keepers – moving from a "women-centred" to a "women-led" model shifted the intervention *and* the outcomes. For example, as noted earlier, more structure was provided within the circle, nurses were provided with stronger knowledge of Indigenous women's experiences, and the principles underlying the iHEAL intervention were tailored to fit with women's experiences.

Culture as Care and Healing

Culture is a key determinant of Indigenous people's health (Greenwood et al., 2018); this translates into respecting and valuing Indigenous cultural knowledge, approaches, languages, and ways of knowing and incorporating these into programing and policy development (Ninomiya et al., 2020, p. 3) – all of which is foundational to the Biigajiiskaan program and ROS intervention. At the same time, research has shown that focusing solely on culture without addressing discrimination and structural violence within health care institutions does not address the fundamental challenges faced by Indigenous patients (Greenwood, 2019; Wylie, McConkey, & Carrado, 2019, 2021).

Community Development, Ownership, and Capacity-Building

Greater engagement with local rural Indigenous communities is a goal of Biigajiiskaan. Although several First Nations communities access mental health services in the urban setting and have strong connections to them, it remains a priority to ensure that accessible, culturally safe, trauma- and violence-informed, person-centred services are developed by and for the community.

Quality Care Services

Ongoing program evaluation/research (process and summative) is built into both the Biigajiiskaan program and ROS. For example, phase two of the Biigajiiskaan program evaluation/research is ready to commence. The aims of this phase are to (1) explore ongoing client, team, hospital, and community perceptions of Biigajiiskaan as they relate to cultural safety and accessibility, (2) explore the workplace experiences and reflections of the Biigajiiskaan team, (3) monitor and evaluate Biigajiiskaan services in keeping with what has been identified as important outcomes (e.g., culture as healing), and (4) collect data to support reporting requirements as defined by the program funder. Data (survey and narrative) are collected and shared in keeping with the principles of ownership, control, access, and possession (OCAP) (Schnarch, 2004). For example, for the Biigajiiskaan program a data-sharing agreement is being developed among St Joseph's Health Care London (Lawson Research Institute), Western University, and Atlohsa. In keeping with employment of "culture as healing," Atlohsa also uses the Native Mental Wellness Tool. ROS is a health promotion intervention, and Biigajiiskaan is a program. Both have data collection mechanisms to ensure quality and safety in keeping with Indigenous perspectives.

BOX 3.1.1 AMBER'S JOURNEY: BUILDING PURPOSEFUL RELATIONSHIPS TO TRANSFORM HEALTH CARE

Chantel Antone, Lisa Jackson, and Lloy Wylie

Amber had worked in the field of Indigenous health services for more than a decade, in a province with a dedicated First Nations Health Authority built in partnership with all First Nations in the province and the provincial and federal governments. Basically, her job was to figure out ways to advance First Nations interests in the health care system, taking up the key problems of racism and poor access to high-quality, culturally safe care.

Expanding the presence and roles of Indigenous patient navigators was a big priority. These navigators had unique insight into the needs and gaps in the health care system. Amber learned a lot from her Indigenous colleagues about the challenges they faced as liaisons between the community and the hospital. Community members were often reluctant to come to the hospital, but the navigators were often told by their bosses at the hospital that their work couldn't leave the building. This made community engagement very challenging, if not impossible.

A serious barrier for Indigenous people was that they needed to travel in order to access health care services. Travel to a city is stressful, time-consuming, dangerous, lonely, disorienting, and expensive. Federally funded Non-Insured Health Benefits (NIHBs) wouldn't always cover all the costs, and people rarely had funds for someone to accompany them. On top of that, sometimes after a day of travel and a long wait at the hospital, an appointment would be cancelled with no warning and rescheduled for weeks later. This would then require more travel for the same procedure, leading to questions from the NIHB office as to why the travel needed to be covered again. There were so many gaps to be addressed. Practice changes were needed to improve service coordination, and some of the barriers to practice change were due to policies that were misaligned with Indigenous people's needs. In an ideal world, coordination of services would result in wraparound care that met those complex needs. Although there were still huge gaps, First Nations, and the staff working for them, like Amber, were at the health system planning tables at least for the time being.

Fast-forward a year, and Amber is now in a new province, in a new role as a researcher at a university, with its partner hospitals and health sciences centres. Fresh from the planning tables in her previous role, Amber asked the leadership in her hospital department what was being done to advance Indigenous health equity. She was a bit taken aback by the response – this was an issue for community health, not the hospital, where staff were much too busy delivering "real medical services" to have time for that. Amber knew she needed to talk to the Indigenous people who worked in health care locally to find out the lay of the land. Those staffing and leading Indigenous health care centres and band offices, as well as people working in Indigenous liaison roles in her local area, shared many of the problems she was familiar with from her old job: models of health that don't meet needs, poor access to services in the community setting, a lack of coordination of care, and racism that made many Indigenous people never want to go back to any of the hospitals, even if it meant dying at home. In all of those discussions, Amber heard the same thing over and over again: "People are having bad experiences in those hospitals, and that has to change." There was clearly a gap in understanding between the hospital and the community. It was going to take time to figure out what strategies would be needed to make change.

Embarking on her journey of discovery, Amber started interviewing care providers about their experiences working with Indigenous people. Along the way, she met Jennifer, an Indigenous patient navigator, who was working in the hospital to support Indigenous patients and families. Amber and Jennifer checked in with each other regularly to assess the situation and prepare a plan of action.

Change was slow, and more resources were needed to take on the work of making the hospital a safe place for Indigenous people. Seven years into that partnership, a new staff member, Christine, joined the Indigenous team, doubling its size. The team was feeling good about the potential for real change, especially given the recent attention to racism against Indigenous people in the health care system. Reflecting on factors that enable and support the practice of culturally safe care, Amber, Jennifer, and Christine highlighted the following:

- Creating safe spaces to talk about challenges and potential solutions.
- Learning from similar and different practices, both good and bad, from elsewhere
- Collecting and sharing knowledge and evidence of various kinds to "make the case" and support policy and practice changes toward cultural safety.
- Focusing on systemic racism and how experiences of micro-aggressions and the individual behaviours of service providers fit into these larger social patterns and norms.
- Taking the long view, noting the scope and magnitude of the problem, and accumulating wins as they come along.

In thinking about her journey, Amber now understood how important it was to be an ally. She was able to begin some conversations to test the waters, including in the most difficult spaces and places: those that have not (yet) made space for Indigenous voices. Together the three of them strategized ways to make that space by advancing strategies for Indigenous communities to participate in health service planning and design and for Indigenous staff to express their opinions as well as the community's concerns.

Lessons Learned

All team members, Indigenous and non-Indigenous, involved in the cases and reflections presented here understand and fully support Indigenous self-determination, and most have spent years in the field of Indigenous health research, yet all of us would agree that every project brings new learning and underscores the importance of what is already known. The following considerations may be helpful.

Leadership and Organizational Commitment

The enactment of trauma- and violence-informed care (TVIC) in culturally safe, contextually tailored, and people-centred ways must be supported at the organizational level, and similarly, those providing direct service need to be engaged from the beginning in this work – organizations cannot change without buy-in from those in direct service. Biigajiiskaan has been developing over the past three years; still, it has taken time for awareness of and support for care from within the institution and community to be realized. For example, referrals from the institution and community engagement have shed light on the benefits of ongoing engagement with leadership and direct service staff, much of which has been done through the program lead and other providers who have worked in the institutional setting and who already have strong connections in the community. Similarly, the ROS intervention team has a long-standing relationship with the community of practice – it has taken time and a commitment to ongoing learning for all to build connections with leaders and organizations as well as providers.

Understanding World View Differences

In its third year of development, Biigajiiskaan has faced challenges related mainly to the fundamental difference between the two world views underpinning the program. The policies and associated practices of dominant systems of care are often at odds with Indigenous perspectives – for example, these perspectives diverge in terms of healing, health, and well-being. A strengths-based approach is very different from a deficit-based model when it comes to assessment and treatment, and what is deemed as mental illness by some may be understood as a spiritual journey by another. The danger of re-enacting or inadvertently triggering others' experiences of trauma and violence is always present. Listening, deep reflection, taking pause, and being fully engaged and committed to creating safe spaces and dialogue are all musts. The concept of cultural safety makes us reflect on how power is operating in these circumstances as well as on how to enact the principles of TVIC – leading with strengths-based and capacity-building approaches, providing opportunities for collaboration, and attending to need for ongoing education regarding the harms of trauma and violence.

The Burden of History

The Biigajiiskaan program and the ROS team have been navigating the daily reality of new and evolving forms of colonial relations, both past (the burden of history for Indigenous peoples) and present (neocolonialism). The influence of this factor should not be underestimated and indeed should be anticipated and acknowledged. For example, in the Biigajiiskaan project, that factor has been ever-present as it relates to institutional policies (hospital), the sharing of administrative data-sharing agreements, transfers of funds, and so on. This has impeded program development. At the beginning of the program, the program lead was not paid for months due to this factor.

Contractual Funding

Year-to-year contract funding and living with uncertainty at year-end limit the ability of Indigenous health programs and other NGOs to provide a seamless continuum of access and care. For example, at the time of writing this chapter (fiscal year end), the Biigajiiskaan program leads had to inform the staff as well as those accessing services that the program might lose its funding, even though they had been told otherwise. The funding was in fact allocated a few weeks later; even so, the danger that it might be lost seriously disrupted program services. This is a norm for Indigenous and other NGOs offering health and social support services. Similarly, the research leads of ROS/iHEAL have collaborative relationships with various community health settings, but despite evidence of effectiveness, they have yet to find a sustainable path to move from research funding to program funding.

Conclusion

Many Indigenous peoples and communities are enjoying healthy and prosperous lives, but many are not. Social and structural inequities continue to lead to increasingly poor health for Indigenous peoples. For example, racism and discrimination persist within systems of health and social services, with many recent horrific cases emerging in the news media, and those cases represent the "tip of the iceberg" when it comes to the everyday reality faced by many Indigenous people. It is in this context that we shift attention to the culture of health care and to the enactment of equity- and IND-equity-oriented approaches within this setting at both organizational and provider levels.

KEY MESSAGES AND IMPLICATIONS

- Culturally safe, contextually tailored, person-centred TVIC holds promise for disrupting the status quo.
- The cases presented reflect what can actually be achieved when we attend to the unique features of Indigenous people's health and well-being in genuine, meaningful partnership as Indigenous and non-Indigenous people engaged in this work.

ADDITIONAL RESOURCES

- San'yas, the Indigenous Cultural Safety (ICS) Training Program (https://sanyas.ca/)
- British Columbia: https://sanyas.ca/core-training/british-columbia

- Ontario: https://sanyas.ca/core-training/ontario
- Manitoba: https://sanyas.ca/core-training/manitoba
- EQUIP Health Care: www.equiphealthcare.ca
- Equipping for Equity Online Modules, Module 4 – Cultural Safety: https://equiphealthcare.ca/equipping-for-equity-online-modules/module-4 (free, registration required)

REFERENCES

Aboriginal Nurses Association of Canada (2009). *Cultural competence and cultural safety in nursing education: A framework for First Nations, Inuit, and Métis nursing.* Retrieved from https://www.indigenousnurses.ca/resources/publications/cultural-competence-and-cultural-safety-nursing-education-framework-first

Baba, L. (2013). *Cultural safety in First Nations, Inuit, and Métis public health: Environmental scan of cultural competency and safety in education, training and health services.* Prince George, BC: National Collaborating Centre for Aboriginal Health. Retrieved from https://www.ccnsa-nccah.ca/docs/emerging/RPT-CulturalSafetyPublicHealth-Baba-EN.pdf

Berg, K., McLane, P., Eshkakogan, N., Mantha, J., Lee, T., Crowshoe, C., & Phillips, A. (2019). Perspectives on Indigenous cultural competency and safety in Canadian hospital emergency departments: A scoping review. *International Emergency Nursing, 43*, 133–40. https://doi.org/10.1016/j.ienj.2019.01.004

Browne, A.J. & Varcoe, C. (2019). Cultural and social considerations in health assessment. In A J. Browne, J. MacDonald-Jenkins, & M. Luctkar-Flude (Eds.), *Physical examination and health assessment by C. Jarvis* (3rd Canadian ed.) (pp. 28–45). Toronto, ON: Elsevier.

Browne, A.J., Varcoe, C., Ford-Gilboe, M., Wathen, C.N., Smye, V., Jackson, B.E., ... Blanchet Garneau, A. (2018). Disruption as opportunity: Impacts of an organizational health equity intervention in primary care clinics. *International Journal for Equity in Health, 17*(1), 154. https://doi.org/10.1186/s12939-018-0820-2

Browne, A.J., Varcoe, C., Lavoie, J., Smye, V., Wong, S., Krause, M., ... Fridkin, A. (2016). Enhancing health care equity with Indigenous populations: Evidence-based strategies from an ethnographic study. *BMC Health Services Research, 16*(544). https://doi.org/10.1186/s12913-016-1707-9

Browne, A.J., Varcoe, C., & Ward, C. (2021). San'yas Indigenous cultural safety training as an educational intervention: Promoting anti-racism and equity in health systems, policies and practices. *International Indigenous Policy Journal, 12*(3). http://doi.org/10.18584/iipj.2021.12.3.8204

Brownridge, D.A. (2008). Understanding the elevated risk of partner violence against Aboriginal women: A comparison of two nationally representative surveys of Canada. *Journal of Family Violence, 23*(5), 353–67. https://doi.org/10.1007/s10896-008-9160-0

Daoud, N., Smylie, J., Urquia, M., Allan, B., & O'Campo, P. (2013). The contribution of socio-economic position to the excesses of violence and intimate partner violence among Aboriginal versus non-Aboriginal women in Canada. *Canadian Journal of Public Health, 104*(4), e278–e283. https://doi.org/10.17269/cjph.104.3724

Dion Stout, M. (2012). Ascribed health and wellness, Atikowisi mimýw-ayawin, to achieved health and wellness, Kaskitmaasowin miyw-aýawin: Shifting the paradigm. *Canadian Journal of Nursing Research, 44*(2), 11–14.

Downey, B. (2020). Completing the circle: Towards the achievement of IND-equity – a culturally relevant health equity model by/for Indigenous populations. *Witness: The Canadian Journal of Critical Nursing Discourse, 2*(1), 97–110. https://doi.org/10.25071/2291-5796.59

Dyck, I., & Kearns, R. (1995). Transforming the relations of research: Towards culturally safe geographies of health and healing. *Health & Place, 1*(3), 137–47. https://doi.org/10.1016/1353-8292(95)00020-M

Ermine, M.A., Sinclair, R., Jeffery, B., & Indigenous Peoples' Health Research Centre (2004). *The ethics of research involving Indigenous peoples: Report of the Indigenous Peoples' Health Research Centre to the Interagency Advisory Panel on Research Ethics.* Retrieved from https://www.researchgate.net/publication/317055157_The_Ethics_of_Research_Involving_Indigenous_Peoples

Firestone, M., Syrette, J., Jourdain, T., Recollet, V., & Smylie, J. (2019). "I feel safe just coming here because there are other Native brothers and sisters": Findings from a community-based evaluation of the Niiwin Wendaanimak Four Winds Wellness Program. *Canadian Journal of Public Health, 110*(4), 404–13. https://doi.org/10.17269/s41997-019-00192-6

Ford-Gilboe, M., Wathen, N., Varcoe, C., Herbert, C., Jackson, B., Lavoie, J.G., ... Browne, A.J. (2018). How equity-oriented health care affects health: Key mechanisms and implications for primary health care practice and policy. *The Milbank Quarterly, 96*(4), 635–71. https://doi.org/10.1111/1468-0009.12349

Gerlach, A.J., Browne, A.J., & Greenwood, M. (2017). Engaging Indigenous families in a community-based Indigenous early childhood programme in British Columbia, Canada: A cultural safety perspective. *Health & Social Care in the Community, 25*(6), 1763–73. https://doi.org/10.1111/hsc.12450

Greenwood, M. (2019). Modelling change and cultural safety: A case study in Northern British Columbia health system transformation. *Healthcare Management Forum, 32*(1), 11–14. https://doi.org/10.1177/0840470418807948

Greenwood, M., de Leeuw, S., & Lindsay, N. (2018). *Beyond the social: Determinants of Indigenous peoples' health* (2nd ed.). Toronto, ON: Canadian Scholars' Press.

Greenwood, M., Lindsay, N., & Loewen, D. (2017). Ethical spaces and places: Indigenous cultural safety in British Columbia health care. *Alter Native: An International Journal of Indigenous Peoples, 13*(3), 179–89. https://doi.org/10.1177//1177180117714411

Health Canada. (2015). *First Nations Mental Wellness Continuum Framework – Full Report*. Ottawa, ON. Retrieved from https://thunderbirdpf.org/wp-content/uploads/2015/01/24-14-1273-FN-Mental-Wellness-Framework-EN05_low.pdf

Hogue, M., & Bartlett, C. (2014). Two-eyed seeing: Creating a new liminal space in education. *Canada Education*, 56(3), 30–1.

Kitching, G.T., Firestone, M., Schei, B., Wolfe, S., Bourgeois, C., O'Campo, P., . . . Smylie, J. (2020). Unmet health needs and discrimination by healthcare providers among an Indigenous population in Toronto, Canada. *Canadian Journal of Public Health*, 111(1), 40–9. https://doi.org/10.17269/s41997-019-00242-z

Lynam, J., & Young, R. (2000). Towards the creation of a culturally safe research environment. *Health*, 4(1), 5–23. https://doi.org/10.1177%2F136345930000400101

McCall, J., Mollison, A., Browne, A., Parker, J., & Pauly, B. (2017). The role of knowledge brokers: Lessons from a community-based research study of cultural safety in relation to people who use drugs. *The Canadian Journal of Action Research*, 18(1), 34–51. https://doi.org/10.33524/cjar.v18i1.320

McKenzie, H.A., Varcoe, C., Browne, A.J., & Day, L. (2016). Disrupting the continuities among residential schools, the "sixties scoop," and child welfare: An analysis of colonial and neocolonial discourses, policies and practices, and strategies for change. *International Indigenous Policy Journal*, 7(2), 1–24. https://doi.org/10.18584/iipj.2016.7.2.4

McLane, P., Bill, L., & Barnabe, C. (2021). First Nations members' emergency department experiences in Alberta: A qualitative study. *CJEM: Canadian Journal of Emergency Medicine*, 23(1), 63–74. https://doi.org/10.1007/s43678-020-00009-3

National Aboriginal Health Organization [NAHO]. (2008). *Cultural competency and safety: A guide for health care administrators, providers, and educators*. Retrieved from http://archives.algomau.ca/main/sites/default/files/2012-25_003_019.pdf

Ninomiya, M.M., George, N., George, J., Linklater, R., Bull, J., Plain, S., ... Wells, S. (2020). A community-driven and evidence-based approach to developing mental wellness strategies in First Nations: A program protocol. *Research Involvement and Engagement*, 6(5). https://doi.org/10.1186/s40900-020-0176-9

Papps, E., & Ramsden, I. (1996). Cultural safety in nursing: The New Zealand experience. *International Journal for Quality in Health Care*, 8(5), 491–7. https://doi.org/10.1093/intqhc/8.5.491

Pauly, B., McCall, J., Browne, A.J., Parker, J., & Mollison, A. (2015). Towards cultural safety: Nurse and patient constructions of illicit substance use in hospitalized settings. *Advances in Nursing Science*, 38(2), 121–35. https://doi.org/10.1097/ANS.0000000000000070

Pedersen, J.S., Malcoe, L.H., & Pulkingham, J. (2013). Explaining aboriginal/non-aboriginal inequalities in postseparation violence against Canadian women: Application of a structural violence approach. *Violence Against Women*, 19(8), 1034–58. https://doi.org/10.1177/1077801213499245

Phillips-Beck, W., Eni, R., Lavoie, J.G., Avery Kinew, K., Kyoon Achan, G., & Katz, A. (2020). Confronting racism within the Canadian healthcare system: Systemic exclusion of First Nations from quality and consistent care. *International Journal of Environmental Research And Public Health, 17*(22). https://doi.org/10.3390/ijerph17228343

Polaschek, N.R. (1998). Cultural safety: A new concept in nursing people of different ethnicities. *Journal of Advanced Nursing, 27,* 452–7. https://doi.org/10.1046/j.1365-2648.1998.00547.x

Ramsden, I. (1993). Kawa whakaruruhau: Cultural safety in nursing education in Aotearoa, New Zealand. *Nursing Praxis in New Zealand, 8*(3), 4–10.

Ramsden, I. (2000). Cultural safety/Kawa whakaruruhau ten years on: A personal overview. *Nursing Praxis in New Zealand, 15*(1), 4–12.

Schnarch, B. (2004). Ownership, control, access, and possession (OCAP) or self-determination applied to research: A critical analysis of contemporary First Nations research and some options for First Nations communities. *Journal of Aboriginal Health, 1*(1), 80–95. https://doi.org/10.3138/ijih.v1i1.28934

Smye, V., & Browne, A.J. (2002). "Cultural safety" and the analysis of health policy affecting Aboriginal people. *Nurse Researcher: The International Journal of Research Methodology in Nursing and Health Care, 9*(3), 42–56. https://doi.org/10.7748/nr2002.04.9.3.42.c6188

Smye, V., Varcoe, C., Browne, A.J., Dion Stout, M., Josewski, V., Ford-Gilboe, M., & Keith, B. (2021). Violence at the intersections of women's lives in an urban context: Indigenous women's experiences of leaving and/or staying with an abusive partner. *Violence Against Women, 27*(10), 1586–607. https://doi.org/10.1177/1077801220947183

Urbanoski, K., Pauly, B., Inglis, D., Cameron, F., Haddad, T., Phillips, J., . . . Wallace, B. (2020). Defining culturally safe primary care for people who use substances: A participatory concept mapping study. *BMC Health Services Research,* 20. https://doi.org/10.1186/s12913-020-05915-x

Varcoe, C., Browne, A.J., Ford-Gilboe, M., Dion Stout, M., McKenzie, H., Price, R., . . . Merritt-Gray, M. (2017). Reclaiming Our Spirits: Development and pilot testing of a health promotion intervention for Indigenous women who have experienced intimate partner violence. *Research In Nursing & Health, 40*(3), 237–54. https://doi.org/10.1002/nur.21795

Varcoe, C., Browne, A.J., & Kang-Dhillon, B.K. (2019). Culture and cultural safety: Beyond cultural inventories. In C.D. Gregory, L. Raymond-Seniuk, L. Patrick, & T. Stephen (Eds.), *Fundamentals: Perspectives on the art and science of Canadian nursing* (pp. 243–61). Philadelphia, PA: Lippincott.

Varcoe, C., Ford-Gilboe, M., Browne, A.J., Perrin, N., Bungay, V., McKenzie, H., . . . Dion Stout, M. (2019). The efficacy of a health promotion intervention for Indigenous women: Reclaiming Our Spirits. *Journal of Interpersonal Violence.* https://doi.org/10.1177/0886260518820818

Ward, C., Morton Ninomiya, M.E., & Firestone, M. (2021). Anti-Indigenous racism training and culturally safe learning: Theory, practice, and pedagogy. *International*

Journal of Indigenous Health, 16(1), 304–13. https://doi.org/10.32799/ijih.v16i1.33204

Wuest, J., M., Merritt-Gray, N., Dube, M.J., Hodgins, J., Malcolm, J.A., Majerovich, K., ... Varcoe, C. (2015). The process, outcomes, and challenges of feasibility studies conducted in partnership with stakeholders: A health intervention for women survivors of intimate partner violence. *Research in Nursing and Health, 38*(1), 82–96. https://doi.org/10.1002/nur.21636

Wyatt, R., Laderman, M., Botwinick, L., Mate, K., & Whittington, J. (2016). Achieving Health Equity: A Guide for Health Care Organizations. IHI White Paper [Internet]. Cambridge, MA: Institute for Healthcare Improvement. Available from http://www.ihi.org/resources/Pages/IHIWhitePapers/Achieving-Health-Equity.aspx

Wylie, L., & McConkey, S. (2019). Insiders' insight: Discrimination against Indigenous peoples through the eyes of health care professionals. *Journal of Racial and Ethnic Health Disparities, 6*, 37–45. https://doi.org/10.1007/s40615-018-0495-9

Wylie, L., McConkey, S., & Corrado. A.M. (2019). Colonial legacies and collaborative action: Improving Indigenous peoples' health care in Canada. *The International Indigenous Policy Journal, 10*(5). https://doi.org/10.18584/iipj.2019.10.5.9340

Wylie, L., McConkey, S., & Corrado. A.M. (2021). It's a journey not a checkbox: Indigenous cultural safety from training to transformation. *International Journal of Indigenous Health, 16*(1), 314–32. https://doi.org/10.32799/ijih.v16i1.33240

3.2 The Nexus of Trauma, Violence, Chronic Pain, Substance Use, and Stigma

COLLEEN VARCOE

Providing care that is trauma- and violence-informed requires an understanding of the relationships among trauma, violence, chronic pain, substance use, and stigma. Not all people who experience trauma and violence will develop chronic pain or use substances in ways that interfere with their lives; conversely, not all people with chronic pain or who use substances in such ways have experienced trauma and violence. However, there is a strong correlation between the two, and experiences of violence and trauma, chronic pain, and substance use that interferes with your life are all stigmatizing. Not all people who experience trauma, violence, chronic pain, and substance use issues are economically or socially marginalized, but when they are, the stigma they experience is exponentially worse (see figure 3.2.1). People who experience structural violence and inequities such as racism, poverty, and dispossession (from country, land, or nation) are stigmatized through multiple systems such as the criminal justice system, child protection services, immigration bodies, and health care services. Given that experiences of stigma deter people from services and shape service encounters, this chapter invites you to consider these intersections, with an emphasis on stigma.

By the end of this chapter, readers will have (1) considered the implications of the intersections among trauma, violence, pain, substance use, and stigma for providing TVIC in their practice, (2) further integrated a critical understanding of substance use and substance use stigma, cultural safety, and harm reduction with TVIC, (3) evaluated their own practice with regard to the provision of non-judgmental, non-stigmatizing, culturally safe, harm-reducing services, (4) identified organizational policies and cultures that support such practice, and (5) developed a plan for their ongoing learning.

This chapter is aimed at all service providers who are seeking to make their work and organizations more trauma- and violence-informed. The issue of stigma and its intersections with trauma, violence, chronic pain, and substance use will be relevant to all, and thus are the focus of this chapter; however, a

202 Colleen Varcoe

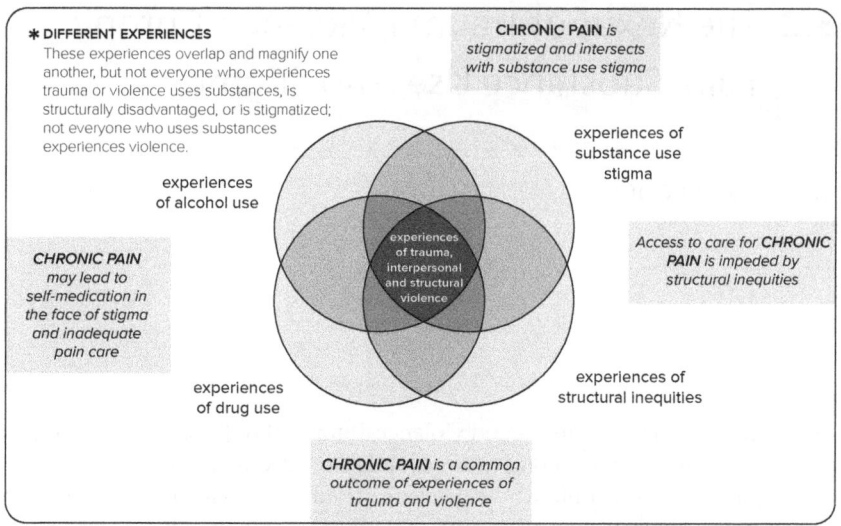

Figure 3.2.1 Chronic pain and differential experiences of harm and stigma. Copyright 2021, the authors.

deeper understanding of each of these will be more relevant to some than to others. For example, the neurobiology of the relationship between trauma and violence and pain will be highly relevant to health care providers but may be less so to others. This chapter will encourage you to identify where you want to deepen your knowledge and direct you to key resources for doing so. For an online learning module that covers the material in this chapter in depth, see the links to key resources at the end of the chapter.

Key Concepts and Their Interrelations

Trauma, Violence, and Chronic Pain

The links between trauma, violence, and chronic pain have a physiological basis, with those experiencing trauma more likely to experience chronic pain (Afari et al., 2014; Gasperi, Afari, Goldberg, Suri, & Panizzon, 2021; Keeshin, Cronholm, & Strawn, 2012; Williams, Cole, Girdler, & Cromeens, 2020). Whether histories of violence are measured among those seeking services for chronic pain, or chronic pain is measured among those experiencing violence, interpersonal violence and chronic pain are highly correlated (e.g., Craner, Lake, Bancroft, & Hanson, 2020; Medina, Erazo, Dávila, & Humphreys, 2011; Wuest et al., 2021). Furthermore, across the lifespan, chronic pain is highly correlated with post-traumatic stress disorder (PTSD) (Benedict, Keenan, Nitz, & Moeller-Bertram, 2020; Manhapra, Stefanovics, Rhee, & Rosenheck, 2021; Sprang, Bush, Coker, & Brancato, 2020). Keeshin and colleagues (2012) summarized that (a) specific neurobiochemical changes are associated with exposure to violence and abuse, (b) several biological pathways have the potential to lead to the development of future illness, and (c) common physiological mechanisms may moderate the severity, phenomenology, or clinical course of medical illnesses in individuals with histories of exposure to violence or abuse (p. 41).

Because of the disproportionately high prevalence and levels of chronic pain among those who have experienced trauma and violence, it can be used to indicate where TVIC is most crucial. Specifically, this understanding can direct providers to consider the impact of stressful life events among people with chronic pain and to address pain concerns among those who have experienced or are experiencing trauma and violence (Gasperi et al., 2021). As an individual provider, you can develop a high level of alertness that those presenting with chronic pain may have experienced violence and trauma and that those with trauma histories may be living with pain.

Chronic pain is itself stigmatizing, and when coupled with some forms of substance use (e.g., use of prescriptions beyond what is prescribed, injection drug use), pain stigma and substance use stigma intersect. This can be seen most easily in health care providers' harmful dismissal of people in pain as "drug seeking" and the disbelief those people face regarding whether they are actually in pain (Dassieu, Kaboré, Choinière, Arruda, & Roy, 2020; Dassieu, et al., 2021). Because such stigmas intersect with racism, classism, and other forms of discrimination, certain groups of people are more likely to experience such dismissal. Given the evidence, service providers can assume that a high proportion of people living with chronic pain will have histories of trauma and violence; furthermore, given the dynamics of stigma, providers can assume that people living with chronic pain will have faced disbelief, dismissal, and discrimination. Making assumptions is part of thinking and decision-making, but assumptions should be checked for both their basis and their impact. Practising based on evidence-based assumptions about trauma, violence, and chronic pain means treating every person as the "most traumatized" and practising as though pain is a common outcome of trauma and violence.

Trauma, Violence, and Substance Use

The relationship between all forms of interpersonal violence, including child maltreatment, sexual assault, and intimate partner violence, and increased and/or problematic substance use has been shown consistently across age groups (Angelone, Marcantonio, & Melillo, 2018; Fletcher, 2021; Ganson et al., 2021; Gezinski, Gonzalez-Pons, & Rogers, 2021; Golder, Connell, & Sullivan, 2012;

Levin et al., 2021). The effects of different forms of interpersonal violence are cumulative and include the risks for harmful substance use (Afifi et al., 2020; Merrick et al., 2017; Pereda & Gallardo-Pujol, 2014). Thus, service providers should consider that people having difficulties with substance use may have histories of trauma and violence and that people with such histories may struggle with substance use issues.

Like the relationship between trauma and chronic pain, the relationship between trauma and substance use is physiological. The physiological evidence of neurobiological changes associated with substance use has led to the "brain disease model of addiction" dominating research, health care, policy, and public understanding (Field, Heather, & Wiers, 2019; Racine, Sattler, & Escande, 2017). However, this model has been much criticized. Lewis (2017) and others argue that the brain disease model does not explain the fact that most people with "substance use disorder" recover and that a developmental learning theory of addiction is more plausible: "Because trauma – whether physical, psychological, or sexual – is often considered the root cause of long-term anxiety and depression; and post-traumatic stress disorder (PTSD) is highly correlated with substance use … addiction can be viewed as a form of self-medication that works against psychological suffering" (p. 9). Approaching people with this understanding sets up service providers to be more compassionate with those they serve and to avoid blame or judgment.

Chronic Pain and Substance Use

The management of chronic pain in Canada is in dismal straits. The Canadian Pain Task Force (2019) found that many people live with unmanaged pain but that the burden of chronic pain is not shared equally among Canadians. Pain is more common among older adults, females, Indigenous peoples, veterans, and populations affected by social inequities and discrimination, and people in these groups face significant discrimination (Craig et al., 2020; Wallace et al., 2021). People who live with chronic non-cancer pain report facing disbelief about and downplaying of their pain by health care providers and high levels of unmet need, and they often resort to using substances, including alcohol, opioids, and stimulants, to treat their pain (Beliveau et al., 2021; Boissoneault, Lewis, & Nixon, 2019; Degenhardt et al., 2021; Martel, Shir, & Ware, 2018). The Canadian Pain Task Force noted that anxiety over opioids has also led to unmanaged pain, which in turn has led people to use illegal substances to manage their pain.

Given the associations between trauma and violence and pain, and the associations between trauma and violence and substance use, it is not surprising that studies of people who use drugs show a high prevalence of chronic non-cancer pain (Bicket et al., 2020; Dassieu et al., 2020; John & Wu, 2020). For example, in a recent Canadian study of a community-based sample of people who use illicit drugs, 45 per cent reported chronic non-cancer pain, and of these, over 20 per cent used substances other than prescribed pain medication to relieve pain and 29 per cent had been refused pain medication by a physician (Kaboré et al., 2020). Chronic pain contributes significantly to the unmet care needs for people who use drugs (Moallef et al., 2020).

Substance Use Stigma

Many people use substances, but not all are stigmatized. Substance use stigma is experienced by people who use certain drugs (e.g., methamphetamines), use certain routes (e.g., injection), and ingest certain forms of alcohol (e.g., non-beverage alcohol). Such stigma is experienced more by people who are exposed to scrutiny or who are visible when using (e.g., people who do not have private homes). It is also experienced by people who are targeted by others with stereotypes that work in tandem with racism, classism, and other forms of stigma. This can be seen most obviously in the pernicious stereotypes targeted toward Indigenous peoples and toward those doing street-level sex work. TVIC is essential in relation to anyone likely to experience substance use stigma, for at least three reasons. First, any person who has experienced such stigma will be more reluctant to seek care and less trusting of the care they receive. Thus, service providers must work to convey respect and build trust if the services they offer are to be effective. Second, those persons who do use substances in ways that may be harmful are much more likely to have a history of trauma and to be dealing with ongoing violence. Thus, they are at greater risk of services being retraumatizing. Third, common public discourse that treats substance use as a "choice" harmfully seeps into policies and services, shaping these to be primarily at the level of the individual (e.g., safe supply; provider education). Service providers who understand the relationships among violence, trauma, substance use, and stigma can contribute not only to safer services for individuals but also to public discourse and wider and more effective policies, such as those related to safe, affordable housing and decriminalization of drug use.

Reclaiming Our Spirits (ROS): A Case Example

For more than a decade, a research team has been evolving an intervention – iHEAL –to support women in the process of leaving an abusive partner (Ford-Gilboe, Merritt-Gray, Varcoe, & Wuest, 2011; Wuest et al., 2015). The intervention has built explicitly on an understanding of the cumulative health effects of violence, which include chronic pain (Ford-Gilboe et al., 2009; Wuest et al., 2009; Wuest et al., 2010). In partnership with Indigenous women, Elders and scholars, and building on team members' research with Indigenous communities (e.g., Browne et al., 2016; Smye et al., 2020; Varcoe, Brown, Calam, Harvey, & Tallio, 2013), the team has developed a version of the intervention that integrates Indigenous knowledge and is designed specifically for Indigenous women (Varcoe et al., 2017). Key features include attention to the impacts of colonization and Indigenous-specific racism, as well as related training for the nurses who deliver the intervention, guidance in all matters from Indigenous Elders and scholars, integration of Indigenous traditions and ceremonies, meaningful relationships with Indigenous organizations, and access to guidance from Elders for the women, including a regular Elder-led circle (see also chapter 3.1). Throughout, we intentionally took a TVIC approach. The first offering provided by ROS was to Indigenous women living in highly marginalizing social and economic conditions. The women had all experienced extensive and multiple forms of violence, including structural violence in the form of systemic racism as well as (for most) policy-induced poverty and state care during childhood through either residential school, "Indian Day School," hospitals, and/or foster care. The women had high levels of chronic pain, and many identified as having a problem related to substance use. All of this established a context in which it was essential to situate TVIC at the nexus of chronic pain, substance use, and stigma.

TVIC at the Nexus

Considering the intersections among trauma, violence, pain, substance use, and stigma deepens and extends each of the principles of TVIC. *Understanding trauma and violence (including interpersonal and structural violence), and its impacts on people's lives and behaviours* (principle 1) means understanding the relationship between trauma and violence, pain, and substance use. Doing so helps shift providers' understanding of substance use from a "choice" model to a trauma model. It also helps providers be attentive to the likelihood that people presenting with chronic pain may have trauma histories, and that people who have trauma histories will have a high likelihood of pain. In ROS we asked women about chronic pain at the beginning of the intervention. As in our previous studies with women experiencing violence, the women had very high levels of disabling pain; nurses did frequent pain assessments and worked to support the women in management of their pain. The women's levels of pain did not diminish through the intervention; however, they repeatedly commented that they greatly appreciated the nurses' attention to their pain and acknowledgment of the role their experiences of violence played in causing the pain – they felt better understood, and if they were using non-prescription substances, they did not feel judged. Thus, attention to pain contributed to trusting relationships.

To *create emotionally, culturally, and physically safe environments for service users and providers* (principle 2), those providers must understand the pervasive nature and harmful impact of pain and substance use stigma and its intersections with other forms of stigma and discrimination; they must also strive to convey trustworthiness. The women in ROS, as Indigenous women, faced substance use stigma daily. Whether they used drugs or not, or drank alcohol or not, they were assumed across health and social services to do both. Their efforts to seek pain relief, be it via prescriptions or non-pharmacological modalities, were met with scepticism or worse, and service providers accused them of "drug-seeking." The nurses regularly accompanied women to appointments to try to mitigate the stigma they experienced; at the same time, they tried to shift how other service providers viewed the women.

To *foster opportunities for choice, collaboration, and connection* (principle 3) providers need to examine their biases toward chronic pain (i.e., what constitutes "legitimate" pain) and substance use (i.e.., who uses, what level of use is "acceptable" and so on) and work to develop and convey sincere understanding, empathy, and respect. Understanding the intersections of violence with chronic pain, substance use, and stigma can help service providers shift away from seeing substance use as a simple "choice" and begin to respect and support people's agency. In ROS, the nurses and Elders faced considerable challenges related to substance use, especially in circles, because each woman had a different relationship with substance use – some used, some did not, and some held stigmatizing attitudes toward one another. The nurses and Elders had to be accepting of the women's individual decisions, even while creating safety in groups, and this required negotiation among the women and with the nurses and Elders.

To *provide strengths-based and capacity-building ways to support service users* (principle 4), providers need to recognize the extant strengths and capacities that people deploy to survive stigma and the trauma and violence they have experienced. In ROS we did not focus on the women's substance use, although a high proportion of them identified themselves as "having a problem." Instead, we focused on each woman's health and well-being and on her own priorities, explicitly taking a strengths-based and capacity-building approach. Although it was not the goal of the intervention, many of the women sought treatment for substance use and/or changed their patterns. One woman said, "I don't drink on Wednesdays, because I know I am coming here on Thursdays."

Conclusion

The key messages below summarize specific strategies for applying a TVIC approach to care, with a focus on what this can look like when serving those experiencing trauma, violence, chronic pain, and substance use issues, and the interrelated forms of stigma associated with each. An important learning from our ongoing work has been the profound effect on attitudes and practices that this "nexus-focused" understanding brings. In evaluating TVIC education (Wathen, MacGregor, & Beyrem, 2021), for example (see also chapter 4.6), one of the most common "ah ha" moments experienced by a variety of health and social service providers and leaders is that trauma and violence cause physical, emotional, and spiritual pain and that those in pain have various ways to cope, including, in some cases, substance use in ways that cause further harms in their lives. Similarly, in the EQUIP Health Care study in primary care settings (see chapter 2.1), changes in practice toward TVIC and equity-promoting care supported service users in feeling more confident and capable in managing their health, which was related to small but important decreases in chronic pain disability (Ford-Gilboe et al., 2018). This reframing from judgment to understanding, respect, and compassion is exactly the kind of shift that a TVIC lens can offer.

KEY MESSAGES AND IMPLICATIONS

- Assume that a high proportion of people experiencing trauma and violence will experience chronic pain, and assume that a high proportion of people experiencing chronic pain will have experienced trauma and violence. Similarly, assume that a high proportion of people experiencing substance use stigma will have experienced trauma and violence; this means that service providers and organizations should be prepared to address both trauma and violence, and pain, simultaneously, and that a harm reduction/substance use health approach is indispensable to TVIC.
- Inquire about pain for all service users. This is useful information for every service provider, regardless of role. Such inquiry will convey your knowledge and acceptance and will provide a foundation for more effective service. (Try it out! Ask the next five people you work with if they experience pain, and see what happens.)
- Assume that people living with chronic pain will have faced disbelief, dismissal, and discrimination; assume that people who are labelled as substance-using will have experienced stigma and discrimination, particularly if they face poverty, housing instability, racism, and other forms of structural violence.
- Inquire about and acknowledge people's experiences of stigma. (Try asking: "Do you ever have trouble getting the help you need?")
- Recognize chronic pain. Acknowledge the challenges of living with chronic pain and dealing with stigma.
- Support people in their own analysis of their experiences and the interrelations between the trauma and violence they have experienced, the pain they may experience, and the challenges related to substances they may experience.
- Counter the stereotype of "drug seeking" with "seeking pain relief."
- Review organizational practices and language. Start with using the EQUIP Health Care "Rate Your Organization Tool" for substance use health and harm reduction.

3.2 The Nexus of Trauma, Violence, Chronic Pain, Substance Use, and Stigma

ADDITIONAL RESOURCES

- EQUIP Pathways e-Learning Module: https://equiphealthcare.ca/online-courses
- EQUIP Chronic Pain resources: https://equiphealthcare.ca/projects/chronic-pain
- Reclaiming Our Spirits video: https://youtu.be/hQcmRmBYNqY
- EQUIP Health Care "Rate Your Organization Tool" for substance use health and harm reduction: https://equiphealthcare.ca/projects/pathways/resources
- Substance use health resources:
  o Canadian Harm Reduction seminars with the Canadian Drug Policy Coalition (CDPC): https://stimulusconference.ca/stimulus-connect
  o American National Harm Reduction Coalition: https://harmreduction.org/our-work/training-capacity-building/online-training-institute
  o Community Addictions Peer Support Association (CAPSA): https://capsa.ca
- Pain BC Pain Education Hub: https://www.painbc.ca/health-professionals
- EQUIP-GTV TVIC Foundations Curriculum: https://equiphealthcare.ca/tvic-foundations

REFERENCES

Afari, N., Ahumada, S.M., Wright, L.J., Mostoufi, S., Golnari, G., Reis, V., & Cuneo, J. G. (2014). Psychological trauma and functional somatic syndromes: A systematic review and meta-analysis. *Psychosomatic Medicine*, 76(1), 2–11. https://doi.org/10.1097/PSY.0000000000000010

Afifi, T.O., Taillieu, T., Salmon, S., Davila, I.G., Stewart-Tufescu, A., Fortier, J., ... MacMillan, H.L. (2020). Adverse childhood experiences (ACEs), peer victimization, and substance use among adolescents. *Child Abuse & Neglect*, 106, 104504. https://doi.org/10.1016/j.chiabu.2020.104504

Angelone, D.J., Marcantonio, T., & Melillo, J. (2018). An evaluation of adolescent and young adult (re)victimization experiences: Problematic substance use and negative consequences. *Violence Against Women*, 24(5), 586–602. https://doi.org/10.1177/1077801217710001

Beliveau, C.M., McMahan, V.M., Arenander, J., Angst, M.S., Kushel, M., Torres, A., ... Coffin, P.O. (2021). Stimulant use for self-management of pain among safety-net patients with chronic non-cancer pain. *Substance Abuse*, 1–8. https://doi.org/10.1080/08897077.2021.1903654

Benedict, T.M., Keenan, P.G., Nitz, A.J., & Moeller-Bertram, T. (2020). Post-traumatic stress disorder symptoms contribute to worse pain and health outcomes in veterans with PTSD compared to those without: A systematic review with meta-analysis. *Military Medicine*, 185(9–10), e1481–e1491. https://doi.org/10.1093/milmed/usaa052

Bicket, M.C., Park, J.N., Torrie, A., Allen, S.T., Weir, B.W., & Sherman, S.G. (2020). Factors associated with chronic pain and non-medical opioid use among people who inject drugs. *Addictive Behaviors*, *102*, 106172. https://doi.org/10.1016 /j.addbeh.2019.106172

Boissoneault, J., Lewis, B., & Nixon, S.J. (2019). Characterizing chronic pain and alcohol use trajectory among treatment-seeking alcoholics. *Alcohol*, *75*, 47–54. https://doi.org/10.1016/j.alcohol.2018.05.009

Browne, A.J., Varcoe, C., Lavoie, J., Smye, V.L., Wong, S., Krause, M., . . . Fridkin, A. (2016). Enhancing health care equity with Indigenous populations: Evidence-based strategies from an ethnographic study. *BMC Health Services Research*, *16*(544), 1–17. https://doi.org/10.1186/s12913-016-1707-9

Canadian Pain Task Force. (2019). *Chronic pain in Canada: Laying a foundation for action*. Retrieved from https://www.canada.ca/content/dam/hc-sc/documents /corporate/about-health-canada/public-engagement/external-advisory-bodies /canadian-pain-task-force/report-2019/canadian-pain-task-force-June-2019 -report-en.pdf

Craig, K.D., Holmes, C., Hudspith, M., Moor, G., Moosa-Mitha, M., Varcoe, C., & Wallace, B. (2020). Pain in persons who are marginalized by social conditions. *Pain*, *161*(2), 261–5. https://doi.org/10.1097/j.pain.0000000000001719

Craner, J.R., Lake, E.S., Bancroft, K.E., & Hanson, K.M. (2020). Partner abuse among treatment-seeking individuals with chronic pain: Prevalence, characteristics, and association with pain-related outcomes. *Pain Med*, *21*(11), 2789–98. https://doi.org /10.1093/pm/pnaa126

Dassieu, L., Heino, A., Develay, É., Kaboré, J.-L., Pagé, M.G., Hudspith, M., . . . Choinière, M. (2021). Conversations about opioids: Impact of the opioid overdose epidemic on social interactions for people who live with chronic pain. *Qualitative Health Research*. https://doi.org/10.1177/10497323211003063

Dassieu, L., Kaboré, J.-L., Choinière, M., Arruda, N., & Roy, É. (2020). Painful lives: Chronic pain experience among people who use illicit drugs in Montreal (Canada). *Social Science & Medicine* (1982), *246*. https://doi.org/10.1016/j.socscimed .2019.112734

Degenhardt, L., Hungerford, P., Nielsen, S., Bruno, R., Larance, B., Clare, P.J., . . . Campbell, G. (2021). Pharmaceutical opioid use patterns and indicators of extramedical use and harm in adults with chronic noncancer pain, 2012–2018. *JAMA Network Open*, *4*(4), e213059. https://doi.org/10.1001/jamanetworkopen.2021.3059

Field, M., Heather, N., & Wiers, R.W. (2019). Indeed, not really a brain disorder: Implications for reductionist accounts of addiction. *The Behavioral and Brain Sciences*, *42*, e9. https://doi.org/10.1017/S0140525X18001024

Fletcher, K. (2021). A systematic review of the relationship between child sexual abuse and substance use issues. *Journal Of Child Sexual Abuse*, *30*(3), 258–77. https:// doi.org/10.1080/10538712.2020.1801937

Ford-Gilboe, M., Merritt-Gray, M., Varcoe, C., & Wuest, J. (2011). A theory-based primary health care intervention for women who have left abusive partners. *Advances in Nursing Science*, *34*(3), 198–214.

3.2 The Nexus of Trauma, Violence, Chronic Pain, Substance Use, and Stigma

Ford-Gilboe, M., Wathen, C.N., Varcoe, C., Herbert, C., Jackson, B., Lavoie, J., ... Browne, A.J. (2018). How equity-oriented health care affects health: Key mechanisms and implications for primary health care practice and policy. *Millbank Quarterly, 96*(4), 635–71. https://doi.org/10.1111/1468-0009.12349

Ford-Gilboe, M., Wuest, J., Varcoe, C., Davies, L., Merritt-Gray, M., Campbell, J., & Wilk, P. (2009). Modelling the effects of intimate partner violence and access to resources on women's health in the early years after leaving an abusive partner. *Social Science & Medicine, 68*(6), 1021–9. https://doi.org/10.1016/j.socscimed.2009.01.003

Ganson, K.T., Murray, S.B., Mitchison, D., Hawkins, M.A.W., Layman, H., Tabler, J., & Nagata, J.M. (2021). Associations between adverse childhood experiences and performance-enhancing substance use among young adults. *Substance Use & Misuse, 56*(6), 854–60. https://doi.org/10.1080/10826084.2021.1899230

Gasperi, M., Afari, N., Goldberg, J., Suri, P., & Panizzon, M.S. (2021). Pain and trauma: The role of criterion A trauma and stressful life events in the pain and PTSD relationship. *The Journal of Pain*. https://doi.org/10.1016/j.jpain.2021.04.015

Gezinski, L.B., Gonzalez-Pons, K.M., & Rogers, M.M. (2021). Substance use as a coping mechanism for survivors of intimate partner violence: Implications for safety and service accessibility. *Violence Against Women, 27*(2), 108–23. https://doi.org/10.1177/1077801219882496

Golder, S., Connell, C.M., & Sullivan, T.P. (2012). Psychological distress and substance use among community-recruited women currently victimized by intimate partners: A latent class analysis and examination of between-class differences. *Violence Against Women, 18*(8), 934–57. https://doi.org/10.1177/1077801212456991

John, W.S., & Wu, L.-T. (2020). Chronic non-cancer pain among adults with substance use disorders: Prevalence, characteristics, and association with opioid overdose and healthcare utilization. *Drug and Alcohol Dependence, 209*, 107902. https://doi.org/10.1016/j.drugalcdep.2020.107902

Kaboré, J.-L., Dassieu, L., Roy, É., Jutras-Aswad, D., Bruneau, J., Pagé, M.G., & Choinière, M. (2020). Prevalence, characteristics, and management of chronic noncancer pain among people who use drugs: A cross-sectional study. *Pain Med, 21*(11), 3205–14. https://doi.org/10.1093/pm/pnaa232

Keeshin, B.R., Cronholm, P.F., & Strawn, J.R. (2012). Physiologic changes associated with violence and abuse exposure: An examination of related medical conditions. *Trauma, Violence & Abuse, 13*(1), 41–56. https://doi.org/10.1177/1524838011426152

Levin, Y., Lev Bar-Or, R., Forer, R., Vaserman, M., Kor, A., & Lev-Ran, S. (2021). The association between type of trauma, level of exposure, and addiction. *Addictive Behaviors, 118*. https://doi.org/10.1016/j.addbeh.2021.106889

Lewis, M. (2017). Addiction and the brain: Development, not disease. *Neuroethics, 10*(1), 7–18. https://doi.org/10.1007/s12152-016-9293-4

Manhapra, A., Stefanovics, E.A., Rhee, T.G., & Rosenheck, R.A. (2021). Association of symptom severity, pain, and other behavioral and medical comorbidities with diverse measures of functioning among adults with post-traumatic stress disorder. *Journal Of Psychiatric Research, 134*, 113–20. https://doi.org/10.1016/j.jpsychires .2020.12.063

Martel, M.O., Shir, Y., & Ware, M.A. (2018). Substance-related disorders: A review of prevalence and correlates among patients with chronic pain. *Progress in Neuro-Psychopharmacology & Biological Psychiatry, 87*, 245–54. https://doi.org/10.1016 /j.pnpbp.2017.06.032

Medina, N.T., Erazo, G.E.C., Dávila, D.C.B., & Humphreys, J.C. (2011). Contribution of intimate partner violence exposure, other traumatic events, and posttraumatic stress disorder to chronic pain and depressive symptoms. *Investigacion & Educacion en Enfermeria, 29*(3), 174–86. Retrieved from http://www.scielo.org.co/pdf/iee /v29n2/v29n2a02.pdf

Merrick, M.T., Ports, K.A., Ford, D.C., Afifi, T.O., Gershoff, E.T., & Grogan-Kaylor, A. (2017). Unpacking the impact of adverse childhood experiences on adult mental health. *Child Abuse & Neglect, 69*, 10–19. https://doi.org/10.1016/j.chiabu.2017 .03.016

Moallef, S., Homayra, F., Milloy, M.J., Bird, L., Nosyk, B., & Hayashi, K. (2020). High prevalence of unmet healthcare need among people who use illicit drugs in a Canadian setting with publicly funded interdisciplinary primary care clinics. *Substance Abuse*, 1–7. https://doi.org/10.1080/08897077.2020.1846667

Pereda, N., & Gallardo-Pujol, D. (2014). One hit makes the difference: The role of polyvictimization in childhood in lifetime revictimization on a southern European sample. *Violence and Victims, 29*(2), 217–31. Retrieved from https://connect .springerpub.com/content/sgrvv/29/2/217

Racine, E., Sattler, S., & Escande, A. (2017). Free will and the brain disease model of addiction: The not so seductive allure of neuroscience and its modest impact on the attribution of free will to people with an addiction. *Frontiers in Psychology, 8*, 1850. https://doi.org/10.3389/fpsyg.2017.01850

Smye, V., Varcoe, C., Browne, A.J., Dion Stout, M., Josewski, V., Ford-Gilboe, M., & Keith, B. (2020). Violence at the intersections of women's lives in an urban context: Indigenous women's experiences of leaving and/or staying with an abusive partner. *Violence Against Women*, 1–22. https://doi.org/10.1177/1077801220947183

Sprang, G., Bush, H.M., Coker, A.L., & Brancato, C.J. (2020). Types of trauma and self-reported pain that limits functioning in different-aged cohorts. *Journal of Interpersonal Violence, 35*(23–4), 5953–75. https://doi.org/10.1177 /0886260517723144

Varcoe, C., Brown, H., Calam, B., Harvey, T., & Tallio, M. (2013). Help bring back the celebration of life: A community-based participatory study of rural Aboriginal women's maternity experiences and outcomes. *BMC Pregnancy & Childbirth, 13*(1), 1–10. https://doi.org/10.1186/1471-2393-13-26

Varcoe, C., Browne, A.J., Ford-Gilboe, M., Dion Stout, M., McKenzie, H., Price, R., ... Merritt-Gray, M. (2017). Reclaiming Our Spirits: Development and pilot testing of a health promotion intervention for Indigenous women who have experienced intimate partner violence. *Research In Nursing & Health, 40*(3), 237–54. https://doi.org/10.1002/nur.21795

Wallace, B., Varcoe, C., Holmes, C., Moosa-Mitha, M., Moor, G., Hudspith, M., & Craig, K.D. (2021). Towards health equity for people experiencing chronic pain and social marginalization. *International Journal for Equity in Health, 20*(1), 1–13. https://doi.org/10.1186/s12939-021-01394-6

Wathen, C.N., MacGregor, J.C.D., & Beyrem, S. (2021). Impacts of trauma- and violence-informed care education: A mixed method follow-up evaluation with health & social service professionals. *Public Health Nursing, 38*(4), 645–54. Retrieved from https://onlinelibrary.wiley.com/doi/abs/10.1111/phn.12883

Williams, J.R., Cole, V., Girdler, S., & Cromeens, M.G. (2020). Exploring stress, cognitive, and affective mechanisms of the relationship between interpersonal trauma and opioid misuse. *PLoS One, 15*(5). https://doi.org/10.1371/journal.pone.0233185

Wuest, J., Ford-Gilboe, M., Merritt-Gray, M., Varcoe, C., Lent, B., Wilk, P., & Campbell, J. (2009). Abuse-related injury and symptoms of posttraumatic stress disorder as mechanisms of chronic pain in survivors of intimate partner violence. *Pain Medicine, 10*(4), 739–47. https://doi.org/10.1111/j.1526-4637.2009.00624.x

Wuest, J., Ford-Gilboe, M., Merritt-Gray, M., Wilk, P., Campbell, J.C., Lent, B., ... Smye, V. (2010). Pathways of chronic pain in survivors of intimate partner violence. *Journal of Women's Health (15409996), 19*(9), 1665–74. https://doi.org/10.1089/jwh.2009.1856

Wuest, J., Merritt-Gray, M., Dube, N., Hodgins, M.J., Malcolm, J., Majerovich, J.A., ... Varcoe, C. (2015). The process, outcomes, and challenges of feasibility studies conducted in partnership with stakeholders: A health intervention for women survivors of intimate partner violence. *Research in Nursing & Health, 38*(1), 82–96. https://doi.org/10.1002/nur.21636

Wuest, J., O'Donnell, S., Scott-Storey, K., Malcolm, J., Vincent, C.D., & Taylor, P. (2021). Cumulative lifetime violence severity and chronic pain in a community sample of Canadian men. *Pain Medicine, 22*(6), 1387–98. https://doi.org/10.1093/pm/pnaa419

3.3 Enhancing Public Understanding: Shifting Narratives on Trauma, Violence, and Mental Health

NADINE WATHEN AND JESSICA CARSWELL

This chapter explores how core concepts of TVIC are, or could be, understood by the general public, as well as the role of media in constructing these understandings. Two case studies are presented that examine this issue from various perspectives – broadly through media analyses and deliberative dialogue techniques, as well as more proximately through interviews with those tasked with educating both service users and the general public about mental health and substance use. We use the cases to explore how attitudes, beliefs, and broader narratives and discourses about trauma and violence and associated mental health issues both are constructed (through media and other means) and are played out in terms of the lived/living experiences of all involved. We examine community/social/structural and organizational/service delivery contexts (case 1), with additional emphasis on policy contexts (case 2) and the key role of major media in reinforcing specific narratives (case 2). The goals are to understand how prevalent beliefs shape our realities and to provide strategies for reconstructing narratives about trauma, violence, mental health, and related social problems through emerging knowledge mobilization strategies.

By the end of this chapter, readers will (1) have a better understanding of potentially harmful discourses related to trauma, violence, mental health, and related social problems and how media can perpetuate these, (2) consider how these narratives affect individual and community-level attitudes and actions, (3) see how service agencies can promote TVIC awareness and anti-discriminatory practices among clients and the public, including various barriers and facilitators to these processes, and (4) think about how to prioritize and counter problematic narratives that act as barriers to improved public understanding of these issues.

Why Public Narratives Matter

A social-ecological understanding of trauma, interpersonal and structural violence, and related forms of stigma (Dahlberg & Krug, 2002; Heise, 1998) situates their causes and consequences at multiple levels, from individual to societal, rooted in beliefs and norms about, for example, gender roles, mental health, or interpersonal violence. "Upstream" efforts to counteract the impacts of trauma and violence must attend to the stigmatizing attitudes, and often harmful attendant behaviours, that enable and perpetuate violence and trauma (Krug, Dahlberg, Mercy, Zwi, & Lozano, 2002).

To use gender-based violence (GBV) as an example, recent results from the national Survey of Safety in Public and Private Spaces (SSPPS; Savage & Cotter, 2019) indicate that while Canadians' perceptions of gender roles and norms are moving in a generally progressive direction, there is still work to do. For example, while most Canadians surveyed believed that people should be able to express their gender as they choose, men are significantly less likely to believe this than women (78% vs 85%); the same pattern was seen regarding supporting a transgender family member. Similarly, fewer than half (47%) of men indicate that people who report sexual assault are always telling the truth (compared to 62% of women); and while most disagree with the statement that "violence between partners can be excused if people get so angry they lose control," men are more likely than women to agree (9% vs 6%) (SSPPS; Savage & Cotter, 2019, survey item ID PA_040).

These kinds of beliefs, articulated in everyday and media narratives, have real impacts on people's lives. For example, transgender people are far more likely to experience most forms of violence, including IPV (Jaffray, 2020) – perhaps not surprising when, as we saw above, 15 to 22 per cent of Canadians don't believe that people should be free to express their gender as they choose. Similarly, media accounts of substance use, such as those that depict people who use substances as violent, or as responsible for their own decisions, without considering the contexts of their lives, reinforce stigmatizing beliefs, which limits the chances of recovery for those using stigmatized substances (Lloyd, 2013; Webster, Rice, & Sud, 2020). These harmful narratives, themselves a form of structural violence (see chapter 1.2) are therefore a key target for TVIC thinking and action. Narratives, for our purposes, are defined as common messages to the public about the issues being considered. These may or may not be "true," but they form the basis of people's thinking and actions as they relate to trauma, violence, mental health, and substance use.

Case Descriptions

Case 1: Educating the Public about TVIC: Learnings from a Mental Health Agency

Creating safe and inclusive spaces and services for trauma- and violence-exposed individuals is a community-wide endeavour. In this project, we partnered with a community-based mental health organization (see box 3.3.1) known to be a community leader in TVIC implementation, inter-organizational TVIC training, and public education/mental health promotion. The prevalence of trauma, violence, mental ill health, and substance use issues in communities across Canada (Elliott, Bjelajac, Fallot, Markoff, & Reed, 2005; van Ameringen, Mancini, Patterson, & Boyle, 2008) suggests that a community-based mental health agency is an ideal site for exploring the potential value and impact of integrating TVIC information into public-facing materials. Furthermore, the multiple compounding forms of stigma experienced by those with mental health challenges (variously including unwarranted assumptions about the relationship between mental health problems and violence, poverty, and criminality) can lead to reduced access to, and quality of, the services needed to maintain good health (Public Health Agency of Canada, 2019). This emphasizes the need to challenge how stigmatizing beliefs and practices perpetuate violence and poor health and to create positive alternatives at individual, organizational, and broader societal levels.

Our partnered research investigated, from an organizational perspective, how to integrate TVIC into both the delivery and the content of public mental health promotion efforts, as well as client-facing psychoeducation, and produced recommendations for agency uptake and action. Using semi-structured interviews and document review, we explored staff perceptions and experiences related to TVIC education and training, as well as perceived barriers and facilitators that could impact the organization's ability to effectively deliver TVIC public and psychoeducation. Documents provided context and insight into the formal goals and actions of the agency in relation to TVIC and public and psycho-education (Carswell, 2020).

Key findings addressed multiple and at times overlapping themes specific to the four TVIC principles (see chapter 1.5), as well as the important influence of stigma and implicit bias on how staff, clients, and the general public engage with those with mental health or substance use challenges. First, participants noted that lack of understanding among the general public about the impacts of trauma and violence on mental health, addictions, and other health and social issues is a major barrier to sharing TVIC information with the community (principle 1). They also emphasized ways to ensure the physical and emotional safety (principle 2) of those receiving TVIC-related information, as well as those delivering it – for example, by creating welcoming and non-judgmental signage and other information in physical and virtual/online spaces. This was tied to barriers related to organizational capacity to effectively create and deliver this form of information and education and to the need to ensure that TVIC educators feel they have the expertise and adequate support from the organization to do this work. There was also the perceived risk that TVIC public and psycho-education could create an expectation of care that the organization would be unable to meet and thus cause further harm to people seeking care.

In terms of principle 3, we found that public education about TVIC must promote inclusivity, collaboration, and connection among community members. Building mutual respect and reciprocity can reduce the negative effects of stigma on learners and create educational environments that promote power-sharing. In the context of psychoeducation specifically, giving choice and control over TVIC information-sharing is key. This can help both staff and clients strengthen their sense of agency and power, especially in service contexts where personal agency may be limited.

Finally, TVIC public and psycho-education and information must focus on individuals' strengths and ability to recover (principle 4). Case 1 findings pointed to the potential for broader TVIC education to perpetuate stigma and the labelling of trauma- and violence-exposed individuals as weak or having deficits. Language encouraging learners to engage with the personal narratives of those with lived/living experience can help create deeper understanding of and empathy about the impacts of trauma and violence. For example, strategies arising from this study and included in the related tool (see Additional Resources, below) included ensuring (a) that people are supported to learn about and honour personal and collective resilience and to build together toward awareness, skills, and hope (individual-level care strategy for principle 4), and (b), at an organizational level (principle 2), that people with lived experience of trauma, violence, and mental health or substance use issues are involved in planning the organization's safety and inclusion strategies.

BOX 3.3.1 CASE 1: DESCRIPTION OF AGENCY SETTING

- Provides community-based mental health supports to individuals age 16+.
- Provides a range of services including crisis supports, clinical services, housing supports, peer support, and community and public education.
- Engaged in organizational implementation of TVIC for 10+ years.
- Has a staff-led TVIC committee that initiates and oversees organizational TVIC-related initiatives.

Case 2: Public Narratives on Gender-Based Violence

Case 2 draws on a multi-phase research and integrated knowledge mobilization study – "Shifting GBV Narratives" – that first identified, through media analysis and environmental scan, prevalent myths and narratives about intimate partner violence (IPV), the most common form of gender-based violence (GBV). These narratives were discussed with federal Canadian policy actors in early 2020, using a deliberative dialogue process (Boyko, Kothari, & Wathen, 2016) to set priorities for the development of counter-narratives.

The first stage of the study identified problematic narratives by conducting an analysis of how IPV is framed and discussed in major Canadian media alongside an environmental scan of prevalent myths and misunderstandings about IPV produced by advocacy groups and, in some instances, reported in long-form journalism (Kingston, 2019). These findings were summarized in an issue brief and pre-circulated to a group of policy actors representing twelve Canadian federal government departments, convened by Women and Gender Equality Canada (WAGE), which sat on the Government of Canada's Interdepartmental Coordinating Committee on Gender-Based Violence. The day-long dialogue resulted in a prioritized list of narratives (see box 3.3.2), which were found to most impact Canadians' beliefs about IPV and to be remediable via new counter-narratives created based on emerging evidence from the Canadian population-based SSPPS (https://www.statcan.gc.ca/eng/survey/household/5256).

BOX 3.3.2 POLICY-IDENTIFIED PRIORITY NARRATIVES/MYTHS ON IPV

- IPV happens to everyone the same way.
- Victim-blaming.
- "Why doesn't she just leave?"
- Exonerating perpetrators/perpetration.

Constructing more trauma- and violence-informed, thoughtful, and evidence-supported narratives requires rigorous and comprehensive identification and analysis of existing harmful narratives and, importantly, guided and critical discussion of what the messages are, where they come from, their impacts, and their "intentionality" (i.e., how they might be operating to maintain power and privilege for certain groups). For example, "Why doesn't she just leave?" is a common narrative among those who wish to situate the problem of intimate partner violence within individuals and to absolve themselves, and society, of any role or responsibility. It cross-cuts all four TVIC principles, in that it emphasizes a lack of awareness about the immediate impacts of IPV on the survivor (her mental and physical health; her access to resources) and how this connects to broader social constructs of IPV (as a "private issue" and a legitimate way for men to control their partners and enact their masculinity) (principle 1). It also obscures the fact that taking any action to end the violence might carry increased risk of danger, especially when we know that "leaving" is the time of highest risk for femicide (principle 2) (Spencer & Stith, 2020). Finally, it makes invisible the fact that most women have found many ways to keep themselves and their children as safe as possible in the context of the violence in their lives, and that directing her to "just leave" does not acknowledge this strength, nor does it take into account that in most cases, there are no immediate pathways to safe, affordable housing – "leaving" is not actually an option, let alone a "choice" (principles 3 and 4).

Our deliberative dialogue process allowed participants to forge links among individual, community, and structural factors that produce, replicate, and reinforce the narratives that often guide the response that abused women experience when trying to address the violence in their lives. Encountering these messages in the public sphere, and experiencing them from health and social services, poses a significant barrier to help-seeking. After all, why would a woman seek help if she is likely to be blamed for the abuse experience, the abuser will be explicitly and/or implicitly exonerated, her experience will be minimized and/or homogenized, and the best advice given is "just leave"?

Communicating about TVIC in a Trauma- and Violence-Informed Way

In this section we reflect on how our empirical findings supporting a TVIC approach to narratives about trauma, violence, and associated mental health issues are framed for and by the general public and how anti-stigmatizing counter-narratives can be developed in a trauma- and violence-informed way.

Fear can lead to stigmatizing attitudes and practices (Jackson-Best & Edwards, 2018), and it is well-established that stigma leads to poor health outcomes (Public Health Agency of Canada, 2019; Turan et al., 2019). In case 1, stigma and fear were seen as key factors that could impact the success of TVIC public- and psycho-education. Furthermore, organizations, service providers, clients, and public education efforts were linked together. As seen in the deliberative dialogue process in case 2, (mis)education and (lack of) awareness at one level directly influences the others. Thus, the considerations for adapting and applying TVIC principles and practices for the public and for psychoeducation are rooted in the interconnections among all levels of the social ecology.

Case 2, on IPV narratives, highlights the link between interpersonal violence and structural violence, and especially gendered violence and its intersections with other individual and social factors, including misogyny and patriarchy. A TVIC approach to re-messaging, based on better evidence, avoids (re)traumatizing survivors of violence and situates the problem where it belongs – in the structures that support, enable, and even glorify the perpetration of violence as well as those who choose to use violence.

Practical Strategies/Guidance for Individuals and Organizations

Here we offer specific strategies for general communication and client education for individuals and organizations, as well as policy actors and media outlets, regarding trauma- and violence-informed messaging to the public.

Strategies for Individuals

1. *Tap into your own knowledge.* Think about the ways in which you may already implicitly be utilizing TVIC principles and practices in your work and consider finding opportunities to more explicitly integrate TVIC content into your written and verbal exchanges with people, your reports, your public- and client-facing materials, and so on. For example, instead of saying "You're back again?," try "It's good to see you! How can I help today?" Instead of charting "Drug seeking," try "Patient described uncontrollable pain; options discussed."
2. *Create a dialogue.* Try not to assume what people know; deliver information in a way that is free of jargon and invites a discussion and/or critical reflection. To ensure emotional safety, provide opportunities for breaks, debriefing, and so on, including, as appropriate, links to further supports. For example, instead of "What's wrong? Have you been using?," try "How are things going – you look like you're having some trouble."
3. *Turn learning inwards.* Consider the ways in which trauma and violence have impacted your own life, through vicarious trauma and/or first-hand experience, and how this may affect your interactions. This can help foster a "we" rather than "us and them" dynamic and enhance feelings of empathy, connectivity, and shared human experience.
4. *Prioritize your own well-being.* Find ways to nurture your own health and well-being, especially after exposure to difficult or stressful situations or content within and outside of the workplace.

Strategies for Organizations and Policy Actors

1. *Utilize the power of narrative.* Include storytelling as part of internal and external TVIC education efforts. Incorporating the expertise of lived/living experience may help reduce stigmatizing practices and foster connection and relationship-building among staff, individuals seeking support, and community members. An example of a resource we created to narrate, in an evidence-based and TVIC way, the experiences of abused women is called "IPV Journeys to Safety" and is freely available (Wathen, MacGregor, Ford-Gilboe, Jack, & Varcoe, n.d. – see link below). It synthesizes research

on women's experiences, using a narrative approach and graphic design to emphasize the help-seeking process, the kinds of things women think about when making decisions, and how care providers can offer safer, more empathetic and trauma- and violence-informed responses. For example, instead of "Why don't you leave?," a provider could ask "What would it take to support you in being safe, and how can I help?"

2. *Build on existing organizational strengths.* Identify ways to leverage existing resources, supports, and initiatives (e.g., advisory committees, existing programs, internal/external communication platforms, inter-organizational partnerships); if TVIC education is already present, expand on current efforts to make it an explicit component of the organization's work.

3. *Create a culture of TVIC.* Reflect on the organization's mission and mandate and consider ways to embed TVIC principles, practices, and content into internal and external communications. Think about how the organization wants people (including staff) to "feel" and what it wants them to "know" about its services and position in the community.

4. *Make your organization's TVIC approach explicit.* Examine client, staff, and public communication materials and explore opportunities to make your organization's TVIC approach explicit and clearly understood. This should be done in a creative and accessible way that emphasizes the strengths and capacity of people who have experienced trauma and violence. The goal is to help everyone (clients, caregivers, direct service staff, organizational leaders, etc.) understand what safe and equitable care is and equip people with the knowledge and information necessary to challenge harmful or inequitable attitudes and practices.

5. *Create accountability measures.* Generating community and service user awareness about their right to safe and equitable care means that the organization must create effective measures for accountability and feedback. Consider developing a feedback tool for people to report their experiences and opinions about the services/information they receive, aligning questions with the TVIC principles, including those related to implicit bias and stigma/discrimination (see Additional Resources below).

6. *Support staff well-being.* Create a strong support system for staff that provides formal and informal debriefing opportunities and promotes self-care but also provides organizational supports for vicarious trauma and compassion fatigue (see Additional Tools and Resources below).

7. *Cultivate partnerships.* Explore opportunities to build bridges with other organizations to support a more integrated and consistent TVIC approach to service provision throughout the community. Use these partnerships as vehicles for system transformation and knowledge exchange.

Strategies for Media

1. *Resist the spectacular.* Gory details draw eyeballs and clicks, but they are potentially retraumatizing, especially given the high rates of trauma and violence in the general population. Focusing solely on the spectacular obscures the more mundane but no less harmful experiences of structural and interpersonal violence, stigma, fear, and isolation encountered by the vast majority of people experiencing these traumas. Resisting the spectacular means weaving in contextual details and telling stories about the daily, grinding, but less spectacular conditions people face.
2. *Provide context, and name the actual problem and its cause(s).* Excellent examples of best practices in journalism exist, including "Fixed It" for reporting on sexual and gender-based violence (Gilmore, 2019), and media resources from, for example, the World Health Organization on safe and appropriate reporting of suicide (World Health Organization, 2017).

Lessons Learned

As we reflect back on our work and provide guidance to others with a focus on public-facing efforts at communication, the following considerations may be helpful.

1. *Partnership and collaboration.* Our cases emphasize how important it is to ask and answer questions alongside those who can make results actionable. We suggest taking the time to foster respectful, trusting, and mutually beneficial partnerships with key stakeholders and potential knowledge users when exploring TVIC-related public education. Using the principles and practices of TVIC to guide this work is beneficial to ensuring safe and equitable working relationships. We often start new collaborative work by articulating values, goals, processes, and desired outcomes, then formalizing these in a "basis of unity" document, which goes beyond simple "terms of reference." (See Additional Tools and Resources below.)
2. *An ecological lens.* As noted, guiding norms and narratives – and their impacts – are an interplay of individual, organizational/community, and structural factors. A good starting place for undertaking narrative-shifting work is needs assessment, tailored to the context and mapped to specific areas of change or concern. Emerging solutions, in our case 2 articulated as counter-narratives, can then be more effectively developed and tailored to specific purposes and audiences.
3. *Leadership and organizational commitment.* As discussed in section 2 of this volume, efforts to integrate TVIC always require both individual and organizational commitment. Providers cannot be left, unsupported, to do this

difficult work. Similarly, organizations cannot change without buy-in from those in direct service. The same is true for public-facing communications. Journalists themselves do not approve stories or write headlines – editors do this, and editorial policy is set by the publisher. The actual or perceived lack of commitment or support from leadership to implement and sustain TVIC practices can create tension within an organization and lead to the frustration or disengagement of those providing direct service. Case 1 highlighted the possible benefits of increasing communication and transparency between leadership and direct service staff and the need to reinforce leadership's consideration of, and commitment to, both patient and staff well-being. Demonstrating organizational commitment to the implementation of TVIC could also include encouraging leadership to increase their own knowledge and practice of TVIC and dedicate resources to TVIC initiatives, including ongoing staff training and education, including board education.

4. *Walking the talk.* Finally, providing public-facing TVIC content, including how this content and related strategies are developed (i.e., through research, journalistic practice, etc.) must itself be done in a TVIC way. For example, when conducting our IPV media analysis, exposure to often horrifying (and glorified) details of violence against women and children took an emotional toll on the research team. We ensured opportunities for formal and informal debriefing and split up the more difficult coding to reduce this burden. During the deliberative dialogue with policy actors, we began by acknowledging the difficult nature of the material and ensuring that people felt safe, including to leave, take breaks, and so on. Similarly, in case 1, we ensured the well-being of participants beyond the Research Ethics Board requirements, by, for example, paying additional attention to emotional safety when discussing potentially difficult topics (e.g., vicarious trauma). Also, we strived to ensure that the research process was collaborative and enabled shared-decision making with our research partners. The investigation itself was rooted in a strengths-based and capacity-building approach in that it sought to build upon and extend the agency's ongoing TVIC-related work.

Conclusion

Neoliberal ways of thinking, especially the relentless downloading of responsibility to individuals and away from publicly funded services and systems, have permeated all aspects of how we view and talk about social problems. We are expected to solve our own problems and are framed as "bad citizens" (lazy, wasteful, undeserving, etc.) if we don't. While recent world events, especially the COVID-19 pandemic, have finally started to reveal the fallacy of assuming that everyone has the same financial, social, physical, and mental/emotional resources to navigate the world, we still see how easy it is for mass media, politicians, and others to fall back into these ways of thinking and speaking. This is reflected in the kinds of narratives we've reviewed above. Intentionally incorporating a TVIC approach will begin to redress these harmful practices; we all have a role to play.

KEY MESSAGES AND IMPLICATIONS

- How we communicate about social problems – individually, in groups, and through mass media – frames how people understand them and can dictate potential action or inaction. Stigmatizing and discriminatory language, especially victim-blaming and "othering"/dehumanizing narratives, are a significant barrier to positive social change.
- Embedding a TVIC lens in communication efforts can result in a positive shift toward destigmatizing experiences, behaviours and entire groups of people. Explicitly considering all four TVIC principles and the role of implicit bias in our language choices provides an opportunity to create positive, actionable responses for and with individuals seeking care, but also for public policy.
- Equipping the public, including individuals, their caregivers, community advocates, and so on, with knowledge about TVIC and people's right to safe and equitable care can help hold organizations, service providers, and governments accountable for providing safe, equity-oriented services. This can help drive system transformation from the ground up and amplify the voices of those who have been underrepresented, underserviced, or oppressed by health and social service systems.

ADDITIONAL RESOURCES

- Intimate Partner Violence: Journeys to Safety: https://gtvincubator.uwo.ca/resources
- TVIC for Client and Public Education: https://gtvincubator.uwo.ca/resources
- EQUIP Health Care Resources for Organizational and System Leaders: https://equiphealthcare.ca/equip-my-organization
- EQUIP Equity Talk Pocket Cards: https://equiphealthcare.ca/files/2019/12/pc_equity-talk-Dec-13-2017.pdf
- Preventing, Recognizing, and Addressing Vicarious Trauma: A Tool for Primary Health Care Organizations and Providers Working with Individuals: https://gtvincubator.uwo.ca/resources
- Sample Basis of Unity document: http://dvatworknet.org/about/basis-of-unity
- The Shared Humanity Project: http://www.sharedhumanity.ca

REFERENCES

Boyko, J.A., Kothari, A., & Wathen, C.N. (2016). Moving knowledge about family violence into public health policy and practice: A mixed method evaluation of a deliberative dialogue. *Health Research Policy and Systems, 14*, 31. https://doi.org/10.1186/s12961-016-0100-9

Carswell, J.M. (2020). *Fostering a trauma- and violence-informed community: Developing strategies to inform public education.* (2020). Electronic thesis and dissertation repository. 7290. https://ir.lib.uwo.ca/etd/7290

Dahlberg, L.L., & Krug, E.G. (2002). Violence – a global public health problem. In E. Krug, L.L. Dahlberg, J.A. Mercy, A.B. Zwi, & R. Lozano (Eds.), *World report on violence and health* (pp. 1–22). Geneva, Switzerland: World Health Organization.

Elliott, D.E., Bjelajac, P., Fallot, R.D., Markoff, L.S., & Reed, B.G. (2005). Trauma informed or trauma-denied: Principles and implementation of trauma-informed services for women. *Journal of Community Psychology, 33*(4), 461–77. https://doi.org/10.1002/jcop.20063

Gilmore, J. (2019). *Fixed it: Violence and the representation of women in the media.* Melbourne, Australia: Viking.

Heise, L.L. (1998). Violence against women: An integrated, ecological framework. *Violence Against Women, 4*(3), 262–90. https://doi.org/10.1177/1077801298004003002

Jackson-Best, F., & Edwards, N. (2018). Stigma and intersectionality: A systematic review of systematic reviews across HIV/AIDS, mental illness, and physical disability. *BMC Public Health, 18*, 919. https://doi.org/10.1186/s12889-018-5861-3

Jaffray, B. (2020). Experiences of violent victimization and unwanted sexual behaviours among gay, lesbian, bisexual, and other sexual minority people, and the transgender population, in Canada, 2018. *Juristat, Catalogue no. 85-002-X.* Ottawa, Canada: Statistics Canada. Retrieved from https://www150.statcan.gc.ca/n1/pub/85-002-x/2020001/article/00009-eng.htm

Kingston, A. (2019, September 17). We are the dead: A months-long *Maclean's* investigation into intimate-partner violence reveals how systems, politicians, and people have failed women and girls. *Maclean's Magazine.* Retrieved from https://www.macleans.ca/news/canada/we-are-the-dead/

Krug, E., Dahlberg, L.L., Mercy, J.A., Zwi, A.B., & Lozano, R. (Eds.). (2002). *World report on violence and health.* Geneva, Switzerland: World Health Organization.

Lloyd, C. (2013). The stigmatization of problem drug users: A narrative literature review. *Drugs: Education, Prevention, and Policy, 20*(2), 85–95. https://doi.org/10.3109/09687637.2012.743506

Public Health Agency of Canada (2019). *The Chief Public Health Officer's report on the state of public health in Canada 2019 – Addressing stigma: Towards a more inclusive health system.* Retrieved from https://www.canada.ca/en/public-health/corporate/publications/chief-public-health-officer-reports-state-public-health-canada/addressing-stigma-toward-more-inclusive-health-system.html

Savage, L., & Cotter, A. (2019). Perceptions related to gender-based violence, gender equality, and gender expression. Juristat Bulletin Catalogue no. 85-005-X. Ottawa: Statistics Canada. Retrieved from https://www150.statcan.gc.ca/n1/pub/85-005-x/2019001/article/00001-eng.htm

Spencer, C.M., & Stith, S.M. (2020). Risk factors for male perpetration and female victimization of intimate partner homicide: A meta-analysis. *Trauma, Violence, & Abuse, 21*(3), 527–40. https://doi.org/10.1177/1524838018781101

Turan, J.M., Elafros, M.A., Logie, C.H., Banik, S., Turan, B., Crockett, K.B., ... Murray, S.M. (2019). Challenges and opportunities in examining and addressing intersectional stigma and health. *BMC Medicine, 17*(1), 7. https://doi.org/10.1186/s12916-018-1246-9

Van Ameringen, M., Mancini, C., Patterson, B. & Boyle, M.H. (2008). Post-traumatic stress disorder in Canada. *CNS Neuroscience & Therapeutics, 14*, 171–81. https://doi.org/10.1111/j.1755-5949.2008.00049.x

Wathen, C.N., MacGregor, J.C.D., Ford-Gilboe, M., Jack, S., & Varcoe, C. (n.d.). *Intimate partner violence journeys to safety: A synthesis of qualitative research.* Western University, London, ON. Retrieved from https://gtvincubator.uwo.ca/resources

Webster, F., Rice, K., & Sud, A. (2020). A critical content analysis of media reporting on opioids: The social construction of an epidemic. *Social Science & Medicine, 244.* https://doi.org/10.1016/j.socscimed.2019.112642

World Health Organization (2017). *Preventing suicide: A resource for media professionals, update 2017.* Geneva, Switzerland: WHO. Retrieved from https://www.who.int/publications/i/item/WHO-MSD-MER-17.5

3.4 Emerging Considerations for Trauma- and Violence-Informed Care: Lessons from Post-Genocide Rwanda

AIMÉE JOSÉPHINE UTUZA, VINCENT SEZIBERA, AND HELENE BERMAN

When horrific events happen, trauma affects not only the direct survivors or witnesses but future generations as well. This has been widely documented in many contexts and is especially relevant when we consider the aftermath of genocide. Many scholars have written about the physical and emotional consequences of genocide and the lifelong scars these events leave, which may or may not be visible. To a lesser extent, the strengths and sources of resilience exhibited by survivors have also been described.

In this chapter, we address emerging considerations for implementing trauma- and violence-informed care (TVIC) and related activities in developing countries, with special attention to Rwanda. As a country that is still healing from the 1994 genocide against the Tutsi people, Rwanda offers a unique opportunity to contemplate the relevance of TVIC. Indeed, the post-genocidal impacts of trauma have affected all Rwandans and all facets of their society. We will illustrate this by examining the intersections between gender and violence. A great deal has been written about women who have experienced gender-based violence, as well as their vulnerabilities to various forms of violence, but less attention has been paid to this phenomenon in relation to genocide. It is our premise that there is, in fact, considerable overlap – that the risks associated with gender-based violence are greatly heightened in a post-genocidal context. Moreover, we assert that the risks are "different" from those faced by women in non-genocidal contexts. We will explore this idea and then conclude the chapter with a broader discussion about the implications and opportunities that a TVIC lens can offer to Rwanda and in other post-conflict contexts. Finally, we highlight the need for a "paradigm shift" – that is, for a fundamental rethinking of how trauma and gender-based violence are best addressed in Rwanda. To set the stage, we begin with a brief overview of the Rwandan genocide.

The Historical Context: The 1994 Genocide against the Tutsi People in Rwanda

The genocide in Rwanda was carried out over one hundred days, beginning in April 1994. It is estimated that by the time it ended in July of that year, approximately one million Tutsi were killed and mass sexual violence had been committed against Tutsi women and girls (Nicolaisen, 2019). The genocide was the culmination of a decades-long campaign of politicization of ethnicity by Belgian colonizers (divide and rule) and, later, by the two regimes (first and second republics) that followed the nation's independence in 1962. This social and political polarization was intended to incite division and hatred toward the Tutsi people. Through processes of dehumanization – which included characterizing the Tutsi people as animals or cockroaches – the Tutsi were deliberately positioned as dangerous and "less than human." Their total isolation and the systematic discrimination against them set the stage for the genocide that followed (Mukimbiri, 2005).

Rwanda had been a German colony until the First World War. After that war, until 1962, Rwanda had been a Belgian colony. During the period of Belgian rule, colonial policies encouraged animosity between the Hutu, the country's largest ethnic group, and the Tutsi, the second-largest. The Belgians viewed the Tutsi minority as superior and favoured them for leadership positions. Ethnic divisions and stereotypes were orchestrated by the Belgians; both the colonial administrators and Roman Catholic hierarchy carried out policies meant to deepen tensions between the Hutu and the Tutsi (Bizimana, 2001). In 1959, following what became known as the Social Revolution, several hundred people, most of them Tutsis, were killed (Chrétien, 2003). Several thousand others were forced to flee the country, and many houses were burned down. Hutu peasants participated in the arson and looting and, very importantly, in hunting down and killing Tutsi. After 1959, it became evident that some Hutu leaders were plotting to exterminate their fellow Rwandans due to their Tutsi ethnicity as it had been fabricated by the Belgians.

By 1962, when Rwanda gained independence, the Hutu community was consolidating its power and excluding Tutsi from all government positions. Escalating violence caused around 120,000 Rwandans, most of them Tutsis, to flee into exile in neighbouring countries. By the end of the 1980s about 350,000 Rwandans had become refugees, resettling primarily in Burundi, Uganda, Zaire (now the Democratic Republic of the Congo), and Tanzania. The Tutsi refugees continued to push for their right under international law to return to Rwanda, but the government of Rwanda at that time remained silent, as did the international community. In response to the reluctance of the international community to act, the Rwandan Patriotic Front (RPF) was founded in December 1987 in Kampala, Uganda, as a political and military movement composed mostly of Tutsi refugees. Its primary aim was to advocate and ultimately fight for the return of the Tutsi refugees and the rule of law and democracy in Rwanda. As its last option (known as option Z), the RPF engaged in a liberation war against the then government of Rwanda.

The signing of the Arusha peace agreements in 1993 seemed to have brought an end to the conflict between the then Hutu-dominated government and the opposition RPF. That peace was, however, a tenuous illusion. Human rights violations continued, and later evidence demonstrated that extremist elements of the Hutu majority government, while talking peace, were in fact planning a campaign to exterminate Tutsis and moderate Hutus. On 6 April 1994, the mysterious deaths of the presidents of Burundi and Rwanda in a plane crash ignited a systematic genocide in which one million people were killed in three months (Wielenga & Harris, 2011).

Gender-Based Violence as a Weapon of War during the Genocide

Though numbers vary, it is estimated that between 250,000 and 500,000 women were raped during the genocide in Rwanda (Sharlach, 1999). Those who perpetrate genocide use rape and sexual violence as weapons for killing and humiliation, as well as to deliberately infect victims with the HIV/AIDS virus. The rape and torture of women as a weapon of war, the literal and figurative use of women's bodies to do battle, is by no means unique to Rwanda. As Christina Lamb (2020) poignantly wrote about rape, "it's the cheapest weapon known to man. It devastates families and empties villages. It turns young girls into outcasts who wish their lives over when they are hardly begun. It begets children who are daily reminders to their mothers of their ordeal and are often rejected by their community as 'bad blood'" (p. 12). It is estimated that between 10,000 and 25,000 children were born from acts of rape that occurred during the genocide (Kahn & Denov, 2019).

The gendered norms that make rape such a powerful and effective way to destroy communities, and indeed nations, have prevailed in virtually every genocide and war in recorded history, including the First and Second World Wars, the Holocaust, Cambodia, Vietnam, and Bosnia. In essence, gender-based violence (GBV) in times of war and genocide is viewed as an "unfortunate" but inevitable outcome. Understanding the gendered dynamics of genocide and violence in the context of war is thus a critical component of any trauma- and violence-informed approach.

Violence directed against women and girls came to be a predominant feature of the 1994 genocide against the Tutsi people in Rwanda. It took many forms (Hamel, 2016). The perpetrators not only violated women and girls, infected them with HIV, and mutilated and killed many, but also used verbal and emotional terror against the Tutsi in general, and especially against the most vulnerable groups, notably women and girls. Sexual violence in the context of war and genocide is intended to achieve several purposes, including to humiliate, to dominate, and to instil fear. It also results in the dispersal and/or forcible relocation of the civilian members of a community or ethnic group (Hamel, 2016). The UN Security Council recognizes rape and other forms of sexual violence as serious international crimes. The International Criminal Tribunal for Rwanda (ICTR, 2014) investigated and prosecuted sexual violence and rape committed during the genocide against the Tutsi in Rwanda, calling these crimes perhaps the gravest of international atrocities committed against girls and women during that period.

According to the 1993 Declaration on the Elimination of Violence against Women, gender-based violence includes acts that result in "physical, sexual or psychological harm or suffering to women, including threats of such acts, coercion or arbitrary deprivation of liberty, whether occurring in public or in private life" (Russell, Lim, Kim, & Morse, 2016, p. 721). The violence that was inflicted on women and girls during the 1994 genocide in Rwanda was consistent with this definition; it was a multifaceted phenomenon that included physical violence, psychological violence, and especially sexual violence, carried out intentionally over prolonged periods of time with intense hatred and animosity. Sexual assaults were enacted with the explicit purpose of killing Tutsi, especially Tutsi women. Where death did not occur, the women (and often their children) were left with HIV infection, unwanted pregnancy, physical injury, and permanent scarring that was both physical and emotional (Russell et al., 2016). No one among the targeted group expected to escape from the atrocities. The few women and girls who did survive lived with rejection from society and a deep sense of humiliation and shame. Whether women were victimized themselves or were forced to witness the rape and sexual torture of others, including their daughters or mothers, the long-term effects were widespread and severe. Most notably, post-traumatic stress disorders have been extensively reported as endemic among the population of Rwanda in general, and especially among women and girls (Munyandamutsa, Nkubamugisha, Gex-Fabry, & Eytan, 2012).

In his paper "'We Are Going to Rape You and Taste Tutsi Women,'" Mullins (2009) wrote about the rape-related narratives of witnesses who spoke at the ICTR. Mullins classified sexual assaults experienced by women and girls into three categories: opportunistic rapes, sexual enslavement, and genocidal rapes. Opportunistic rapes are sexual assaults that arise out of the general chaos and confusion of a military engagement. Sexual enslavement is a form of repetitive rape that is inflicted more than once, often over a prolonged period. In this kind of sexual assault, the victims, who are mostly women and girls, are held captive as "sexual abuse slaves" (pp. 726–7), typically for weeks or months.

The third category discussed by Mullins is "genocidal rape" (p. 728). Tutsi women and girls were viewed as an easy target for race elimination. It was thought that rape could be a means for the perpetrators to achieve this political objective. Once it was ensured that women could no longer reproduce, the total extinction of the Tutsi people could become reality. This form of genocidal rape was carried out by those who led the genocide, especially military personnel. According to Wood (2018), soldiers often participated in rape and other forms of sexual violence because they had been indoctrinated to do so. Seeing a companion soldier doing cruel things served as a powerful motivating factor. Through the power of indoctrination, the new cohort of fighters internalized what it meant to be a "successful" combatant (Wood, 2018). Rather than being a single act, genocidal rape was more commonly carried out through multiple acts of mutilation, humiliation, and dehumanization. In some cases, these acts were done in combination with various forms of public humiliation, including public nudity, something that is considered particularly shameful in Rwandan society. This was especially troubling for women who were mothers (Mullins, 2009).

In their article "The Lived Experience of Genocide Rape Survivors in Rwanda," Mukamana and Brysiewicz (2008) reported that women and girls suffered not only as direct victims of torture but also as witnesses. This observation is consistent with those of others, who have noted in other contexts that witnesses to violence experience many of the same harmful effects as those who are abused directly (Berman, 1999). With respect to Rwanda, torture was inflicted upon women as they were forced to watch their family members, including their children and partners, being physically and psychologically abused and, in some cases, killed. Some mothers witnessed the rape and mutilation of their daughters and of other close relatives, which left them with unbearably painful psychic scars along with a complete loss of hope.

Addressing Gender-Based Violence in Post-Genocidal Rwanda

The physical and emotional harms associated with the genocide continue to be a dominant feature in the daily lives of women and girls. Moreover, the long-term effects are experienced not just by those who were direct victims or witnesses to the horrors that took place during the genocide; we see also intergenerational impacts of trauma. Many of the children who were born in the aftermath of rape have grown up without an awareness of the circumstances surrounding their birth (Torgovnik, 2019). Their discovery – typically during the teen years or in early adulthood – of their lineage and relationship to the genocide often triggers a range of adverse physical, mental, and psychosocial sequelae. Today, these children are young adults, and many of them suffer from continuous and complex traumas associated with their status in the society and the stigma that comes with being a "child of rape" (Denov & Piolanti, 2019).

Putting the Problem in Context: The Numbers

The prevalence of gender-based violence (GBV) in Rwanda is largely consistent with the numbers reported globally – approximately one out of every three women have experienced some form of GBV, including domestic and sexual violence, in their lifetime. The Rwanda Demographic Health Survey (RDHS), conducted by the National Institute of Statistics of Rwanda in collaboration with the Ministry of Health, found that cases of violence against women more than doubled between 2005 and 2010, from 16 to 35 per cent (National Institute of Statistics of Rwanda [NISR], Ministry of Health [MOH], & ICF International, 2012; NISR, MOH, & ICF International, 2015). The same trend was observed in 2015 (NISR et al., 2015). According to the 2010 RDHS, among the 5,008 women aged fifteen to forty-nine surveyed, 22 per cent said they had suffered from sexual violence, and 41 per cent reported that they had experienced physical violence at some point in their life (NISR et al., 2012). Among the 3,042 survey participants who were ever married, 56 per cent had been abused by their husband or partner or by their former husband or partner, while 18 per cent had been a victim of sexual violence at the hands of their husband or partner. There is also considerable evidence that girls and young women endure multiple forms of violence at disturbingly high rates. According to a report from the Rwanda Ministry of Health (2016), 18 per cent of females have experienced physical, sexual, and/or emotional abuse before the age of eighteen. This early exposure is strongly linked to later prevalence of attempted suicide and suicidal ideation. Additionally, women and girls are being subjected to financial violence and sexual harassment in the post-genocide period (Abbott & Malunda, 2016).

Toward a Legal and Policy Framework

In the more than twenty-six years since the genocide, the Government of Rwanda has made various efforts to reduce and prevent the occurrence of gender-based violence and to support those who have been impacted (Richters, Rutayisire, Sewimfura, & Ngendahayo, 2010). This includes myriad programs and policies that have been developed and are operating to this day. Despite these efforts, the social and cultural norms that allow violence against women to thrive persist. In the absence of fundamental structural change, efforts to prevent, resist, and overcome gender-based violence risk being limited in scope and duration. Rwanda's commitment to ending violence against women was evident long before the 1994 genocide. In 1981, Rwanda ratified the Convention on the Elimination of all Forms of Discrimination against Women (CEDAW) (UN, Human Rights Office of the Commissioner, 1979). The importance of this convention lies in the recognition that women have rights and must enjoy equality with men. According to the convention, the multifaceted reality of women's lives must be considered holistically, with attention to the economy, nutrition, and health.

The first wave of measures to address gender-based violence in post-genocide Rwanda built on this foundation and included judicial reform and police training. As well, specialized services for victims of GBV and other forms of violence – including domestic violence, violence against children and child defilement, and human/sex trafficking – were established. In 2005 the Ministry of Gender and Family Promotion (MIGEPROF) published its National Policy for Family Promotion, whose specific mission was to protect families against gender-based violence and to strengthen existing measures to protect vulnerable groups, mainly children and mothers. The development of this national policy was based on the key aspirations of the Government of Rwanda toward its 2020 Vision and on the 2013 Constitution, which requires the State of Rwanda to enact appropriate legislation and institutions for the protection of the family, especially mothers and children, to ensure that families flourish. The policy was instrumental in establishing strategies for reducing inequalities and disparities between men and women and, importantly, for reducing poverty by increasing domestic incomes. Little has been published regarding the links between poverty reduction, women's empowerment, and the elimination of GBV; however, Cherry and Hategekimana (2013) observed that "there is a positive correlation between the implementation of security sector reform and women's economic and social solidarity work in cooperatives and a reduction in GBV" (pp. 110–11).

The Strategic Plan for the Implementation of the National Gender Policy (2010) articulated clear strategies for reducing poverty and gender inequality in Rwanda. Moreover, the text supported the establishment of centres that would provide counselling and guidance for victims of family violence. This led to the founding of the Isange One Stop Centres. This same policy considered the social injustices that have affected women for many centuries and that have led to structural violence against women, including the violations and rapes suffered during the 1994 genocide. Internationally recognized today as one of the most comprehensive approaches to preventing and addressing GBV, the Isange Centres offer psychological and legal supports to victims of GBV in a holistic manner. There are currently forty-four centres located in district hospitals throughout Rwanda (Rwanda National Police, n.d.). The central operating mechanism is communication, with information provided by the victim, family members, or community members, including health workers, community police, and volunteers.

The services available in the centres have provided invaluable support to those who have experienced violence, mainly women and children. Even so, the Isange One Stop Centres face challenges, including a shortage of funding and human resources. As well, there is a need for ongoing education and awareness, and this is often beyond the scope of what the centres can provide. Lastly, the stigma that continues to be associated with GBV deters women from coming forward and seeking help, thus sustaining a culture of silence (Lambrecht, 2020).

"Law No. 59/2008 of 10/09/2008" is another important piece of legislation; this one focuses on preventing GBV and punishing its perpetrators. It broadens earlier conceptualizations of GBV, identifies forms of GBV that had not previously been recognized as such, including conjugal rape, and recognizes GBV as grounds for divorce. The same law includes an item on the protection of children, with specific mention of human trafficking, and has provisions designed to ensure respect and social justice for women and girls who experience violence.

The National Policy in Opposition to GBV was enacted in 2010. This policy explicitly mentions the harmful effects of traditional social norms that consider women less powerful than men. This policy highlights positive Rwandan culture-based values that can support positive responses to, and the prevention of, GBV in the community. The policy framework is based on the stated premise that women, girls, and families cannot achieve or succeed as long as GBV persists. Importantly, the policy also recognizes the need to involve men and boys in all efforts to end GBV (Ministry of Gender and Family Promotion, 2010).

Healing and Resilience in the Aftermath of Genocide

In post-genocide Rwanda, genocidal violence and healing from trauma will always be at the centre of efforts to achieve peace, unity, reconciliation, and socio-economic development. As Rieder and Elbert (2013) wrote, the genocide in Rwanda has had lasting effects, such as trauma and impaired mental health and psychosocial functioning among survivors, former prisoners, and their children. In a recent study, Mutuyimana and colleagues (2019) reported persistent PTSD manifestations in mothers who survived the genocide as well as in their offspring, equally among the non-targeted group of mothers and the 1959 refugees who returned to the country after the genocide. Such findings corroborate previous evidence on the transmission of parental post-traumatic stress disorder (PTSD) to offspring through epigenetic processes such as methylation status of the glucocorticoid receptor (GR) gene (*NR3C1*) from a sample of survivors of the genocide in Rwanda (Perroud et al., 2014). This study found that mothers exposed to the genocide, as well as their children, had lower cortisol and glucocorticoid receptor gene levels and higher mineralocorticoid receptor

3.4 Emerging Considerations for Trauma- and Violence-Informed Care

(MR). The imbalance in the two receptors is a risk factor for stress- and anxiety-related disorders. The vulnerability is therefore assumed to be transmitted from parents surviving the genocide to the next generation via epigenetics. The shared vulnerability to post-genocide distress was also seen among Holocaust survivors; here, research found that their children had distinct difficulties in coping with stress and demonstrated a higher vulnerability to PTSD than the offspring of people from the general population with emotional problems (Kellerman, 2001).

At a social level, living with neighbours who committed genocide is likely to permanently trigger traumatic memories of the violence and trauma associated with genocide; it is assumed that this undermines one's sense of security and safety. In the immediate aftermath of the Rwandan genocide, survivors continued to live alongside their perpetrators. Nine years later, the country introduced a system of national community-based judicial courts called "Gacaca." This traditional jurisdiction in Rwanda, which worked toward reconciliation by telling the stories related to the genocide, remained operational until 2012. A premise of the Gacaca court system was that these courts would promote "restorative justice," which would, in turn, strengthen the processes of unity and reconciliation. This would occur by providing a platform for truth-telling, forgiveness, and punishment of the 1994 genocide perpetrators (Official Gazette of the Republic of Rwanda, 2004). The courts were also meant to foster healing among survivors who were grieving the losses they had endured. This healing would be achieved, in part, by receiving information from perpetrators about the circumstances surrounding the deaths of loved ones, by survivors learning who had killed them and how, and by hearing the perpetrators repent (Doughty, 2011).

The Gacaca courts were closed June 2012. It was assumed, however, that Gacaca would survive beyond its closing, as a concept or as a practice (Rwagatare, 2012). Several factors support this assumption. First, the Gacaca process was a clear sign that Rwandans are resilient and capable of finding culturally informed ways of resolving conflict, including the most tragic and painful one, namely the 1994 genocide. The Gacaca process is unique because it is part of Rwandan heritage; therefore, the people already believe in it. Also, many believe that Gacaca has marked two very important contradictory, but also in many ways complementary, aspects of the history of the Rwandan people: it is inevitably linked to the most tragic and painful period – the 1994 genocide – and most people will see it solely in that way; but it has also served to reveal the depth and strength of character of the Rwandan people. Rwandans have had to dig deep into their culture and traditions to develop a workable solution to the unique problems the genocide has brought in its wake.

The significance of Gacaca went beyond rendering justice and reconciliation. Gacaca was considered to be an exceptional healing opportunity for both victims and perpetrators of the genocide. As King (2011) emphasized:

> Many Rwandans were optimistic about the Gacaca concept. Both Hutu and Tutsi had high expectations for it; they hoped it could bring them back together and help restore relationships. On the one hand, Tutsi survivors wished to know details about how and where their family members had been killed and who had killed them. They also wanted to at least have the perpetrators admit what they had done and apologize. The Hutu also welcomed the Gacaca idea and contributed to information gathering in the hope that the truth would come out, set the innocent free, oblige the guilty to acknowledge the suffering of the victims, who would offer forgiveness before guaranteeing a reduced sentence to those who confessed. (p. 136)

In the same vein, mental health practitioners found Gacaca to "be a promising alternative approach to the imported models that tended to focus on the individual and ignore the collective nature of psychosocial trauma" (King, 2011, p. 136).

Despite the efforts of UN agencies to provide legal tools for punishing the genocide's perpetrators, genocide prevention remains historically problematic. The genocidal events in Darfur, Rwanda, and Bosnia in the 1990s are tangible examples of that assertion. In most of these, genocide was accompanied by mass violence among citizens. Turmoil, non-existent security, and lack of social and systemic support continue in those places to be a huge burden to citizens, and all of this has led to intergenerational traumatic disorders, especially for the most vulnerable, including women and children. Given that genocide is at its root a social issue as well as a universal political concern, it is crucial to examine the global possibility of preventing genocide and ensuring the long-term protection of vulnerable populations (Vollhardt & Bilewicz, 2013).

The Gacaca courts played an important role in processes of healing and recovery as well as in fostering resilience. This idea is supported by research conducted by Dushimirimana, Sezibera, and Auerbach (2014), who found that many people viewed Gacaca as a source of safety and a means to achieve rebuilding and resilience. The Gacaca courts also played a concrete role in promoting healing in a country where there are not enough health and justice professionals and where there is limited capacity to manage the significant post-genocidal mental health effects, including PTSD, depression, and suicide.

While the Gacaca courts served a very important role in healing, reconciliation, and resilience, they had their limitations. Many women and girls who experienced GBV were reluctant to disclose what they had endured because of the stigma and shame they encountered, and continue to encounter, from their families and communities. There is also evidence that some women who were raped and subsequently became pregnant remained connected to their perpetrators – indeed, in some cases they married them. Coming forward to tell their stories heightened their risk of harm, isolation, further shame, and discrimination from family and the community more broadly.

Rethinking Approaches and Perspectives while Shifting the Paradigm

To move from individually focused interventions to a system that pays more attention to family, systemic trauma, and TVIC, a paradigm shift is needed. Health care and social service providers have developed and implemented a range of effective individual and group therapeutic measures to address PTSD and other adverse health sequelae of GBV, and these have undoubtedly led to a significant improvement in the mental health of those seeking treatment. However, we contend that these approaches need to be complemented by societal and structural changes that can foster resilience and healing, individually and collectively, and that disrupt the underlying conditions that allow violence to persist and thrive.

Staub (2013) has described a process for building peaceful communities that stresses the importance of progressive change and the promotion of reconciliation in the development of harmonious societies. According to Staub, this can only be achieved when approaches such as TVIC are embedded in the system at multiple levels and across multiple sectors. Considering the complexity of GBV in Rwanda, it is not enough to deal with its causes and consequences at the individual or interpersonal level. Nor is an approach that emphasizes biological weaknesses, deficits, or pathology sufficient. Rather, meaningful efforts must be made to challenge the root causes of the problem, as well as the deeply entrenched social and structural inequities and norms that support and sustain ideologies and practices of oppression, marginalization, and, indeed, gender-based violence.

The genocide committed against the Tutsi in Rwanda caused injuries at the individual *and* community level. The sexual violence inflicted on women and girls during the genocide left indelible physical and psychological wounds on survivors. We should also note that the status of "victim of sexual violence" is itself a form of injury, as is the stigma it carries. In a culture in which sexuality is experienced as taboo, victims of sexual violence live with feelings of shame and guilt as well as post-traumatic stress.

After the genocide, the Rwandan government put in place various programs and policies aimed at preventing and punishing GBV crimes, including sexual violence. An analysis of the policies and laws in place in Rwanda reveals that these texts are based on the assumption that sexual and gender-based violence is a consequence of discrimination against, and oppression of, women. In this understanding, the strategies in place focus on raising awareness about gender equality, promoting women through their integration into decision-making structures and bodies, increasing the financial capacity of women to guarantee their independence from men, and so forth. While many of these efforts are not unique to Rwanda, several important actions in that country have been quite distinct. For example, Rwanda has established national gender machinery

(NGM) institutions, which include the Ministry of Gender and Family Promotion (MIGEPROF), the Gender Monitoring Office (GMO), the National Women's Council (NWC), and the Rwanda Women Parliamentary Forum (FFRP). NGM bodies have invested in several education and intervention programs aiming at thorough change in the management of GBV. Various programs have been launched to raise awareness of GBV and to change mindsets. Regarding the latter, efforts to engage boys and men have been strengthened through #HeForShe outreach campaigns, an invitation for men to stand in solidarity with women for gender equality, and other home-grown initiatives such as "Umugoroba w'Ababyeyi" (literally "Parents' Evening"). These latter gatherings are meant to bring together parents to address any GBV or child abuse cases within the community. We also note the legislature's desire to severely punish crimes of gender-based and sexual violence, as a form of preventing and discouraging these kinds of offences. These strategies are bearing fruit; even so, the statistics for reported cases of GBV and sexual violence are increasing day by day.

Policies and practices aiming to address the consequences of the genocide – in particular, gender-based and sexual violence – should integrate TVIC. Such approaches emphasize policies and practices that recognize the connections between violence, trauma, and negative behaviours and health outcomes. TVI approaches expand on the concept of trauma-informed approaches to account for the broader systemic inequities that influence and contribute to interpersonal experiences of trauma and violence.

Conclusion

The lessons we can learn about trauma, healing, and recovery in the aftermath of the genocide against the Tutsi people in Rwanda have a relevance that extends far beyond geographic boundaries. While certain aspects are uniquely applicable to a post-genocidal context, we contend that many of the ideas presented throughout this chapter may offer insights about other countries and communities that have endured individual and collective pain and suffering. As we know from the Rwandan experience, as well as from other modern-day atrocities, the impacts of trauma persist for many years after horrific events are over. The consequences affect successive generations, giving rise to the phenomenon commonly referred to as intergenerational trauma. Although the effects are often invisible, they impact identity and development, as well as the broader social, political, and structural fabric of daily life. Given our increasingly interconnected world, efforts to incorporate TVIC should be undertaken through a global lens, one that simultaneously considers distinct local realities and contexts, as well as shared realities. In the absence of such coordinated and comprehensive approaches, the impacts of genocide, violence, and trauma will continue to limit the human rights and lives of those who are most vulnerable.

KEY MESSAGES AND IMPLICATIONS

- Genocide doesn't only kill people; it kills nations (Waintrater, 2003). In Rwanda, there is widespread recognition that the effects of trauma are pervasive throughout society. However, there is less agreement as to how it is best addressed, and the notion of TVIC has not, thus far, been introduced.
- Despite this gap, we contend that TVIC has tremendous relevance across many sectors, including health, education, gender and family promotion, and justice.
- Ongoing efforts to protect, nurture, and sustain health, to create a context where gender-based violence is no longer a part of daily life, must work in concert with cultural values and strategies that promote equitable social relationships, social structures, and community functioning (Zraly & Nyirazinyoye, 2010).
- There is a clear need to articulate the problem of gender-based violence with the goal of preventing it. The implementation of TVIC in Rwanda offers a meaningful and relevant approach to achieving this goal.

REFERENCES

Abbott, P., & Malunda, D. (2016). The promise and the reality: Women's rights in Rwanda. *African Journal of International and Comparative Law, 24*(4), 561–81. https://doi.org/10.3366/ajicl.2016.0173

Berman, H. (1999). Stories of growing up amid violence by refugee children of war and children of battered women living in Canada. *Image: The Journal of Nursing Scholarship, 31*(1), 1–12. https://doi.org/10.1111/j.1547-5069.1999.tb00422.x

Bizimana, J.D. (2001). *L'Eglise et le genocide au Rwanda: Les Peres Blancs et le negationnisme*. Paris, France: L'Harmattan.

Cherry, J., & Hategekimana, C. (2013). Ending gender-based violence through grassroots women's empowerment: Lessons from post-1994 Rwanda. *Agenda, 27*(1), 100–13. https://doi.org/10.1080/10130950.2013.793895

Chrétien, J.P. (2003). *The great lakes of Africa*. New York, NY: Zone Books.

Denov, M., & Piolanti, A. (2019). Mothers of children born of genocidal rape in Rwanda: Implications for mental health, well-being, and psycho-social support interventions. *Health Care for Women International, 40*(7–9), 813–28. https://doi.org/10.1080/07399332.2019.1571593

Doughty, K.C. (2011). Contesting community: Legalized reconciliation efforts in the aftermath of genocide in Rwanda (Doctoral dissertation). *Retrieved from Publicly Accessible Penn Dissertations*. (333)

Dushimirimana, F., Sezibera, V., & Auerbach, C. (2014). Pathways to resilience in post-genocide Rwanda: A resources efficacy model. *Intervention*, *12*(2), 219–30. https://psycnet.apa.org/record/2014-29718-005

Hamel, M.E. (2016). Ethnic belonging of the children born out of rape in post-conflict Bosnia-Herzegovina and Rwanda. *Nations and Nationalism*, *22*(2), 287–304. https://doi.org/10.1111/nana.12151

International Criminal Tribunal for Rwanda (ICTR). (2014). United Nations international residual mechanism for criminal tribunals. Retrieved from https://unictr.irmct.org/en/documents

Kahn, S., & Denov, M. (2019). "We are children like others": Pathways to mental health and healing for children born of genocidal rape in Rwanda. *Transcultural Psychiatry*, *56*(3), 510–28. https://doi.org/10.1177%2F1363461519825683

Kellerman, N.P.F. (2001). Perceived parental rearing behaviors in children of Holocaust survivors. *Israel Journal of Psychiatry*, *38*(1), 58–68. Retrieved from https://pubmed.ncbi.nlm.nih.gov/11381585/

King, R.U. (2011). Healing psychosocial trauma in the midst of truth commissions: The case of Gacaca in post-genocide Rwanda," *Genocide Studies and Prevention: An International Journal*, *6*(2), 134–51. Retrieved from https://scholarcommons.usf.edu/gsp/vol6/iss2/5

Lamb, C. (2020). *Our bodies, their battlefields: War through the lives of women.* New York, NY: Scribner.

Lambrecht, I. (2020). Failing women? Structural violence's relevance in responses to sexual violence: A case study of Rwanda. *Undergraduate Journal of Global Citizenship*, *3*(2), 2. Retrieved from https://digitalcommons.fairfield.edu/jogc/vol3/iss2/2

Ministry of Gender and Family Promotion. (2005). *National Policy for Family Promotion.* Retrieved from https://www.ilo.org/dyn/natlex/docs/ELECTRONIC/92985/117299/F-1037879932/RWA-92985.pdf

Ministry of Gender and Family Promotion. (2010). *National Gender Policy.* Retrieved from https://www.ilo.org/dyn/natlex/docs/ELECTRONIC/94009/110188/F-1576743982/RWA-94009.pdf

Mukamana, D., & Brysiewicz, P. (2008). The lived experience of genocide rape survivors in Rwanda. *Journal of Nursing Scholarship*, *40*(4), 379–84. https://doi.org/10.1111/j.1547-5069.2008.00253.x

Mukimbiri, J. (2005). The seven stages of the Rwandan genocide. *Journal of International Criminal Justice*, *3*(4), 823–36. https://doi.org/10.1093/jicj/mqi070

Mullins, C.W. (2009). "We are going to rape you and taste Tutsi women": Rape during the 1994 Rwandan Genocide. *The British Journal of Criminology*, *49*(6), 719–35. Retrieved from https://core.ac.uk/download/pdf/60554071.pdf

Munyandamutsa, N., Nkubamugisha, P.M., Gex-Fabry, M., & Eytan, A. (2012). Mental and physical health in Rwanda 14 years after the genocide. *Social Psychiatry and Psychiatric Epidemiology*, *47*(11), 1753–61. https://psycnet.apa.org/doi/10.1007/s00127-012-0494-9

3.4 Emerging Considerations for Trauma- and Violence-Informed Care 241

Mutuyimana, C., Sezibera, V., Nsabimana, E., Mugabo, L., Cassady, C., Musanabaganwa, C., & Kayiteshonga, Y. (2019). PTSD prevalence among resident mothers and their offspring in Rwanda 25 years after the 1994 genocide against the Tutsi. *BMC Psychology, 7*(1), 1–7. https://doi.org/10.1186/s40359-019-0362-4

National Institute of Statistics of Rwanda (NISR), Ministry of Health (MOH), & ICF International. (2012). *Rwanda Demographic and Health Survey 2010.* Calverton, MD: NISR, MOH, and ICF International. Retrieved from http://dhsprogram.com/pubs/pdf/FR259/FR259.pdf

National Institute of Statistics of Rwanda (NISR), Ministry of Health (MOH), & ICF International. (2015). *Rwanda Demographic and Health Survey 2014–15.* Rockville, MD: NISR, MOH, and ICF International. Retrieved from https://dhsprogram.com/pubs/pdf/FR316/FR316.pdf

Nicolaisen, V. (2019). The systematic use of sexual violence in genocide: Understanding why women are being targeted using the cases of Rwanda and the former Yugoslavia (Dissertation). Retrieved from http://urn.kb.se/resolve?urn=urn:nbn:se:uu:diva-394662

The Official Gazette of the Republic of Rwanda. (2004). *Organic Law N.16/2004.* Retrieved from https://www.refworld.org/cgi-bin/texis/vtx/rwmain/opendocpdf.pdf?reldoc=y&docid=52f22c704#:~:text=This%20organic%20law%20establishes%20organization,penal%20code%20of%20Rwanda%2C%20but

The Official Gazette of the Republic of Rwanda. (2008). *Law No. 59/2008 of 10/09/2008 on prevention and punishment of gender-based violence.* Retrieved from https://www.refworld.org/docid/4a3f88812.html

Perroud, N., Rutembesa, E., Paoloni-Giacobino, A., Mutabaruka, J., Mutesa, L., Stenz, L., ... Karege, F. (2014). The Tutsi genocide and transgenerational transmission of maternal stress: Epigenetics and biology of the HPA axis. *The World Journal of Biological Psychiatry, 15*(4), 334–45. https://doi.org/10.3109/15622975.2013.866693

Richters, A., Rutayisire, T., Sewimfura, T., & Ngendahayo, E. (2010). Psychotrauma, healing, and reconciliation in Rwanda – the contribution of community-based sociotherapy. *African Journal of Traumatic Stress, 1*(2), 55–63. Retrieved from https://hdl.handle.net/11245/1.367021

Rieder, H., & Elbert, T. (2013). Rwanda – lasting imprints of a genocide: Trauma, mental health, and psychosocial conditions in survivors, former prisoners, and their children. *Conflict and Health, 7*(1), 1–13. https://doi.org/10.1186/1752-1505-7-6

Russell, S.G., Lim, S., Kim, P., & Morse, S. (2016). The legacy of gender-based violence and HIV/AIDS in the postgenocide era: Stories from women in Rwanda. *Health Care for Women International, 37*(7), 721–43. https://doi.org/10.1080/07399332.2015.1083026

Rwagatare, J. (2012, June 19). The courts have closed, but Gacaca lives on. *The New Times.* Retrieved from https://www.newtimes.co.rw/section/read/54142

Rwanda Ministry of Health. (2016). *Violence Against Children and Youth Survey: Findings from a national survey, 2015–2016.* Retrieved from https://www.unicef.org/rwanda/media/181/file/Violence-against-Children-Youth-Survey-2015-16.pdf

Rwanda National Police. (n.d.). *Isange One Stop Center Model* [PowerPoint slides]. Retrieved from https://darpg.gov.in/sites/default/files/Rwanda.pdf

Sharlach, L. (1999). Gender and genocide in Rwanda: Women as agents and objects of genocide. *Journal of Genocide Research, 1*(3), 387–99. https://doi.org/10.1080/14623529908413968

Staub, E. (2013). Building a peaceful society: Origins, prevention, and reconciliation after genocide and other group violence. *American Psychologist, 68*(7), 576–89. https://psycnet.apa.org/doi/10.1037/a0032045

Torgovnik, J. (2019, March 30). Rwanda's children of rape have come of age. *The New York Times.* Retrieved from https://www.nytimes.com/2019/03/30/opinion/rwandas-children-of-rape-have-come-of-age.html

United Nations, Human Rights Office of the Commissioner. (1979). *Convention on the Elimination of All Forms of Discrimination against Women.* Retrieved from https://www.ohchr.org/en/professionalinterest/pages/cedaw.aspx

Vollhardt, J.R., & Bilewicz, M. (2013). After the genocide: Psychological perspectives on victim, bystander, and perpetrator groups. *Journal of Social Issues, 69*(1), 1–15. https://doi.org/10.1111/josi.12000

Waintrater, R. (2003). *Sortir du génocide: Témoigner pour réapprendre à vivre.* Paris. France: Payot.

Wielenga, C., & Harris, G. (2011). Building peace and security after genocide: The contribution of the gacaca courts of Rwanda. *African Security Review, 20*(1), 15–25. https://doi.org/10.1080/10246029.2011.561008

Wood, E.J. (2018). Rape as a practice of war: Toward a typology of political violence. *Politics & Society, 46*(4), 513–37. https://doi.org/10.1177%2F0032329218773710

Zraly, M., & Nyirazinyoye, L. (2010). Don't let the suffering make you fade away: An ethnographic study of resilience among survivors of genocide-rape in southern Rwanda. *Social Science & Medicine, 70*(10), 1656–64. https://doi.org/10.1016/j.socscimed.2010.01.017

3.5 Thinking through Gaps and Support Needs: What Newcomer and Migrant Worker Interventions Teach Us about Trauma- and Violence-Informed Care

SUSANA CAXAJ, JENNIFER SANDU, AND TANAZ JAVAN

Drawing on research and practice experiences, this chapter provides strategies for implementing trauma- and violence-informed care (TVIC) in both the settlement service sector and, more broadly, with diverse migrant populations in Canada. We focus on how to integrate TVIC into organizations serving newcomers, many of whom are highly traumatized, and on how to work with and provide support for the migrant agricultural workforce. We also provide insight into how TVIC principles can be applied as an evaluation tool for programs and initiatives already implemented or being considered. Our case studies can guide organizations that have already implemented programs or services in assessing and possibly (re)aligning them with TVIC principles.

The needs of migrant populations, be they immigrants, refugees, or temporary foreign workers, are diverse and often complex. Yet an examination of how to provide them with services reveals that there are commonalities among these groups, however unique they are. When we apply a TVIC framework, we are compelled to think through both the lived realities and the larger structural barriers faced by these diverse groups. By the end of this chapter, the reader will (1) understand the intersections of life events and social, political, and economic factors that uniquely shape the support and care needs of diverse migrant populations, (2) identify factors of particular significance to diverse migrant populations, especially in terms of prior history of trauma, violence, precarious status, discrimination, and existing networks of support, (3) know how TVIC principles can be applied to supporting refugee and migrant worker populations in Canada, (4) use TVIC principles to assess whether existing programs and services are trauma- and violence-informed, and (5) identify interpersonal and organizational values, attitudes, and practices that can champion a TVIC approach to delivering support to diverse migrant populations.

Providing Support for Diverse Migrant Populations: Two Case Studies

Case 1: A Support Model for Migrant Farm/Agricultural Workers

Based on our past research on support networks and services available to migrant agricultural workers (Caxaj, Cohen, & Marsden, 2020; Caxaj & Cohen, 2021a, 2021b), we developed what we called a support model intervention to better address the needs and the gaps in access and service delivery for migrant agricultural workers. British Columbia's Okanagan Valley, known for its orchards and vineyards, is a prominent destination for migrant agricultural workers under Canada's Seasonal Agricultural Worker Program (SAWP). SAWP brings a large contingent of migrant agricultural workers into Canada through a circular migration process whereby workers are permitted to work on a specific farm through a bilateral agreement between the host country (Canada) and a sending country (Mexico and several Caribbean nations) for a maximum period of eight months. As prior research has documented, this group experiences various barriers to accessing services and protections; it also faces systemic discrimination (McLaughlin, Hennebry, & Haines, 2014; Preibisch & Hennebry, 2011; Pysklywec, McLaughlin, Tew, & Haines, 2011). The need for SAWP is one outcome of free trade policies that have largely displaced local economies in the global South; thus, migrant agricultural workers can also be viewed as "economic migrants." Austerity and a lack of resources in their countries of origin make it still harder for them to assert their rights while working and living in Canada (Basok, Bélanger, & Rivas, 2014; Horgan & Liinamaa, 2017).

Our prior research made clear that the needs of this population are difficult to understand within the parameters of a single sector. For example, a migrant agricultural worker who is injured on the job needs support to navigate Workers' Compensation (and to report the injury) but also needs access to independent and accurate translation at the point of care and to be served by clinicians who understand that migrant agricultural workers are entitled to the same workplace injury protections as other workers in Canada (Caxaj & Plamondon, 2020; Colindres, Cohen, & Caxaj, 2021). Furthermore, since migrant agricultural workers may be medically repatriated, and their tenure in Canada may be contingent on their employment (Orkin, Lay, McLaughlin, Schwandt, & Cole, 2014; Vosko & Casey, 2019), they need access to people who understand immigration law so that they are aware of their rights. To work toward a multisectoral approach to service delivery, we developed strong partnerships with organizations with different skill sets and capacities. Partner organizations included Kelowna (BC) Community Resources, a settlement organization with an office that focuses on immigrant services, and the Migrant Workers Centre, a legal organization that provides legal services to temporary migrant labourers.

We also worked closely with a low-barrier health care clinic, Outreach Urban Health, to begin to address the many barriers workers face as they try to access timely and continuous health services.

Key activities of the intervention were carried out by two key support staff: an outreach worker and a legal advocate. The outreach worker visited and made connections with workers, oriented them to services, accompanied them as they navigated various services, and provided both language and cultural interpretation for migrant agricultural workers requiring various types of support. A typical day for the outreach worker involved several farm visits, outreach to workers at locally frequented grocery stores, fielding intake phone calls to answer workers' questions, referring workers to appropriate resources, and accompanying workers to medical appointments.

The legal advocate worked closely with the outreach worker to respond to any legal queries or concerns raised by migrant agricultural workers, and as necessary, to provide legal advice and representation. A typical day for the legal advocate involved conversing with several workers about their concerns and assessing to what degree those concerns had a solution in law, making referrals to non-legal but essential services that might support the pursuit of a legal claim, and submitting applications and reports on workers' behalf. As is reflected in prior literature (see above and also Caxaj, Cohen, Buffam, & Oudshoorn, 2020; Hennebry, McLaughlin, & Preibisch, 2016; Robillard, McLaughlin, Cole, Vasilevska, & Gendron, 2018), migrant agricultural workers face many barriers: they struggle to understand what services are available, to access those services, to find culturally relevant and language-appropriate care, and to understand and assert their legal rights. So it was important that staff be able to anticipate the complexity of barriers faced by this group while also demonstrating a great deal of accountability for each individual's cultural safety. A notable aspect of the support model was that both organizations were able to secure matching funding (in addition to the baseline research funding provided through the Vancouver Foundation); this enabled them to supplement and increase the impact of their initial interventions. Importantly, this meant we were able to hire the two staff on a full-time rather than part-time basis; it also gave us the resources to expand our social outreach activities and to develop comprehensive networking events, information workshops, and resource fairs for migrant agricultural workers. Because these events were always coupled with a culturally appropriate recreational component, such as soccer matches, BBQs, and so on, they were well-attended and had the additional benefit of building rapport and trust in the community, thus making more migrant agricultural workers aware of the services that were available.

A TVIC lens. Though not explicitly designed as a "TVIC intervention," our partnered and community-based model of service delivery, with continuous input from migrant agricultural workers, did exemplify many of the core principles of TVIC. In the next section, we illustrate how we used TVIC principles in retrospect to rejig our guiding values and principles in carrying out this work.

Principle 1: Understand trauma and violence as well as their impacts on people's lives and behaviour. A core principle of TVIC encourages organizations to be aware of the prevalence of trauma and violence and understand the impact of these on individuals' lives. TVIC expands on the concept of TIC and recognizes the importance of historical (collective and individual) and ongoing (interpersonal and systemic/structural) violence (chapters 1.2, 1.5). We had to *understand the impact of trauma and violence on the lives of migrant agricultural workers* in order to work toward effective service delivery. For instance, given the limited reporting of workplace abuses and violations among this population in the past, employer associations and government agents had often assumed that this reflected adequate legal protections. Yet through consistent rapport-building, and opportunities to circumvent stifling formalities in outreach and intake protocols, our support staff were able to build more meaningful relationships with workers that fostered the trust necessary to consider pursuing reports or legal claims. In other words, our work reflected that this population was structurally disadvantaged in service-seeking due to their experiences of coercion and precarity. By showing flexibility in outreach and accompanying workers in ways that safeguarded their well-being as they navigated formal systems that could be triggering, intimidating, and inaccessible, our team was able to anticipate these barriers to workers' assertions of their legal rights.

Principle 2: Create emotionally, culturally, and physically safe environments for all clients and providers. Creating welcoming environments and intake procedures is another important aspect of TVIC. Note that service providers do not need to know their clients' histories of trauma and violence in order to provide trauma- and violence-informed services. Rather, the structure and culture of organizations should create a space for everyone to receive safe and respectful care. All members of our team played an important role in *creating emotionally and physically safe environments* for migrant agricultural workers. For instance, given that migrant agricultural workers are typically housed on their employers' property (which is also their worksite), they often report being burdened by a high degree of surveillance and control. Our legal advocate, outreach worker, and program evaluation lead provided opportunities for workers to meet away from the farm. We also normalized and humanized the need for connection through invitations to discuss issues "over a cup of coffee," or by accompanying them on their weekly grocery trips into town. These settings provided a sense of care and respect for individuals, many of whom would not have had experiences with anyone in Canada outside their work environment and had good reason to believe that any interaction with an individual "off the farm" could be seen as "trouble-making" and perhaps even prohibited by their employer (Beaumont, 2020).

Principle 3: Foster opportunities for choice, collaboration, and connection. TVIC emphasizes the importance of policies and procedures that foster flexibility and shared decision-making. By listening to what their clients require and privileging their voices, service providers can provide better options tailored to their needs. Clearly, this population required us to *integrate choice and the greatest level of autonomy into services* we offered. Migrant agricultural workers sought the services they needed, indicating their preferences for who should be involved (whether it meant legal or health service delivery). For instance, some women required medical attention for their reproductive health and, understandably, preferred female interpretation/accompaniment. In these situations, our program evaluation coordinator and specialized volunteer supports in the region were able to accompany workers with the help of our outreach worker. In other cases, workers had disclosed serious experiences of abuse or medical distress and preferred for the program evaluation coordinator (whose role was primarily data collection) to accompany them throughout the process of pursuing further services. This request was often a result of the rapport and trust they had already built with this person, the energy and momentum required to share one's story, and in some cases, needs unique to the worker's circumstances. It was important to honour these requests, because we did not want to participate in workers' retraumatization by having them explain their stories over and over again; doing so would have created further obstacles for workers to get the support they needed. Besides heightening migrant agricultural workers' sense of choice when accessing support through our team, these strategies strengthened the impact of our service delivery by bringing additional partners and collaborators into the process.

Principle 4: Use a strengths-based and capacity-building approach to support clients. It is essential to allow sufficient time for building meaningful relationships. Through these interactions, providers can recognize the intentions and efforts of their clients and work with them to showcase their clients' strengths. When initiating outreach, maintaining relationships, seeking program evaluation feedback, and so on, the centrality of *building authentic relationships that honour the strengths of this population* was key to all that we achieved. Organized events, workshops, and data collection always prioritized addressing workers' isolation and working toward community connections, even if the aim was to increase knowledge about resources or services.

Furthermore, celebrating workers' talents, cultures, and interests through soccer tournaments, culturally important foods, and face-to-face time getting to know people fostered a sense of collaboration among workers and service providers. This allowed us to anticipate barriers (e.g., low literacy skills) and then overcome them by developing culturally significant ways to transform the services offered. This informed how we partnered with our collaborators, including those in health services, and ensured that we valued the strong volunteer sector, which had experience adopting these types of services to the community.

Case 2: London, Ontario, Newcomer Clinic

In 2015, the Government of Canada began resettling more than 40,000 Syrian refugees (Immigration, Refugees, & Citizenship Canada, 2019). This extraordinary time was the impetus for strengthening partnerships, innovative practices, and capacity-building to meet the needs of the Syrian resettlement initiative and, by proxy, future resettlement communities in Canada. During this time, the London (Ontario) Cross Cultural Learner Centre (CCLC), a settlement agency and resettlement assistance program (RAP) service provider organization that provides immediate and essential services to newly arrived government-assisted refugees, joined forces with the London InterCommunity Health Centre (LIHC) to meet the immediate health care needs of Syrian newcomers.

After the needs encountered during the immediate settlement period began to recede, CCLC and LIHC identified the need to continue to collaborate, especially given the increasingly complex histories and health and social needs of government-assisted refugees (GARs) and the expanding resettlement commitments made in the local community. Thus, the Newcomer Clinic was established, located at CCLC in Jeremiah's House, a reception centre and short-term accommodation for newly arrived GARs. The clinic is staffed by clinicians from LIHC and provides care during refugees' first six months in Canada. Its two primary areas of focus are (1) completing early health assessments for newcomers, and (2) providing acute care for newcomers, some of whom have never accessed primary care, have undiagnosed or uncontrolled medical issues, or have arrived with complex medical needs and medication records (London InterCommunity Health Centre, 2021).

The Newcomer Clinic staff work alongside case managers to provide culturally integrated and coordinated care that addresses the clients' often complex medical and mental health care needs. Case managers commonly have gone through the immigration process themselves, and this aids in rapport-building; it also fosters empowerment practices and circumvents language barriers; these things are all especially important during initial resettlement.

The clinic plays many important roles, with an emphasis on providing safe and compassionate care from the newcomers' first days in Canada. Newcomers develop trusting relationships with health care and settlement staff, who provide immediate necessary services as well as a bridge to the health care system and community services as they integrate. The clinicians and case managers work in tandem to support the transition from initial primary health care to permanent primary health care in the community. This provides continuity of care and support for the long-term health, well-being, and integration of individuals and families.

A TVIC lens. The groundwork of building a strong and supportive collaborative partnership during the Syrian resettlement initiative helped our teams reinforce TVIC principles and evolve our collective understanding of the impacts of trauma and the unique needs of trauma survivors (principle 1). This paved the way for the complex resettlement process for the Yazidi community. In 2017, the Government of Canada began resettling more than 1,200 Yazidi refugees in London, Toronto, Winnipeg, Calgary, and other communities in Canada (Standing Committee on Citizenship and Immigration, 2018). This resettlement was in response to the 2014 massacre conducted by the Islamic State, which had set out to systematically eradicate the Yazidi, an ethnic minority group that had been persecuted and marginalized for generations; their historical and ongoing experiences of severe trauma and violence meant that an especially intricate resettlement and integration process was required in Canada. A history of collaborating to bring various perspectives to the table allowed for a greater understanding of the nuances and impact of forced migration and resettlement distress.

After resettling these communities, our TVIC foundation then provided a vehicle for navigating various health care and settlement challenges in the context of the COVID-19 pandemic. For example, during COVID-19, the Middlesex-London Health Unit (MLHU) collaborated with Newcomer Clinic staff and the CCLC to develop a health promotion campaign to disseminate tailored and targeted public health messaging to the Yazidi community. Leveraging the clinic partnership, we were able to build a collaborative campaign with core service providers and leaders based on awareness and knowledge of the community's pre-migration trauma, its strengths and cultural characteristics, and its experiences with resettlement. This highlighted the importance of cross-sectoral collaboration and of providing information in a trusting and inclusive way that was attuned to the unique facets of the Yazidis' culture and resettlement journey.

Another TVIC strategy arising from the Yazidi resettlement process was a protocol developed around the anniversary of the Yazidi genocide, a collectively triggering event characterized by complex grief over separation from family members back home, some of whose whereabouts were unknown. The protocol included expanded clinic hours, streamlined processes, and additional availability of case managers and wellness counsellors. This consistent commitment to discussing and addressing ongoing resettlement challenges and structural barriers, and to instituting enhanced culturally integrated processes, has helped us be both proactive and responsive to the needs of newly arrived GARs.

The Newcomer Clinic creates welcoming and safe spaces for those newly arrived in London (principle 2). For example, the clinic has been co-located at the CCLC so as to provide multidisciplinary care at a single site, so that new arrivals are wrapped within a supportive network. This reduces the barriers to care and provides opportunities for teams to consistently communicate, coordinate services, and support one another. One very valuable strategy has been to hold monthly meetings between the primary care team and CCLC staff. These regular check-ins allow for feedback, rapid response to evolving situations, updates regarding expected arrivals, and trust-building among agencies. This trust has fostered an environment where team members feel valued no matter what their role and allows for constructive bi-directional feedback between CCLC and LIHC staff. Our partnership allows for improved client care because each provider, whether from primary care or the settlement agency, is able to leverage their unique skills, role, life experience, and understandings from interacting with the client or the client's cultural group in order to create an environment in which newcomers can thrive in their new life in Canada.

COVID-19 continues to challenge and reshape how we provide health care services in the Newcomer Clinic. TVIC offers a lens for approaching equitable and adaptive service delivery. This has included temporarily relocating the clinic out of a congregate setting and developing new protocols and practices – for example, COVID-19 staff and client safety protocols for Jeremiah's House. In 2021, this included working closely to support the vaccine roll-out for recently resettled clients. The teams worked tirelessly together to transition, navigate, and mitigate these changes in ways that supported individual and family resettlement in an adverse time, acknowledging the heightened and often disproportionate challenges faced by new arrivals.

Given our partnership, we are constantly aware of the context and nuances in people's integration journeys and of the need to provide meaningful and collaboratively based choices and connections (principle 3). For example, a vital element of effective service delivery in the context of the clinic and in working with newcomers is access to interpretation services. This is crucial to consider, for too often there is a lack of universal and standardized approaches to providing interpretation.

Berry (1997) highlights a conceptual framework that incorporates various factors in individual adaptation processes both prior to and during acculturation. One important factor involves looking at an individual's society of origin, namely their economic situation, political context, and demographic location (Berry, 1997). Looking at the Yazidi resettlement process as it relates to access to interpretation, while many in the community speak Arabic and Arabic interpreters are often more available than Kurmanji interpreters, Arabic can often represent the language of Yazidi people's oppressors and their experiences of being marginalized in their home countries. However, unless one knows the context of pre-migration experiences, one could easily overlook the need to provide vital and informed options in accessing interpretation services in a post-migration context. When we realize this, we as service providers are able to provide better-informed trauma- and violence-informed options, so as to foster safety and (re)instil people's sense of power and control over their lives.

Fostering strength and resilience is pivotal for refugee health and resettlement (principle 4). It is important to maximize resiliency, however adverse the circumstances. It is crucial to acknowledge the strength it takes for people to overcome pre- and post-migration stressors, historical and ongoing experiences of trauma and violence, health and social inequities, and subsequent distress. George (2012) notes that "refugee resiliency serves to counter the social construction of forced migrants as victims without agency, and enables refugees, despite their traumatic experiences, to succeed in the new society" (p. 432). So it is important to acknowledge the sheer tenacity and perseverance of refugees throughout their migration experiences. Reflecting on the Yazidi resettlement process and our work with GARs at the Newcomer Clinic, we surmised that a strengths-based approach can simply mean focusing on the person's ability to attend medical appointments and navigate complicated transportation systems or other immediate challenges in their initial adjustment to life in Canada. But it is also important to pay attention to system-level issues that can strengthen resilience (Wylie, Corrado, Edwards, Benlamri, & Murcia Monroy, 2020). Barriers can include limited transcultural knowledge, skills, and practices among care providers, as well as systemic time constraints (Wylie et al., 2018). All of this points again to the need for collaborative approaches and for systems and structures for collectively supporting clients.

Exploring protective factors can also help refugees navigate their integration journeys. Although this can be delicate given pre-migration experiences, in the context of the Yazidi resettlement process, understanding cultural factors, such as their communal and collective nature, underscores the importance of family, community, and social interventions in the post-migration context. Examples of these strategies have included celebrating Yazidi New Year, supporting community leaders, and encouraging group therapeutic and recreational activities.

Practical Strategies to Implement TVIC for Newcomers

Active Listening, Orientation to Structural Factors, and Anticipating Barriers

There are various approaches that can help foster relationship-building and resilience with newcomer clients using a TVIC lens. One of those pivotal practices is understanding clients' unique migration histories and resettlement journeys. This does not necessarily require self-disclosure, but it does require that providers approach their practice with cultural humility and with openness to listening, understanding, and learning. For example, regarding the Yazidi resettlement process, barriers to family reunification were a major stressor and factor in their recovery and integration. It can be useful to understand this in terms of Hoggett and Thompson's (2012) idea of socially structured feelings, or emotions in a political context. Hoggett and Thompson's work "adds to an understanding of the relationship between external structures and the inner world of feelings, including the feelings associated with loss, hurt and injustice" (Allan, 2015, p. 1706). So it is important to understand the impacts and intersections of broader systems, policies, and social determinants of health on newcomer well-being and their overall integration process.

Likewise, the community-based intervention launched to serve migrant agricultural workers confirmed what the literature has established – that this population not only faces practical barriers to accessing services but also may be navigating workplace abuse, coercion, deportability, and isolation, including familial separation. So the real possibility of being retriggered or further alienated as a result of a cumbersome or repetitive intake processes can be a real hindrance to breaking a cycle of violence experienced by this group.

Beyond the intake process, offering services without a solid understanding of structural and systemic challenges faced by this group may fail to address the fundamental needs of these clients. So an ability to anticipate these barriers (Caxaj & Cohen, 2019) and to orient oneself to the many factors that perpetuate vulnerability and precarity among temporary workers is necessary for effective services to this group to be provided.

Invest in Staff and Infrastructure to Promote Longevity and Address Risk of Vicarious Trauma

From an organizational perspective, CCLC has continued to learn from our Newcomer Clinic. Working with clients who have faced extreme trauma and violence, including genocide, has impacts on not only direct service settlement and health care staff, but also on others in the circle of care, including interpreters and community leaders. These compassionate individuals, often volunteers, play essential roles in supporting the integration of newcomers but seldom have access, for example, to teams for debriefing support or counselling or to other services funded by an organization. It is important for organizations to consider this and to support the shared well-being of newcomers' support networks. We have also learned the value and benefit of providing "in house care," not only to build trust and safety but also to better help understand clients' needs and provide coordinated care. Our experiences have highlighted the need to connect on different levels (provincial, national, international) to evolve and share our understanding and practices working with refugee populations. As we deal with increased complexity, understanding the unique needs of newer resettlement groups and best practices to support them not only supports the clients themselves but also the well-being of service providers.

Likewise, our support model intervention with migrant agricultural workers confirmed the need to recruit and foster the strengths of very dedicated staff and the network of volunteers working with this group. Our prior research has discussed how individuals who can effectively and compassionately carry out this work have tremendous empathic abilities and are highly versatile and flexible in addressing a variety of issues that may come up when supporting an individual migrant agricultural worker (Caxaj & Cohen, 2021a). However, as with the Newcomer Clinic experience, our intervention did require a lot of energy and commitment among support staff, and there were times when staff were overwhelmed and emotionally drained.

Furthermore, a tension in carrying out this work is being aware that many very skilled and dedicated individuals are engaging in unpaid work to support this group, and that while this is an incredible strength of the community, it also points to very serious gaps in government funding and organizational commitment within the formal service sector (Caxaj, Cohen, & Marsden, 2020). By building a community of practice that honoured these abilities and sought to "lighten the load" of both formal and informal support actors, we were able to gain the trust of, and develop solid partnerships with, these people. We must, however, continue to explore how to better fund the services that are made available to this population and develop a more formalized structure to support paid service staff that includes their support network and extends it beyond a largely volunteer base.

Lessons Learned

Both projects illuminate the relevance of community education activities and strategies that build wider connections within local communities to support integration and capacity beyond a particular sector (settlement, health, etc.). They have also shown us the power contained in advocacy and grassroots efforts. For example, the support model for migrant agricultural workers highlights the pervasiveness of rights violations and challenges the narrative of the "one bad apple" in the farming community that can impede necessary change. In the case of the Newcomer Clinic, staff have demonstrated this by bringing the challenges of family reunification of the Yazidi resettlement process to the forefront. We have also learned of many unintended but positive and intangible outcomes of having an enhanced and strengthened partnership model. For example, at the clinic this approach has fostered clients' abilities to leverage non-primary health care programs to support their overall health and well-being. In the support model project, through the provision of services, we have seen migrant agricultural workers begin to internalize and take up resources and better know the options available to support them.

We would advise others taking up similar projects to anticipate and embrace ways to be collaborative. Celebrating the experience and skill sets of the people who can contribute will yield richer insights, better support for staff, and greater comprehensiveness in the execution of services. This collaborative environment is crucial, not only for clients but also for building a community of practice for staff that anticipates the intensity and importance of their work. Be adaptive and flexible. There will always be problems, whether we are addressing complexity in client experiences or resource management challenges. Many of these challenges will be iterative and even "trial and error." Yet if staff are empowered and have the flexibility required to meet the needs of their clients and to overcome the many barriers they face, faith in the program will grow, and staff will flourish, knowing that they have made a true difference. At a wider level, however, decision-makers must invest in continuous and predictable funding models to lessen the pressure on staff and client populations alike to do less with more. In the meantime, organizations can work across sectors and learn from grassroots volunteers, who have significant potential to transform services and support for these populations.

Limitations to consider related to the support model have to do with the nuances of where this project was carried out. Future projects may confront new realities based on the networks of support that exist in different regions. Furthermore, while the intervention reached hundreds of workers, there are thousands in the region, some of whom likely still don't know about the services offered by our team. For the Newcomer Clinic, there are still limitations in some categories of refugees accessing services, or in case managers' ability to transition people from the clinic's short-term program to permanent primary health care in the community. In the case of both projects, there is a continual need for research and enhanced evidence-based practices to help us better serve the unique clients who are seeking our help. The work is never done, but the collaborative commitment is always there to tackle the next hurdle along the way.

Moving forward, projects like the ones we have presented will require new approaches to address the needs and challenges that have been exacerbated by COVID-19. Adapting to a virtual world and new technologies can certainly be part of the solution, but such approaches also come with new barriers such as restricted access to equipment, lack of computer literacy, and the requirement for virtual interpretation. For example, in the case of the Newcomer Clinic,

COVID-19 prompted the exploration of telemedicine to provide choices and create safe virtual environments for clients. In the case of migrant agricultural workers, this population has been uniquely disadvantaged by inadequate action to address the limited digital and material resources available to them. COVID-19 has disproportionately impacted this population, and this in turn sheds light on important system-imposed vulnerabilities, such as those relating to housing regulation, access to health services, and cultural/language navigation. With increased attention to these issues, there may be unique opportunities for service providers across various sectors to work together to address them.

Conclusion

There is a continual need to address broader issues that affect migrant and refugee populations, such as access to universal and standardized interpretation, equitable access to health care, mental health stigma, and precarious work or status. Many scholars and advocates have been vocal in emphasizing the importance of opportunities for permanent residence as a way to address many of the vulnerabilities faced by those with precarious status. This is an important structural factor for migrants and refugees, because living in Canada as someone who is "deportable" can contribute to underreporting abuse, exploitative living and working conditions, and fear leading to delayed help-seeking. Policies that enhance opportunities to end closed work permits and extend permanent residence may be beneficial to migrant labourers and asylum-seekers alike. Furthermore, government policies and practices that foster coordination and partnerships across jurisdictions and sectors can provide significant support to front-line organizations that wish to provide services in a trauma- and violence-informed manner.

KEY MESSAGES AND IMPLICATIONS

- TVIC can help organizations anticipate and address structural barriers faced by migrants and refugees in how they plan and deliver services.
- Building capacity across sectors, and acknowledging and fostering the skill sets of both formal and informal support networks, supports TVIC for newcomers.
- Integrating cultural safety and an awareness of the unique histories of each client throughout all aspects of service delivery ensures appropriate and person-centred care.
- There is an urgent need for policy change to sustain the work of support services and to address underlying vulnerabilities that determine the health and well-being of these diverse populations.

REFERENCES

Allan, J. (2015). Reconciling the "psycho-social/structural" in social work counselling with refugees. *British Journal of Social Work, 45*(6), 1699–716. https://doi.org/10.1093/bjsw/bcu05

Basok, T., Bélanger, D., & Rivas, E. (2014). Reproducing deportability: Migrant agricultural workers in southwestern Ontario. *Journal of Ethnic and Migration Studies, 40*(9), 1394–413. https://doi.org/10.1080/1369183X.2013.849566

Beaumont, H. (2020, 20 July). Coronavirus sheds light on Canada's poor treatment of migrant workers. *The Guardian.* https://www.theguardian.com/world/2020/jul/20/canada-migrant-farm-workers-coronavirus

Berry, J.W. (1997). Immigration, acculturation, & adaptation. *Applied Psychology: An International Review, 46*(1), 5–68. https://doi.org/10.1111/j.1464-0597.1997.tb01087.x

Caxaj, C.S., & Cohen, A. (2019). "I will not leave my body here": Migrant farmworkers' health and safety amidst a climate of coercion. *International Journal of Environmental Research and Public Health, 16*(15), 2643. https://doi.org/10.3390/ijerph16152643

Caxaj, C.S., & Cohen, A. (2021a). Emerging best practices for supporting temporary migrant farmworkers in western Canada. *Health & Social Care in the Community, 29*(1), 250–8. https://doi.org/10.1111/hsc.13088

Caxaj, C.S. & Cohen, A. (2021b). Relentless border walls: Challenges of providing services and supports to migrant agricultural workers in British Columbia. *Canadian Ethnic Studies, 53*(2), 41–67. https://doi.org/10.1353/ces.2021.0010

Caxaj, S., Cohen, A., Buffam, B., & Oudshoorn, A. (2020). Borders and boundaries in the lives of migrant agricultural workers: Towards a more equitable health services approach. *Witness: The Canadian Journal of Critical Nursing Discourse, 2*(2), 92–103. https://doi.org/10.25071/2291-5796.69

Caxaj, S., Cohen, A., & Marsden, S. (2020). Supports for migrant farmworkers: Tensions in (in)access and (in)action. *International Journal of Migration, Health and Social Care, 16*(4). https://doi.org/10.1108/IJMHSC-03-2020-0017

Caxaj, C.S., & Plamondon, K. (2020, March 2). Nurses' role in improving health care access for migrant agricultural workers. *Canadian Nurse.* Retrieved from https://www.canadian-nurse.com/blogs/cn-content/2020/03/02/nurses-role-in-improving-health-care-access-for-mi

Colindres, C., Cohen, A., & Caxaj, C.S. (2021). Migrant agricultural workers' health, safety, and access to protections: A descriptive survey identifying structural gaps and vulnerabilities in the interior of British Columbia, Canada. *International Journal of Environmental Research and Public Health, 18*(7), 3696. https://doi.org/10.3390/ijerph18073696

George, M. (2012). Migration traumatic experiences and refugee distress: Implications for social work practice. *Clinical Social Work Journal, 40,* 429–37. https://

link.springer.com/article/10.1007/s10615-012-0397-y. https://doi.org/10.1007
/s10615-012-0397-y
Hennebry, J., McLaughlin, J., & Preibisch, K. (2016). Out of the loop: (In)access to health care for migrant workers in Canada. *Journal of International Migration and Integration, 17*(2), 521–38. https://doi.org/10.1007/s12134-015-0417-1
Hoggett, P., & Thomson, S. (Eds.) (2012). *Politics and the emotions: The affective turn in contemporary political studies*. London: Continuum.
Horgan, M., & Liinamaa, S. (2017). The social quarantining of migrant labour: Everyday effects of temporary foreign worker regulation in Canada. *Journal of Ethnic and Migration Studies, 43*(5), 713–30. https://doi.org/10.1080/1369183X.2016.1202752
Immigration, Refugees, & Citizenship Canada. (2019). *Syrian Refugee Resettlement Initiative: Looking to the future*. Retrieved from https://www.canada.ca/en/immigration-refugees-citizenship/services/refugees/welcome-syrian-refugees/looking-future.html
London InterCommunity Health Centre. (2021). *Newcomers clinic*. Retrieved from https://lihc.on.ca/programs/newcomers-clinic/
McLaughlin, J., Hennebry, J., & Haines, T. (2014). Paper versus practice: Occupational health and safety protections and realities for temporary foreign agricultural workers in Ontario. *Perspectives Interdisciplinaires sur le Travail et la Santé, 16*(2). https://doi.org/10.4000/pistes.3844
Orkin, A.M., Lay, M., McLaughlin, J., Schwandt, M., & Cole, D. (2014). Medical repatriation of migrant farm workers in Ontario: A descriptive analysis. *CMAJ Open, 2*(3), e192. https://doi.org/10.9778/cmajo.20140014
Preibisch, K., & Hennebry, J. (2011). Temporary migration, chronic effects: The health of international migrant workers in Canada. *Canadian Medical Association Journal, 183*(9), 1033–8. https://doi.org/10.1503/cmaj.090736
Pysklywec, M., McLaughlin, J., Tew, M., & Haines, T. (2011). Doctors within borders: Meeting the health care needs of migrant farm workers in Canada. *Canadian Medical Association Journal, 183*(9), 1039–42. https://doi.org/10.1503/cmaj.091404
Robillard, C., McLaughlin, J., Cole, D.C., Vasilevska, B., & Gendron, R. (2018). "Caught in the same webs" – service providers' insights on gender-based and structural violence among female temporary foreign workers in Canada. *Journal of International Migration and Integration, 19*(3), 583–606. https://doi.org/10.1007/s12134-018-0563-3
Standing Committee on Citizenship and Immigration. (2018). *Report of the Standing Committee on Citizenship and Immigration: Road to recovery: Resettlement issues of Yazidi women and children in Canada*. Retrieved from https://www.ourcommons.ca/Content/Committee/421/CIMM/Reports/RP9715738/cimmrp18/cimmrp18-e.pdf
Vosko, L.F., & Casey, R. (2019). Enforcing employment standards for temporary migrant agricultural workers in Ontario, Canada: Exposing underexplored layers of vulnerability. *International Journal of Comparative Labour Law and Industrial*

Relations, *35*(2), 227–54. Retrieved from http://www.kluwerlawonline.com/abstract.php?area=Journals&id=IJCL2019011. https://doi.org/10.54648/IJCL2019011

Wylie, L. Corrado, A.M., Edwards, N., Benlamri, M., & Murcia Monroy, D.E. (2020). Reframing resilience: Strengthening continuity of patient care to improve the mental health of immigrants and refugees. *International Journal of Mental Health Nursing*, I(1), 69–79. https://pubmed.ncbi.nlm.nih.gov/31478332/. https://doi.org/10.1111/inm.12650

Wylie, L., Van Meyel, R., Harder, H., Sukhera, J., Luc, C, Ganjavi, H., ... Wardrop, N. (2018). Assessing trauma in a transcultural context: Challenges in mental health care with immigrants and refugees. *Public Health Reviews*, *39*(22). https://doi.org/10.1186/s40985-018-0102-y

SECTION FOUR

Bringing It All Together

Section 4 highlights strategies for embedding TVIC approaches in organizational and system-level protocols and policies. Drawing on research and evaluation, as well as case work, the chapters demonstrate TVIC's potential impact on and across systems of care. We also provide an overview of our foundational TVIC e-learning curriculum and its development, as well as evaluation considerations, including how to define and measure the success of TVIC interventions.

SECTION FOUR

Bringing It All Together

4.1 How Organizations Take Up Trauma- and Violence-Informed Care

TANAZ JAVAN, JENNIFER SANDU, AND NADINE WATHEN

This chapter summarizes "lessons learned" from our current work examining organizational implementation of TVIC in two social service settings. Using an established implementation model – Active Implementation Frameworks (AIFs) – we provide process learnings with attention to the important contextual factors, including tailored facilitation, that support effective uptake and embedding of TVIC. Our hope is that by the end of the chapter, readers with an interest in implementing TVIC in their settings will have access to a structured approach (the AIFs), as well as guidance based on our experiences.

Implementation science is defined as "the scientific study of methods to promote the systematic uptake of clinical research findings and other evidence-based practices into routine practice" (Improved Clinical Effectiveness through Behavioural Research Group, 2006, p. 1). While this definition emphasizes clinical research, the field reaches beyond traditional clinical sites to examine the interactions among interventions, providers, and contexts at the individual, organizational, and policy/system levels, both within and beyond health care settings (Bauer, Damschroder, Hagedorn, Smith, & Kilbourne, 2015).

Various frameworks have been developed to study how interventions are taken up by health and social services and what indicators ensure successful implementation (Fixsen, Naoom, Blase, Friedman, & Wallace, 2005). There are three main approaches in the literature to understanding how organizations come to adopt new interventions: diffusion (letting it happen), dissemination (helping it happen), and implementation (making it happen) (Greenhalgh, Robert, Macfarlane, Bate, & Kyriakidou, 2004). In the "letting it happen" or diffusion approach, most often an organization becomes interested in taking up an intervention as "a good idea." This "taking up" usually occurs informally, meaning that issues of fidelity (commitment to fully deliver the intervention as designed) and sustainability (ongoing use of the intervention) may not be fully addressed (Greenhalgh et al., 2004). "Helping it happen," or dissemination, entails investigating organizational readiness and system influences and encourages more active approaches to "taking up," such as developing websites and guidelines and providing training to encourage providers to use the intervention in service delivery (Greenhalgh et al., 2004). Dissemination can be effective and result in higher fidelity and sustainability compared to the diffusion approach (authors have noted a 5% to 15% greater chance of success in fidelity and sustainability of an intervention using dissemination strategies versus diffusion; Greenhalgh et al., 2008); however, it is still far behind more active, "making it happen" implementation approaches, which are up to 80 per cent successful (Fixsen et al., 2001). When "making it happen," an organization adapts the new intervention to its own cultural and structural requirements and the outcome is the actual use of the intervention and full integration of its components into practice (Greenhalgh et al., 2004). Active implementation approaches address the gap in the literature on understanding how the interaction between complex systems and complex interventions impacts the implementation process, as well as the implications of these interactions on fidelity and sustainability (Fixsen et al., 2005; Greenhalgh et al., 2004).

Implementation is challenging in large part because evidence-based interventions are often complex, that is, they have multiple interacting components that act both independently and interdependently, making implementation a non-linear process (Medical Research Council, 2008). In addition, the contexts in which they are implemented are also complex (Fixsen, Blase, Naoom, Van Dyke, & Wallace, 2009a; Shiel, Hawe, & Gold, 2008). Some industries are complicated by nature, an example being the pharmaceutical industry when it develops a new vaccine, which involves a series of testing stages, followed by production, the establishment of supply chains, and so on (Ogden & Fixsen, 2014). In their own way, health and social services are complex (as opposed to complicated) because they encompass both clients and providers, each with unique needs and experiences. Their interactions are bounded by organizational factors such as budgets, policies and procedures, and "the way we've always done things." Organizations themselves are constrained or enabled by system-level factors, including funding sources, regulatory bodies, policies, and legislation. Thus, while Fixsen and colleagues (Fixsen, Blase, Naoom, & Wallace, 2009b) note that "the intervention is the practitioners" (p. 532), meaning that what the service user experiences at the point of care is embodied in the individual provider, it is important to recognize that practitioners and their practices are shaped in large part by what is (and is not) supported and incentivized by the organization, which itself is bounded by system-level factors (Hawe, 2015a).

Thus, an intervention is designed with certain outcomes in mind but is often tested in ideal contexts that have been designed to give it the best chance of success (e.g., by ensuring sufficient staff and other resources during testing, and by selecting sites and participants best placed to benefit). In "real world" settings, these supports may not exist, with the result that implementation often deviates from the original design when a complex system adopts it. This means that the complexity of the system in which the complex intervention is implemented also plays a critical role. Thus, implementing successful changes in a system depends on understanding the nature and diversity of the activities in that system (Greenwood-Lee, Hawe, Nettel-Aguirre, Shiell, & Marshall, 2016). In addition, factoring in the providers and their roles draws attention to the social relationships that shape the system. These social relationships can play a key role in how change happens, since the new intervention is likely to create new social roles, bridge existing gaps (and/or create new ones), and impact existing social dynamics overall (Hawe, 2015a, 2015b). Implementation of a complex intervention in health and social services requires attention to the providers' expertise, incorporation of the intervention into their daily practices and routines, and recognition of variation among services and of the dynamic between the complex intervention and the complex system in which it is implemented, "conceived as evolving networks of person-time-place interaction" (Hawe, 2015a, p. 310).

In 2005, the National Implementation Research Network published an extensive literature review on approaches to implementation (Fixsen et al., 2005). Based on that review, Fixsen and colleagues developed the Active Implementation Frameworks (AIFs), which include five implementation dimensions, or "frameworks": usable intervention criteria, stages of implementation, implementation drivers, improvement cycles, and implementation teams. We used AIF dimensions to guide the implementation of TVI approaches in two diverse settings.

Usable Interventions

The first framework of the AIFs is concerned with determining what an intervention is and what it means to implementers and service providers (Fixsen et al., 2009a). In this stage, "what 'it' is that must be done well to produce the desired results" (Fixsen et al., 2009a, p. 219) should be fully grasped by the service providers so that there will be effective implementation at the practice level. Organizations need to develop a deep understanding of the essential concepts of TVIC and its articulated principles. It is also necessary to understand how organizations intend to operationalize these principles based on the needs of their settings, staff, and service users.

Stages of Implementation

The AIFs define implementation as "a specific set of activities designed to put into practice an activity or program of known dimensions" (Fixsen et al., 2005,

p. 5). These activities take place over time and in multiple stages that overlap and are revisited when necessary (Fixsen, Blase, Metz, & Van Dyke, 2013). AIFs have continued to develop into multidimensional frameworks and been applied to various contexts in implementation research. As mentioned earlier, AIFs assume a non-linear and interconnected process for intervention implementation (Fixsen et al., 2005), as well as a multi-stage framework for demonstrating different points in the implementation process. These stages overlap and may reoccur, and activities during one stage may be repeated as the activity in the next stage begins (Fixsen et al., 2005). These stages and the exemplar activities/outputs within each are described below (see also table 1 in Metz et al., 2015).

Stage 1: Exploration and adaptation. The exploration stage is crucial to building a solid foundation for implementation. A deep understanding of the intervention helps clarify what to expect and how the results of the implementation could affect the organization. Articulating potential impacts, facilitators, and barriers will help the implementation team anticipate and overcome challenges. Many organizations expect to implement an evidence-based intervention in a "plug and play" manner. Such an expectation can end the implementation process in its infancy if the organization is not prepared to face the uncertainty and challenges that accompany the implementation of complex interventions. So this stage is crucial in setting expectations though careful examination of the intervention, the implementation process, required resources, and potential barriers (Fixsen et al., 2013). To achieve consensus in expectations, organizations can build connections with individuals or groups (purveyors) representing the intervention, who actively work with the organization to ensure successful implementation with high fidelity and desired outcomes (Fixsen et al., 2005).

Also, when an organization has identified a potential intervention, it does not mean that every component will match their needs; context plays a crucial role in implementation logistics. Therefore, during the exploration and adaptation stage, organizations need to outline the intervention components in order to assess which aspects are suitable and decide whether sufficient fidelity can be achieved to ensure that the anticipated benefits will be realized. Clarifying the details of an intervention is essential because it can help the organization use the intervention effectively to achieve important, preidentified outcomes. Mapping the intervention's core principles and strategies with desired outcomes and expectations, and committing to intervention fidelity, must underpin implementation. This means that organizations need to consider the potential fit between the target population, the organization, and available resources, on the one hand, and the program's key principles and underlying theories as well as the proposed model, on the other. Potential barriers such as funding streams, staff patterns, and required organizational, cultural, and structural shifts also need to be examined.

Stage 2: Installation. The installation stage begins with creating and/or acquiring the resources needed to shift the practice into alignment with the new intervention's principles. Purveyors and experts help the organization establish and/or repurpose the competency and organizational drivers necessary for high-fidelity implementation. The establishment of these competency drivers also prevents the intersection of the new intervention with the existing infrastructure. Organizations can avoid confusion and less effective implementation by evaluating and repurposing previously developed programs and routines that may interfere with the new intervention (Bertram, Blase, & Fixsen, 2015).

Implementation drivers. Since AIFs focus on finding common indicators of a successful implementation and on *how* interventions can be reinforced in practice, this approach can further illuminate the interactions among contextual factors that enable successful implementation (Fixsen et al., 2013). Implementation drivers or core implementation components are "the building blocks of the infrastructure needed to support practice, organizational and system change" (Metz et al., 2015, p. 416). They underpin the interactive process that is integrated into the system to maximize the influence on the fidelity of provider behaviours and organizational culture (Fixsen et al., 2009a). There are three different types of implementation drivers, and each includes structural factors and activities that ensure high fidelity and sustainability of the intervention: *competency drivers*, *organizational drivers*, and *leadership*.

Competency drivers are mostly focused on the facilitator mechanisms that can enable staff and providers to improve their ability to deliver the desired outcomes. The four competency drivers are *staff selection, training, coaching,* and *evaluation* (Fixsen et al., 2009b; Metz et al., 2015). AIFs pay particular attention to the selection of staff who are qualified to carry out the intervention. Qualifications include compatible academic background and experiences, but other factors as well such as willingness to learn, commitment to moral values and social justice, good judgment, and empathy, all of which are especially important in the context of TVIC and health equity interventions. Ongoing coaching and consultation are other necessary steps for effective implementation; workshops and training can teach new skills to providers; ongoing coaching is better tailored to the contextual factors of each organization, such as the types of services they provide and the needs of their clients (Fixsen et al., 2009b). Also, coaching can provide encouragement and help motivate staff to apply their new skills (Metz et al., 2015). Performance evaluations provide valuable insights for organizations as staff strive to practise their new skills in effective ways; they also provide quality improvement feedback to trainers (Metz et al., 2015).

Organizational drivers focus on evaluating the implementation progress of the entire organization. To that end, specific quality improvement indicators and organizational fidelity assessment targets are suggested (Fixsen et al., 2009b). Outcomes can then be shared in a user-friendly decision support data system to facilitate decision-making and quality improvement at the policy and practice levels in the organization (Fixsen et al., 2013).

Leadership drivers refer to leaders' abilities to apply appropriate strategies when facing technical versus adaptive challenges; these drivers play an essential role in the implementation process. Technical challenges, such as those related to logistics or staffing, are usually better-defined and have a clear path to solutions, whereas adaptive challenges, such as learning and change capacity, can be defined from multiple and sometimes competing perspectives, leading to multiple viable solutions. Leaders should be able to distinguish between the two, for it has been shown that mistaking one for the other can impact their ability to support staff and sustain outcomes.

Stage 3: Initial implementation. This stage often brings a sense of excitement and enthusiasm to use the new skills learned during the installation stage. However, challenges can arise: it is difficult to change set ways of doing things and incorporate change effectively (Bertram et al., 2015). Challenging the status quo and existing power dynamics, when coupled with the complexity of implementation, creates disruption. So it is essential to have structural support to learn from mistakes and approach these challenges systematically. Support from leadership in addressing these issues is critical; their participation creates top-down and bottom-up accountability (Fixsen et al., 2013).

Stage 4: Full implementation. Full implementation occurs when practitioners are comfortable providing high-quality service aligned with the new intervention principles and these new practices become the standard (Bertram et al., 2015). Implementation drivers are fully established and supported and are regularly evaluated for improvement. Note that without careful development and repurposing of available resources and establishment of implementation drivers, full implementation may be delayed and the implementation process may need to revisit previous stages (Fixsen et al., 2013). The implementation team plays a crucial role in the fidelity and sustainability of the intervention. The support and coaching provided by the implementation team is a facilitating factor for full implementation.

Organizational Cases and Contexts

TVIC implementation was examined in a settlement agency and a police service; these are described briefly in box 4.1.1 (see also chapters 2.6 and 3.5). The settlement service sought to implement TVIC because of the increases in the numbers, complexity, and trauma needs of newly arrived refugees as well as the impact that vicarious trauma was having on staff and volunteers. The police service was interested in TVIC due to increased awareness of the impact of direct and vicarious trauma and violence, especially officer-involved domestic violence, on the mental health and well-being of its members, specifically an increase in suicide and operational stress and moral injuries among police officers. In both cases, leadership committed itself to shift their organization's culture and structure to support better practices, especially for clients facing marginalization; to prevent and/or mitigate the effects of vicarious trauma; and to promote staff well-being. For example, policing has traditionally reinforced a "suck it up" and "don't ask, don't tell" approach to operational stress injuries; leadership recognized TVIC as a strategy to support a shift in organizational culture around the stigma associated with the mental health impacts of police work, while also providing education about trauma and violence highly relevant to their service mission. Also, TVIC education was seen as a way to motivate staff to use mental health services provided by the organization that were not being effectively promoted or used. In both organizations, TVIC was viewed as a "container" or framework for bringing otherwise disconnected issues and services together and creating an emotionally and physically safe place for staff to access supports of various kinds.

BOX 4.1.1 CASE ORGANIZATIONS

Case 1: Settlement Service (see also chapter 3.5)

- A one-stop, multi-service support network for newcomers that provides integration services and supports and promotes intercultural awareness and understanding.
- Annually serves ~8,000 newcomers; volunteers contribute >13,000 hours per year.
- Vision: A more welcoming community where newcomers can succeed.
- Organizational values are inclusion, compassion, empowerment, advocacy, and accountability. (https://lcclc.org)

Case 2: Police Service (see also chapter 2.6)

- Mission: To ensure the safety and well-being of the communities served.
- Vision: To be respectful and responsive to the evolving needs of the community through a strategic and collaborative partnership.
- Values: Professionalism, excellence, integrity, inclusiveness, transparency, accountability, diversity, and trust.
- A mid to large sized police service with over 600 sworn members and 300 civilians employed and an annual budget of over $120M and over 28,700 Criminal Code cases in 2019. (https://www.londonpolice.ca/en/about/Reports-and-Statistics.aspx)

TVIC Implementation Activities

Initial interactions with the two organizations focused on how they came to understand the concept of TVIC for their service context and how this understanding led to formal implementation decisions. Following their initial explorations, each organization undertook, with expert facilitation, specific steps. These were tracked and recorded by the first author as part of a larger evaluation study. Insights relevant to TVIC implementation are noted below.

Implementation and Integration of TVIC Principles

The AIFs provided a staged way to think about implementation processes. These stages, as outlined earlier, are exploration, installation, and initial and then full implementation. The two organizations we looked at were in different stages when we engaged them: the settlement service in the installation stage, the police service in the exploration stage. Next, we provide a brief narrative of each service's TVIC implementation process.

Police service. When we started our collaboration with the police service, they were seeking and reviewing information and exploring available options. At this stage, organizations seek to build connections with individuals or groups (purveyors) representing the potential intervention (TVIC) to ensure a successful implementation with high fidelity and desired outcomes (Fixsen et al., 2005). We noted this in the police service in the following activities.

To assess the fit of TVIC with their needs, the police service established a staff-led and leadership-supported mental health and well-being committee. This bottom-up approach resonated with staff because the decisions made by this committee were not perceived as being imposed by the senior executives. The committee was tasked with creating new approaches regarding mental health and shifting the dominant culture of "show no weakness" to one of resiliency and open discussions around mental health. A focus was on informing staff of the impacts of trauma and violence and providing the care and support needed by staff who were experiencing their effects. The committee was confident that learning about trauma and violence would enable staff to become more aware of the prevalence of trauma and structural violence in individuals' lives and that this knowledge would be applied in their community service responses.

By building partnerships with local mental health and violence prevention experts, the committee learned about TVIC and its core principles. The first of the four TVIC principles requires organizations and individuals to understand trauma and both interpersonal and structural violence and their impact on people's lives and behaviour; this helps staff and leaders create a culture that recognizes their impacts and provide training and support to mitigate those

4.1 How Organizations Take Up Trauma- and Violence-Informed Care

impacts. Given the starting point of the police service, TVIC was a seen as a good fit, aligned with their goal, which was to shift their organizational culture.

After the decision was made to proceed, a clear plan was developed and tasks and timelines to facilitate an effective implementation were established. The close collaboration between the police service implementation team and the external facilitators ensured that at every step, decisions were made based on the core principles of TVIC. For instance, this collaboration succeeded in modifying TVIC training for the organization's needs. The team created short videos based on police officers' everyday jobs to enable staff to identify symptoms of PTSD. The team reviewed the scenarios in several meetings to map them with TVIC principles, seeking ways to affirm and validate these experiences using a strengths-based approach. These meetings also:

- clarified what implementation of TVIC means and entails for the organization;
- recognized that TVIC implementation is not limited to training staff, but also entails significantly shifting the structure and culture of the organization so that a TVIC approach is reflected in decision-making on all levels;
- adjusted language from trauma- and violence-informed *care* to trauma- and violence-informed *practices* to make it more compatible with police services;
- created new training materials, including videos, and modified existing materials to meet needs;
- developed online training sessions to accommodate COVID-19 specific restrictions; and
- designed new tools to evaluate implementation progress (interviews, surveys).

To involve leadership and the remaining members of the wider mental health and wellness committee in the implementation process, the committee organized two training sessions, with feedback iteratively applied to subsequent sessions. These training sessions were received very positively, and the inputs from leadership and the mental health and wellness committee were encouraging. The new training curriculum was well-received by both parties, which felt that the material aligned with stated goals, which were to enhance members' well-being and raise awareness about trauma and violence. This support encouraged the implementation team to move forward with the training sessions for all staff (civilians and sworn members).

At the time of writing, the organization was in the initial implementation stage, establishing the drivers and providing structural support for the process. Competency drivers and organizational drivers have been developed and established. Ongoing weekly training sessions for the members and data collection through interviews and surveys ensure competency drivers. Also, members are encouraged to provide input through a previously established feedback loop to inform the implementation team of members' perceptions of the TVI training. The purveyors offer coaching and support by conducting biweekly meetings with the implementation team. These meetings are crucial to helping the organization build enough confidence to act independently and complete the implementation process in the eventual absence of purveyors. Currently, these meetings are also focused on recruiting staff across the organization to involve themselves in the TVI committee to ensure the fidelity and sustainability of the intervention.

Settlement service. In recent years, especially preceding the COVID-19 pandemic, the mid-sized city served by this service has taken steps to become a trauma- and violence-informed community. In November 2017, the Centre for Research on Health Equity and Social Inclusion (CRHESI), a university/community partnership, held a meeting to invite local organizations to initiate a conversation about TVIC. The settlement agency discussed here took part, and their participation in the meeting sparked an interest in implementing TVIC in their organization. The settlement agency found that the principles of TVIC aligned with their mission of providing sufficient support and care for their staff, especially given the recent increases in arrivals of refugees from particularly dangerous contexts, which included the plight of Yazidi women and children fleeing interpersonal and structural violence (i.e., rape and genocide) in northern Iraq.

The CRHESI meeting initiated the exploration stage, with the settlement agency contacting our team of researchers at Western University. CRHESI also partnered with a local mental health service provider in the community that has pioneered the implementation of TVIC in London. Through that partnership, the settlement agency decided that TVIC was a good match for their organization, fitting well with the structural and cultural changes they anticipated. The initial implementation started with forming a TVIC implementation team, which included the organization's executive director. Note that the leadership's involvement and commitment provided tremendous support for the team and the implementation process. The TVIC committee also invited the managers and senior staff across the organization to involve themselves. The installation stage began with planning two introductory training sessions for staff.

The TVIC committee had regular meetings to ensure that structural supports were in place and that there was a space to discuss the operationalization of TVIC principles. (Several years later, those meetings are still being held.) Establishing the committee also created a policy–practice loop that helped the organization collect data and evaluate the implementation process. The TVIC committee coached and supported managers to operationalize TVIC in their departments and provided an opportunity for practitioners to reflect on incorporating TVIC into their practice; again, a formal feedback mechanism

4.1 How Organizations Take Up Trauma- and Violence-Informed Care

ensured that the implementation committee was aware of, and could co-create solutions to, any challenges arising from implementation. For example, based on feedback, the organization provided complementary training on debriefing, self-care, and mindfulness. The embodiment of TVIC's core principles in the organization also raised awareness about the importance of providing structural support for staff to practise self-care. For instance, when staff are not given enough time for a break, the notion of self-care becomes irrelevant; thus, structural changes are necessary to complement individual efforts, and vice versa. Recognizing that to meet its goals of implementation fidelity and sustainability requires allocation of sufficient resources (Fixsen et al., 2005), the settlement agency also started providing training for new full-time and contract-based employees, thus opening another pathway to sustainability of the intervention.

Note also that the implementation process is not linear and usually happens organically. Expecting an intervention to become part of routine practice over a short period can create disappointment and stall momentum. Patience and endurance are essential for the successful implementation of complex interventions in complex settings (Fixsen et al., 2005). This ecological perspective underscores that the interaction between intervention and context creates particular types of experiences for individuals unique to each setting; space is required for embracing the uncertainty and disruption that generally accompany change (Browne et al., 2018; McLaren & Hawe, 2005). Flexibility and open-mindedness allow mistakes to be made and provide opportunities to adjust. In this process, the core principles of TVIC can serve as a road map. For instance, the settlement agency became aware of the importance of providing training for its contractors, who were not included in the initial training sessions. However, contractor training costs had not been budgeted, which meant that the team had to backtrack to an earlier stage of implementation and allocate appropriate resources to address this gap.

Another critical factor in successful implementation is the presence of champions in the organization. For example, in the TVIC context, social workers often find that TVIC's core principles are well-aligned with their professional and personal values, and they are excited about making cultural and structural shifts. Champions can be the driving force behind implementation when disruptions and challenges arise – they help keep the momentum going. In the settlement agency, the TVIC committee's leader, and managers, were very enthusiastic about implementing TVIC in their agency, and their commitment and effort were significant drivers to achieving full implementation.

At the time of writing, the agency is in the full implementation stage, with TVIC fully operationalized, and core principles have been embedded in organizational policies, practices, and decision-making. For instance, when the COVID-19 pandemic started, the TVIC committee was confident enough to deal with the issues that arose. Providing support and care for the staff is an ongoing agenda item for the committee, and this has resulted in less pandemic-related impact on the organization than might otherwise have been the case. In addition, being aware of the impact of trauma and structural violence, practitioners understand how the isolation and lack of social support from COVID-19 measures can impact their clients. This awareness has opened them to alternative ways of providing service, including video calls, which have become routine practice to ensure a minimum level of social contact.

Practical Strategies for Implementing TVIC

A key learning from our cases is the crucial role of context. It is important to understand the unique history, present circumstances, and other salient factors of the organization and of those seeking care. With this understanding, service becomes more adaptive, because an eye is kept out for changes to practices, procedures, and policies that impact service users in the context of violence and trauma experiences. These nuanced factors inform and shape organizational and provider-level interactions and decision-making. Being attuned to client needs, circumstances, and behaviours, and to societal and structural factors, allows TVIC approaches to be tailored so that they best serve clients and support providers. These shifts may seem subtle, but they can be impactful and profound. For example, it is not uncommon that refugees were held in forced confinement prior to resettlement; so, during an in-office visit, having the settlement counsellor ask their client if they would like to keep the door slightly open is a trauma- and violence-informed action. In this example, the worker is attuned to the client's potential history without the need for disclosure, and this creates a psychologically safe environment that allows choices and reasserts power and control, things often negated during a forced migration.

Fundamental to TVIC is attention to provider well-being, both through opportunities for self-care and by building resiliency through organizational supports. At the settlement service, this was integral to building resiliency within the organization – what could leadership do to support their staff? For example, leaders more regularly communicated about, and reinforced access to, the Employee Assistance Program (EAP); they also provided wellness sessions for staff, such as yoga and guided meditation. They also trained staff in debriefing. All of this was facilitated by an agency with a rich history of working with refugee trauma survivors. At a structural level, staff were encouraged to exercise peer debriefing and work it into their daily routines and schedules.

Multiple resources are available to police service members to support them through their daily encounters with trauma and violence, but these are not always used. Strategies such as peer support programs play an essential role in supporting members, and such programs, with their emphasis on unity and teamwork, align well with police work. To reinforce and complement its peer

4.1 How Organizations Take Up Trauma- and Violence-Informed Care

support program, this organization has recently hired a psychologist as part of its TVIC implementation work.

It is also crucial to train everyone involved in the organization and commit to structural change to reinforce and support new practices among individual providers. Training the entire organization, from volunteers to receptionists to leaders and board members, recognizes the integral role everyone plays in becoming a trauma- and violence-informed organization. TVIC can be as simple as a smile and a warm welcome from reception staff, or it can mean a worker delving deeper into why their client is constantly late for appointments as well as acknowledging what it took for them to get there. When staff are building knowledge, awareness, and skills related TVIC, a whole-organization approach acknowledges their inherent value and responsibility in organizational transformation. This itself is trauma- and violence-informed.

The settlement service prides itself on the compassionate care of its staff and volunteers, many of whom have their own immigration experiences. Training staff in TVIC allowed for a reflective process of examining one's own experiences, and the connections and strengths this process provides to newcomer clients, while simultaneously fostering willingness to learn and value everyone's unique settlement and integration experiences.

Embedding these shifts in practice requires that organizations support such changes. TVIC provides the opportunity for compassionate care and effective service delivery, both to service providers and to organizations. However, both individual-level practice and organizational policies must go hand-in-hand. It is equally important to consider, as an organization, what happens when service providers are trained in TVIC but the organization itself does not follow suit or in some cases requires more long-term planning to implement larger organizational changes. Without alignment, organizations run the risk of increased staff frustration, moral distress, or burnout. For example, in the case of the settlement service, organizational growth led to office spaces becoming increasingly confining for some staff and clients. From a TVIC perspective, the physical environment became an impediment to providing safe and welcoming services. However, making changes to address this requires time, resources, planning, and communication. Thus, the lesson is to communicate with staff that such changes are being addressed and to give regular progress updates.

Every organization has its own starting point and its own journey. At the beginning of that journey, a key consideration is the organization's readiness for change. TVIC provides a vehicle for positive change, but it is also a vehicle for disruption (ideally, for the better). It requires self-awareness, open and courageous conversations in addressing operational issues, resources to support these changes, and a great deal of accountability on the part of service providers and organizational leaders. So it is vital to take an honest look at the organization's aptitude for change and at what is needed in order to manage change.

Lastly, as you start this process it can be daunting and at times overwhelming. This is where the importance of partnerships is emphasized, including mentoring by other organizations. Finding partners who can help measure TVIC's impact on the organization, or provide ongoing support regarding evidence-based best practices, is another consideration; we have found partnering with content and research experts a valuable approach to assessing and documenting organization-level outcomes, as well as sectoral/system-level impacts. Look beyond your walls and build partnerships to mutually support your implementation process. It's helpful to know what has worked for other organizations and what can be tailored to the unique needs of your sector, community, and organization.

Lessons Learned

Hindsight is 20/20, and with time and experience many lessons have been and continue to be learned. For example, retrospectively, it would have been important to further chart how the two case organizations monitored and evaluated progress toward implementation milestones. Were there key success indicators? How do we know when we have become a TVIC agency? Here is where academic partnerships can be leveraged to support monitoring and evaluation. This also allows for more feedback from staff, volunteers, and clients to ensure that your organization stays nimble during implementation. Key questions to discuss during the exploration stage, and throughout implementation, are provided in box 4.1.2.

BOX 4.1.2 INITIAL AND ONGOING QUESTIONS

- What are the priorities and how do you determine them?
- What is success, and how do you define and assess it?
- How will you evaluate your progress?
- How will you structure the work?
- What resources will it take to move forward?
- How will you engage staff?
- Do you have leadership buy-in? Board buy-in? Staff buy-in?

Other factors we continue to reflect on include how, as organizations, we are continually engaging and communicating with staff and clients. Given competing operational priorities, complexity, diverse client experiences, and shifting policy and funding parameters, how do we keep TVIC alive and well in the forefront of people's minds and in the organization as a whole? How do we begin to embed TVIC in our practices and policies? These questions became especially relevant as the service environment was rocked by COVID-19 restrictions. All of our practices – in policing, settlement services, and beyond – have since been examined, including how to serve people facing vulnerability and marginalization remotely, mediated by technology, instead of face-to-face, while keeping everyone physically, emotionally, and culturally safe.

We have learned that constant messaging of organizational commitment to TVIC is key to supporting this collective work. For example, a TVIC newsletter has been developed by the settlement service that shares updates, resources, and professional development opportunities related to TVIC across the agency. The COVID-19 pandemic also reaffirmed the need to support staff wellness, for example, by providing virtual wellness sessions on mental health and isolation, as well as practical strategies for working remotely with children. As well, the settlement service developed a program questionnaire to check in with staff regarding clients and their own self-care needs. The police services also developed a survey to assess their members' knowledge of trauma and violence and their awareness of available services. Another survey was planned to evaluate training sessions. The implementation team made itself available to members interested in having one-on-one confidential interviews to share their concerns and feedback.

Our primary lesson learned is that finding what works for your organization, tailoring communications about the intervention to meet your organizational needs, and top-down and bottom-up support for the overall integration process are key to ensuring successful implementation of TVIC. These steps demonstrate to all actors in the organization the value of, and accountability and commitment to, TVIC. Transformational change takes time as well as continual self-reflection, individually and as an organization. It takes focus and feedback to effectively align practices and policies with TVIC. At times, this is a disruptive process, for it involves unlearning and rewriting behaviour, processes, and policies. This will not come naturally for everyone, and there may be uncertainty and hesitancy, especially in the early stages. So it is important to have self-compassion as individuals and as an organization, as this is a collective learning process. It is also important along the way to collect and share positive examples and success stories. Simple acts and successes make a difference and reinforce the change management process. They can be deeply empowering, meaningful, and motivating in showing how TVIC has a positive impact on providers and service users. Successes help bring us together in this work and weather any storms.

Conclusion

Effective implementation of TVIC is a complex task that requires up-front and ongoing planning, engagement of all members of the organization (including direct service and ancillary staff, volunteers, and leaders), and strategic supports and resources, including tools, training activities, and assessment approaches, all of these determined by and adapted to the context. The AIFs provide a useful and flexible model to help organizations think through the various stages, from identifying and finding potential interventions, to assessing their fit, to implementing them in iterative stages. The AIFs encourage organizations to create a "practice to policy cycle" to embed changes to ensure cultural and structural sustainability (Fixsen et al., 2013).

KEY MESSAGES AND IMPLICATIONS

- Each stage of the implementation needs to be deeply explored. It is especially important that the exploration stage be robust, so that all involved parties are fully aware of what TVIC offers and what it will take to fully implement it.
- Implementation takes time and is not a linear process. Being patient, iterative, and flexible supports success.
- Leadership commitment and involvement are crucial, and furthermore, staff and direct service workers must be involved in helping operationalize the intervention. Creating a policy–practice loop is essential.
- Most often, not-for-profit organizations act within a project/task-oriented framework; however, implementation of TVIC is an ongoing process with no end point.

ADDITIONAL RESOURCES

- EQUIP Organizational Implementation Tools: https://equiphealthcare.ca/equip-my-organization
- Equipping for Equity Online Modules: https://equiphealthcare.ca/equipping-for-equity-online-modules
- Active Implementation Research Network (AIFs): https://www.activeimplementation.org

REFERENCES

Bauer, M.S., Damschroder, L., Hagedorn, H., Smith, J., & Kilbourne, A.M. (2015). An introduction to implementation science for the non-specialist. *BMC Psychology*, 3(1), 1–12. https://doi.org/10.1186/s40359-015-0089-9. https://bmcpsychology.biomedcentral.com/articles/10.1186/s40359-015-0089-9

Bertram, R.M., Blase, K.A., & Fixsen, D.L. (2015). Improving programs and outcomes: Implementation frameworks and organization change. *Research on Social Work Practice*, 25(4), 477–87. https://doi.org/10.1177/1049731514537687. https://journals.sagepub.com/doi/abs/10.1177/1049731514537687

4.1 How Organizations Take Up Trauma- and Violence-Informed Care

Browne, A.J., Varcoe, C., Ford-Gilboe, M., Wathen, C.N., Smye, V., Jackson, B.E., ... Blanchet-Garneau, A. (2018). Disruption as opportunity: Impacts of an organizational-level health equity intervention in primary care clinics. *International Journal for Equity in Health, 17*, 154. https://doi.org/10.1186/s12939-018-0820-2

Fixsen, D., Blase, K., Metz, A., & Van Dyke, M. (2013). Statewide implementation of evidence-based programs. *Exceptional Children, 79*(2), 213–30. https://doi.org/10.1177/001440291307900207l

Fixsen, D.L., Blase, K.A., Naoom, S.F., Van Dyke, M., & Wallace, F. (2009a). Implementation: The missing link between research and practice. *NIRN Implementation Brief, 1*, 218–27. https://www.aucd.org/meetings/205/15097/NIRN_brief_1_2009.pdf

Fixsen, D.L., Blase, K.A., Naoom, S.F., & Wallace, F. (2009b). Core implementation components. *Research on Social Work Practice, 19*(5), 531–40. https://doi.org/10.1177/1049731509335549

Fixsen, D.L., Naoom, S.F., Blase, K.A., Friedman, R.M., & Wallace, F. (2005). *Implementation research: A synthesis of the literature (FMHI #231).* Tampa, FL: University of South Florida, Louis de la Parte Florida Mental Health Institute, National Implementation Research Network. https://nirn.fpg.unc.edu/resources/implementation-research-synthesis-literature

Greenhalgh, T., Robert, G., Macfarlane, F., Bate, P., & Kyriakidou, O. (2004). Diffusion of innovations in service organizations: Systematic review and recommendations. *The Milbank Quarterly, 82*(4), 581–629. https://doi.org/10.1111/j.0887-378X.2004.00325.x

Greenhalgh, T., Stramer, K., Bratan, T., Byrne, E., Mohammad, Y., & Russell, J. (2008). Introduction of shared electronic records: Multi-site case study using diffusion of innovation theory. *BMJ, 337*, a1786. https://doi.org/10.1136/bmj.a1786

Greenwood-Lee, J., Hawe, P., Nettel-Aguirre, A., Shiell, A., & Marshall, D.A. (2016). Complex intervention modelling should capture the dynamics of adaptation. *BMC Medical Research Methodology, 16*(1), 51. https://doi.org/10.1186/s12874-016-0149-8

Hawe, P. (2015a). Lessons from complex interventions to improve health. *Annual Review of Public Health, 36*, 307–23. https://doi.org/10.1146/annurev-publhealth-031912-114421

Hawe, P. (2015b). Minimal, negligible, and negligent interventions. *Social Science & Medicine, 138*, 265–8.

Improved Clinical Effectiveness through Behavioural Research Group (ICEBeRG). (2006). Designing theoretically informed implementation interventions. *Implementation Science, 1*, 4. https://doi.org/10.1186/1748-5908-1-4

McLaren, L., & Hawe, P. (2005). Ecological perspectives in health research. *Journal of Epidemiology & Community Health, 59*(1), 6–14. https://www.ncbi.nlm.nih.gov/pmc/articles/PMC1763359. https://doi.org/10.1136/jech.2003.018044

Medical Research Council. (2008). *Developing and evaluating complex interventions.* London, UK: MRC.

Metz, A., Bartley, L., Ball, H., Wilson, D., Naoom, S., & Redmond, P. (2015). Active implementation frameworks for successful service delivery: Catawba county child well-being project. *Research on Social Work Practice, 25*(4), 415–22. https://doi.org/10.1177/1049731514543667

Ogden, T., & Fixsen, D.L. (2014). Implementation science: A brief overview and a look ahead. *Zeitschrift für Psychologie, 222*(1), 4. https://doi.org/10.1027/2151-2604/a000160

Shiell, A., Hawe, P., & Gold, L. (2008). Complex interventions or complex systems? Implications for health economic evaluation. *BMJ, 336*(7656), 1281–3. https://doi.org/10.1136/bmj.39569.510521.AD

4.2 Strategies, Tools, and Resources for Integrating Trauma- and Violence-Informed Care across Settings

COLLEEN VARCOE, NADINE WATHEN, ANNE-MARIE SANCHEZ, AND SCOTT COURTICE

As exemplified throughout the cases in sections 2 and 3 of this volume, embedding trauma- and violence-informed, equity-oriented care in any setting requires understanding the key contextual factors that underpin and/or influence service delivery, including organizational values, mission, and mandate, along with more proximate considerations such as resource availability and the ability to be flexible in budgeting, scheduling, and so on, as well as the ability of leaders and staff to learn and integrate new skills and approaches. Across all contexts, however, there is a need for specific (to task), tailorable, and useful tools and strategies to actually implement TVIC.

This chapter briefly summarizes and provides links to key tools and resources developed by the Gender, Trauma and Violence Knowledge Incubator (GTV Incubator), EQUIP Health Care, and other relevant initiatives to support TVIC education and practice, organizational policy, and the ongoing sustainability of these new approaches. We offer our "TVIC Action Kit," which structures these tools and resources into a staged yet flexible and tailorable approach to implementation and is loosely based on existing implementation approaches, especially the Active Implementation Frameworks (AIFs; see chapter 4.1). The intent is to support organizational thinking and action when implementing trauma- and violence-informed services.

Self-implementation efforts by a Community Health Centre, as well as the experiences of individuals and small groups of TVIC champions, are used as case examples to highlight how to get started and how to use the Action Kit to support practice improvement. By the end of this chapter, the reader will know where to access key tools and resources, how implementation can work in "real world" settings, and how to begin the process of "equipping for TVIC."

Overview of Tools, Resources, and Strategies to Support Uptake of TVIC

Our collective efforts in developing, implementing, and evolving TVIC are grounded in the original research from EQUIP Health Care (see chapter 2.1).

As a research *and* implementation program, EQUIP was and is concerned with producing and making available tools and resources to support practice. Building from EQUIP's work, the GTV Incubator has further supported the development of tools tailored to various services. We therefore have two primary, interlinked clearing houses for our freely available TVIC-specific and related resources (see links at end of this chapter). Each has suites of tools that are useful for a general understanding of TVIC and TVIC education and offers approaches to implementing and assessing TVIC uptake at the individual and organizational levels. Each also provides access to the TVIC Action Kit. Because we understand TVIC as oriented toward equity and social justice and as requiring structural analysis and changes, these tools are consistent with the integration of equity-oriented approaches more broadly, as well as with the integral concepts of cultural safety/anti-racism and harm reduction/substance use health. Individuals can "lead" with the concept of TVIC or with one of these other conceptual entry points. As various authors have argued throughout this handbook, you can't have TVIC without cultural safety and harm reduction, and vice versa.

Who Can Initiate TVIC Implementation?

Implementing TVIC requires both individual and organizational commitment and action; however, its actual implementation can start with anyone, at any level of the organization. Thus, the tools and steps we provide are broadly useful. Individuals can take the initiative within their organizations or professions to deepen their understanding and promote a TVIC approach, or entire organizations can do so. Typically, organizational-level initiatives begin with a passionate and dedicated individual. For example, Dr Trystan Nault is a physician and family medicine resident at the University of British Columbia (UBC) who is working to bring TVIC to the practice of his colleagues. His plan to work in partnership with his family medicine mentors started with a TVIC workshop in mid-2021 for other family medicine residents that embedded this way of being and doing within an equity-oriented framework. His goal is to expand the work to specific organizations and even the entire health authority within which he works. Similarly, organizational levels of implementation typically require "buy-in" and leadership from a range of people within the organization. For example, Dr Anas Manouzi is a pediatric emergency physician at BC Children's Hospital and a Hudson Scholar in Equity, Diversity and Inclusion, who has a mandate to integrate equity-oriented care, which signals some level of organizational commitment.

The best approach to building from individual- to organizational-level commitment will depend on those involved, their positions within the organization, and the organization's overall mindset. For example, Ms Pam Rardon is the site director for West Coast General Hospital in Port Alberni, BC. As a nursing leader, she has extensive knowledge of the groups the hospital serves in the community, and she has relationships with other key leaders. Her process started with assembling a team consisting of a physician lead and another administrative leader in her setting. Dr Manouzi, for his part, conducted a series of interprofessional virtual learning sessions in an effort to "build momentum" for change (about thirty people from diverse roles and professions across the hospital have participated in each session), and Dr Nault has built a learning program for his colleagues from the "grassroots" and sought support from leadership in his residency program with the goal of demonstrating "proof of principle" before considering what's next. Innovators have a keen eye for taking the opportunities available to them, and the tools and resources we have developed are designed to support these individuals and teams, wherever they're able to get started.

How Do You Start Implementing TVIC?

The best process for initiating and implementing TVIC must be tailored to context (a core principle of equity-oriented care; see chapter 2.1); the starting point also depends on the context. But regardless of context, we have identified a series of steps that are useful to take. At EQUIP Health Care, with additional TVIC-specific tools from the GTV Incubator, we have gathered all relevant resources into a series of steps – an Action Kit – that can be used to implement equity-oriented health care starting at any conceptual entry point, including TVIC. The TVIC Action Kit provides processes and tools to help organizations "get started" or strengthen their existing efforts. While the Action Kit is intended for use by organizations, individuals will find it useful to see their own efforts within a larger plan. For the purposes of this chapter, we highlight selected key tools within the steps.

Phase 1: Examine and Explore

As seen in figure 4.2.1, it is helpful to carefully plan the implementation of any new intervention, especially one that touches on all aspects of organizational culture and service delivery. While phases and steps can be mapped (per figure 4.2.1, based on the AIFs; see chapter 4.1), it is equally important to consider the fundamental human processes involved in adapting and embedding a complex intervention in a complex adaptive system. In this section, we briefly review implementation considerations and phases/steps, building on learnings from our various implementation studies, with a focus on some of the intangibles that can lead to success, or failure. For example, we have learned about the key role of buy-in from both leadership and direct service

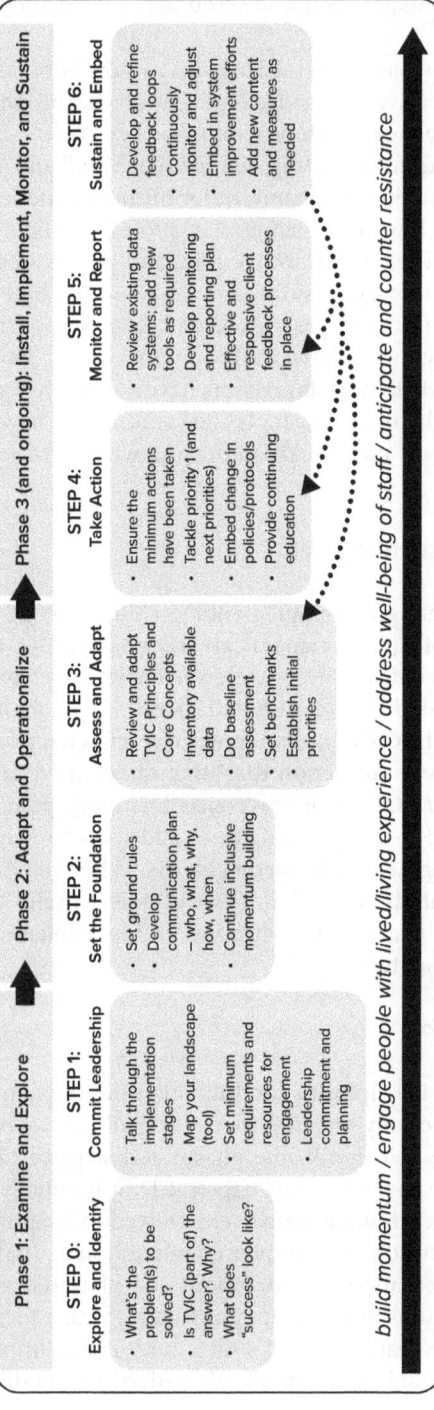

Figure 4.2.1 TVIC action kit – phases and steps. Copyright 2021, the authors.

levels, as well as the need to harness enthusiasm and build momentum for implementation. Building buy-in and momentum are not separate steps, but strategies that can be employed at any time, by anyone. They can be formal activities, such as Dr Manouzi's virtual seminars, or Ms Rardon's planning meetings, or an informal sharing of ideas among colleagues one-to-one or in meetings – for example, in the group chat Dr Nault shares with his colleagues. Getting buy-in, or preferably "ownership" over the commitment to TVIC, and building momentum can be supported by a wide range of information and discussion tools we have developed. For example, the TVIC-specific Rate Your Organization tool supports both building momentum among colleagues and mapping the context that is part of phase 1 and that continues throughout.

Step 0 (Zero): Explore and identify. How and why do organizations or individual actors decide, in the first place, that something like TVIC is needed? In our experience, this can happen all at once – for example, due to a tragic event, such as harm or death arising from poor policy or structurally incompetent practice, as we've seen in recent cases of racist health care practice in Canada, such as the deaths of Mr Brian Sinclair[1] and Ms Joyce Echaquan.[2] Or it can happen over time, as service providers begin to buckle under the weight of unacknowledged and unmediated vicarious trauma, compassion fatigue, and moral distress (see chapter 1.4), as we've recently seen during the COVID-19 pandemic.[3] Finally, change can be mandated, for example, in increasing calls for equity-oriented care, tied to accountabilities to redress health and social inequities. Regardless of the precipitating circumstances, we've found that TVIC, especially when conjoined with the other key dimensions of equity-oriented care (cultural safety/anti-racism and harm reduction/substance use health; see chapter 2.1), resonates as a solution to whatever problems or needs are identified. Given this, and consistent with the AIFs' initial "exploration stage," our "Step 0" involves asking the following types of questions: What's the problem(s) to be solved? Is TVIC (part of) the answer? Why? What does "success" (broadly defined) look like? We've called this "Step 0" not to indicate that these processes begin in a void or with a "blank slate," but to reinforce the fact that organizations, and their members, need to understand where they're at before they can take a first step on a path to change. In our EQUIP Emergency research, for example, we found that each of three emergency departments had unique strengths and challenges in relation to equity and TVIC; thus, a formal effort to enhance equity needed to begin in different places.[4]

Step 1: Commit leadership. As our examples above suggest, leadership can start from anywhere – committed individuals from any discipline or role can initiate change. The process will vary depending on where the initiators are positioned in the organization, with the keys to success being partnerships, inclusion, and diversity. As the chapters throughout this handbook have shown, there must be both top-down and bottom-up leadership on the implementation team, with people at all levels of the organization engaged toward developing and sustaining a TVI culture; importantly, people with lived experiences of trauma and violence (including structural violence) need to be part of the mix. Discussing the nature of change and the stages of implementation is a useful initial conversation. For example, chapter 4.1 demonstrated how the AIFs – including a focus on "leadership drivers" – were useful to two diverse organizations as they implemented TVI approaches.

Map your landscape. Every service setting has its own unique context, and every organization has its own strengths and challenges when it comes to the uptake of TVIC. In all settings, a key first step is some form of contextual analysis. We recommend that this begin with a structured consideration of (a) the population served and (b) organizational characteristics, including values, mandate, and mission. This context analysis, coupled with the factors that precipitated an exploration of TVIC in the first place (see Step 0), is an initial step, but it should continue throughout the implementation process. For example, in research on equity in primary care clinics, the EQUIP Health Care team supported each clinic to develop a "context profile"[5] (see also chapter 2.1). More recently, in research with emergency departments (EDs), the team found it useful to consider how the sites, and EDs more generally, were being positioned in local media (Thomas et al., 2021). How staff and service users perceive one another and the organization will shape the process toward TVIC; it matters how confident, comfortable, fearful, and/or cautious service users are in relation to the service.

From a TVIC perspective, the context analysis focuses on trauma and violence experiences and their impacts among the population served, as well as the organizational features that are conducive to or work against TVI approaches. Who are the people most likely to have experienced trauma and violence? For example, do you serve populations who experience racism? Are there groups who are newcomers from war-torn countries? What is the history of the Indigenous people in your area? What are the factors that expose people to ongoing violence? Also, what are the income levels of the people you serve? Do you serve a proportion of women parenting in poverty? Does your organization's mandate easily align with TVIC principles, or do values such as "efficiency" override values such as "effectiveness" and "compassion"? Who are the likely champions of TVIC within your organization? Do you already have processes in place to take direction from people with lived experiences of trauma and violence? Do an initial "mapping" of your landscape and then deepen that analysis as you go. To support initial context analysis, we have created a Map Your Landscape tool (see link below).

Phase 2: Adapt and Operationalize

Once needs have been identified and it has been decided that TVIC will be implemented, further assessment is required (of both TVIC as an intervention and the context in which it is to be fitted) with regard to any adaptations that will be necessary to make it work. Steps 2 and 3, therefore, map onto the "Installation" phase of the AIFs (chapter 4.1). A cautionary note: "minimum requirements" must be set for what the intervention will include (see box 4.2.1). In our experience, when organizations "cherry-pick" the easier aspects of the TVIC principles and related strategies, full implementation and its desired effects and outcomes are not realized. For example, sites that make their waiting rooms more welcoming with local Indigenous art (a popular strategy) are not changing anything when they do not back that up by developing meaningful relationships with local Indigenous communities and by providing Indigenous-specific anti-racism education that includes a clear understanding of the impacts of colonialism, residential schools, and how these forms of structural violence show up in site-specific client health outcomes. In fact, they may be doing additional harm by making what in effect are false promises that things will change, when really all that's changed is the art. Similarly, energizing direct service staff to become trauma- and violence-informed in their practice without commensurate and supportive changes to policy and protocols, or attention to supporting staff experiencing vicarious trauma, may only increase moral distress as staff try to work in new ways without the supports they require (see chapter 1.4).

BOX 4.2.1 MINIMUM RESOURCE REQUIREMENTS FOR TVIC ACTION

- Resources to allow staff representatives from diverse roles to meet on a regular basis over a minimum of a year (a leading working group of six to eight seems to work well; meeting monthly seems to maintain momentum).
- A leader with line authority committed to working directly and consistently with the working group.
- Support from the executive level of the organization.
- Resources for all staff to participate in education (e.g., see link to the TVIC Foundations Curriculum below; it takes between five and seven non-consecutive hours), and regular opportunities for interprofessional conversations about applying this education.
- Formalized and authentic strategies for seeking and incorporating ideas and feedback from people with lived experience of trauma and violence.

Step 2: Set the foundation. Setting the foundation means engaging the entire organization. At a minimum, this means communicating to everyone the intention of the work, the processes you are planning to use, and opportunities for their involvement. Using whatever forms of communication exist in your organization, as opposed to creating something purpose-built, will help streamline the process. For example, in the EDs we worked with in EQUIP, one site used ten-minute morning "huddles" and their existing monthly newsletter; another used regular staff meetings. We also learned that emphasizing strengths and capacity, rather than pointing repeatedly to problems, helped sustain enthusiasm and build momentum. The goals of this step are to (1) build and keep buy-in, ownership, and momentum, (2) build in "quick wins" and make those visible, and (3) show progress and success.

Step 3: Assess and adapt. Assessing the organization in multiple ways contributes to identifying the strengths, opportunities, aspirations, and results (e.g., a SOAR analysis) imagined for a TVIC implementation within your organization, assessing readiness, and setting goals and priorities. Taking a deep dive into where you are starting requires both information and dialogue. In research in primary care, the EQUIP Health Care research team found that interprofessional conversations were the most impactful strategy for change; more important than education was attention to the "so what" of such education for practice across diverse roles (Levine, Varcoe, & Browne, 2020). Something like the Rate Your Organization tool (see link below) can help start conversations among diverse stakeholders.

A more in-depth assessment strategy is to conduct a Trauma Review (see link below). We suggest that staff do this on their own as an initial step, then with one another, and finally (and crucially) with the people for whom they want to improve care. The EQUIP team found that in one ED setting, staff were shocked at the condition of patient washrooms; some of the staff had worked in the setting for years yet had never looked in the washrooms, or looked through a TVIC lens. We found in another setting that "walking through" the setting with an Indigenous Elder led to staff feeling defensive, uncomfortable, and angry, even though the Elder was only observing and saying how she felt in the setting, without suggestion of criticism.

Assessments can also include surveys of staff and patients. For example, the police service described in chapter 4.1 surveyed its members. The EQUIP research team has gathered survey data from patients and staff in both primary health care and ED settings and provided that information to the implementation teams. Gathering information through multiple strategies provides a SOAR analysis and allows the implementation team to set priorities for action.

Phase 3 (and Ongoing): Install, Implement, Monitor, and Sustain

Once TVIC has been adapted and operationalized (phases 1 and 2), it's time to implement. The following three steps may not be as linear as outlined in figure

4.2.1; however, the types of activities described, when there is authentic and ongoing attention to momentum, buy-in, and clear and well-timed communication, will prepare the ground for implementation success, including feedback loops for monitoring, reporting, and continuous improvement.

Step 4: Take action. The actions taken will depend on the priorities identified by the implementation team. Regardless of the priorities, typically actions will include (1) assessing the need for and providing access to education, (2) creating interprofessional opportunities for dialogue, (3) identifying the changes required in policy and practice, and (4) embedding changes in policy. For example, as we have described elsewhere (Browne et al., 2018; Ford-Gilboe et al., 2018), in our intervention in primary care settings we provided mandatory education on TVIC but then learned that the education was not necessarily at the right level for some (Levine et al., 2020). More importantly, across all sites staff found that interprofessional discussions of the "so what" for their practice, including the provision of data from their own sites, were more powerful than education alone. There are numerous TVIC learning opportunities (e.g., see link to TVIC Foundations Curriculum below), but we advise couching this education in meaningful conversations about how to *enact* TVIC in the specific setting and the development of policies to support doing so. For example, in several settings, with input from medical office assistants and receptionists, it was found that changing how people were received and appointments were scheduled was one of the most powerful ways of enacting TVIC; these changes variously made people feel more welcome and respected and reduced their exposure (in line-ups and waiting rooms) to trauma triggers.

Step 5: Monitor and report. Being able to show progress is key to maintaining momentum. Staff and service users alike appreciate having input and seeing that input enacted; success will breed success. Monitoring and reporting will vary with the context, but we advise that regardless of that context, you (1) use pre-existing monitoring processes as much as possible, (2) select indicators of success and benchmarks that will be meaningful in the specific context, (3) establish a baseline of where you are starting on a few key indicators, and (4) monitor indicators of the well-being of both the people using and the people providing services. For example, in our research with primary care settings, we found that the clinics had useful data – such as social histories of foster care or residential school attendance for Indigenous people – that could signal trauma histories, but that the data had not been summarized or shared with staff. Through our research we provided trauma scores for a large sample of people accessing care, which staff found "eye-opening"; but ongoing, the clinics could use social histories as approximations of the extent of trauma among the people they are serving. In our ED research, we selected the variable of staff sick leave as a baseline, reasoning that while not all staff sick time is related to vicarious trauma, TVIC might reduce vicarious trauma, which might then be reflected in sick time. Depending on the type of organization you are working in, there may be wider data collection and processing mechanisms you can draw upon. For example, most health and social service settings conduct or contribute to surveys on "patient experiences of care" or "client satisfaction."

Beyond using data that are already collected, and monitoring those data, consider assessing the experiences of staff and those being served in ways that reflect TVIC. Various tools are available to measure and monitor TVIC and related concepts (see chapter 4.6). For the broader concept of equity-oriented care, we have developed the Equity Oriented Health Care Scale (EHoCS; see link below) for use in primary care, and we are developing one for more episodic health care encounters, such as ED visits. We also used the EHoCS to adapt a widely used trauma-informed care assessment tool, the ARTIC, adding a broader range of elements addressing structural violence and its impacts on care (Rodger et al., 2020).

Step 6: Sustain and embed. Maintaining momentum is ultimately aimed toward a "new normal" of a culture of TVIC. Regardless of setting, this will be supported by (1) communicating, celebrating, and making successes visible, (2) continuously aligning policies and funding decisions with a TVIC orientation, and (3) seeking out and addressing new priorities. Again, using available approaches and media is a good starting place. A highly visible centrepiece of action may be possible. For example, at St Paul's Hospital ED, staff collaborated with the Indigenous Health Team to commission and install art by a local Indigenous artist, with the aim of expressing welcome and safety to the Indigenous people served. The resulting art transformed the waiting area for everyone. This process created new interdisciplinary relationships and was linked to appreciable changes in service that reflected a TVIC approach to Indigenous patients.

Case Study: Using Online Resources to Implement TVIC at the London InterCommunity Health Centre

London InterCommunity Health Centre (LIHC) has been a key partner in our ongoing efforts to develop relevant teaching, learning, and application tools for TVIC and equity-oriented health care (EOHC). LIHC leaders (Sanchez, Courtice) have been implementing these processes using the online "Equipping for Equity Modules." (see link below). In this case study, they describe LIHC and why they decided to implement EOHC and TVIC, outline key activities and lessons learned, and offer advice for other organizations considering this kind of work.

As a Community Health Centre (CHC), LIHC's mandate is to provide comprehensive primary health care and health promotion for individuals, families, and communities. The mission is to provide inclusive and equitable health and social services to those who experience barriers to care. We also foster the participation of individuals and the communities we serve. LIHC's values – social justice, equity, caring, inclusion, and respect – are at the core of our work. As one of the largest CHCs in Ontario, LIHC provides a breadth of programs that go far beyond traditional primary care. This includes mental health supports, diabetes education and care, physiotherapy, respiratory therapy, refugee health, trans health, newcomer programing, supports for isolated seniors, francophone health promotion, and community development.

LIHC is known to respond to the needs of its community as they arise. In the past five years alone, we have developed the following: a safer opioid supply program for people who use street drugs; a physiotherapy program for people without extended health benefits, which reduces reliance on opioids and other medications for pain management; a Trans Health program for people on their gender journey; a clinic for government-assisted refugees to provide health assessments upon arrival as well as primary care services for up to six months or until a family physician is found (see chapter 3.5); TeamCare for primary care physicians who are not practising in a team-based model whose marginalized, complex patients could benefit from these supports; and low-barrier infectious disease services for highly marginalized individuals who face barriers to accessing hospital-based infectious disease specialists. Specialists offer clinics at LIHC, and we provide street-level outreach to support treatment.

Every client faces unique barriers to accessing health care and supports within the system at large. Most LIHC clients have an annual income of $14,999 or less. Many do not have access to a phone or email, and many are homeless. Other clients require added supports such as interpretation or transportation (taxi vouchers or bus tickets), and some are looking for basic needs (food, clothing, harm reduction kits). The populations served are members of the community who are often pushed to the margins by our society and its governing systems. For clients, this alone can cause ongoing trauma and distrust toward institutions and agencies.

LIHC's Goals in Implementing TVIC

LIHC staff already had a natural disposition to understanding health equity. The organization even has a Health Equity Charter, which places equity in the forefront of the work. However, it was less clear whether all staff understood health equity at a deeper level and whether staff had a consistent appreciation for the three primary components of equity-oriented health care: (1) TVIC, (2) harm reduction, and (3) culturally safe care. While most staff had a good surface understanding of health equity, it was less clear whether they understood how they themselves could shape the client experience through a health equity lens. Furthermore, while health equity was something the organization viewed as removing barriers to care for clients, not enough thought was being put into how staff were experiencing equity-oriented care within their own roles and that of the organization as a whole. So the leadership team agreed to embark on this process to accomplish the following goals: (1) strengthen the organization's commitment to health equity, (2) deepen staff understanding of TVIC, harm reduction, and culturally safe care, and how they are interconnected, (3) through client and staff feedback, develop tools and training to embed health equity in LIHC's planning and everyday work, and (4) begin to shift the organization's thinking to focus on both what the clients need and what staff require to provide equity-informed care.

Implementing TVIC at LIHC

LIHC's implementation activities are outlined in box 4.2.2. While this work predated the TVIC Action Kit outlined above, we can see from the focus and staging of activities that many of the same steps and processes were relevant, especially in terms of leadership, communication, contextual tailoring, and grounding in the lived experience of service users.

BOX 4.2.2 LIHC'S KEY IMPLEMENTATION ACTIVITIES

Phase 1 – Leadership engagement and organizational awareness: Exploring, identifying, committing

- Leadership completed the EQUIP Rate Your Organization tool (link below), first independently and then as a group. This created a communal lens to look through when assessing where there was room to improve.
- Communication to staff (all-staff meeting and email) introduced the concept of EQUIP Health Care and its Equipping for Equity Modules (link below).
- The Community Advisory Council (a group of service users and other community stakeholders) and members of the leadership team conducted Equity/Trauma Reviews (link below) or "walk-throughs" of LIHC during which they physically went through the space and reflected on questions designed to prompt thinking about whether and how (or not) the environment was a welcoming, safe space for clients and staff.

Phase 2 – Determining baseline and setting the foundation

Staff Survey

- Customized survey, using EQUIP questions, to reflect the design and realities of LIHC services including more opportunity for reflections and comments than previous surveys.

- Survey deliberately focused on staff wellbeing, role clarity, and staff level of understanding re: health equity, TVIC, and cultural safety.
- All responses were stripped of identifying information and analyzed independent of leadership. The goal was for staff to feel safe and provide honest answers.

Client Survey

- *Accessibility*
    o Based on EHoCS and using simplified language (compared to usual client satisfaction surveys) to make it accessible.
    o Translated into multiple languages.
    o Volunteers engaged with clients to support them in survey completion.
    o Clients were given a $5 gift card as a token of appreciation.
- *Safe Space*
    o A room with drinks and snacks was dedicated to complete the survey; there was no time limit.
    o Volunteers were encouraged to allow time for comments and observations from clients.
    o Same-day social work was available in case clients felt triggered or overwhelmed.

Analysis

- An independent research analyst de-identified and aggregated the data.
- The quantitative data was summarized in charts and the qualitative data was summarized by theme; salient quotes were highlighted.

Phase 3 – Embedding TVIC & Health Equity in Practice and Professional Development

   o Based on the results of the two surveys; LIHC prioritized all-staff training on grief and on crisis intervention.

Looking to the future: embedding and sustaining

   o Results from staff and client surveys were also part of LIHC's stakeholder feedback for our strategic planning process.
   o This allowed for equity-oriented care to become a prevalent theme for the development of the LIHC's strategic directions from both a client and staff perspective.
   o EQUIP Health Care questions and processes are now embedded in LIHC's ongoing client experience survey in order to not lose sight of equity-oriented care.

Practical Strategies for Services Interested in Implementing TVIC

Box 4.2.3 outlines key "lessons learned" from LIHC's experience; below we integrate their lessons with those of others presented in this volume, with the goal of providing concrete initial and ongoing steps and guidance to support TVIC implementation using tailored tools and resources.

BOX 4.2.3 THE LIHC EXPERIENCE: LESSONS LEARNED

- Contextual analysis identified that leadership team members were not always aligned in understanding equity-oriented care, particularly the importance of focusing on the structures, systems, and policies that create challenges for staff to practise in this way.
- This analysis created the conditions for solution-oriented, generative conversations about areas of strength, as well as opportunities for improvement. It is important to create the time and space to do this step well before rolling out to the rest of the staff.
- The EHoCS client tool, and the EQUIP-based staff survey, gave far richer client and staff feedback than our traditional surveys. Both align perfectly with the quadruple aim of health system improvement, which supported broader organizational planning and caused us to adjust our client satisfaction survey and employee engagement practices.
- It is important to align this work with existing strategic planning and quality improvement systems so that action can flow from learnings. To sustain front-facing worker buy-in, analysis must be followed by action.

Next Steps:

- Operationalize our strategic plan, which focuses on equity-oriented care; specifically, this translated into two strategic directions: (1) health equity champions, and (2) a supportive and engaging workplace.
- Implement quality improvement initiatives based on client feedback (e.g., focus on improving coordinated care planning and discussing the social determinants of health with clients on an ongoing basis).
- Develop a training schedule that will focus on TVIC and cultural safety.

Conclusion

This chapter has outlined practical strategies, supported by tailorable resources and tools, to implement TVIC. The LIHC case example demonstrates that any organization, even those already steeped in the values of equity and social justice, can benefit. The tools, resources, and processes are highly tailorable to fit almost any service context.

NOTES

1. http://ignoredtodeathmanitoba.ca/index.php/2017/09/14/report-on-inquest-into-the-death-of-brian-sinclair
2. https://www.theglobeandmail.com/canada/article-quebec-coroner-finishes-echaquan-inquest
3. https://www.cma.ca/sites/default/files/pdf/Moral-Distress-E.pdf
4. https://equiphealthcare.ca/publications
5. https://equiphealthcare.ca/projects/primary-health-care/research-sites

KEY MESSAGES AND IMPLICATIONS

- The exploration stage of TVIC implementation is often triggered by local events and/or champion(s). TVIC, as part of equity-promoting practice and policy, is seen as a good way to address the root causes of poor practices or outcomes and to shift organizational culture.
- To implement TVIC, start with specific and measurable objectives and a structured work plan. The TVIC Action Kit can be very helpful and can be adapted to suit.
- Create a safe way for clients and staff to provide honest feedback.
- Overcommunicate. Ensure that you can execute and then implement in a timely manner. Build in opportunities for "quick wins" and make these visible to build and sustain momentum.
- Embed TVIC in professional development and all-staff training; our TVIC educational tools and e-learning can help.
- Find multiple ways to keep TVIC and equity at top of mind. If possible, embed it in your operations plan and/or strategic planning.

ADDITIONAL RESOURCES

- GTV Incubator TVIC Resources: https://gtvincubator.uwo.ca/resources
  o TVIC Tool: https://gtvincubator.uwo.ca/wp-content/uploads/2021/05/GTV-EQUIP-Tool-TVIC-Spring2021.pdf
  o Trauma Review Exercise: https://gtvincubator.uwo.ca/wp-content/uploads/2021/07/GTV_TraumaReviewExercise_July2021.pdf
  o Vicarious Trauma Tool: https://gtvincubator.uwo.ca/wp-content/uploads/2021/07/EQUIP-GTV-Tool-Vicarious-Trauma-Nov-25-2019.pdf

- EQUIP Organizational Tools: https://equiphealthcare.ca/equip-my-organization
  - Equity Action Kit: https://equiphealthcare.ca/equity-action-kit
  - Map Your Landscape tool: https://equiphealthcare.ca/resources/map-your-landscape
  - Rate Your Organization (RYO): https://equiphealthcare.ca/resources/toolkit/rate-your-organization
  - SOAR Analysis: https://equiphealthcare.ca/resources/toolkit/organization-tools/soar-analysis-worksheet
  - Equity-oriented Health Care Scale: https://equiphealthcare.ca/resources/toolkit/equity-oriented-health-care-scale
- EQUIP-GTV TVIC Educational Resources
  - TVIC Foundations Curriculum: https://equiphealthcare.ca/tvic-foundations
  - EQUIP Equipping for Equity Modules: https://equiphealthcare.ca/equipping-for-equity-online-modules

REFERENCES

Browne, A.J., Varcoe, C., Ford-Gilboe, M., Wathen, C.N., Smye, V., Jackson, B.E., . . . Blanchet-Garneau, A. (2018). Disruption as opportunity: Impacts of an organizational-level health equity intervention in primary care clinics. *International Journal for Equity in Health*, *17*(154). https://doi.org/10.1186/s12939-018-0820-2

Ford-Gilboe, M., Wathen, C.N., Varcoe, C., Herbert, C., Jackson, B., Lavoie, J., . . . Browne, A.J. (2018). How equity-oriented health care affects health: Key mechanisms and implications for primary health care practice and policy. *Milbank Quarterly*, *96*(4), 635–71. https://doi.org/10.1111/1468-0009.12349

Levine, S., Varcoe, C., & Browne, A.J. (2020). "We went as a team closer to the truth": Impacts of interprofessional education on trauma- and violence-informed care for staff in primary care settings. *Journal of Interprofessional Care*, 1–9. https://doi.org/10.1080/13561820.2019.1708871

Rodger, S., Bird, R., Hibbert, K., Johnson, A.M., Specht, J., & Wathen, C.N. (2020). Initial teacher education and trauma and violence informed care in the classroom: Preliminary results from an online teacher education course. *Psychology in the Schools*, *57*(12), 1798–814. https://doi.org/10.1002/pits.22373

Thomas, K., Browne, A.J., Jiao, S., Dooner, C., Wright, P., Slemon, A., . . . Varcoe, C. (2021). Media framing of emergency departments: A call to action for nurses and other health care providers. *BMC Nursing*, *20*(1), 1–12. https://doi.org/10.1186/s12912-021-00606-2

4.3 Development of a Core Trauma- and Violence-Informed Care e-Learning Curriculum

EUGENIA CANAS, SAMRIDHI PRADHAN, AND NADINE WATHEN

This chapter describes the process of developing an online core curriculum for TVIC, focusing on the question of how to deliver TVIC education *in a TVIC way*. It begins with a review of the core competencies we developed for TVIC education at the individual provider level, including the mapping of gaps and opportunities for the introduction of evolving priorities in TVIC pedagogy. These priorities include (a) implementation of TVIC principles in educational content and form, (b) application of the concepts of moral distress, implicit bias, and interprofessional collaboration as drivers for individual and organizational action on TVIC, and (c) use of transformational learning theory as a framework for the development of both foundational and context-specific learning opportunities. As described in this chapter, developing a foundational TVIC online curriculum involved multiple, iterative phases of consultation with community- and university-based experts in TVIC, health and social service providers, and educators. Alongside a process of curating and customizing TVIC resources for the online environment, we sought to translate the practical knowledge of expert TVIC facilitators into meaningful, self-directed learning experiences.

We begin the chapter by reviewing the core competencies for TVIC education at the individual provider level, including our mapping of gaps and opportunities for the introduction of evolving priorities in TVIC pedagogy. The chapter then (a) describes in detail our process of curriculum-mapping in relation to core competencies, (b) documents how we sought to integrate the wisdom of our group of TVIC expert workshop facilitators with transformative learning theory and instructional design methods in professional education, (c) reflects on how this process and the final curriculum serve values-oriented and principles-based work, and (d) concludes with considerations and lessons learned for application in future context-specific approaches to TVIC education, and for taking a trauma- and violence-informed approach to teaching and learning in other areas, such as substance use, suicide, and child maltreatment, where content has considerable traumatizing potential.

Trauma- and Violence-Informed Care Education

Given the nature and potential impact of the subject matter, and the prevalence of trauma and violence (direct and vicarious) among our anticipated learners, a core principle was to develop a curriculum and delivery platform about TVIC that was itself trauma- and violence-informed. This was especially important since the design was driven by the needs of individual online learners, interacting with the content on their own.

In what follows, we describe this process of building the TVIC curriculum, which is freely available online[1] and consists of seven sections that combine written and video-based core content delivery with interactive, case-based activities. As it relates to building capacity among a broadly imagined audience of health, education, and social service providers, curricular content is the foundational theoretical, empirical, and practical understandings of TVIC as outlined in section 1 of this handbook, inflected with examples from the various settings described in sections 2 and 3 and articulated into an e-learning environment.

Establishing the Need and the Focus

The need for a broadly and freely available formal online curriculum arose from several intersecting realizations. First, through our work on EQUIP Health Care (chapter 2.1), we became aware of the demand for this kind of training. EQUIP researchers were increasingly being asked to provide workshops and webinars on our approach to equity-oriented health care and, especially, trauma- and violence-informed, culturally safe care. It became clear that we could not meet this demand by relying on in-person sessions. The Gender, Trauma and Violence Knowledge Incubator at Western University[2] (GTV Incubator) arose to fill this gap, initially with a "train the trainer" model. Concurrent with our research-based activities, community- and university-based experts in London, Ontario, were delivering related sessions in different contexts, from domestic violence services to community mental health and addictions services. A group of us came together to discuss and evolve core TVIC content, and community facilitators started to take the lead in providing training locally, regionally, and in other parts of Canada, with academics initially in support and eventually receding to focus more on developing the evidence base for TVIC. As previously noted, many of the chapters in this volume describe work undertaken by Incubator members to adapt and test TVIC in multiple settings.

In 2020, with the experience of more than a dozen workshops behind us, we undertook an evaluation of those in-person training sessions. We found that, consistent with our pre- and post-session evaluations, the education was having an impact on people's knowledge, attitudes, and, to some extent, practices (Wathen, MacGregor, & Beyrem, 2021; see also chapter 4.5). This coincided with a funding opportunity from the Public Health Agency of Canada that allowed us, as part of a larger project to update EQUIP materials so as to embed an explicit focus on substance use stigma, to develop core TVIC education as well as a specific sub-module (not described here) on the intersections of trauma, violence, chronic pain, substance use, and stigma (see chapter 3.2).

Given these experiences, we anticipated that our learners would be coming from a broad range of health and social service settings, including education, policing, public health, primary and acute health care, domestic violence services, and mental health and addictions. The curriculum would have to address this breadth by carefully selecting cases that would resonate with a diverse audience, in clear, non-discipline-specific language accessible to many kinds of staff and, potentially, peer workers and volunteers.

Our Process

The first step was to draft our Core Competency Framework for the curriculum (box 4.3.1). The list of learning objectives and outcomes spanned knowledge, skills, and attitude domains, and each of these was further operationalized into core competencies. All of them emphasized the integration of the four TVIC principles to prioritize knowledge, awareness of history and context, safety, agency, strength, and choice, while also encouraging self-care and organizational support for providers. This guiding document was developed through a consultative process with curricular and TVIC experts from the GTV Incubator and EQUIP and was informed by our experience delivering TVIC workshops.

At the core of our framework is the recognition that TVIC places the responsibility for the physical, cultural, and emotional safety of the person attending services on the organizations and professionals providing care. This focus on the relationship between the individual and the organization played a significant role in the curriculum's design, which pushes individual learners to reflect on how they would feel/act in a particular situation and continually invites them to reflect on their organization and interprofessional team as key factors in the delivery of TVIC.

BOX 4.3.1 TVIC CURRICULUM: CORE COMPETENCY FRAMEWORK

Learning Objectives and Outcomes

Trauma- and violence-informed care means that the responsibility for the physical, cultural, and emotional safety of the person accessing care or services rests with the organizations and professionals providing care. This can be thought of as a universal approach to ensuring that individuals do not suffer further harm when seeking care and are helped in ways that are based on their strengths and capacities and offer meaningful choice and collaboration. This is differentiated from trauma-specific services, where interventions are provided to those identified with trauma symptoms, and expands on trauma-informed practice, where the focus is on individual-level traumatic experiences and responses. TVIC includes explicit attention to structural and systematic violence, with a focus on people's life conditions as well as their trauma and violence experiences.

Knowledge: Those who provide trauma- and violence- informed safe care know:

1. The prevalence of different types of trauma and violence and the physiological, psychological, and social impacts of these on physical and emotional well-being, including the cumulative effects of violence and trauma over the lifespan.
2. How social and structural factors, including health and social care practices and policies, focus ongoing harm against certain people and groups and can contribute to their ongoing experiences of violence and trauma, and their effects.
3. That common actions by providers, and/or environmental conditions, may be retraumatizing for people who have experienced various forms of structural or interpersonal violence and trauma, and their effects.
4. That an environment that is safe for the most traumatized person will be safe for all people and care providers, regardless of their histories.

Skills: Those who provide trauma- and violence-informed and culturally safe care can:

1. Create emotionally, culturally, and physically safe care spaces and contribute to trauma and violence-informed policies that support doing so.
2. Respect the person's experience by using strengths-based and collaborative approaches to discuss realistic and appropriate strategies to support the person's active involvement in their own well-being.
3. Perform self-care practices, and access organizational supports, to promote personal well-being in the face of their own trauma and violence histories, and of exposure to others' experiences.
4. Advocate for policies and practices that support safety and well-being within and beyond their organizations.

Attitudes: Those who practise in a trauma- and violence-informed, culturally safe way and are aware of the impact of trauma and violence on people's health and well-being, demonstrate:

1. A respectful, non-stigmatizing and non-judgemental attitude towards all people.
2. Compassion and positive regard for people while promoting safe decisions and behaviours.
3. The ability to examine, with humility, their own role in the dynamics and impact of structural violence and stigma.
4. A commitment to structural competency, including continuous learning, teaching, and advocacy.

Core Competencies
Health and social service providers who provide trauma-and violence-informed care can:

1. Demonstrate structural competence, understanding the influence of social and system-level factors (including policies, economic structures, and social hierarchies) on individuals' experiences, and structural humility, recognizing that individuals can participate in structural change, but will be limited in their impact.
2. Provide emotionally, physically, and culturally safe, competent, high-quality care.
3. Describe the core elements of trauma- and violence-informed care.
4. Maintain and enhance practices and policies that promote safety, including their own well-being.
5. Demonstrate a non-judgmental, anti-discriminatory, and non-stigmatizing attitude as a fundamental aspect of their professional roles.

A second important aspect entailed framing TVIC as a universal approach to ensuring that individuals are safe and do not suffer further harm when seeking care, and are helped in ways that are based on their strengths and capacities. TVIC must also offer meaningful choice and collaboration when decisions are made. In implementing the learning program, all of this meant underscoring the differences between TVIC and both trauma-specific services (where specialized interventions are provided to those identified with trauma symptoms) and trauma-informed practices (where the focus is on individual-level traumatic experiences and responses and mitigating further harm within a service or setting). In form and in content, we sought to reinforce that TVIC includes explicit attention to structural and systemic violence, with a focus on people's life conditions as well as their previous and ongoing experiences with trauma and violence.

Of the utmost importance to the community of scholars and service providers who contributed to this curriculum was the need to *walk the talk* of such a framing of TVIC. In other words, a universal approach had to be universally accessible, at no cost to anyone wanting to learn. In the same vein, the process of learning about TVIC could not cause harm in and of itself. Establishing safety in the way content was delivered to learners, with a focus on their strengths and capacities, while offering meaningful choice within the curriculum, was a priority from the start. The rest of our story about developing this curriculum concerns how this was accomplished in a self-directed online environment where the audience might be anyone, anywhere.

Mapping Core Content from Training Workshops into Curriculum

After creating the Core Competency Framework, we reviewed and inventoried all of the GTV Incubator and EQUIP-based TVIC resources, using curriculum-mapping as a tool for discerning which learning outcomes were already supported and which were underrepresented in the existing materials. This mapping and gap analysis helped us better understand the kinds of interactive and facilitated activities that had been field-tested in workshops and begin to imagine how they could be adapted for a self-directed online learning environment.

Capturing the Tacit Knowledge of TVIC Facilitators

As we assessed what already existed to inform TVIC training within the existing array of resources, it became clear that expertise in facilitating TVIC workshops was integral to their effectiveness. Our plans for this online curriculum could not include facilitation; even so, it was important to understand what elements of facilitation could be imported into self-directed learning. To that end, we undertook interviews with all of those who had conducted our TVIC workshops and asked them about the "essential ingredients" of their interactions in those face-to-face sessions. Three elements emerged as crucial. First, learners could only learn to the degree that it felt safe for them to do so. If they felt blamed and shamed, or forced to justify past actions, these learners would only shut down. Our facilitators underscored that moral distress, that is, "the experience of being seriously compromised as a moral agent in practicing in accordance with accepted professional values and standards" (Varcoe, Pauly, Webster, & Storch, 2012, p. 59), is a common experience in these fields. "It must be brought to the forefront," said one of our colleagues, "how hard it is to do this work. I ask: 'How many people have felt this way?' I want to create that place of safety and a feeling that 'I'm not labouring through this alone.'" Another of our facilitators said:

Recognizing some of this stuff may be triggering to some people here, and I can't even anticipate what's going to be triggering, or what's going to be triggering for *you* ... We all have some level of violence in our lives. And those that haven't, that's also not a shame. But you also have to go further than that. [You have to] put yourself in the shoes of the person who's experienced the most trauma in the room; a person who came to Canada as a refugee, has seen war, has been in violent relationships. You want to speak to them – and you want to speak to the person who's never had any of that in their lives.

Second, learners know what is happening in their context – they hold expertise that is tied to the particular conditions of those they serve, their organizations, and their own internal resources. For our facilitators, humility was a crucial element, which might involve saying to a group of learners, "*You* tell *me* how it is." In expressing their own humility, facilitators recognize the strengths and capacities of the participants, invite their choice and control, and abandon a "power over" stance in relation to them.

Third and finally, we learned that people need practical, feasible, and accessible tools that empower them to act when they see the opportunity. One described this need in the groups she had facilitated: "People say things like: 'I don't know what to say, what to do.' They're afraid they're going to create discomfort. Afraid of doing the wrong thing. It's so important to take out the shame and blame."

Pedagogical Considerations

Adult learning as a distinct conceptual field has been defined as "the process of using a prior interpretation to construe a new or revised interpretation of the meaning of one's experience to guide future action" (Mezirow, 1996, p. 162). Given our intended audience, this constituted a core framing for the curriculum. Transformative learning (TL), also known as transformational learning, is an approach to adult learning that Nemec (2012) defines as learning that can bring about a shift in learner's perspectives. Learners achieve this transformation by examining, through a critical lens, the assumptions, values, and beliefs they hold as well as the systems in which they operate. TL can transform the knowledge, views, opinions, beliefs, and meanings that adults have acquired over their lifespan into a newer or revised perspective. Adult educators should at least comprehend this approach even if they choose not to adopt it (Imel, 1998; Christie, Carey, Robertson, & Grainger, 2015).

A meta-review of forty peer-reviewed journal articles by Taylor (2007) emphasized that TL as a pedagogical approach can contribute to bringing perspective change among learners in various disciplines. TL encourages learners to critique their thought processes and points of view as well as the experiences that shaped them. It allows them to reassess the validity of their previous learning. Taylor's meta-review suggested that specific steps or directions are needed to ensure that learners have the necessary skills to act on their new learning; it also highlighted the significant role of relationships in TL (for support, trust, friendship, and intimacy). Taylor (2007) also suggests that using audiovisual media in TL can assist participants who sometimes lack the necessary verbal skills and reflexive ability to adequately describe their beliefs, values, and/or feelings. Educators and learners play equally important roles in TL; together, they co-create and sustain the learning environment (Taylor, 1998). Similarly, Nemec (2012) highlighted six key factors that are critical for TL to occur: motivation to learn, a safe learning environment, trust among learners and trainers, training providing experience rather than mere exposure to knowledge, dialogue, and adequate time.

Table 4.3.1 shows Mezirow's (1996) ten phases of TL, that is, what a learner undergoes or experiences when personal transformation through TL occurs. Some examples of how we aligned our TVIC curriculum follow. The idea of a disorienting dilemma (phase 1) highlights that an individual's "world view" is deeply ingrained in their thought processes and can only be shifted through a powerful human catalyst. As noted earlier, our experience delivering TVIC education tells us that this catalyst is often framed as moral distress – the awareness of a profound and harmful dissonance between how individuals and organizations *want* to act and how they *do* act. This can come to light in various ways, including rising incidence of vicarious trauma and compassion fatigue, often described as a feeling of "burnout," poor or declining outcomes and/or satisfaction among service users, and a sense that organizational and/or professional mandates are not being met.

Critical self-examination and reflection (phases 2 and 3) involves questioning the integrity of the deeply held assumptions and beliefs that are based on one's prior experiences. Critical reflection can help learners examine their abilities, beliefs, assumptions, and values in ways that can bring significant change (Kitchenham, 2008; Nemec, 2012; Taylor, 2007). In our workshops, we found that while the leaders convening the session were "there" in terms of identifying potential sites for change, many in our audiences were not. Beginning sessions by acknowledging the moral distress and emotional labour faced by many in helping professions – and that these feelings and thoughts are not unique (phase 4) – was found to be an important initial discussion in the workshops and so was embedded in our online curriculum.

The latter phases, at least up to phase 9, we embedded in the curriculum in various ways, as outlined below. The final phase, reintegrating into life with the transformed approach, was beyond the scope of curriculum development, though we hope to conduct follow-up evaluations of its effectiveness, as we did with the TVIC workshops (Wathen et al., 2021).

Table 4.3.1 Transformative learning phases

Phase 1 – A disorienting dilemma.
Phase 2 – Self-examination with feelings of guilt or shame.
Phase 3 – Critical assessment of epistemic, sociocultural, or psychic assumptions.
Phase 4 – Recognizing that discontent and the process of transformation are shared and that others have negotiated a similar change.
Phase 5 – Exploring options for new roles, relationships, and actions.
Phase 6 – Planning a course of action.
Phase 7 – Acquiring knowledge and skills for implementing plans.
Phase 8 – Provisionally trying new roles.
Phase 9 – Building competence and self-confidence in new roles and relationships.
Phase 10 – Reintegration into one's life on the basis of conditions dictated by one's perspective.

Creating Opportunities for Meaningful Online Learning and Self-Reflection

There is an increasing body of scholarly literature on the effectiveness of online learning compared to face-to-face instruction (Sitzmann, Kraiger, Stewart, & Wisher, 2006). According to Hamad, Serna, Morrison, and Fleming (2010), asynchronous distance learning allows the user to access course materials in their own space and time, and at their own pace, an approach that aligns well with the preferences of adult learners (Knowles, 1990). Web-based learning can also reinforce the transformative learning process in several ways (Taylor, 2007), especially by providing direct, active, and meaningful experiences to the learner, including using simulations so that they can learn through case studies, real-life examples, exercises, and so on. Such simulations can provide safe but relevant experiences and prepare learners to implement new skills in real-world settings. Similarly, methods that promote or mimic interaction can promote critical reflection, a key phase of TL (Kolagani, 2019).

An online environment also offers advantages for trauma- and violence-informed learning experiences. These include learner-controlled pacing, choice in ordering of content, selection of a safe, private, and comfortable learning environment, and the ability to harness other tools and resources in real-time (e.g., concurrent internet searches for additional information). To realize effective integration of TL in an e-learning environment, we began by engaging an experienced instructional designer with the requisite technical skills, who had worked with team members on a related project (developing on online graduate-level university course in health equity). A working group from the GTV Incubator that included both content and curriculum design experts guided the work of the instructional designer. Consistent with our emphasis on creating a trauma- and violence-informed, user-based learning environment, we prioritized making the learning platform as welcoming and usable as possible, mixing various modes of delivery with opportunities to test new knowledge and, via a Notebook feature (described below), a place for personal reflection. As outlined in the overview of the TVIC Curriculum (box 4.3.2), informal quizzes and points of reflection were interspersed throughout, often specific to TVIC strategies as they would apply to the cases presented. These informal checks were designed to prepare the learners for the more formal assessment activities at the end of each section, as well as for the culminating assessment following section 7, required to obtain the Certificate of Completion.

BOX 4.3.2 TVIC CURRICULUM CONTENTS

Section 1: Getting Started

1. Welcome
2. How This Program Works
3. About Us [videos]
4. The TVIC Community and You

Section 2: Trauma- and Violence-Informed Care

1. Learn key concepts and evidence relating to trauma and violence [video].
2. Learn the TVIC principles [video].
3. Reflect on a case from a trauma- and violence-informed lens.
   a Additional Notebook-only exercise – [case].
4. Think of yourself and your interactions as part of interventions [case and quizzes].

Section 3: TVIC in Individual Practice

1. Learn about moral distress and implicit bias [videos].
2. Replay case from section 2 using a TVIC approach [cases and quizzes].
3. Explore other short cases to consider new ways of interacting [cases and quizzes].

Section 4: TVIC Principles at Work

1. Consider how TVIC principles may be applied in practice in various contexts.
   a. Recap four principles.

2. Reflect on your own role with regard to creating awareness, safety, choice, and a strengths-based approach [case].
3. Explore organizational level applications [case and quizzes].

Section 5: Organizational Change for TVIC

1. Organizational Uptake of TVIC [videos].
2. Vicarious Trauma/Compassion Fatigue [videos].
3. Bringing back the case from section 4 to demonstrate key concepts [case and quizzes].

Section 6: Team-Based TVIC Practice

1. Interprofessional, team, and reflective practice – how to orient to TVIC [videos].
2. Case re: connection between organizational and professional culture and TVIC [case and quizzes].
3. Reflect on your practice as part of an interdependent team.

Section 7: Full Case and Final Assessment

1. Assess progress on skills and core-competencies through a full case.
2. Review the Team Case Debrief [video].
3. Complete the Final Assessment => Certificate of Completion.

Each section links to relevant resources, and each has a brief end-of-section assessment.

The downloadable Notebook feature is also integrated at specific points for self-reflective exercises, with the competencies for that section recapped, and links to resources.

Lessons Learned

Aspirations versus Technical Realities in Implementation

It is not easy to match the values-driven aspirations of a group committed to this type of practice with the technological affordances of a Web-based platform designed for a large institution. For our curriculum, it became clear that the most sustainable, cost-effective, and secure means of hosting the content was the Canvas learning management system (LMS) at the University of British Columbia, home of the EQUIP Health Care resources (chapter 2.1). The system allowed for non-university-affiliated users (i.e., anyone) to securely join and, over time, complete the curriculum at their own pace. By saving an individual's login information and self-assessment progress, Canvas allows learners to choose when and where they complete the curriculum; this means they can process the content at their own pace as well as return to previous sections for review or reflection. After the final section and successful completion of the final assessment, learners have the option to request a Certificate of Completion.

The decision to build this curriculum in H5P (an open-access html-based content development platform) and house it on Canvas came at the cost of other technological freedoms in terms of design and user experience. These had to be negotiated in accordance with TVIC principles to prioritize a strengths-based and choice-rich experience. For example, early on, a pedagogical priority had entailed prompting the learner to reflect in a Notebook. In a facilitated learning environment, to support emotional safety, such reflections are debriefed as a group or processed with the support of a facilitator. In the context of self-directed learning, facilitation wasn't possible, so the point of the Notebook was to capture the learner's reflections to improve content delivery and understand our audience. Programing restrictions on Canvas further meant that this Notebook would be a freestanding resource, a downloadable, fillable workbook that learners could complete and keep for their records. This restriction prompted us to use the Notebook as another program "takeaway," in addition to key messages/content, a recap of learning objectives and competencies, and reflection questions for each section of the curriculum.

The Canvas framework also enabled us to program design features. The curriculum had been envisioned as a beautiful and humanistic online space that would provide learners with a warm and welcoming online experience. However, neither H5P nor Canvas on the UBC server allows for alterations in design and navigation features, and this significantly restricts colours, font styles, and background options. We therefore sought other ways to inject a human touch, and hired an artist to draw custom images for each learning case. The resulting images were inspired by careful reflection on the principles and "ways of doing" TVIC and by discussion of the concerns and possibilities presented in each case. We meant these to convey how much more there is to a story, beyond what fits in case or briefing notes. For example, in illustrations of "Fatima's story," the images convey the strong relationship between mother and children (figure 4.3.1).

We then, to the extent possible, used colours from the image palette for slides and other visuals. However, menu colours, navigation buttons, and the like remained at pre-set values.

Curriculum(a) for Individuals, Organizations and Systems Moving to TVIC

The process of developing this curriculum raised interesting questions regarding what it means to promote change at individual, organizational, and systems

Figure 4.3.1 Sample case illustration. Copyright 2021, the authors.

levels. While our pedagogical approach focused on the interplay between individuals' experiences and their context, at the core of transformational learning and TVIC itself is the idea that change starts with what a person does and specifically with the ways they think, speak, and act differently in the place where they are. This stance of consistently asking the individual to act does does not reflect the belief that individuals are solely responsible for the conditions of their lives or the lives of others. Our parallel commitment to a socio-critical examination of the systemic and structural factors in people's access to health and well-being runs counter to that assumption. Making a meaningful curriculum, then, required drawing attention to the systemic and structural forces that create trauma and violence while also highlighting where, especially for service users, individual provider actions were key for disrupting such cycles of trauma, violence, and marginalization. We hope the curriculum leads to experiences in which an individual acting as "the intervention," safely and supported by their organization, brings about interprofessional and organizational shifts, which can then be taken up to transform policies, structures and, ultimately, systems.

Conclusion

In this chapter, we described how we developed an online TVIC curriculum through a process of multiple, iterative phases of consultation with community- and university-based experts, various sectors in public and community health and social services, and education experts. Transformational learning theory served as a guiding framework to create a learning environment that balanced understanding new constructs with individual application and self-reflection. This meant troubling our own assumptions and being able to imagine our own efficacy in promoting change where we work. To that end, what had been learned in previous live TVIC workshops was crucial. The practical experience of TVIC facilitators, collected through interviews with them and through recorded videos with the TVIC community, became content for the platform, and was essential to creating meaningful, self-directed learning experiences. Our next steps will be to evaluate the impact of the curriculum on its stated core competencies and learning objectives and outcomes and to assess the extent of its reach into various sectors.

NOTES

1 https://equiphealthcare.ca/tvic-foundations
2 https://gtvincubator.uwo.ca

KEY MESSAGES AND IMPLICATIONS

- Our process, based on transformational learning, was very well-suited to this specific content and is potentially relevant for curriculum development for any complex or challenging topic.
- Centring the learner and their safety, well-being, agency, choice, and strengths has led us to what we hope is a flexible, engaging, and ultimately impactful learning experience.

ADDITIONAL RESOURCES

- TVIC Foundations Curriculum: https://equiphealthcare.ca/tvic-foundations
- GTV Incubator: https://gtvincubator.uwo.ca

REFERENCES

Christie, M., Carey, M., Robertson, A., & Grainger, P. (2015). Putting transformative learning theory into practice. *Australian Journal of Adult Learning, 55*(1), 9–30. https://ajal.net.au/putting-transformative-learning-theory-into-practice/

Hamad, C.D., Serna, R.W., Morrison, L., & Fleming, R. (2010). Extending the reach of early intervention training for practitioners: A preliminary investigation of an online curriculum for teaching behavioral intervention knowledge in autism to families and service providers. *Infants and Young Children, 23*(3), 195. https://doi.org/10.1097%2FIYC.0b013e3181e32d5e

Imel, S. (1998). Transformative learning in adulthood. *ERIC Digest*, 200.

Kitchenham, A. (2008). The evolution of John Mezirow's Transformative Learning theory. *Journal of Transformative Education, 6*(2), 104–23. https://doi.org/10.1177%2F1541344608322678

Knowles, M. (1990). *The adult learner: A neglected species*. Houston: Gulf Publishing.

Kolagani, S. (2019, May 16). Leveraging the power of transformative learning in eLearning. [Blog post]. Retrieved from https://blog.commlabindia.com/elearning-design/transformational-learning-elearning

Mezirow, J. (1996). Contemporary paradigms of learning. *Adult Education Quarterly, 46*(3), 158–72. https://doi.org/10.1177/074171369604600303

Nemec, P.B. (2012). Transformative learning. *Psychiatric Rehabilitation Journal, 35*(6), 478–9. doi: https://doi.org/10.1037/h0094585

Sitzmann, T., Kraiger, K., Stewart, D., & Wisher, R. (2006). The comparative effectiveness of web-based and classroom instruction: A meta-analysis. *Personnel Psychology, 59*(3), 623–64. https://doi.org/10.1111/j.1744-6570.2006.00049.x

Taylor, E.W. (2007). An update of transformative learning theory: A critical review of the empirical research (1999–2005). *International Journal of Lifelong Education, 26*(2), 173–91. https://doi.org/10.1080/02601370701219475

Taylor, E.W. (1998). *The theory and practice of transformative learning: A critical review*. Information series no. 374. ERIC Clearinghouse on Adult, Career & Vocational Education. Retrieved from https://files.eric.ed.gov/fulltext/ED423422.pdf

Varcoe, C., Pauly, B., Webster, G., & Storch, J. (2012). Moral distress: Tensions as springboards for action. *HEC Forum, 24*, 51–62. https://doi.org/10.1007/s10730-012-9180-2

Wathen, C.N., MacGregor, J.C.D., & Beyrem, S. (2021). Impacts of trauma- and violence-informed care education: A mixed method follow-up evaluation with health & social service professionals. *Public Health Nursing*. Retrieved from https://onlinelibrary.wiley.com/doi/abs/10.1111/phn.12883

4.4 Thinking Structurally: Using Trauma- and Violence-Informed Care to Reimagine Service Systems

MARGARET MACPHERSON AND NADINE WATHEN

This chapter will consider the potential of trauma- and violence-informed (TVI) interventions to address persistent issues in the violence response ecosystem. Issues to be explored include the fragmented approach to service, especially for older women experiencing domestic violence, and insufficient resourcing from governments. When funding is inadequate, operating costs rely on donations and time-limited project grants; this leads to precarious work environments and interorganizational competition for scarce government and non-government funds. We will specifically examine how policies and services respond to the abuse of older adults and to domestic violence in two distinct and siloed sectors; as we will discuss, trauma and violence are baked into systems, from top to bottom. Exploring our societal response to interpersonal violence can tell us a lot about intrinsic issues that are more difficult to see and the work that needs to be done to move toward prevention. Understanding how TVI thinking can provide a collaborative bridge across systems will also help advance more integrated approaches to service, to the ultimate benefit of those seeking care. A systems approach is the best way to achieve TVI results with fewer resources and in more lasting ways (Stroh, 2015).

Preventing interpersonal violence – including domestic violence and elder abuse/abuse of older people (see box 4.4.1) – is a large project of social change that requires broad engagement and persistent repeatable actions over time. The trope "everyone has a role to play" is often heard in anti-violence campaigns. While the idea is sound, the goal behind it cannot be achieved without clarity of roles and identification of specific actions. We hope that by the end of this chapter, readers will be inspired to identify their contribution points and next steps with TVI principles as a concrete guide to action, with application of this thinking for the systems and sectors in which they work. To anchor the discussion at the sector level, two questions will be explored: (1) Can collective work to become trauma- and violence-informed serve as a bridge between traditionally siloed sectors that must often compete for funding? And (2) can alignment mitigate the structural violence that service users describe as "re-traumatizing" and/or "revictimizing" when they are seeking service?

BOX 4.4.1 KEY DEFINITIONS

- Domestic violence,* also referred to as spousal violence or intimate partner violence (IPV), involves couples of any age or gender. It includes physical, psychological, emotional, sexual, and financial forms of violence and is placed in a larger context of violence against women (VAW) or gender-based violence (GBV). Women are most often the victims of serious injury, hospitalization, and death.
- Abuse of older adults includes neglect as well as physical, psychological, emotional, sexual, and financial forms of violence. It is often included under "family violence," as spouses and other family members (predominantly adult children and even grandchildren) are most often the perpetrators.
- "Elder abuse" is a contentious term in collectivist communities, including many religious communities and Indigenous communities, for whom the term "Elder" has a specific meaning and place. Because governments use the term, it is widely used. *Ignoring cultural significance is the first example of structural violence in this chapter.*

Each of these questions points to different albeit interrelated kinds of trauma and violence as well as to opportunities for tailored interventions at the sectoral, organizational, and individual levels. Thus, throughout the chapter, we will be discussing the connections among individual and sector issues in the context of the broader society. If the adoption of TVI principles can build bridges between sectors dedicated to addressing individual impacts, then perhaps, as a society, we can move upstream toward more strategic goals: prevention, equity, and healing for everyone involved.

Consistent with this multilevel way of thinking about causes, consequences, and responses to violence, the World Health Organization (WHO) promotes an ecological framework, one that is based on evidence that no single factor can explain why some people or groups are at higher risk of interpersonal violence. This framework views interpersonal violence as the outcome of interactions among many factors at four levels – individual, relationship, community, and societal (Heise, 1998). Figure 4.4.1 presents an adapted version of WHO's ecological framework indicating the primary factors, across levels, related to experiences of elder abuse (EA) and domestic or intimate partner violence (DV/IPV).

---

* "Family violence" is a broader term that includes violence against children and others in the family or home.

312　Margaret MacPherson and Nadine Wathen

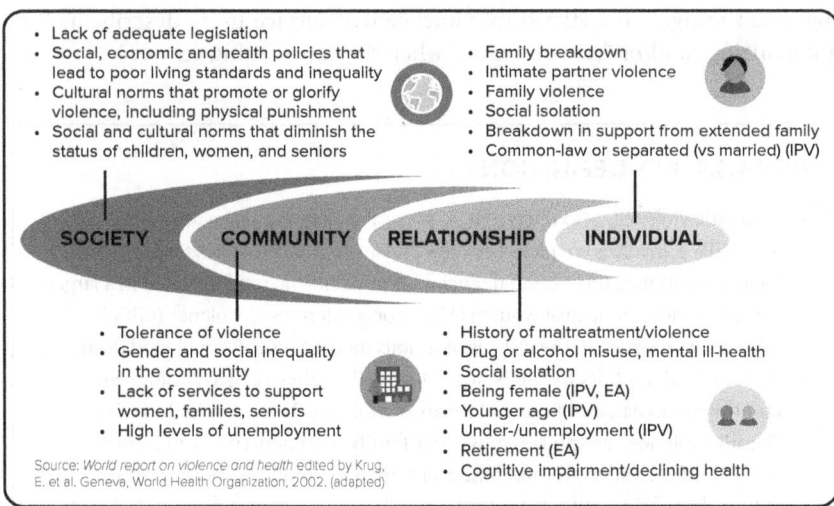

Figure 4.4.1　Ecological model on DV/IPV and EA. Copyright 2021, the authors, design by J. MacGregor.

Thus, "the interaction among many factors" creates the conditions for both interpersonal violence and potential remedies. There are two sides to every coin. The conditions spring from the values, attitudes, and beliefs that are internalized within us and within our organizations and communities, which are then reflected and reified by society (World Health Organization, 2021). TVI principles provide evidence-based, practical levers that can be applied at any level of the system to help facilitate the paradigm shift in world views that is happening, from an unsustainable society to a sustainable one, from inequities to equity.[1] Becoming TVI is hopeful, creative action grounded in a recognition that the personal is political.[2] In the grand scheme of things, how we act matters.

> The changes in which we will be called upon to participate in the future will be both deeply personal and inherently systematic. Yet the deeper dimensions of transformational change represent a largely unexplored territory both in current management research and in our understanding of leadership in general. This blind spot concerns not the what and how – not what leaders do and how they do it – but the who: who we are and the inner place or source from which we operate, both individually and collectively. (Senge, Scharmer, Jaworski, & Flowers, 2004, p. 5)

To insist that discussion of causes and consequences of, and solutions to, interpersonal violence includes the full ecology in Figure 4.4.1 is itself a radical act that asks for something from each of us in accepting social conditions and structural violence as causal factors in violent relationships. To some degree, it requires making a leap from the industrial age[3] world view based on individualism and taking responsibility as creative contributors in an emerging society, leaning into change, while working within the constraints of our current system. Applying TVI principles to domestic violence is not blue-sky dreaming. As we will discuss throughout this chapter, it means being able to embody principles in practice in any environment and to understand TVI as a social contribution. TVI principles are the levers for change and a compass for the journey.

This discussion begins with a consideration of societal-level influences as the backdrop of knowledge, attitudes, and practices/policies that drive what is possible, and probable, at the more proximate levels. Working from the outside in (from societal/systemic to organizational/community to individual/relationship), we will discuss the clustering of organizations into sectors that provide the services, the relationship between service users and professionals, individual professionals who provide service, and individuals who access services. The relationships between the levels of the ecological model are complex and recursive. Understanding how different kinds of structural violence create the conditions for interpersonal violence challenges the entrenched belief that violence in relationships is the problem of a few "bad apples." It bears repeating that structural competency is the "trained ability" to recognize that individual actions are a long way downstream from larger social forces that create the conditions for interpersonal violence (see chapter 1.2). Readers are asked to consider how individual beliefs and actions are influenced and sustained through each of the levels.

The ecological framing is important for this discussion because interpersonal violence is still widely perceived an individual issue, not a societal, public health, or even heath care issue. This stubborn belief persists, despite all evidence to the contrary, because it is deeply rooted in a still dominant world view that sees individuals as static and discrete (able to exercise agency and choice, irrespective of actual social conditions), not as dynamic beings in complex relationships with multiple identities. It is much easier to blame the person who acts violently – or worse yet, the victim – than to consider the relational, community, and societal conditions in which violent behaviour is produced, enabled, and even rewarded. *Individualist explanations are founded on personal responsibility discourse, which attempts to render individuals as particularly blameworthy for their conditions, circumstances, or state of health. This often justifies the application of paternalistic or punitive policies toward them* (see chapter 1.2). A core tenet of TVI principles is that people do not act without reason and that behind every action is a story and a logic. With respect to the violence response system, this is the first test. Are we willing to apply the principles to those who are abusive, controlling, and violent in their relationships?

This is not to say that individuals are not responsible for their actions. They are. But it is possible to hold people accountable for their actions and at the same time offer support and expect change. Rarely are the dots connected through the different levels of the social ecology to show that trauma and violence are often predictable and, it follows, preventable outcomes of inequality, disparity, and discrimination, which can be understood as an interlocking expression of structural violence that contributes to individual acts. Because we are part of the society around us, we are implicated in the problem and also in the solution.

Systems scientist Peter Senge writes: "Who wants to produce any of the deep systemic problems we see in the world? The answer is no one. Yet we are all responsible for it" (Senge, 2017, para. 8). The seemingly intractable gulf between what is wanted in a violence response system and what currently exists has been described as a source of "moral distress" for professionals constrained by budgets and mandates (Varcoe, Pauly, Webster, & Storch, 2012). Senge (2017) concludes that it will take all of us working together to solve our problems. Being willing to reflect on the ways in which we function as carriers of structural violence builds our individual capacity to make choices and foster connections within dysfunctional environments. The commitment to becoming TVI reverses the adage that you are part of the problem if you are not part of the solution. Instead, from a TVI perspective, *you can't be part of the solution if you are not part of the problem*. Like it or not, you are part of the problem when you are the one who has to tell a family that they don't fit within the criteria for service. You become part of the solution when you anticipate and take steps to mitigate the harm in your delivery of the information, possibly connecting them with another service or just taking time to talk with them about options. Once you recognize the ways in which you are unintentionally complicit with the status quo, you can become an active agent in a grassroots groundswell. Same coin, different sides. In a connected world, even small actions can have a big impact.

The Societal Context: Nothing Less than Epoch Change

We are living in a time of great change. A global shift is taking place that promises a more complex understanding of our planet and society. The shift is toward equity and sustainability. The reductionist world view that continues to dominate in North America and Europe values the individual over the collective. Individualism and collectivism have long been positioned in opposition to each other; one is either an individualist or a collectivist. In fact, each of us is both an individual and a member of the collective. Individualism came to dominance in North America and Europe with the Industrial Age and capitalism. Collectivism is the dominant world view of Indigenous peoples and of many other communities around the world. Within individualism, the "rugged individual" has been constructed as the human ideal – it is someone who has risen to success on "his" merit, an independent agent, free to act with impunity, without impacting or being impacted by others or the environment (Eppard et al., 2020). With the advent of the internet and global challenges such as climate change, the individual has been shown not to be so separate and autonomous, but instead part of the whole, interconnected and interdependent within a living system.

The tension between world views has become literally a fight for dominance. That fight took form during the COVID-19 pandemic in the struggle between people who refuse to wear a mask because they believe their rights are at stake and people who wear one because they understand that our collective survival depends on individual actions that, in aggregate, contribute to keeping infection rates down. The individualist understanding of self-interest is limited to oneself. Self-interest in a collective context is an understanding that equity is in everyone's interest. Inevitably, we sink or swim together. The shift in world views is relevant to this discussion because the propensity to anchor the causes and consequences of interpersonal violence at the individual level is rooted in the same belief system as anti-masking. Our societal response to interpersonal violence is structured by these beliefs and made material in the systems and institutions – from health care to criminal justice to journalism – that insist that interpersonal violence is an individual issue.

Structural Violence – Societal Level

Structural violence is inevitable in systems that are built on the assumption that some people matter more than others. Individualism confers value based on identity and material success. A level playing field is assumed; thus, if you are not successful, it must be your own fault. Trauma, from this assumption, cascades in many directions as a form of violence, internalized within ourselves and exteriorized by our systems. Discrimination based on identity (gender, race, class, age) filters into unexamined policies and programs that have real-world impacts on entire populations across the life course.[4] Examples germane to this chapter include the gender wage gap, the lack of research on and investments in services for older people in general (especially in terms of the inadequacies revealed by COVID-19's impacts on long-term care, for example) and for those experiencing abuse, lack of investments for prevention in the violence response sector, growing income inequality, a lack of affordable housing, and the erosion of the social safety net through austerity measures over the past forty years, to name a few.

Increasing numbers of people in Canada and globally are struggling just to survive (MacDonald, 2018). Their daily struggles cause trauma and spawn increased rates of violence in homes and communities (Wilkinson & Pickett,

2009). When structural violence is not acknowledged, their struggles are interpreted as personal failure. There is explicit resentment in public discourse about the need for a safety net in the first place, which explains why it is okay to let it collapse. The "nanny state" is being indicted by many as a social intervention that promotes dependency and disincentivizes people to work (Moore, Yeatman, & Davey, 2015). This belief system was evident in social conservatives' sharp criticism of wage subsidies and paid leave early in the COVID-19 pandemic. Those who hold such views are fearful of human nature that is not policed and that peers beyond the strict boundaries of self-interest. In fact, the pandemic has highlighted the need to use public funds to create safety and invest in the strength, compassion, and resilience of people during a crisis. The pandemic has clearly shown the implications of identity in an individualist society. Women and seniors form a significant part of the demographic on the margins of society, and they have been among the hardest hit by the pandemic (Canadian Women's Foundation [CWF], Canadian Centre for Policy Alternatives, Ontario Nonprofit Network, & Lahey, 2020; United Nations [UN], 2020).

Top-Down: Systemic Ageism and Sexism All the Way to the Ground

The entire human service system operates according to a business model that privileges profits over people (Chomsky, 1999). This business overlay sets the stage for everything that follows and dictates how much service will be doled out in terms of allocations and budgets. The reluctance to adequately fund human services is apparent as governments separate complex human needs into sectors with budget lines that are limited in scope and closely tied to mandates and programs. Compared to the mammoth health, justice, and education ministries, the government departments responsible for seniors and "women's issues" are typically small and underbudgeted and lack power and influence – in many cases they are not formal "departments" or "ministries" but merely "offices" or "units." Clearly, then, ageism and sexism permeate the system ("turtles all the way down"[5]), penalizing everyone who touches the problem. This was expressed in a startling admission by an assistant deputy minister (ADM) during a stakeholder meeting in 2015. As the top bureaucrat responsible for victims' issues in a small unit attached to the massive Ministry of the Attorney General, she was pressed by a group of community leaders to use her power and position to help shift the system toward prevention. Quietly she admitted to the group, "I don't feel very powerful."

Another Stubborn Belief: Interpersonal Violence Is Not a Health Issue

Within governments, elder abuse and domestic violence services are located in separate sectors, both outside of health services. They are not included in standard health care departments or budgets. WHO has clearly recommended that interpersonal violence be treated as a major public health problem that has significant long-term health consequences and costs, yet it is still not accepted as a health issue. Structurally, it remains locked in place as a social service issue and a problem of individual failure.

Competing for Scarce Resources

Governments allocate budgets, which can be thought of as a pie. The pie can be cut into quarters or eighths, but there is only one pie for a sector. In Ontario, Canada's most populous province, funding to respond to abuse of older adults comes from the same pie as for other victim response services. The violence against women (VAW) shelter system has its own pie. The pie system creates territories to protect. New operational or project-based funding can lead to frenzied interorganizational competition – the expression "blood in the water" comes to mind. Scarce funding and the fear of losing what your organization has creates trauma among leaders. Lateral violence in the form of infighting within underresourced sectors is a well-established phenomenon: "When a powerful oppressor has directed oppression against a group for a period of time, members of the oppressed group feel powerless to fight back and they eventually turn their anger against each other" (Middleton-Moz, 1999, p. 116). Throughout the VAW and EA sectors, the forced competition for funding is a result of inadequate resourcing in both, coupled with the need to meet heartbreaking demands for service from the most vulnerable citizens. That there is fighting over the scraps is to be expected. All of the reasons why the sectors are more alike than different, and why they should work together for common goals, are eclipsed by each sector's struggle to survive. For the most part, the material reality of scarcity is never questioned – we are trained to follow the "do more with less" business ethos, as if it is the only possible option.

Sectoral Roots

The separation of sectors also has to do with their roots. Elder abuse has evolved out of geriatrics and gerontology and is still considered a "new" field of study (Dong, 2015). According to professionals working with seniors, the sector is the "poor cousin" to VAW. They consider themselves twenty-five years behind VAW in research and funding. In the discursive pecking order of who matters in society, older people finish behind women.

Domestic violence and violence against women (VAW) services have evolved from a feminist, grassroots movement. The activism that put VAW on the social map and government radar has become increasingly institutionalized and assimilated into the mainstream over the past three decades, and it is now sustained with government funding (Harris, Wathen, & Lynch, 2014). As a result, advocacy has become a dirty word. As far as funders are concerned, agencies should never bite (i.e., critique or even question) the hand that feeds. In many jurisdictions, paternalism is rife in a top-down public service.[6] Not-for-profit organizations providing direct services have been constructed as "parasitic supplicants" (McKenzie, 2015, p. 12) since the 1990s in a public service that, having embraced the business mindset, has abandoned community development for overt paternalism. The funding is just enough for politicians to be able to point to action, but without ever addressing the root causes of structural violence that fuel the hamster wheel demand for services.

Competing Research Paradigms and Gender Perspectives

Three competing research paradigms dominate the respective fields of study in the two sectors: older adult mistreatment informed by social gerontology; older adult protection informed by geriatrics; and intimate partner violence informed by the domestic violence movement. Differing definitions have led to uneven findings, policy responses, programs, and practices that can appear contradictory and confusing as each is linked to different theoretical assumptions. The resulting confusion has confounded the development of an overarching framework, especially for older women, who overlap the two fields (United Nations DESA [UN DESA], 2013).

Elder abuse is characterized by various forms of abuse such as physical, psychological, sexual, and financial, as well as by intentional or unintentional neglect, but rarely considers coercive power dynamics in intimate partner relationships (Brownell, 2015; Nägele, Böhm, Görgen, & Toth, 2010). As men age, they are treated increasingly like women by society, and their rates of victimization go up (Calasanti, Slevin, & King, 2006). Older men experience abuse and neglect at close to the same rates as women. Domestic violence victimization rates at any age are more influenced by gender, with women being the predominant victims (Dong, 2015; Nägele et al., 2010; National Institute for the Care of the Elderly [NICE], 2015; Warmling, Lindner, & Coelho, 2017).

Gender analysis generates an unresolved tension that plays out as a simple opposition: those advocating and working in the elder abuse field view the gender lens as a betrayal of older male victims, while in the VAW sector, the lack of gender analysis is viewed as a betrayal of older women (MacPherson, Reif, Titterness, & MacQuarrie, 2020). Further tension is found in the justice language of "victims" and "perpetrators" common in the VAW sector – language that is skewed to respond only after the fact of violence with a justice intervention. Perpetrators of elder abuse are often family members, most typically spouses and adult sons (NICE, 2015). The idea of labelling the abusive behaviour of an adult child in criminal justice terms is unacceptable for most seniors. They will imperil themselves to protect their children from judgment and justice. Trauma- and violence-informed principles address these tensions by refocusing attention on the humanity of everyone involved and by including "offenders" in their efforts to address problems. This more holistic approach is not new for collectivist communities, in which TVI principles are implicit and the focus is on family-based interventions.

The literature on elder abuse typically does not single out older women as a separate group, nor does it recognize their unique vulnerabilities (Crockett, Brandl, & Dabby, 2015; Pathak, Dhairyawan, & Tariq, 2019). *Domestic violence grown old* is a common phrase and a rationalization for ignoring the issue (i.e., the problem is long-standing and there is nothing to be done about it now) (MacPherson et al., 2020). The unspoken response is to blame the victim for staying in the relationship. The invisibility of domestic violence in elder abuse research creates a domino effect for older women, as funding for services and research generally follows evidence (Dong, 2015). The lack of evidence then supports the myth that domestic violence is not a serious issue for older women. Health care and social service providers working with seniors often have little training in interpersonal violence and are thus more likely to dismiss warning signs, perceiving them as part of the natural aging process (McGarry, Simpson, & Hinchcliff-Smith, 2017; Violence Against Women and Girls [VAWG], 2016). As a result, ageism is pervasive. Until recently, the VAW sector did not consider ageing to be a factor requiring specialized knowledge or services tailored to the unique needs of older people. As a result, most VAW services for abused women have been developed for younger women of reproductive age. Services for male victims of any age are extremely rare. Increasingly, however, VAW services have been adapting to include gender-diverse people.

Older women live in the crosshairs of the two sectors. They are invisible in both sectors for different reasons, which coalesce in a mistaken belief that domestic violence does not occur in, or is not as serious for, older couples. That belief, which amounts to a confirmation bias, is rooted in a research gap. Global domestic violence studies conducted by WHO and the UN have not included women over the age of forty-nine (Ellsberg & Heise, 2005, VAWG, 2016). Older women who are care-dependent or cognitively incapacitated and possibly living in institutions are even more undersampled (UN DESA, 2013).

The workforce in both sectors is comprised mainly of women, who are working in small organizations that are struggling to survive, dependent on fundraising, and competing for project money to cover operational costs (CWF et al., 2020). Turtles and more turtles. The pandemic highlighted the situation of "essential workers" in precarious and multiple part-time jobs, working for low wages and usually without benefits or paid sick leave. It is believed that the costs of providing unpaid care work during the pandemic have set women back decades economically (UN, 2020).

Lessons from the pandemic show us that society has it backwards when it comes to the way we value and reward work. This is especially evident in the violence response sector and the incredible amount of unpaid care work on which society depends (CWF et al., 2020). The further the work from the grit of direct services and caregiving, the higher the pay and the more secure the position. Anthropologist David Graeber writes that "in our society there seems to be a general rule that, the more obviously one's work benefits people, the less one is likely to be paid for it" (Graeber, 2016, para. 14). The senior provincial government bureaucrat responsible for victim issues makes a six-figure salary with an excellent benefit package and a full pension; in stark contrast, the shelter worker and the personal support worker who are providing direct services are too often working multiple minimum-wage part-time jobs to make ends meet, with no benefits or pension. And when these workers "retire," they take their place in the struggling class of older women with even fewer options. The closer you stand to the fire of trauma and violence, the more vicarious trauma you will experience, both from the situations and people you encounter and from the structural violence built into the system that makes demanding work even harder (see chapter 1.4). As women age, their horizons for action diminish and they come to see themselves as having fewer life choices within the scope of decreasing power (McGarry et al., 2017).

When the pandemic first struck, the federal and provincial governments sent $40 million into the VAW shelter system to address the "shadow pandemic" of domestic violence (Lao, 2020). The money flowed with little direction from the top down in an unprecedented and telling "do whatever you have to do" release of funds. There was no pie to fight over. Governments quickly realized that when the crisis comes, it is the people working in the local communities, directly with those who are most exposed to violence, who are the best-situated to respond.

The COVID-19 pandemic response saw no corresponding flow of money to services for elder abuse, partly because there was no infrastructure or dedicated system in place to support those services. The risk of violence and abuse for older people remains deep in the shadows of the "shadow pandemic." The mistreatment of older adults in the long-term care system and congregate care situations has brought about a shameful call to action; meanwhile, violence against older adults in their homes and communities remains mostly hidden. This, even though the majority (91.2%) of older adults live in the community (Statistics Canada, 2011).[7]

In sum, the overall approach to responding to interpersonal violence is crisis-driven. The system tasked with responding to violence is not funded for prevention; we do not engage the violent partner or family member until after they commit a criminal act. At that point it is a strictly criminal justice response, fuel for adversarial relationships. The system is perpetually stuck in crisis mode, and that is the most expensive possible response, one that comes with a never-ending cascade of human, social, and economic costs. It is impossible to calculate the costs of elder abuse because there is so little data and few services are available. The Canadian federal government estimates that violence against women costs $1.1 billion (in 2007 value) annually in direct medical costs alone (Health Canada, 2007). Domestic violence is estimated to cost more than 5 per cent of the global GDP (Vara-Horna, n.d.).

The steady state of crisis response is as bad as the worst-case scenario for the health care sector, which was reached at times during the COVID-19 pandemic, during which spikes in hospitalization outstripped the system's capacity to provide intensive care and sick people had to be triaged to die without treatment. The high trauma impacts on health care workers are recognized as burnout and operational stress. The violence response sector operates under these conditions on a daily basis. For example, the largest shelter in Ontario reported on the organization-level trauma of having to turn away women who were fleeing violence 2,500 times in a one-year period, pre-pandemic (Dubinski & Duhatschek, 2019). We cannot talk about trauma and violence without first recognizing the different kinds of harm caused by the system to those charged with providing service and support. Becoming TVI is not just about clients or the public; it is also about acknowledging and mitigating the harm to service providers caused by structural violence. Healing is needed throughout the violence ecosystem. It is beyond the scope of this chapter to delve any deeper into the history and complexity of how and why our socio-politico-economic systems are unjust to entire populations and steeped in structural violence from top to bottom. It is what it is. However, at a certain point, you have to say, *never mind how the jackass got in the ditch, just get him out.*

Out of The Ditch – The Disruptive Potential of TVIC

Trauma- and violence-informed principles and practices have disruptive and transformative potential for the entire violence response system; they can cut through the bottomless morass of top-down existing conditions. Leaders everywhere can make a commitment to becoming TVI. In a world that is understood to be interdependent and interconnected, every action has an impact and small everyday actions can make the difference, especially when those actions aggregate in organizations and communities.

At an individual level, TVI principles can facilitate a shift for professionals who feel trapped in a dehumanizing system; it can encourage them to take up responsibility as creative agents by never underestimating or relinquishing the power to be humane in every instance. We act as world-builders by investing in people. Equity and healing are the internal drivers.

In a 2017 interview, Senge unpacked the idea that all we can do is what we can do as individuals: "As an individual, my role has always been to be a bridge between practice and ideas" (para. 12). Here he is describing a reversal in the ecological field whereby the individual is the catalyst for social change – not an individual in isolation but an individual who is part of the social field, a member of the whole. To be the change you want in the world is the action. There is no need to wait for permission, policy change, or allocation of funding. Every person is a potential point of constructive disruption in the social system, every encounter is a beginning point when TVI principles can be deployed. Once you understand the forms of structural violence, you can be intentional and strategic in the mitigation of specific kinds of harm for yourself and others. The transformation from powerless victim of circumstance to world-builder can happen to anyone, anywhere, from one moment to the next. The potential cannot be controlled by even the most authoritarian system. That is what makes free will so dangerous to the status quo (Deleuze & Guattari, 1987). Yes, the social container is constructed to privilege profits over people, to blame individuals for their problems, and to assert that some people matter more than others, but within the container there is a lot of room to manoeuvre.

There are many reasons why the DV and EA sectors should be able to find common ground and mutual support on issues, yet the structural violence in the system actively disincentivizes and works against unity and collaboration. As Senge suggests, there is no alternative but to work together to get ourselves out of the mess. We have to be strategic to be effective.

"Organizations and social systems do in fact have a life of their own" (Stroh, 2015, p. 1). Becoming TVI at the relationship and community levels is a "high-leverage intervention" for leaders in every part of the violence response system to take up independently and simultaneously. Systems thinking can help with strategizing (see box 4.4.2; Stroh, 2015, pp. 1–2).

BOX 4.4.2 SYSTEMS THINKING

Applying systems thinking enables you to achieve better results with fewer resources in more lasting ways. It works because it:

- increases your awareness of how you might unwittingly be contributing to the very problems you want to solve;
- empowers you to begin from where you can have the greatest impact on others, by reflecting on and shifting your own intentions, thinking, and actions;
- mobilizes diverse stakeholders to take actions that increase the effectiveness of the entire system over time instead of meeting their immediate self-interests;

- helps you and others anticipate and avoid the negative longer-term consequences of well-intentioned solutions;
- identifies high-leverage interventions that focus limited resources for maximum, lasting, system-wide improvement; and
- motivates and supports continuous learning.

If you are a leader, you can commit to becoming TVI as an organization. Professionals in human services may think they already do this because they have a well-developed trauma focus and are already engaged in equity initiatives. An understanding and analysis of the ecosystem is what's needed to transcend the core values inherent in the individualist world view. Becoming TVI as an organization is about much more than training. It requires a committed, dedicated focus by leadership over time as well as a heart courageous enough to examine and expose the ways an organization inevitably reproduces the status quo. It takes the will and resources to make system and structural changes that address specific harms, within and without.

The pandemic provides a useful starting point for reflecting on how informed the response in your organization has been to collective trauma. What concrete steps were taken to support workers and clients through social isolation, during lockdowns, and in the storm of relentless pressure for service? Did you acknowledge the increased risk for interpersonal violence in the community and with staff working from home? How involved was your organization with community coordination of services? Anecdotal reports from leaders in the violence response sector suggest that in some communities, collaboration among multisector organizations improved during the crisis. It will be important to identify and hold on to ground gained in working together over the course of the pandemic.

TVIC Principles from the Ground Up

We have zoomed out for most of this chapter to describe the powerful societal forces, including poverty, sexism, classism, and racism, that reinforce and perpetuate trauma and violence within the violence response system. Systems are incredibly resilient and will absorb and appropriate change efforts that lack ongoing commitment to critique, engagement, and ongoing learning (Meadows, 2008).

The first TVIC principle is *understand trauma and violence, especially structural violence, and the impacts on people's lives and behaviour – including our own.*

Many professionals in human services gravitate toward equity in principle and practice without the need for theory. It comes naturally to them. In today's circumstances, the challenges more concern how to internalize the principles and then to organize collectively across sectors. The pandemic has provided us with an opening to consider previously unthinkable ideas, such as universal basic income, and meanwhile, ideas about how to correct inequitable wealth distribution are circulating in the public domain. This is the time to lean into collective action. Large, shared goals can invite participation and contribution. Becoming TVI is as much a project of engagement as it is a project of social change.

It is important to engage the entire organization in discussion and build capacity to recognize structural violence and how it is replicated and reified in policies, processes, interactions, and the environment. Begin by assuming that structural violence exists. Be relentless in looking for the ways it manifests harm. In our experience, dedicating an internal team, with explicit mandate and authority to set goals, develop accountability processes, and generally hold the TVI focus over time, is a key driver for successful implementation.

Engaging community partners in discussion about taking a project approach to becoming a "TVI community" is a next-level strategy. As a project, system change can be broken down into steps and goals, making the collective journey visible and achievable. Set clear markers of progress over time and create opportunities to learn from other organizations. Start with a training for leaders on TVIC principles and design the project from there. Many communities already have multisector community tables and networks that are dedicated to violence prevention and response. As discussed throughout the chapter, without intentional intervention, they are likely to be functioning as separate issue tables; however, there are exceptions. Anti-violence coordinating committees provide existing infrastructure to bring people together under the TVI umbrella.

The actions of individuals are enhanced when leaders support them. If individuals' actions can pool and join forces with those of others engaged in similar practice, the joining can become a wave of social change that is then aligned through the TVI core to become institutionalized over time. This has broader implications for service users. When professionals are supported and experience less harm from the work they do, they are better able to support their clients and take steps to mitigate the system's harms. Governments that recognize and respect the importance of community leadership and expertise put stable financial resources into place that can withstand election cycles to support ongoing collective work. System change toward the prevention of interpersonal violence becomes possible. Leadership under a TVI approach is found at all ecological levels (figure 4.4.2).

For example, a regional table of Violence Against Women Coordinating Committees (VAWCCs) in southwestern Ontario set a priority in 2017 to become a TVI region. Cross-sector trainings were organized by the local VAWCCs for their community partners to introduce TVI principles and to initiate community discussion about setting local and regional goals as well as next steps. Subsequent "cultural humility" and senior leadership trainings were held to explore the community-level ability to create physically and emotionally safe environments. Building relationships among service organizations through a shared project is a way to strengthen connections and collaboration in the response system that can have direct implications for service users. Connecting the communities through a regional project is a way to put people to work in their home communities on complex problems that are both unique and shared. Anecdotally, a few leaders have suggested that the pre-COVID TVI workshops set an important tone for the community to respond when the pandemic struck.

Engaging multisector service leaders and staff to identify and discuss the powerful forces that reinforce and perpetuate trauma and violence at all levels of society is the first TVIC principle in action. Evaluations of community workshops have shown there is deep appreciation for the time and space given to professionals to think together about the system and how they are impacted on a daily basis. In many of the rooms there was a palpable connection when the topic of moral distress was introduced. Community-level discussion about how to *create physical and emotional safety* as a community sparked deeper considerations about how individuals in the system can anticipate and reduce the harmful impacts of systemic and structural violence for themselves and for others in their immediate environment. Understanding that safety is a relative term that can never be guaranteed, the third principle – to foster *choice, collaboration, and connection as a practice* – is a way to increase safety and reduce isolation, for those seeking service as well as for professionals. In the informal cross-sector relationships, the strength of service coordination became evident through discussion. Groups heard stories about professionals who intentionally connect with peers in other organizations to build relationships that allow them to facilitate "warm referrals" across agencies in the community and, at times, in the region. The workshops provided opportunities to discuss how these relationships can serve as drivers to build bridges across sectors, inspiring the question, how can we do more of what works? Evaluations of the workshops showed high marks for participants being able to meet, connect, and learn about colleagues and other organizations.

Application of the universal principle to act as if everyone has experienced some form of trauma and violence is another important connector between sectors, supported by the fourth principle – *use a strengths-based and capacity-building approach*. The principle becomes practice when professionals "meet people where they are" and acknowledge the value of life experience as the experts in their own lives.[8] This seemingly small, very do-able step amounts to a

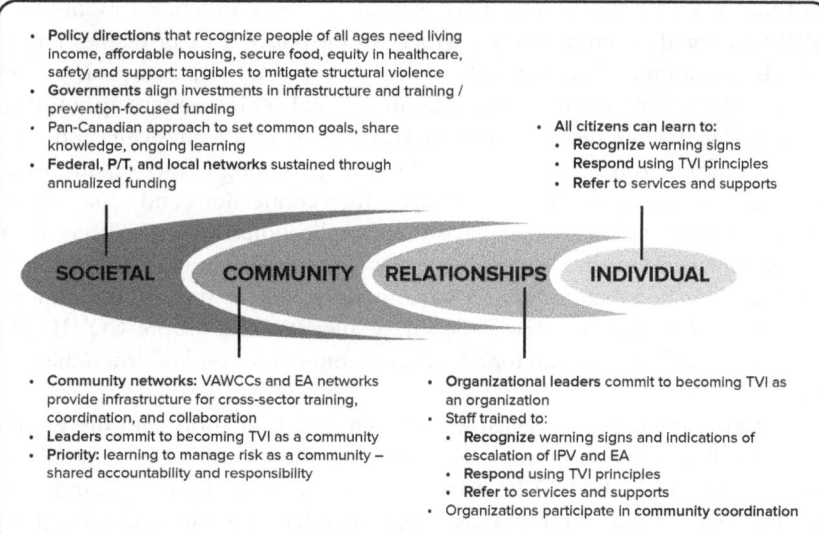

Figure 4.4.2 The ecological framework – a solutions focus. Copyright 2021, the authors, design by M. MacPherson.
P/T = provincial/territorial; VAWCC = violence against women coordinating committee; EA = elder abuse; IPV = intimate partner violence.

fundamental reorientation of the service experience for clients who describe a harmful dichotomy of "us" (who are broken) and "them" (as the experts who can fix). Challenging traditional "us versus them" divides in whatever form they take is a way to acknowledge our common humanity. Implementation of TVI principles challenges the idea that only some people, identified as clients, need help and support with the attending and underlying assumption that people who need help are somehow to blame for their circumstances.

The need to respond to the COVID-19 pandemic pressed the pause button on the initiative; however, by May 2021, there was renewed interest at the regional table to consider how the pre-pandemic workshops may have helped organizations and communities adapt to the crisis. More recent work informed by the lessons of COVID-19 point to the need for more intentional actions that follow from social critique to capitalize on lessons learned from the pandemic and the importance of recognizing ageist attitudes and practices that marginalize older adults within the violence response system as a whole. The initiative is an ongoing voluntary project.

In Alberta, the provincial government is funding an initiative called IMPACT: Domestic and Sexual Violence. IMPACT is a *collective impact* project that brings multisector community partners together under a common goal to achieve primary prevention. IMPACT leaders have reached out and engaged the provincial elder abuse council as a project partner. The initiative stands as an example of what is possible when government partners with community to move the entire violence response system toward prevention. People involved with the project describe a working relationship with civil servants, politicians, academics, and community leaders as respectful and beneficial, with little top-down direction or micro-management from funders. Although it is not explicitly a TVI project, a quick scan of the website indicates that TVI principles are embedded throughout.[9]

Prevention: Where the Rubber Hits the Road

If murder is the final irrevocable act of interpersonal violence that links domestic violence and elder abuse, then learning to prevent the worst possible outcome is a common goal that can unite the sectors and move society toward prevention. Informing violence prevention initiatives with TVI thinking is not yet explicit in practice, so there is a lot of room for innovation and ideas about how to integrate the two.

In both projects described above, important, innovative actions are under way that can elevate the violence response system. Evidence from reviews of domestic homicides reveals a further collective step that has the potential to unify sectors and communities under broad common goals (see figure 4.4.2). The evidence shows that in cases of domestic homicide, the people who are closest to the family are the first to see what is happening but don't know what to do. They are neighbours, friends, family members, and co-workers. The Ontario Domestic Violence Death Review Committee (DVDRC) has recommended broad public education to increase awareness and to teach all Canadians to recognize the warning signs of domestic and family violence, how to respond safely and supportively, and where to find help in the community (Domestic Violence Death Review Committee, 2003).

"Recognize – Respond – Refer" is the learning outcome for the Ontario campaign Neighbours, Friends and Families (NFF), which was developed in response to the 2003 DVDRC recommendation. NFF has since been expanded and is now a series of campaigns that encompass elder abuse (It's Not Right! Neighbours Friends and Families for Older Adults) and workplace domestic violence (Make It Our Business). The NFF campaigns have common learning outcomes for different audiences. Although not explicitly, these campaigns support TVI principles. The enhancement we are suggesting is to make TVI principles explicit in NFF training and in related violence prevention initiatives. This will help create the common language of equity in principle and practice as well as to build capacity to see aligned but still diverse collective action. Individuals and organization leaders can avail themselves of these existing resources to drive dissemination and engagement in their communities.

Workplace domestic violence legislation is another potential lever. All of the organizations in the violence ecosystem are themselves employers with the responsibility to protect their workers from harm. Communities have set a goal to become TVI; similarly, they could prepare their member organizations to protect their workers from domestic violence. Preparing an entire workforce to "recognize, respond, refer" would meet have meaningful implications for the broader community. One manager in a rural manufacturing plant described it this way: "We have 1,000 employees in this small town. If we teach everyone to respond safely and effectively to warning signs of domestic violence, it will have a huge impact on this community. Employers in all sectors are potential community partners in the prevention of domestic violence" (personal communication to M. MacPherson).

Everyone has a role to play. The task for leaders in the violence response ecosystem is to put their good minds together to figure out how to achieve the broad goals of public education and engagement by working together, first to internalize TVIC, in order to lead by example, and then to work to engage others. The project approach discussed above for becoming TVI is a logical extension of a long-term progression.

Conclusion

Society is a system of networks and relationships. Everyone belongs to it and contributes to the whole state, knowingly or not. More "knowing" interventions are needed. Becoming TVI is a process that asks us to contribute first by understanding and reflecting on our stories, behaviours, experiences, biases, privileges, and assumptions and then doing everything in our power to support others through specific strategies focused on safety, collaboration, and person-centred approaches, especially as they involve validating and valuing the strength that individual people, organizations, and even sectors bring to complex challenges like violence prevention and response. Understanding the ways that trauma and violence are perpetuated through systems can help us make conscious choices to work differently – to reduce the harm and to heal.

We cannot consider interventions in the violence response system without first acknowledging how pervasive the impacts of structural violence are for those working within the system. Leadership at the organizational and community levels is needed to invest energy to support ongoing, and safe, TVI learning and development. Embedding TVI principles and practices into the institutional memory of the violence response sector is a shared project that can mitigate the harms experienced by service users and providers. Education on ageism and elder abuse can be included. To prevent violence at any age, we must learn to recognize and manage risk as a community. The trajectory is found in the ecological reversal that grows from a grassroots movement.

Margaret Mead famously referenced the power of a small group to change the world. Organizational leader Leandro Herrero suggests that implicit in Mead's words is the idea that people who are thoughtful and committed to change are also organized. He writes: "Never doubt that a small group of thoughtful, committed, *organized* citizens can change the world; indeed, it's the only thing that ever has" (para. 1). Herrero goes on to contend that passion, commitment and intention are not enough. We need to be organized with a "clear platform" for change (Herrero, 2016).

It is impossible to imagine how such a clear platform could ever be imposed in an individualist top-down society. It only becomes thinkable in a society that grows out from a deep understanding that all people and their unique contributions to the well-being of society are needed if we are to survive this time of great change. It requires a keen understanding at a system level of the impacts of trauma and violence, commitment to creating safety for ourselves and others, taking steps to support meaningful choice and strategic connections, and, ultimately, a strengths-based leap of faith in humanity and enduring resilience. We hope it is possible at the end of this chapter to imagine the journey toward becoming trauma- and violence-informed from wherever you are in the service system and to see your effort as a vital contribution to society.

Imagine the potential when these small groups are connected through equity-based principles, working to prevent all forms of violence across varied and diverse jurisdictions. Social change is much less overwhelming when the responsibility for safety and support is shared. Many who work in the violence response sector already share a big vision: putting themselves out of work. Perhaps through local and regional projects to become trauma- and violence-informed and educating and engaging all Canadians to recognize, respond, and refer, we can finally imagine ourselves as a whole and peaceful society.

NOTES

1 The UN has identified seventeen Sustainable Development Goals and the 2020–30 decade as the time for urgent action to tackle growing poverty, to empower women and girls, and to address the climate emergency. See https://www.un.org/sustainabledevelopment/sustainable-development-goals.
2 "The personal is political" is a political argument that has been used as a rallying cry for the student movement and second-wave feminism since the late 1960s. It underscores the connections between personal experience and broader social and political structures.

3 The Industrial Age is a period of history that encompassed the changes in economic and social organization that began around 1760 in Great Britain and later in other countries, characterized chiefly by the replacement of hand tools with power-driven machines such as the power loom and the steam engine, and by the concentration of industry in large establishments. While it is commonly believed that the Industrial Age was supplanted by the Information Age in the late twentieth century, a view that has become common since the revolutions of 1989, much of the Third World economy is still based on manufacturing. It is thus debatable whether civilization has left the Industrial Age already or is still in it and in the process of reaching the Information Age. Wikipedia.
4 We are focused on sex and age in this chapter but recognize that the intersections of marginalization and discrimination include race, class, ethnicity, ability, sexual orientation, gender, and ability.
5 "Turtles all the way down" is an expression of the problem of infinite regress. The saying alludes to the mythological idea of a World Turtle that supports a flat Earth on its back. It suggests that this turtle rests on the back of an even larger turtle, which itself is part of a column of increasingly large turtles that continues indefinitely. Wikipedia.
6 The Cambridge Dictionary defines paternalism as the practice of controlling, especially employees or citizens, in a way similar to that of a father controlling his children, by giving them what is beneficial but not allowing them responsibility or freedom of choice.
7 According to the 2011 Canadian census, 91.2 per cent of older Canadians live in private households or dwellings.
8 Meeting someone "where they are" means bridging the gap between your own expectations and judgment to appreciate where the other person is coming from, without judgment. It is practised with intentional, honest listening to glimpse the other person's hopes, values, needs, and desires. To "meet them where they are" is a skill everyone can learn.
9 https://impact.sagesse.org

KEY MESSAGES AND IMPLICATIONS

- TVIC Principles are relevant at the sectoral and system levels and can serve as an organizing framework for cross-sectoral collaboration and change.
- Collective, organized action is required to enable and enact change.
- TVIC-based change, linked to cross-sectoral collaboration, will provide better experiences for service users and providers, while also identifying opportunities for both prevention and response.

ADDITIONAL RESOURCES

- Neighbours, Friends & Families: http://neighboursfriendsandfamilies.ca
  o Voisin-es, amis-es et familles: https://voisinsamisetfamilles.ca

- o Kanawayhitowin: http://www.kanawayhitowin.ca
- o NFF – Immigrant and Refugee Communities: https://www.immigrantandrefugeenff.ca
- It's Not Right! Neighbours, Friends & Families for Older Adults: http://itsnotright.ca
- Make It Our Business (workplace domestic violence): http://www.makeitourbusiness.ca

REFERENCES

Brownell, P. (2015). Older women and intimate partner violence. *The Encyclopedia of Adulthood and Aging*, 1–5. https://doi.org/10.1002/9781118521373.wbeaa152

Calasanti, T., Slevin, K., & King, N. (2006). Ageism and feminism: From "et cetera" to center. *NWSA Journal*, 18(1), 13–30. https://doi.org/10.2979/NWS.2006.18.1.13

Canadian Women's Foundation (CWF), Canadian Centre for Policy Alternatives, Ontario Nonprofit Network, & Lahey, K. (2020). Resetting normal: Funding a thriving women's sector. *Canadian Centre for Policy Alternatives*. Retrieved from https://www.policyalternatives.ca

Chomsky, N. (1999). *Profit over people: Neoliberalism and global order*. New York, NY: Seven Stories Press.

Crockett, C., Brandl, B., & Dabby, F.C. (2015). Survivors in the margins: The invisibility of violence against older women. *Journal of Elder Abuse & Neglect*, 27(4–5), 291–302. http://vawnet.org/sites/default/files/assets/files/2016-10/JEAN-Invisibility OlderWomen.pdf

Deleuze, G., & Guattari, F. (1987). *A thousand plateaus: Capitalism and schizophrenia*. Minneapolis, MN: University of Minnesota Press.

Domestic Violence Death Review Committee. (2003). *2002–2003 Annual Report to the Chief Coroner*. Toronto: Office of the Chief Coroner. Retrieved from http://cdhpi.ca/sites/cdhpi.ca/files/2003_Annual_Report_0.pdf

Dong, X.Q. (2015). Elder abuse: Systematic review and implications for practice. *Journal of the American Geriatrics Society*, 63(6), 1214–38. https://doi.org/10.1111/jgs.13454.

Dubinski, K., & Duhatschek, P. (2019, June 11). Ontario's largest women's shelter is struggling to keep up with service demands. *CBC News*. Retrieved from https://www.cbc.ca/news/canada/london/thousands-of-women-turned-away-from-shelter-due-to-lack-of-beds-anova-says-1.5169732

Ellsberg, M., & Heise, L. (2005). *Researching violence against women: A practical guide for researchers and activists*. Washington, DC: World Health Organization, PATH. Retrieved from https://www.who.int/reproductivehealth/publications/violence/9241546476/en

Eppard, L., Rank, M., Bullock, H., Chomsky, N., Giroux H., Brady, D., & Schubert, D. (2020). *Rugged individualism and the misunderstanding of American inequality*. Bethlehem, PA: University Press Copublishing Division, Lehigh University Press.

Graeber, D. (2016). Why capitalism creates pointless jobs. *Evonomics: The Next Evolution of Economics*. Retrieved from https://evonomics.com/why-capitalism-creates-pointless-jobs-david-graeber

Harris, R.M., Wathen, C.N., & Lynch, R. (2014). Assessing performance in shelters for abused women: Can "caring citizenship" be measured in "value for money" accountability regimes? *International Journal of Public Administration, 37*, 737–46. https://doi.org/10.1080/01900692.2014.903273

Health Canada. (2007). *Violence against women: Impact of violence on women's health*. Ottawa: Health Canada.

Heise, L.L. (1998). Violence against women: An integrated, ecological framework. *Violence Against Women, 4*(3), 262–90. https://doi.org/10.1177/1077801298004003002

Herrero, L. (2016, Feb. 19). The missing word in the famous Margaret Mead quote. Retrieved from https://leandroherrero.com/the-missing-word-in-the-famous-margaret-mead-quote

Lao, D. (2020, April 4). Coronavirus: Trudeau announces $40M for women's shelters, $10M for Indigenous women and kids. *Global News*. Retrieved from https://globalnews.ca/news/6778731/coronavirus-womens-indigenous-assault-centres

MacDonald, D. (2018). Born to win: Wealth concentration in Canada since 1999. Canadian Centre for Policy Alternatives. Retrieved from https://www.policyalternatives.ca

MacPherson, M., Reif, K., Titterness, A., & MacQuarrie, B. (2020). Older women and domestic homicide. In P. Jaffe, K. Scott, & A. Straatman (Eds.), *Preventing domestic homicides: Lessons learned from tragedies* (pp. 15–37). Cambridge, UK: Elsevier Academic Press.

McGarry, J., Simpson, C., & Hinchliff-Smith, K. (2017). Older women, domestic violence and mental health: A consideration of the particular issues for health and healthcare practice. *Journal of Clinical Nursing, 26*(15–16), 2177–91. https://doi.org/10.1111/jocn.13490

McKenzie, H. (2015). The long shadow of Mike Harris. Canadian Centre for Policy Alternatives Ontario Office, *OnPolicy, 12*. Retrieved from https://www.policyalternatives.ca

Meadows, D. (2008). *Thinking in systems: A primer*. White River Junction: Chelsea Green Publishing.

Middleton-Moz, J. (1999). *Boiling point: The high cost of unhealthy anger to individuals and society*. Deerfield Beach, FL: Health Communications Inc.

Moore, M., Yeatman, H., & Davey, R. (2015). Which nanny – the state or industry? Wowsers, teetotallers, and the fun police in public health advocacy. *Public Health, 129*(8), 1030–7. https://doi.org/10.1016/j.puhe.2015.01.031

Nägele, B., Böhm, U., Görgen, T., & Tóth, O. (2010). *Intimate partner violence against older women – Summary report*. Daphne Project. Retrieved from https://www.ipvow.org/media/reports/summary_report_final.pdf

National Institute for the Care of the Elderly (NICE). (2015). *Into the light: National survey on the mistreatment of older adults*. Retrieved from https://cnpea.ca/images/canada-report-june-7-2016-pre-study-lynnmcdonald.pdf

Pathak, N., Dhairyawan, R., & Tariq, S. (2019). The experience of domestic violence among older women: A narrative review. *Maturitas, 121*, 63–75. https://doi.org/10.1016/j.maturitas.2018.12.011.

Senge, P. (2017, Jan. 12). There are no heroes: Peter Senge on system leadership. *MIT Leadership Centre*. Retrieved from https://yourlearningresource.wordpress.com/2017/09/24/there-are-no-heroes-peter-senge-on-system-leadership

Senge, P., Scharmer, O., Jaworski, J., & Flowers, B.S. (2004). *Presence: An exploration of profound change in people, organizations, and society*. New York, NY: Random House.

Statistics Canada. (2011). *Census*. Retrieved from https://www12.statcan.gc.ca/census-recensement/2011/as-sa/98-312-x/98-312-x2011003_4-eng.cfm

Stroh, D. (2015). *Systems thinking for social change: A practical guide to solving complex problems, avoiding unintended consequences and achieving lasting results*. White River Junction: Chelsea Publishing.

United Nations. (2020). *Policy brief: The impact of COVID-19 on women*. Retrieved from policy_brief_on_covid_impact_on_women_9_apr_2020_updated.pdf (un.org)

United Nations DESA [UN DESA]. (2013). *Neglect, abuse, and violence against older women*. Retrieved from https://www.un.org/esa/socdev/documents/ageing/neglect-abuse-violence-older-women.pdf

Vara-Horna, A.A. (n.d.). *The costs of intimate partner violence against women to business in Colombia and Mexico: South–south cooperation from Peru to develop scientific competencies in the measurement of the costs of violence against women*. Peru: San Martin de Porres University (USMP).

Varcoe, C., Pauly, B., Webster, G., & Storch, J. (2012). Moral distress: tensions as springboards for action. *HEC forum: An Interdisciplinary Journal on Hospitals' Ethical and Legal Issues, 24*(1), 51–62. https://doi.org/10.1007/s10730-012-9180-2

Violence Against Women and Girls [VAWG]. (2016). *Brief on violence against older women*. Retrieved from https://www.un.org/esa/socdev/documents/ageing/vawg_brief_on_older_women.pdf

Warmling, D., Lindner, S., & Coelho, E. (2017). Intimate partner violence prevalence in the elderly and associated factors: Systematic review. *Ciencia & Saude Coletiva, 22*(9), 3111. doi:10.1590/1413-81232017229.12312017.

Wilkinson, R., & Pickett, K. (2009). *The spirit level. Why greater equality makes societies stronger*. New York, NY: Bloomsbury Press.

World Health Organization. (2021). The ecological framework. *Violence Prevention Alliance*. Retrieved from https://www.who.int/violenceprevention/approach/ecology/en

4.5 But Does It Work? Evaluating T(V)IC Initiatives

NADINE WATHEN, JENNIFER MACGREGOR, AND BRENNA SCHMITT

This chapter reviews strategies and measurement tools used to evaluate TVIC initiatives, including individual training and education and organizational uptake and implementation. Since TVIC as articulated in this volume is a relatively new construct, we draw on existing literature on trauma-informed care/practice (TIC/P) and summarize relevant approaches from completed and ongoing evaluation activities among the initiatives reviewed in previous sections (collectively, T(V)IC). By the end of this chapter, the reader will understand the state of evidence in this area, with a focus on considerations for those wanting to assess the impact of TVIC on individuals and on organizational practices and policies.

Intervention Research in T(V)IC

Trauma-informed interventions generally involve at least one of three elements: (1) workforce development (e.g., staff training on the impacts of trauma), (2) practice change (e.g., tailoring care to client needs; implementing vicarious trauma mitigation strategies), and (3) organizational change (e.g., adjusting physical environments, integrating trauma-informed policies and procedures) (Avery et al., 2020; Hanson & Lang, 2016). Although often considered alongside trauma-informed approaches (e.g., Fondren, Lawson, Speidel, McDonnell, & Valentino, 2020), interventions focused solely on trauma screening, assessment, or treatment (i.e., "trauma-specific" services) will not be discussed here.

Most T(V)IC intervention research to date assesses how staff/providers are assessed in relation to trauma-informed strategies. Purtle (2020) reviewed twenty-three research articles of this kind, set in a variety of contexts – child welfare, psychiatric hospitals, medical settings (e.g., emergency departments), a juvenile justice facility, and a school – and identified common topics in the trainings (which ranged in duration from one hour to multiple days), such as the effects of trauma, how to avoid retraumatizing clients, and strategies for staff self-care.

Most of the studies in Purtle's (2020) review used single-group, before/after designs to evaluate impacts on staff knowledge, attitudes, and behaviour/behavioural intent, and most found at least one significant improvement post-training. No two studies used the same instrument to measure these outcomes. Longer trainings generally had larger effect sizes, and a number of studies found that improvements were maintained over time. Significant improvements were also found for related outcomes, including staff safety, self-reported trauma-informed practices, and frequency of trauma screening. Fewer than half the studies measured client outcomes (i.e., using administrative data or directly from clients); that said, significant improvements were found by some studies. For example, one study reported reduced use of seclusion and restraint in a psychiatric hospital setting two years after a TIC intervention. Of the two studies examining patient perceptions of care, one study found improvements, and one did not.

Some of the interventions in Purtle's (2020) review had additional components beyond training, such as changes to the physical environment, wellness programs to promote staff self-care, and checklists to encourage trauma-informed practice. Indeed, as articulated in previous chapters, successful T(V)IC implementation requires integration of individual education and support, leadership buy-in, structural and policy changes, and resourcing. Unfortunately, other than Purtle (2020), reviews useful for making recommendations regarding T(V)IC interventions are difficult to find. For example, Avery and colleagues (2020) reviewed four school-wide trauma-informed interventions that each involved the three elements described above. However, limitations of the studies prevented the authors from drawing clear and generalizable conclusions.

There are significant gaps in the evidence regarding the effectiveness (in any element) of T(V)IC interventions, and the optimal strategies for implementing trauma-informed education in various settings remain unclear (Purtle, 2020; Wheeler & Phillips, 2019). To be maximally effective, trauma-informed approaches must be integrated into systems (e.g., to ensure buy-in and funding) and linked to "wraparound" services and collaboration across sectors and organizations (Avery et al., 2020; McKenna & Holtfreter, 2020). Related to this, more research is needed on T(V)IC interventions in education (e.g., Avery et al., 2020; Rodger et al., 2020; see chapter 2.4) and criminal justice settings (Branson, Baetz, Horwitz, & Hoagwood, 2017; McKenna & Holtfreter, 2020).

Several other points specific to T(V)IC intervention research are worth noting. First, a common barrier to evaluation in this area is the lack of consensus regarding what a "trauma-informed" approach actually is. A number of authors have suggested that a unified concept or "common lexicon" of T(V)IC would improve measurement, facilitate appropriate research synthesis, and provide a better foundation for making evidence-informed decisions (Donisch, Bray, & Gewirtz, 2016; Hanson & Lang, 2016). Second, for progress in this area to be truly trauma-informed, service users and staff at various levels must be meaningfully involved throughout evaluation processes (Browne et al., 2018; Roche et al., 2020).

More broadly, the evidence base for T(V)IC interventions suffers from many of the same gaps as are present in other areas of research and evaluation. For example, stronger research designs with outcomes measured longitudinally and with validated instruments are needed, and so are studies examining the extent to which T(V)IC interventions actually improve the lives of service users (Avery et al., 2020; Purtle, 2020). Other familiar gaps include the present lack of understanding of barriers to and facilitators of implementation in different contexts. Ideally, there should be tailored interventions in diverse samples of service users, providers, and organizations (Avery et al., 2020; Champine, Lang, Nelson, Hanson, & Tebes, 2019).

Measurement Considerations

Drawing on the results of a scoping review conducted by the authors, this section describes established tools for measuring T(V)IC (including vicarious trauma), their use, how existing tools map onto the principles of TVIC, instrumentation gaps, and recommendations for improving TVIC measurement. The intent is to provide a guide and outline practical considerations for those looking to assess the uptake and impact of TVIC in their own context.

Measurement of T(V)IC is an emerging area of study (Champine et al., 2019). Related constructs (e.g., shared decision-making, patient-centred care) have been examined in more depth, but we are aware of no review of measures for TVIC as it is defined in this handbook. So we have conducted a systematic scoping review of measures with the goal of (1) describing existing validated measures and (2) mapping the measures according to the principles of TVIC as we articulate them (Wathen, Schmitt, & MacGregor, 2021). The thirteen T(V)IC measures that met our inclusion criteria are briefly described in table 4.5.1.[1]

All were validated in US-based samples that generally lacked gender and/or ethnic diversity. Validation samples were from various sectors, including child welfare, education, health care, law enforcement, human services, and domestic violence services. The measures varied in length from 10 to 100 items, and most were published in 2016 or later. Most had not been used much or at all in subsequent published research, with the exception of the ARTIC (Baker, Brown, Wilcox, Overstreet, & Arora, 2016).

Most measures we reviewed were designed to be completed by service providers rather than service users. Some had different versions depending on context. For example, the ARTIC (Baker et al., 2016) has education and human services/health care versions. The measures assessed a variety of constructs related to T(V)IC. Two that we reviewed were focused on vicarious trauma (Hallinan et al., 2019; Sprang, Ross, Miller, Blackshear, & Ascienzo, 2016) but explicitly measured it from the perspective of trauma-informed organizations. Similarly, one measure assessed trauma-informed self-care practices (Salloum, Choi, & Stover, 2018).

Table 4.5.1 Trauma- (and violence-) informed measures

Name (author, yr)	Description	Strengths	Weaknesses
ARTIC scale (Baker et al., 2016)	• 45, 35, or 10* items measuring central components of attitudes supportive of TIC implementation	• More validated and used in subsequent research than other measures • Different versions for use in human service/health care vs education sectors • Short-form available	• Purchase required • Measures mostly principles 1 and 2
TICOMETER (Bassuk et al., 2017)	• 35 items measuring the level of TIC in health and human service organizations	• Some items across all 4 principles (but did not have access to all items)	• Author permission required • Has not been used for data collection in subsequent research
CPC (Clark et al., 2008)	• 26 items measuring consumer's perceptions of care and satisfaction with services for co-occurring disorders and/or trauma-related disorders	• Some items across all 4 principles • Available in published journal article (may require article purchase) • Used for data collection in subsequent research	• May not be useful in other contexts
TIP Scales (Goodman et al., 2016)	• 20* items measuring the extent to which survivors perceive DV programs to be trauma-informed; 2 supplemental scales	• Some items across all 4 principles • English and Spanish versions • Available in published journal article (may require article purchase) • Used for data collection in subsequent research	• May not be useful in other contexts
VT-ORG (Hallinan et al., 2019)	• 63* items measuring employee perceptions of whether an organization is vicarious trauma-informed	• 4 versions: law enforcement, fire services, emergency medical services, and victim services • All versions freely available (in public domain)	• Measures mostly principles 1 and 2; many items do not map to any principle • Has not been used for data collection in subsequent research

(Continued)

Table 4.5.1 Trauma- (and violence-) informed measures (*Continued*)

Name (author, yr)	Description	Strengths	Weaknesses
Knowledge, Attitudes, and Practices of Trauma-Informed Practice Survey (King et al., 2019)	• 21 items measuring knowledge, attitudes, and practices re: TIC among health care professionals within health care setting	• Some items across all 4 principles • Over half the items measure principle 1 • Available in published journal article (open access)	• Few items for principles 2–4 • Has not been used for data collection in subsequent research
TSRT (Chadwick Center for Children and Families, 2013; Lang et al., 2016)	• 100 items* measuring child welfare workers' perceptions of agency/agency staff understanding of and capacity to use TIP	• Some items across all 4 principles • Used for data collection in subsequent research • Original version freely available online from CTISP (see Additional Resources); revised version available from Lang et al. (2016) by request • Short form available from Connell et al. (2019) by request	• Many items do not map to any principle • May not be useful in other contexts
Child Welfare Trauma-Informed Assessment Tool (Madden et al., 2017)	• 11 items measuring the use of TIC among frontline child welfare service providers	• Available in published journal article (may require article purchase)	• Measures mostly principles 1 and 2 • Has not been used for data collection in subsequent studies
TISCI (2nd ed.) (Richardson et al., 2010, 2012)	• 18 items measuring extent to which child welfare systems function in a trauma-informed manner; designed for measuring change from training initiatives	• Used for data collection in subsequent research • Available from authors by request	• Measures mostly principles 1, 2, and 3

(*Continued*)

Table 4.5.1 Trauma- (and violence-) informed measures (*Continued*)

Name (author, yr)	Description	Strengths	Weaknesses
TISC-R (Salloum et al., 2018)	• 10 items measuring trauma-informed self-care practices used by professionals	• Available in published journal article (may require article purchase) • Used for data collection in a subsequent study	• Measures principle 1 and 2 only
STSI-OA (Sprang et al., 2016)	• 40 items measuring the extent to which an organization is STS-informed and responds to the impacts of STS in an organization	• Freely available (in public domain)	• Measures mostly principle 2 • Has not been used for data collection in subsequent research
Measure of TIC Foundational Knowledge (Sundborg 2019)	• 30 items measuring foundational knowledge related to TIC	• Available in published journal article (may require article purchase)	• Only measures principle 1 • Has not been used for data collection in subsequent research
TIAA THRIVE (2011)	• 35–42* items measuring children's behavioural health agency performance related to TIP for the purpose of informing change efforts and benefiting the overall system for youth and families	• 3 versions: Agency, Youth, and Family • Some items for all 4 principles (but mostly 2 and 3; varies by version) • Freely available (in public domain)	• Has not been used for data collection in subsequent research

Note: ARTIC = attitudes related to trauma-informed care; CPC = consumer perceptions of care; DV = domestic violence; STS = secondary traumatic stress; STSI-OA = secondary traumatic stress informed organizational assessment; TIAA = system of care trauma-informed agency assessment; TIC = trauma-informed care; TICS = trauma-informed climate scale; TIP = trauma-informed practice; TISC = trauma-informed self-care; TISCI = trauma-informed system change instrument; TSRT = trauma system readiness tool; VT-ORG = vicarious trauma organizational readiness guide

* Number of items varies by version or whether supplemental scales are used. Adapted from Wathen et al., 2021 © the authors.

Two measures were used to examine client perceptions of care (Clark et al., 2008; Goodman et al., 2016); otherwise, they assessed capacity to implement T(V)IC (Baker et al., 2016; Lang, Campbell, Shanley, Crusto, & Connell, 2016), T(V)IC practice (Bassuk, Unick, Paquette, & Richard, 2017; Richardson, Coryn, Henry, Black-Pond, & Unrau, 2012; THRIVE, 2011), T(V)IC knowledge only (Sundborg, 2019), or a combination of knowledge, attitudes, and/or practice (King, Kuan-Lang, & Chokshi, 2019; Madden, Scannapieco, Killian, & Adorno, 2017).

Our review involved a unique process to help us understand how well each of the core constructs included in our conceptualization of TVIC is covered across available measures. To this end, we mapped all items in each of the identified measures to our four TVIC principles. Principle 1 (understand trauma and violence, including structural and interpersonal violence, and its impacts on people's lives and behaviour) and principle 2 (create emotionally and physically safe environments for all clients and providers) were by far most commonly represented among the 499 items coded. Although principle 1 was most commonly addressed, the extent to which structural violence was addressed was minimal, and no items measured implicit bias.

Overall, and consistent with Champine and colleagues (2019), we suggest that researchers and providers "build upon, adapt, and study" (p. 433) existing measures when possible and appropriate, rather than developing new ones. This was the approach taken by Rodger and colleagues (see chapter 2.4; Rodger et al., 2020), who evaluated the impact of TVIC education among teacher candidates using the education version of the ARTIC (Baker et al., 2016), augmented with questions from the Equity-Oriented Health Care Scale (EHoCS) developed to assess TVIC and related concepts in the EQUIP Primary Health Care research program (Browne et al., 2015; Ford-Gilboe et al., 2018). However, this may not be feasible for all, given that some measures we reviewed require purchase and place limits on their use and reporting (see table 4.5.1). Moreover, our "mapping" of the measures by the TVIC principles revealed large gaps when it came to principles 3 (foster opportunities for choice, collaboration, and connection) and 4 (use a strengths-based and capacity-building approach to support clients) and provider implicit bias (see chapter 1.3). Items getting at structural issues such as the social determinants of health, racism, stigma, and discrimination (i.e., the "V" in TVIC; see chapter 1.2) were also noticeably scarce. Clearly, then, the most urgent area for future research is the development and validation of a measure that comprehensively includes all aspects of TVIC, including a focus on structural competence and implicit bias.

Case Example – The Impact of TVIC Educational Workshops

This section describes the evaluation of a set of "basic" or introductory TVIC workshops provided to health and social service providers in various settings with the aim of demonstrating how these kinds of evaluations can be implemented, as well as providing empirical support for the use of TVIC education to effect practice change. The workshops were facilitated by members of the Gender, Trauma, and Violence Knowledge Incubator (GTV Incubator; https://gtvincubator.uwo.ca/), a university/community partnership to enhance TVIC practice and research. Details of the workshops and the evaluation are provided in box 4.5.1. A full description of the workshop evaluation method and results is available elsewhere (Wathen, MacGregor, & Beyrem, 2021).

BOX 4.5.1 CASE EXAMPLE – THE IMPACT OF TVIC EDUCATIONAL WORKSHOPS

Workshops

- Content based on theoretical, empirical, and experiential knowledge from the EQUIP research program (see chapter 2.1) and expertise of GTV Incubator members.
- Half- to full-day sessions conducted from 2017 to 2019, covering:
    1. "Trauma 101": the prevalence and impact of trauma across the lifespan, focusing on complex and chronic forms such as interpersonal violence, and health outcomes.
    2. "What the 'V' Adds – Structural Violence": applying an explicit equity and social justice lens, helping people make the shift from "what's wrong in the person's head" to "what's happened, and is still happening, to this person."
    3. "Principles and Strategies": the four TVIC principles (see chapter 1.5).

A video of an example workshop is available at https://equiphealthcare.ca/tvic-workshop

Evaluation

- Purpose: to assess the longer-term impact of the workshops on individual knowledge and practices and on organizational strategies.
- Method: a mixed-method study with sixty-seven online survey participants (late 2019) and seven semi-structured interviews (late 2019–early 2020).
- Analysis: survey data analysed descriptively, content analysis used for interview transcripts to identify key themes, with focus on impacts, barriers, and facilitators at individual and organizational levels.
- Participants: most survey participants and interviewees had six or more years of experience in their organization (or a similar one); most worked in a community or social services organization or in primary health care, public health, education, etc.

We found that most survey participants indicated that the workshop had an impact on how they think about their practice. The most common area of change was in their views regarding the links among violence, trauma, behaviour, pain, and substance use. Also, all interviewees reported increased knowledge and/or awareness. For example, a few had "ah ha!" moments when they suddenly understood something better. Others said that the workshop helped "reinforce" or "enhance" knowledge they already had, or that it "planted a seed" for further understanding.

More than half of survey participants indicated their practice had changed in at least one of five ways. The most common related to how they now spoke with people initially and/or through the care process. Interviewees also reported various tangible changes related to interacting with people, including improvements in communication (verbal and non-verbal, e.g., avoiding jargon and "starting a conversation with a smile") and in how they completed referrals or documentation (e.g., taking better notes so that individuals wouldn't need to repeatedly describe a traumatic experience). Other changes included treating people like individuals or "human beings" rather than like "patients"; focusing on the quality of care and how things are done rather than on numbers and assessments; and improved relationships between staff and service users. Most interviewees noted that understanding TVIC leads to better care, for example: "It cannot do any harm. It can only prevent harm. So, it's a win–win situation."

More than half the survey participants reported at least one type of organizational change. The most common was new well-being supports for staff who experience vicarious trauma or related distress due to their work. Supporting this, interviewees reported changes to the physical environment, inclusion of TVIC in clinical curriculum, being more understanding of or taking responsibility for "no-shows," and attempting to make TVIC an ongoing topic of discussion among staff. Much like the survey participants, interviewees also reported improvements related to vicarious trauma or more generally the supportiveness of their workplace. For example, one interviewee noted that staff were more likely to check in with one another in a more thorough way. Notably, all but one interviewee mentioned challenges related to implementing organizational change – for example, a lack of resources or support from leadership.

Overall, the survey participants reported being quite committed to becoming trauma- and violence-informed, and most were very interested in receiving follow-up TVIC education. Consistent with these findings, all interviewees discussed how TVIC education should be foundational for anyone working in health or social services.

Lessons Learned: Evaluating TVIC in Your Organization and/or Practice

A key finding from existing reviews of T(V)IC intervention studies, and our own evaluation of TVIC workshops, indicates that this kind of education is an important first step, for both individuals and organizations, in embedding core concepts about trauma and violence and their impacts. Achieving principle 1 (knowledge and understanding) requires a foundation in these basics. Some research, including ours, shows that this new knowledge can shift attitudes and has the potential to change practices; however this latter outcome – actual behaviour change among individuals and in organizations, linked to changes in client outcomes – is less well-established.

Educational efforts, however, need to focus explicitly on aspects of systemic violence and structural competence, not just the individual experiences and impacts of trauma. In our reviews of both interventions and measures, we found that supporting a shift from "what's wrong in the person's head" to "what's happened and is still happening in their lives" is where the most impact can be had but where the least effort is currently placed. In the dozens of workshops we and our colleagues have conducted, we have found that the most important "ah ha" moments happen when learners are encouraged to see how individual experiences, social/system expectations, and structural conditions are all linked. For example, we found that knowledge about the intersections of trauma and violence, pain, and substance use (see chapter 3.2) was the most commonly reported new learning among participants (Wathen et al. 2021), a finding also reported by Levine, Varcoe, & Browne (2020).

High-profile instances of discrimination in Canadian health care settings have led to an emphasis on the impacts of stigma and implicit bias on the health of individuals and communities (Chief Public Health Officer of Canada, 2019; chapter 1.3). These issues underpin recent discourse and growing public awareness regarding, for example, systemic racism in health care and how this impacts individual interactions; they also situate the organization and the broader system (including health provider education) as part of the problem, and the solution. However, in our review of existing T(V)IC measures (Wathen et al., 2021), few explicitly included these issues. While some interventions with a T(V)IC focus include these forms of systemic violence (Varcoe et al., 2019; Browne et al., 2015), most do not (Purtle, 2020). Integrating this structural lens into T(V)IC intervention and measurement work is therefore a key priority in research and practice. However, these processes must themselves be embedded thoughtfully and in a trauma- and violence-informed way – intervening and measuring without contextualizing can do more harm than good (Varcoe et al., 2009).

Conclusion

Those seeking to implement TVIC in their own practice and/or organization can begin with educational interventions that emphasize the prevalence, causes, and consequences of trauma and violence among individuals, and in society. Emphasizing the structural aspects can shift thinking; indeed, emerging evidence shows that this can be a precursor to shifts in action, which, when implemented consistently and in a person-centred way, may be linked to improved health outcomes (Ford-Gilboe et al., 2018; Wathen & Mantler, 2022). However, education is necessary but not sufficient; additional intervention components are required to support sustained individual and organizational practice change (Varcoe et al., 2019). New measures are being created to more holistically capture the range of concepts we have constructed as "TVIC" (Rodger et al., 2020), but additional work in this area, and ongoing evaluation of new TVIC interventions, are required.

NOTE

1 We are aware of one new measure developed since completing our review, the Organizational Trauma-Informed Practices tool (O-TIPS; Manian, Rog, Lieberman, & Kerr, 2022).

KEY MESSAGES AND IMPLICATIONS

- Research supports T(V)IC education for staff/providers to improve their knowledge and attitudes. Some studies evaluating TVIC show a link to actual practice changes and improved health outcomes, but more research is needed.
- While education is necessary, it is not sufficient. True practice change requires various intervention components and a commitment to organizational change, supported by appropriate resources.
- Integrating a structural lens, especially a focus on stigma and implicit bias, into TV(I)C intervention and measurement work is a key priority in research, measurement and practice.
- Most available measures of T(V)IC require further validation, especially with diverse samples. While some T(V)IC principles are adequately represented in the measures, others are not. A measure that comprehensively assesses all aspects of TVIC is needed.

ADDITIONAL RESOURCES

- Measuring Trauma- (and Violence-) Informed Care: Summary of a Scoping Review. (infographic): http://gtvincubator.uwo.ca/resources
- System of Care Trauma-informed Agency Assessment (Thrive Initiative, 2011): https://www.maine.gov/dhhs/ocfs/cbhs/webinars/documents/SOC-TIAA-Agency.pdf
- System of Care Trauma-informed Agency Assessment: Family Version (Thrive Initiative, 2011): https://www.maine.gov/dhhs/ocfs/cbhs/webinars/documents/SOC-TIAA-Family.pdf

- System of Care Trauma-informed Agency Assessment: Youth Version (Thrive Initiative, 2011): https://www.maine.gov/dhhs/ocfs/cbhs/webinars/documents/SOC-TIAA-Youth.pdf
- Secondary Traumatic Stress-Informed Organizational Assessment (University of Kentucky, Center on Trauma & Children, n.d.): https://www.uky.edu/ctac/stsioa
- Trauma System Readiness Tool (Chadwick Center for Children and Families, 2013): https://ctisp.wordpress.com
- Vicarious Trauma – Organizational Readiness Guide (US Department of Justice, Office for Victims of Crime, n.d.): https://ovc.ojp.gov/program/vtt/what-is-the-vt-org

REFERENCES

Avery, J.C., Morris, H., Galvin, E., Misso, M., Savaglio, M., & Skouteris, H. (2020). Systematic review of school-wide trauma-informed approaches. *Journal of Child & Adolescent Trauma*, 1–17. https://doi.org/10.1007/s40653-020-00321-1

Baker, C.N., Brown, S.M., Wilcox, P.D., Overstreet, S., & Arora, P. (2016). Development and psychometric evaluation of the Attitudes Related to Trauma-Informed Care (ARTIC) Scale. *School Mental Health*, 8(1), 61–76. http://dx.doi.org/10.1007%2Fs12310-015-9161-0

Bassuk, E.L., Unick, G.J., Paquette, K., & Richard, M.K. (2017). Developing an instrument to measure organizational trauma-informed care in human services: The TICOMETER. *Psychology of Violence*, 7(1), 150–7. https://psycnet.apa.org/doi/10.1037/vio0000030

Branson, C.E., Baetz, C.L., Horwitz, S.M., & Hoagwood, K.E. (2017). Trauma-informed juvenile justice systems: A systematic review of definitions and core components. *Psychological Trauma: Theory, Research, Practice, and Policy*, 9(6), 635–46. https://doi.org/10.1037/tra0000255

Browne, A.J., Varcoe, C.M., Ford-Gilboe, M., & Wathen, C.N., on behalf of the EQUIP Team. (2015). EQUIP Healthcare: An overview of a multi-component intervention to enhance equity-oriented care in primary health care settings. *International Journal for Equity in Health*, 14, 152. doi:10.1186/s12939-015-0271-y

Browne, A.J., Varcoe, C., Ford-Gilboe, M., Wathen, C.N., Smye, V., Jackson, B.E., ... Blanchet Garneau, A. (2018). Disruption as opportunity: Impacts of an organizational health equity intervention in primary care clinics. *International Journal for Equity in Health*, 17, 154. https://doi.org/10.1186/s12939-018-0820-2

Chadwick Center for Children and Families. (2013). Trauma System Readiness Tool [PDF file]. Retrieved from https://ctisp.wordpress.com

Champine, R.B., Lang, J.M., Nelson, A.M., Hanson, R.F., & Tebes, J.K. (2019). Systems measures of a trauma-informed approach: A systematic review. *American Journal of Community Psychology*, 64(3–4), 418–37. https://doi.org/10.1002/ajcp.12388

Chief Public Health Officer of Canada. (2019). *Report on the state of public health in Canada 2019: Addressing stigma: Towards a more inclusive health system*. Ottawa,

Canada: Public Health Agency of Canada. Retrieved from https://www.canada.ca/en/public-health/corporate/publications/chief-public-health-officer-reports-state-public-health-canada/addressing-stigma-toward-more-inclusive-health-system.html. Accessed 24 September 2020.

Clark, C., Young, M.S., Jackson, E., Graeber, C., Mazelis, R., Kammerer, N., & Huntington, N. (2008). Consumer perceptions of integrated trauma-informed services among women with co-occurring disorders. *The Journal of Behavioural Health Services & Research*, 35(1), 71–90. https://doi.org/10.1007/s11414-007-9076-0

Connell, C.M., Lang, J.M., Zorba, B., & Stevens, K. (2019). Enhancing capacity for trauma-informed care in child welfare: Impact of a statewide systems change initiative. *American Journal of Community Psychology*, 64(3–4), 467–80. https://doi.org/10.1002/ajcp.12375

Donisch, K., Bray, C., & Gewirtz, A. (2016). Child welfare, juvenile justice, mental health, and education providers' conceptualizations of trauma-informed practice. *Child Maltreatment*, 21(2), 125–34. https://doi.org/10.1177%2F1077559516633304

Fondren, K., Lawson, M., Speidel, R., McDonnell, C.G., & Valentino, K. (2020). Buffering the effects of childhood trauma within the school setting: A systematic review of trauma-informed and trauma-responsive interventions among trauma-affected youth. *Children and Youth Services Review*, 109(1). https://doi.org/10.1016/j.childyouth.2019.104691

Ford-Gilboe, M., Wathen, C.N., Varcoe, C., Herbert, C., Jackson, B.E., Lavoie, J.G., ... Browne, A.J. (2018). How equity-oriented care affects health: Key mechanisms and implications for primary care practice and policy. *The Milbank Quarterly*, 96(4), 635–71. https://doi.org/10.1111/1468-0009.12349

Goodman, L.A., Sullivan, C.M., Serrata, J., Perilla, J., Wilson, J.M., Fauci, J.E., & DiGiovanni, C.D. (2016). Development and validation of the trauma-informed practice scales. *Journal of Community Psychology*, 44(6), 747–64. https://doi.org/10.1002/jcop.21799

Hallinan, S., Shiyko, M.P., Volpe, R., & Molnar, B.E. (2019). Reliability and validity of the Vicarious Trauma Organizational Readiness Guide (VT-ORG). *American Journal of Community Psychology*, 64, 481–93. https://doi.org/10.1002/ajcp.12395

Hanson, R.F., & Lang, J. (2016). A critical look at trauma-informed care among agencies and systems serving maltreated youth and their families. *Child Maltreatment*, 21(2), 95–100. https://doi.org/10.1177%2F1077559516635274

King, S., Kuan-Lang, D.C., & Chokshi, B. (2019). Becoming trauma informed: Validating a tool to assess health professional's knowledge, attitude, and practice. *Pediatric Quality and Safety*, 4(5). https://doi.org/10.1097%2Fpq9.0000000000000215

Lang, J.M., Campbell, K., Shanley, P., Crusto, C.A., & Connell, C.M. (2016). Building capacity for trauma-informed care in the child welfare system: Initial results of a statewide implementation. *Child Maltreatment*, 21(2), 113–24. https://doi.org/10.1177%2F1077559516635273

Levine, S., Varcoe, C., & Browne, A.J. (2020). "We went as a team closer to the truth": Impacts of interprofessional education on trauma- and violence-informed care for staff in primary care settings, *Journal of Interprofessional Care*. Retrieved from https://www.tandfonline.com/doi/full/10.1080/13561820.2019.1708871

Madden, E.E., Scannapieco, M., Killian, M.O., & Adorno, G. (2017). Exploratory factor analysis and reliability of the Child Welfare Trauma-Informed Individual Assessment Tool. *Journal of Public Child Welfare*, 11(1), 58–72. https://doi.org/10.1080/15548732.2016.1231653

Manian, N., Rog, D.J., Lieberman, L., & Kerr, E.M. (2022). The Organizational Trauma-Informed Practices tool (O-TIPS): Development and preliminary validation. *Journal of Community Psychology*, 50(1), 515–40. https://doi.org/10.1002/jcop.22628

McKenna, N.C., & Holtfreter, K. (2020). Trauma-informed courts: A review and integration of justice perspectives and gender responsiveness. *Journal of Aggression, Maltreatment & Trauma*, 1–21. https://doi.org/10.1080/10926771.2020.1747128

Purtle, J. (2020). Systematic review of evaluations of trauma-informed organizational interventions that include staff trainings. *Trauma, Violence, & Abuse*, 21(4), 725–40. https://doi.org/10.1177%2F1524838018791304

Richardson, M.M., Coryn, C.L.S., Henry, J., Black-Pond, C., & Unrau, Y. (2012). Development and evaluation of the Trauma-Informed System Change Instrument: Factorial validity and implications for use. *Child and Adolescent Social Work Journal*, 29(3), 167–84. https://doi.org/10.1007/s10560-012-0259-z

Richardson, M.M., Coryn, C.L.S., Henry, J., Black-Pond, C., & Unrau, Y. (2010). Trauma Informed System Change Instrument (TISCI, 2nd Ed.). Southwest Michigan Children's Trauma Assessment Centre.

Roche, P., Shimmin, C., Hickes, S., Khan, M., Sherzoi, O., Wicklund, E., ... Sibley, K.M. (2020). Valuing All Voices: Refining a trauma-informed, intersectional, and critical reflexive framework for patient engagement in health research using a qualitative descriptive approach. *Research Involvement and Engagement*, 6(1), 42. https://doi.org/10.1186/s40900-020-00217-2

Rodger, S., Bird, R., Hibbert, K., Johnson, A.M., Specht, J., & Wathen, C.N. (2020). Initial teacher education and trauma and violence informed care in the classroom: Preliminary results from an online teacher education course. *Psychology in the Schools*, 57(12), 1798–814. https://doi.org/10.1002/pits.22373

Salloum, A., Choi, M. J., & Stover, C. (2018). Development of a trauma-informed self-care measure with child welfare workers. *Children and Youth Services Review*, 93, 108–16. https://doi.org/10.1016/j.childyouth.2018.07.008

Sprang, G., Ross, L., Miller, B.C., Blackshear, K., & Ascienzo, S. (2016). Psychometric properties of the Secondary Traumatic Stress-Informed Organizational Assessment. *Traumatology*, 23(2), 165–71. https://psycnet.apa.org/doi/10.1037/trm0000108

Sundborg, S.A. (2019). Knowledge, principal support, self-efficacy, and beliefs predict commitment to trauma-informed care. *Psychological Trauma: Theory, Research, Practice and Policy*, 11(2), 224–31. https://psycnet.apa.org/doi/10.1037/tra0000411

THRIVE. (2011). *System of Care Trauma-Informed Agency Assessment (TIAA) Overview.* Retrieved from https://www.hca.wa.gov/assets/program/trauma-informed-self-assessment-tiaa.pdf

Varcoe, C., Browne, A.J., Wong, S., & Smye, V.L. (2009). Harms and benefits: collecting ethnicity data in a clinical context. *Social Science & Medicine, 68*(9), 1659–66. https://doi.org/10.1016/j.socscimed.2009.02.034

Varcoe, C., Bungay, V., Browne, A.J., Wilson, E., Wathen, C.N., Kolar, K., ... Price, R. (2019). EQUIP Emergency: Study protocol for an organizational intervention to promote equity in health care. *BMC Health Services Research, 19*(1), 687. https://doi.org/10.1186/s12913-019-4494-2

Wathen, C.N., MacGregor, J.C.D., & Beyrem, S. (2021). Impacts of trauma- and violence-informed care education: A mixed method follow-up evaluation with health and social service professionals. *Public Health Nursing, 38*(4), 645–54. https://onlinelibrary.wiley.com/doi/abs/10.1111/phn.12883

Wathen, C.N., & Mantler, T. (2022). Trauma- and violence-informed care: Orienting intimate partner violence interventions to equity. *Current Epidemiology Reports, 9,* 233–44. https://doi.org/10.1007/s40471-022-00307-7

Wathen, C.N., Schmitt, B., & MacGregor, J.C.D. (2021). Measuring trauma- (and violence)-informed care: A scoping review. *Trauma, Violence & Abuse.* Online first: https://doi.org/10.1177/15248380211029399

Wheeler, K., & Phillips, K.E. (2019). The development of trauma and resilience competencies for nursing education. *Journal of the American Psychiatric Nurses Association.* https://doi.org/10.1177%2F1078390319878779

Conclusion

NADINE WATHEN

This collection has presented a critical, intersectional way to think about implementing trauma- and violence-informed care (TVIC) in diverse contexts and from multiple starting places and perspectives. In this final chapter, I reflect on what it means to be trauma- and violence-informed, situate the need for change in current world events and circumstances that have made this kind of shift increasingly imperative, and provide advice, based on the collective wisdom articulated in this text, on what it takes to get there.

TVIC as a Call to Action

Adding the "V" to existing models of trauma-informed practice is, at its core, a political act. Specific attention to structural and interpersonal violence means that we must confront the inequities baked into our policies, protocols, systems, and sectors and recognize that these inequities shape our practices, often to the detriment of specific groups, but in ways that ultimately harm us all.

COVID-19 has demonstrated that while a virus is not racist or discriminatory, policy responses to it are; myriad data have shown that racialized groups globally, and in Canada especially Black and Indigenous people, face the greatest risk of illness and death, as well as the least access to vaccines and other supports, including, among other things, paid sick days. Domestic violence has surged to new levels, and inequities are apparent across social locations, especially when it comes to developing and implementing strategies to address disease transmission. For example, those in congregate settings, especially long-term care, homeless shelters, and prisons, were deemed expendable from the outset of the pandemic, with little effort made to protect them, and there was initial and ongoing resistance to basic science (e.g., aerosol transmission, masking) that could have shifted responses to save lives. These violent policy responses, and the despair arising from them, intersect with pre-existing pandemics, in which we can include overdose deaths from toxic street drugs, gender-based violence, poverty, and homelessness, to create a "syndemic" situation, that is, the "simultaneous occurrence of diseases and their determinants that promote and enhance the overall negative effects on health and other conditions experienced by individuals and populations" (Fronteira et al., 2021, p. 2).

But the cost is not only to those seeking care; indeed, as we have seen starkly highlighted throughout the COVID-19 pandemic, the toll on those *providing* services may pose the greatest risk to our systems of care going forward. In Canada as elsewhere, service providers and leaders are being crushed by moral injury, burnout, and overt violence perpetrated against them by angry and distraught service users, by organizations and governments that have done the bare minimum, if anything, to protect them from COVID-19 itself, from harassment by anti-vaccination proponents, and from dangerous understaffing and overwork. In Ontario, Canada, for example, legislation passed by a majority Conservative government in the midst of the pandemic capped pay increases for nurses at below cost-of-living increases, an additional show of disrespect that has many leaving the profession, resulting in a crisis in the health care workforce that will take years to address, if it ever can be addressed (Canadian Institutes for Health Information, 2021).

What We're Working For, and Against

We position TVIC as a philosophical framework but also a tailorable and action-oriented set of strategies and tools – that is, an intervention – that can begin, one care interaction at a time, to improve things. TVIC is values-based work that requires us to examine our own personal and institutional attitudes, assumptions, and biases. It means being honest about the world we live in and where potentially harmful and stigmatizing beliefs reside, as well as the impact these beliefs, operationalized through actions, have on those seeking services, especially those facing various barriers to care.

TVIC is not easy work, but it's work worth doing. If nothing else, the pandemic has laid bare the structural inequities, racism, gender and sexual inequality, ableism, and other forms of stigma and discrimination that have existed, and been growing, for decades. As noted earlier, we have an exhausted and traumatized health and social service workforce, teachers and nurses are leaving their professions in droves, and children have fallen behind, with many schools apparently lacking plans to catch them up. TVIC alone will not pull us out of this collective trauma, but it can help us to remember the basic values that brought us into the various professions we inhabit and to take a clear-eyed look at the ways of thinking and doing that seem to drive our care systems. From challenging business-oriented quality improvement models applied in places and ways that undercut human processes of care, to refocusing on effectiveness instead of efficiency, we now have an opportunity for a rethink.

The concept of shared humanity, discussed in chapter 1.3, is fundamentally what TVIC is about – a desire to really understand what we're doing and why and to provide safe and respectful care with and for those we serve, while also caring for ourselves and our co-workers. TVIC helps us see and value the humanity in others, taking into account how skin colour, language, gender, sexual orientation, ability, and other social dimensions advantage and disadvantage groups and individuals variously. It helps us counter the structures and influences that foster othering and exclusion, or deeming some worthy and some unworthy of our care. We are challenged to broaden our lens beyond looking for "what's wrong with this person" to considering "what's happened, and is still happening" to them, and, crucially, "what are the economic, political and social dynamics that keep it all in place, and who benefits?" Finally, a TVIC approach trusts those closest to the work to know what to do and how to deploy resources for those ends.

A key lesson across the volume is the importance of context and the complex interactions among context, culture, and practice. There is, and always will be, a fundamental role for individual interaction – what does the service user, patient, client, or student experience in a moment of care, and how does the care provider, teacher, officer, or other staff member feel about the care they provide (or don't provide). TVIC is based on the notion that the individual service provider embodies and enacts the intervention – that is, is TVIC's "face" – at least from the perspective of the care seeker. Every moment in a care space, and every encounter with a staff member in that space, shapes the person's experience of care. Who feels welcomed, safe, and supported, and who does not? Why? What does trauma look like in a waiting area, a classroom, a treatment room? How can we ensure that we don't make things worse? How can we make all people feel deserving, heard, strong? These are the questions underpinning TVIC encounters, and they're predicated on providers and organizations noticing and taking into account what's happening with and to people in their broader life contexts and reconnecting with our human values: respect, compassion, empathy – that is, *care*.

As also discussed across chapters, organizations must themselves, via their leaders and staff, undertake self-reflection and close examination of their contexts to articulate their goals and determine what success looks like. While many TVIC-specific strategies do not add financial or other resource costs, the work must be intentional and structured into organizational practices and policies. Sufficient staffing is required for organizations to meet their mandates; those that are understaffed and otherwise underresourced are unlikely to be able to integrate TVIC. Thus, to provide TVIC, individuals must be supported by a well-aligned structure, working in common cause with the organization's core objectives. Using case examples, we learned of different ways that teams and organizations provide this support, including by examining and updating policies and protocols, rethinking time use to enable as much flexibility as possible (e.g., in appointment length), and using good judgment (e.g., in timing of tasks), while recognizing the impacts of vicarious trauma and mitigating these with organizational supports. This last includes shifting language and removing negative social judgments about vicarious trauma, moral distress, and burnout. These attempts to mitigate harms to staff, even when in process and/or imperfect, can themselves shift the culture to one of care and compassion, helping to lessen moral distress and identify structural changes that might further do so. When the carers feel cared for, they provide better care.

COVID-19 has underscored the need to think upstream when it comes to sectors and systems and to attend carefully to social and structural factors, including firmly held narratives and beliefs. Safe and affordable housing is less expensive, in the long run, than people experiencing homelessness and its ill effects and accessing emergency departments when they can't find primary or community care. Neoliberal expectations related to "bootstraps" and "rugged individualism" work against universal approaches such as basic income and social housing. The need to examine not only our biases and assumptions but also our relative power and privilege and the structures, norms, and narratives that reinforce these was a key lesson across chapters.

Final Thoughts

TVIC is a transformational approach to practice that focuses on people, their care interactions, and the working conditions under which those interactions take place. It is founded on social justice principles and has the specific goal of acknowledging and remediating health and social inequities, one encounter at a time, one policy at a time, one funding decision at a time. It is values-based, engaging the heart and the mind, supporting the enactment of our professional ethics. Importantly, TVIC provides a scaffold, through simple (but not easy) principles, articulated in tailorable strategies for individuals, organizations, and ideally systems of care, founded on the insights and lived and living experiences of those seeking care and service. We have noted in our work with various professions in various contexts the importance of language and expression – not only the words, tone of voice, and eye contact that underpin relational practice with individuals, but also the way of thinking about and articulating both small and large actions. We often use this example: the staff at one of our research sites now acknowledge that because of inflexibility and lack of resourcing, patients are being put on hold repeatedly and for long periods when they telephone for help: "this is structural violence" say reception staff. And family medicine residents have come to realize that fee-for-service payment models often work contrary to their desire to take time with people with complex needs, causing moral distress. Again, structural violence.

TVIC solutions can be small or large, but they are also universal, in the sense that they encompass the breadth of care provided to all service users. Knowing the specifics of someone's trauma and violence experiences is not required to provide structurally competent care for everyone. From creating a safe and welcoming space that reflects local communities, to changing fluorescent lighting to avoid reactivating trauma for people who have had terrible experiences in institutions (this is an example from a child welfare agency serving many Indigenous clients with Residential School experiences), to hiring Elders or supportive peer workers rather than more security guards – there are myriad ways to account for lived and living experience of trauma and violence and previous experiences of poor and harmful practices. The strategies often come from those receiving and providing care but must be implemented and sustained by leaders and systems. The authors of this collection hope that the cases, strategies, and resources provided throughout will spark ideas in your practice. Wherever you, your colleagues, and your organization are right now is the best place to start. We wish you the very best on your TVIC journey.

REFERENCES

Canadian Institutes for Health Information (2021). Health workforce in Canada: Highlights of the impact of COVID-19. https://www.cihi.ca/en/health-workforce-in-canada-highlights-of-the-impact-of-COVID-19

Fronteira, I., Sidat, M., Magalhães J.P, et al. (2021). The SARS-CoV-2 pandemic: A syndemic perspective. *One Health*, *12*. https://doi.org/10.1016/j.onehlt.2021.100228

Contributors

Co-Editors

Nadine Wathen, PhD, is Professor in Western University's Arthur Labatt Family School of Nursing and Canada Research Chair in Mobilizing Knowledge on Gender-Based Violence. She is Academic Director of Western's Centre for Research on Health Equity and Social Inclusion, Research Scholar at the Centre for Research and Education on Violence Against Women and Children, a Fellow of the Canadian Academy of Health Sciences. Her research examines the health and social service sector's response to violence against women, interventions to reduce health inequities, and the science of knowledge mobilization, with a focus on partnerships to enhance the use of research in policy and practice. Wathen convenes the Gender, Trauma & Violence Knowledge Incubator @ Western University, a community-university partnership committed to TVIC education and service delivery, whose members and projects comprise the impetus and content for this volume. She has delivered numerous TVIC workshops with health and social service agencies and led TVIC-specific curriculum development, research, and evaluation activities.

Colleen Varcoe, RN, PhD, is Professor Emeritus at the University of British Columbia School of Nursing. Her clinical background is in emergency and critical care and primary health care. Her research focuses on violence and inequity, with an emphasis on both structural and interpersonal violence. Her completed research includes studies of the risks and health effects of violence, including for rural and Indigenous women. Her current research includes studies to promote equity in primary health care and emergency care and studies of health interventions for women who have experienced violence, most recently for Indigenous women. She is one of the leads for EQUIP Healthcare, which is a knowledge hub for promoting equity in health and health care though trauma- and violence-informed care, cultural safety, and harm reduction. Her contributions to this volume build on a decade of work to integrate attention to structural violence, including systemic racism in health care, and to integrate cultural safety and TVIC within organizations.

Contributors

Chantel L. Antone, RN, BScN, MPEd, is an Indigenous woman from the Oneida Nation of the Thames First Nation community located southwest of London, Ontario. Chantel is a health activist and advocates on behalf of First Nation, Inuit, and Métis patients and families navigating the health system. Her areas of advocacy include ensuring equitable access to health care and social services, addressing racism and discrimination, and collaborating with FNIMU communities across Ontario. Her work examines patient navigation practices to ensure culturally safe care in the cancer system for First Nations, Inuit, Métis, and urban Indigenous patients in Ontario. Chantel has recently been appointed the Senior Director, Indigenous Health, Office of Social Inclusion and Accountability, at a large tertiary hospital. She is a registered nurse and has been working across health and social systems for the past fifteen years.

Helene Berman, RN, PhD, is Distinguished University Professor Emerita in the Arthur Labatt Family School of Nursing, Western University, a Fellow of the Canadian Academy of Nursing, and a Fellow of the Canadian Academy of Health Sciences. Her program of research, supported by more than $7 million in research funding from tri-council agencies and Status of Women Canada, has focused on subtle and explicit forms of violence. She was the inaugural Academic Director of the Centre for Research on Health Equity and Social Inclusion in downtown London, Ontario, an important community engagement initiative for the advancement of knowledge-informed solutions through participatory community action. Actively engaged as a leader in the "professional" aspects of nursing, she served as President of the Nurses Network on Violence Against Women International (2012–14). In recent years, she has been engaged in efforts to address gender-based violence and health equity in Rwanda. Her contributions to this volume build upon this work and contemplate the potential merits of TVIC in the Rwandan context.

Annette J. Browne, RN, PhD, is one of the leads for EQUIP Healthcare, a knowledge hub for promoting equity and social justice in health and health care though trauma- and violence-informed care, cultural safety, and harm reduction. Building on her experience as a clinical nurse who lived and worked within First Nations and Inuit communities, Annette's program of research has generated a body of evidence aimed at improving health care and health outcomes for Indigenous and non-Indigenous people affected by health and social inequities. Working in partnership with communities, health and policy leaders, and clinicians at the point of care, her research focuses on organizational interventions to improve health equity in primary health care settings and emergency departments and on strategies for integrating equity-oriented health care in health systems and policies. Her contributions to this volume are three chapters focused on Structural Violence, Taking Organization-Level Action, and Cultural Safety.

Karen Campbell, RN, PhD, is Assistant Professor at York University's School of Nursing. With more than twenty years as a registered nurse, her clinical background is in public health nursing, with a focus on reproductive and child health. Her program of research is at the intersection of women's health and physical and social geography. She is interested in how community health nursing intervention programs can improve health and quality of life for women experiencing health inequities across diverse settings, including rural communities, and for women with disabilities. Her contributions to this volume included drafting, writing, and editing content for a foundational chapter in section 1.

Eugenia Canas, PhD, was Post-Doctoral Associate with the Faculty of Information and Media Studies at Western University, as well as a Trainee with the Gender, Trauma & Violence Informed Knowledge Incubator. Her doctoral work focused on the impact of service-user involvement on the design and delivery of mental health services. Eugenia's other research and knowledge-translation collaborations included roles in the CIHR grant titled Voices Against Violence: Youth Stories Create Change; the Wisdom 2 Action Network; the Mental Health Incubator for Disruptive Solutions; and the Mental Health Commission of Canada's SPARK Training Institute. Tragically, we lost Eugenia to cancer in June 2021. Her invaluable contributions to this volume stem from her postdoctoral work developing a foundational curriculum for TVIC, alongside a committee of scholars and community experts.

Jessica Carswell, BA(Hons), MHIS, completed her Master of Health Information Science at Western University, working under the supervision of Dr Nadine Wathen, exploring strategies to translate principles and practices of TVIC into materials for public education programing. She has also been involved in various global health- and equity-related initiatives at Western University, including Global MINDS at Western, and was a trainee in the Gender, Trauma & Violence Knowledge Incubator @ Western University. Prior to completing her Master's, she pursued undergraduate honours specialization degrees in psychology and media studies, with a major in criminology. Additionally, Jessica has worked in community-based mental health and addictions services since

2012, in both direct service and leadership capacities. Her contributions to this volume are informed by her Master's thesis work and provide insight into strategies that can help foster a trauma- and violence-informed community through TVIC education and information-sharing.

Susana Caxaj, RN, PhD, is a professor at the Arthur Labatt Family School of Nursing at Western University. Her research is focused on the experiences of diverse migrant populations, including immigrants, refugees, and migrant workers accessing and navigating health and social supports. From 2013 to 2019, Caxaj worked at UBC Okanagan, and she continues to carry out community-based research developing social support interventions with migrant agricultural workers in the province of BC. More recently, Caxaj has been working in partnership with Ontario settlement and migrant support organizations to investigate culturally safe, trauma- and violence-informed, equity-oriented approaches to service for diverse migrant populations. She has also developed federal guidelines to ameliorate the impacts of COVID-19 on vulnerable migrant communities. She is currently working with colleagues across the country to develop national standards for migrant agricultural worker health and safety. Her contributions to this volume are focused on reflecting on how the principles of TVIC can inform community-based and partnered interventions for both newcomers and migrant agricultural workers.

Scott Courtice is Executive Director of the London InterCommunity Health Centre, an organization that provides comprehensive primary health care and social services for people who face barriers to accessing care. Scott is an avid community volunteer, having served as President of the London Cares Homeless Response Services Board of Directors, Chair of the London Public Library Board of Trustees, President of the London Youth Advisory Council Board of Directors, and Chair of the London Chamber of Commerce Government Affairs Committee. His contributions to this volume are based on his executive leadership within a community-based, equity-oriented primary care setting, and on his advocacy for broader systems change to improve the health and well-being of stigmatized and marginalized people and communities.

Francine Darroch, PhD, is an interdisciplinary health researcher at Carleton University. Her feminist participatory action research focuses on leveraging trauma- and violence-informed physical activity to improve quality of life, social connections, community cohesion, and overall health and well-being; these experiences are described in chapter 2.5.

Iloradanon Efimoff (Illy), BA (Hons), MA, PhD, is a Haida and European settler woman from the northwest coast of British Columbia. She recently defended her PhD at the University of Manitoba in Social and Personality Psychology and has started a postdoctoral fellowship at the University of Michigan. Her dissertation research focused on reducing anti-Indigenous racism. Her broader research interests converge on the social psychology of Indigenous well-being and reconciliation. Illy also is engaged in research on Indigenization and Indigenous experiences of racism at postsecondary institutions. She contributes to this volume through her experience working with Indigenous peoples in the community, in organizations, and in institutions, where she has consistently focused on putting Indigenous people first and creating sustainable social change through novel, interdisciplinary, mixed-methods research.

Marilyn Ford-Gilboe, RN, PhD, is Professor and Women's Health Research Chair in Rural Health at the Arthur Labatt Family School of Nursing, Western University. For more than two decades, her research has focused primarily on violence against women, health inequities, and place. This includes leading studies on the effectiveness of trauma- and violence-informed interventions for women experiencing intimate partner violence (IPV) and the integration of effective interventions into services in ways that are inclusive, locally tailored, and sustainable. Her work includes innovations that are delivered in person (e.g., iHEAL, Reclaiming Our Spirits) and as mobile applications (iCAN Plan 4 Safety – now the iHEAL app). She is past President of the Nursing Network on Violence Against Women International and a member of the American Academy of Nursing Expert Panel on Violence. Her contribution to this volume is leading the chapter in section 1 on trauma and violence.

Gabriela Gonzalez Montaner is a research assistant for the Taking Steps: Warrior Women's Wellness program. She works as a research assistant in the School of Nursing at the University of British Columbia. She contributed to chapter 2.5 of this volume.

Paul Gross, MDCM, a family physician, focuses on men's health and HIV. He has a full-time practice at Spectrum Health, a multi-disciplinary primary care clinic near St Paul's Hospital in downtown Vancouver. Since 2009, he has had a small practice in the Downtown Eastside of Vancouver (Vancouver Native Health Clinic, 2009–19; and Kilala Lelum Health Clinic, 2019–21), where he has worked in clinical settings that provide a full range of services to mainly Indigenous people in the community. Paul is the co-founder and medical director of the Dudes Club, an innovative, community-driven men's health program founded in 2010, which incorporates Indigenous approaches to healing and wellness; it has since expanded to more than forty sites throughout British Columbia. He also is Clinical Assistant Professor in the Department of Family Practice at University of British Columbia, where he is involved in teaching family practice residents and doing research in various areas of Indigenous men's wellness. Paul lives in North Vancouver with his wife and two children. His contribution to the handbook includes his experience as a primary care physician who has employed trauma- and violence-informed approaches in everyday practice – in particular, in the context of Indigenous programs/care and the DUDES club.

Lisa Heslop, HBSW, MA, is a doctoral candidate in developmental psychology at the University of Toronto and a research associate at the Centre for Research and Education on Violence Against Women and Children, Western University. Lisa has worked in the area of crisis intervention and violence against women for more than thirty years. Using police administrative data, her program of research explores women's use of force against intimate partners as an act of resistance. Her contributions to this volume included drafting, writing, and editing content for a foundational chapter in section 1.

Kathryn Hibbert, PhD, is Professor and Associate Dean of Teacher Education at Western University. She was the founding Director of the Interdisciplinary Centre for Research on Curriculum as a Social Practice, and a Centre Research Scholar at the Centre for Education Research and Innovation at Western's Schulich School of Medicine and Dentistry. Her research examines multimodal "literacies" and their ability to shape our communications systems across the professions. She views curriculum-making to be a process engaging multiple constituents of a group and has worked with educators in schools, medicine, and nuclear science through the International Atomic Energy Agency. Her contributions to this volume bring together her curriculum and educational experiences working with children and families who have experienced trauma and violence, and curriculum work with other professionals who have experienced trauma. She draws on research and curriculum development experiences working with interdisciplinary teams of first responders to the Fukushima Nuclear Accident in Japan.

Bill Hill – Ro'nikonkatste (Standing Strong Spirit), RPN, MSW, RSW, BEd, is a Mohawk from Six Nations, living outside of London, Ontario. He is an Adjunct Assistant Professor in the Department of Psychiatry, Schulich School of Medicine and Dentistry at Western University. Ro'nikonkatste is also the Director of Indigenous Mental Wellness for Biigajiiskaan: Indigenous Pathways to Mental Wellness, an Indigenous mental health initiative co-led by Atlohsa Family Healing Services and St Joseph's Health Care–London. He has worked at SJHC in mental health since 1982 in Nursing, Social Work, and Education. He has extensive experience in frontline work, including at inpatient admission units and in intensive ambulatory care, such with Assertive Community

Treatment teams. Utilizing his professional experience in Western medicine and his personal and professional knowledge of traditional Indigenous healing methods, he contributes to this volume walking in both worlds, working to create an Indigenous mental health program that acknowledges and integrates the gifts of both forms of treatment in ways that are culturally safe while adhering to a trauma- and violence-informed care ideology.

Susan Jack, RN, PhD, is Professor at the School of Nursing, an Associate Member of the Department of Health Research Methods, Evidence, and Impact, and a core member of the Offord Centre for Child Studies at McMaster University. Her program of research is focused on evaluating community-based approaches to preventing family violence. Building on her professional and educational experiences in public health, she has spent more than a decade developing and evaluating program and curriculum elements for Nurse–Family Partnership, a public health nurse home visitation program for young pregnant individuals and first-time parents. She has also delivered multiple TVIC workshops to public health professionals. From 2016 to 2020, Dr Jack served as President of the Nursing Network on Violence Against Women International. Her contributions to this volume include examining how TVIC principles can be applied in public health contexts.

Lisa Jackson is from the Oneida of the Thames First Nation. Lisa holds a degree in sociology from King's University College and a Harm Reduction Certificate from York University. She is the Indigenous Resource Consultant/Program Project Coordinator for the Indigenous Cancer Program at the South West Regional Cancer Program at London Health Sciences Centre and engages with regional hospital partners and Indigenous communities to enact meaningful change in key areas of building productive relationships, research and surveillance, prevention, screening, palliative and end-of-life care, education, and health equity. She has more than fifteen years' experience in the area of addictions and mental health, having worked as a program coordinator with a local territorial organization that represents seven First Nations in Ontario and as a case worker in a women's and family shelter in London. In this volume, she contributed her wisdom and expertise on providing culturally safe care to Indigenous people in health care settings.

Tanaz Javan, BA (Hons), MSc, PhD, did her doctoral work under the supervision of Dr Wathen and was a trainee in the Gender, Trauma, and Violence Knowledge Incubator at Western University over the course of this book project. Her doctoral research evaluated the implementation and integration of TVIC in community-based health and social services in London, Ontario. Her project used multiple case study methodology to qualitatively explore how organizations at different stages of TVIC implementation take up and integrate these principles and practices. Her contributions to this volume provided insights on the implementation process of TVIC, highlighting the facilitators and barriers for effective implementation. She is currently a college professor at Fanshawe College in London, Ontario, and a research assistant at the Centre for Research and Education on Violence Against Women and Children and the Department of Pathology and Laboratory Medicine, Schulich School of Medicine and Dentistry, Western University.

Viviane Josewski, MSc, PhD, is Assistant Professor with the School of Nursing at the University of Northern British Columbia and a Research Associate with the National Collaborating Centre for Indigenous Health. A white settler and immigrant, she has spent most of her professional and academic life working with urban Indigenous communities in British Columbia, exploring inequities in access to culturally safe care in the areas of mental health and substance use, trauma and violence, including historic and intergenerational trauma and structural violence. In her doctoral research, she explored how different contractual arrangements advance cultural safety and equity in the context of Indigenous mental health and addictions programing and care. Currently, she works with communities to develop, implement, and evaluate Indigenous-led culturally safe health service delivery models. Her contributions to the handbook are twofold: (a) she examines how violence intersects with colonization, race, class, and gender and manifests itself structurally within institutions to re-create situations of trauma and harm; and (b) she discusses concrete examples drawn from her involvement in the above-mentioned research to illustrate how trauma- and violence-informed care can be enacted in the context of Indigenous community-based programing and research.

Sandy Lambert is a member of the TALLCREE First Nation in northern Alberta, but he calls Vancouver home. He has many years of volunteering with not-for-profit organizations and NGOs, attending and organizing HIV/AIDS conferences and research committees/projects nationally. This that has led to the growth of DUDES Clubs off/on reserve, in rural and remote areas.

Heather Lokko, RN, MPH, has worked as a direct service provider, professional practice lead, program manager, and senior leader during her public health career. She is currently the Director of Healthy Start at the Middlesex-London Health Unit in Ontario, a division focused on providing public health interventions that support healthy growth and development. Additionally, she is MLHU's Chief Nursing Officer. In this role, Heather leads the organization's health equity strategy, promotes practice excellence, and provides nursing leadership in the organization and in regional, provincial, and national initiatives.

Heather is the Community Co-Director of the Centre for Research on Health Equity and Social Inclusion, is on the board of directors for the London Intercommunity Health Centre, and is an Adjunct Research Professor at Western University. Heather's extensive expertise in public health, and her experience building individual and organizational capacity to address health inequities, including trauma and violence-informed practice, contributes a perspective on the practical application of TVIC principles and theoretical concepts across many levels of intervention to enhance population health.

Jennifer MacGregor, PhD, is Senior Research Associate at the Arthur Labatt Family School of Nursing at Western University and Community Research Associate at Western's Centre for Research and Education on Violence Against Women and Children. She is a member of the Domestic Violence at Work Network (DVatWorkNet.org) and was a lead researcher on the first Canadian national study on the impacts of domestic violence on the workplace. Her recent projects focus on health and social service sector responses to family violence, evaluation of trauma- and violence-informed care training initiatives, and systematic evidence reviews related to intimate partner violence and work. Her contributions to this volume are particularly informed by her recent work on a scoping review of measurement tools for trauma- and violence-informed care and vicarious trauma.

Susan Macphail has worked in the social service and health sectors for forty years with a focus on advancing equity for all. Working with individuals and communities who experience the intersectionality of factors such as adverse mental and physical health, trauma and violence, homelessness, gender inequity, racism, and colonization and newcomer experiences, has led her to help initiate several innovative programs to promote community wellness and safety. These include the first shelters for women, services for Indigenous families, and housing projects in London. As the previous Director of Community and Women's Programs at Canadian Mental Health Association Middlesex, she worked to develop and implement trauma- and violence-informed approaches. She currently consults, provides training, and presents on trauma- and violence-informed care and cultural humility. Her contributions to this volume include these topics: working collaboratively with and across multiple sectors at the community level, and translating trauma- and violence-informed care into practical and coordinated applications with a view to making systemic and structural changes.

Margaret MacPherson, MA, is Research Associate with the Centre for Research and Education on Violence Against Women and Children at Western University in London, Ontario. She designs projects and curriculum and delivers education and training on community and workplace harassment and violence and abuse of older adults. Apart from her work at the centre, Margaret is a freelance public servant providing leadership, facilitation, and project management on a variety of projects that contribute to the evolution of a peaceful and just society. She is the regional and provincial coordinator for Violence Against Women (VAW) coordinating committee networks. Her contributions to this volume include two chapters on TVIC in policing and as a bridge-builder between sectors.

Michelle Paquette is of mixed Cree and European ancestry. She is raising her five children on the traditional and unceded lands of the Squamish, Musqueam, Tsleil-Waututh, Semiahmoo, Katzie, Kwikwetlem, Kwantlen, Qayqayt and Tsawwassen First Nations. She is currently attending Langara College with a focus on Indigenous Studies. Michelle is happy to be giving back to her community through her work with the Taking Steps Advisory Board. She contributed to chapter 2.5 of this volume.

Lyana Patrick, PhD, is an Indigenous scholar and practitioner from the Stellat'en First Nation and Acadian/Scottish. She has worked as an education specialist for more than two decades, developing curriculum, managing education programs, and evaluating Indigenous health and education initiatives. She has also worked as a community planner, most recently for the City of Vancouver, helping design community engagement for a municipal poverty reduction strategy. Lyana works with communities to develop Indigenous-focused collaborative research models that can transform Indigenous experiences of health, planning, and justice. Currently she is an Assistant Professor in the Faculty of Health Sciences at Simon Fraser University. Her contributions to the handbook include a discussion of examples drawn from her involvement with the DUDES club to illustrate how trauma- and violence-informed care has been and continues to be enacted in the context of Indigenous programing and planning.

Samridhi Pradhan, BPH, MSc, MHIS, completed her Master of Health Information Science at Western University, working under the supervision of Dr Nadine Wathen to map TVIC curriculum. At present, she works as a Research and Evaluation Specialist at United Way Centraide Windsor–Essex County. Previously, she worked for non-governmental organizations based in Nepal. Samridhi's previous research focused primarily on maternal and child health. Her contributions to this volume are informed by her Master's research project and include the theoretical and curriculum-development frameworks that shape the TVIC curriculum described in section 4.

Susan Rodger, PhD, is a psychologist and Professor at the Faculty of Education at Western University, a Research Associate at the Centre for Research and

Education on Violence Against Women and Children, and a Principal Investigator with the Centre for School-Based Mental Health. Her research within the education, health, and child welfare systems examines mental health literacy and trauma- and violence-informed care for teachers, teacher candidates, and foster care providers. Her contributions to this volume are based on her extensive experience integrating and innovating TVIC in the context of K–12 and post-secondary teacher education.

Anne-Marie Sanchez is Director of Strategy, Planning, and Health Systems Integration at the London InterCommunity Health Centre. Prior to her role at the Health Centre, Anne-Marie was a management consultant for non-profits in London, Ontario. Anne-Marie has a passion for equity and was the co-founder of a local grassroots organization, Women & Politics, as well as a member of the Diversity, Inclusion, and Anti-Oppression Advisory Committee for the City of London. Anne-Marie is currently on the executive committee of the Centre for Research on Health Equity and Inclusion and the Health Care Ethics Committee at St Joseph's Health Care. Anne-Marie's contribution to this volume is to share the Health Centre's experience with strengthening the organization's health equity lens in its people-centred care through online tools such as EQUIP.

Jennifer Sandu (Williamson), MSW, RSW, is a social worker and currently the Community Engagement Specialist at the London Cross Cultural Learner Centre (CCLC), a settlement agency in London, Ontario. Jenn focuses her work on building capacity around the needs of newly arrived government-assisted refugees and how to create welcoming and safe spaces for newcomers. Prior to that, Jenn spent time as the Director of Client Services in Windsor supporting individuals living with HIV/AIDS and as a case manager at CCLC working with newly arrived refugees. Her contributions include reflections of the organizational implementation of TVIC and sharing collaborative experiences in the context of communities, settlement, and migration.

Brenna Schmitt, HBSc, is working toward her Master of Science in Occupational Therapy at the University of Toronto. She has an Honours Bachelor of Science from the University of Toronto, with a focus on human biology and health studies. She has worked as a research assistant for the Arthur Labatt Family School of Nursing at Western University and the Mental Health Nursing Research Alliance at Lawson Health Research Institute, Parkwood Institute Research. Her research interests include gender-based and reproductive health service disparities, housing and food justice, and equity-oriented health policy solutions. Her contributions to this volume are informed by her recent work on a scoping review of measurement tools for trauma- and violence-informed care and vicarious trauma.

Matthew Sereda is the Equity and Inclusive Education Learning Coordinator for the Thames Valley District School Board. Previously, Matthew acted as the Safe Schools Learning Coordinator for TVDSB and helped to create and implement the School Within a College Program, a TVDSB initiative designed to re-engage students who had dropped out of high school. Matthew is a recipient of an Atlohsa Peace Award for his work toward Truth and Reconciliation with the See Me Project, a program designed to teach students about Canada's Residential School System and Missing and Murdered Indigenous Women and Girls. Matthew is also a recipient of a Prime Minister's Award for Teaching Excellence for his work with the School Within a College program. His contribution to this volume is as an author of chapter 2.4.

Vincent Sezibera, PhD, is Professor of Psychology (Clinical Psychology) and Director of the Centre for Mental Health, College of Medicine and Health Sciences, University of Rwanda. He is also the founding president of the Rwanda Psychological Society (RPS), a professional organization of psychologists in Rwanda. Prof. Sezibera received his doctorate in Psychology from the Catholic University of Louvain, Belgium. He specializes in post-traumatic stress disorder (PTSD) and child and adolescent traumatic grief. Research areas include the assessment of poor mental health outcomes from social crisis (genocide), domestic violence, intimate partner violence, and medical conditions (HIV, COVID-19). His contributions are based on extensive experience in community education about trauma, resilience and trauma-informed care in Rwanda, and related work in a number of countries, including Benin, Republic of Central Africa, Cameroon, Ivory Coast, and South Africa. His contribution to this volume elaborates on TVIC in a post-genocidal context, with more focus on the use of gender-based violence as a weapon of war and lessons learned in the aftermath of the 1994 genocide against the Tutsi in Rwanda.

Victoria Smye (Vicki), RN, PhD, is Associate Professor and Director of the Arthur Labatt Family School of Nursing at Western University. She has years of clinical experience in mental health and substance use services/care. Her program of research is located at the intersections of violence, gender, poverty, mental health, substance use, and Indigenous health. Vicki's completed studies include critical ethnographic studies exploring the narratives of Indigenous people accessing mental health services and supports; this is to explore the challenges and those aspects of services and care that support health and well-being. Currently, she is engaged in studies to address health inequity through the promotion of cultural safety, trauma- and violence-informed care, and recovery-oriented and harm reduction approaches in mental health settings. Drawing from research exemplars involving Indigenous peoples, Vicki's contributions to this volume include a chapter on integrating TVIC for interventions with Indigenous people, and an examination of how TVIC principles can be applied in culturally safe, contextually tailored, and person-centred ways in mental health care, including those services for persons who use substances, and in social support contexts.

Jacqueline Specht, PhD, is a professor at the Faculty of Education at Western University where she is the director of the Canadian Research Centre on Inclusive Education. Professor Specht's research expertise is located in the areas of inclusive education, teacher development, and psychosocial aspects of individuals with disabilities. She has presented locally, nationally, and internationally for parents, educators, and researchers working with children and youth in the inclusive classroom. Her contributions to this volume are informed by her work in education, where ways of teaching, academic expectations, referral rates for discipline, and segregated programs set up environments of inequity in schools.

Javeed Sukhera, MD, PhD, is Chair of Psychiatry at the Institute of Living and Chief of Psychiatry at Hartford Hospital in Hartford, Connecticut. He is also an Associate Clinical Professor at the Yale University School of Medicine. He was formerly Associate Professor in the Departments of Psychiatry/Paediatrics and a scientist at the Centre for Education Research and Innovation at the Schulich School of Medicine and Dentistry at Western University in London, Ontario. His research focuses on bias recognition and stigma reduction. His contributions to this volume include a chapter on stigma and bias and their intersections with trauma- and violence-informed care.

Aimée Joséphine Utuza, MA, is a health professional from Rwanda, with a master's degree in health promotion from Western University in the area of gender-based violence among women and girls with disabilities in sub-Saharan African countries. Aimée has more than fifteen years' experience working in the health sector in Rwanda in public health, clinical psychology, and mental health nursing and was the senior project manager of the TSAM Project, a four-year partnership project funded by Global Affairs Canada in Rwanda. Aimée, together with her sister, created "Living with Happiness" and "Rwandan Mothers' Team" – two local NGOs that serve women and families in Rwanda. She recently created the "Victorious Ladies" group to support separated and divorced women in Rwanda in the process of achieving a positive mindset, self-love, resilience, and being happy for no reason.

Jessica Webb was a community partner, co-founder, and facilitator of the Taking Steps: Warrior Women's Wellness program in Vancouver. She recently finished her MA in the School of Human Kinetics at the University of Ottawa. She contributed to chapter 2.5 of this volume.

Lloy Wylie, PhD, is Associate Professor in Public Health at Western University and Adjunct Professor in the Faculty of Health Sciences at Simon Fraser University. Her research focuses on health equity, and she has more than fifteen years' experience working on community-based partnership research and education, primarily with Indigenous, immigrant, and refugee communities. Previously, she was the Senior Advisor on Health Systems with the British Columbia First Nations Health Authority, where she brought forward the mandates of BC First Nations' leadership along with research and policy recommendations to plan for organizational and practice changes in health care across BC. Her research focuses on tangible strategies and recommendations for implementing change, examining services within their social, economic, and political contexts to inform the changes required for meaningful reconciliation in health care. She contributed to chapter 2.2 of this volume.